HOCKEY
ALL-STARS

FIREFLY BOOKS

HOCKEY ALL-STARS

THE NHL HONOR ROLL

CHRIS McDONELL

A FIREFLY BOOK

Published by Firefly Books Ltd. 2000

First Printing 2000

U.S. Cataloging-in-Publication Data is available.

Canadian Cataloguing in Publication Data

McDonell, Chris
    Hockey all-stars : the NHL honor roll

ISBN 1-55209-542-8

1. Hockey players – Biography.
2. National Hockey League – Biography. I. Title.

GV848.5.A1M274   2000   796.962'092'2   C00-930878-4

Published in Canada in 2000 by
Firefly Books Ltd.
3680 Victoria Park Avenue
Willowdale, Ontario M2H 3K1

Published in the United States in 2000 by
Firefly Books (U.S.) Inc.
P.O. Box 1338, Ellicott Station
Buffalo, New York 14205

Produced by
Bookmakers Press Inc.
12 Pine Street
Kingston, Ontario K7K 1W1
(613) 549-4347
tcread@sympatico.ca

Design by
Janice McLean

Colour Separations by
Friesens
Altona, Manitoba

Printed and bound in Canada by
Friesens
Altona, Manitoba

The Publisher acknowledges the financial support of the Government of Canada through the Book Publishing Industry Development Program for its publishing activities.

TO MY FAMILY,
ESPECIALLY SUE, QUINN, TARA AND ISAAC

ACKNOWLEDGMENTS

For the past 15 years, Sue Gordon has been my primary support, both in my life and in my work. I would not be the person I am without her. Thank you, Sue, especially for your unflagging patience. Our children, Quinn, Tara and Isaac, have likewise been solidly behind me. While I spent hundreds of hours in front of the computer researching and writing this book, they continued to indulge me when I felt the need to read a hockey story to them at the dinner table. I am blessed to have such wonderful people to love.

Lionel Koffler and Michael Worek of Firefly Books helped shape the idea that became *Hockey All-Stars*. They have been generous with their advice and their faith in me as a writer. I'm grateful that they engaged the talented people of Bookmakers Press to craft another book with me. Tracy Read kept a firm grip on the production process while being a joy to work with. She, Susan Dickinson and Catherine DeLury brought their keen attention to detail and strong editorial skills to the text, helping me be more clear and accurate. If any errors remain, they are mine, for I have had superb assistance. Designer Janice McLean allowed me to feel like a collaborator while continually surprising and delighting me with her creative and lively solutions. This book owes so much to the abilities of these people.

Melanie North provided valuable research assistance, particularly for the stories of the early All-Stars. Poring over old newspapers and assorted archives, she found rich anecdotal material for many of these profiles. Craig Campbell combed the photo vaults of the Hockey Hall of Fame, helping me select the splendid images for this book. His good nature and that of his colleagues Phil Pritchard, Jane Rodney and Tyler Wolosewich made my fruitful research trips to the Hall a pleasure. Pat Park, Director of Media Relations for the Toronto Maple Leafs, provided helpful volumes of NHL information.

My large extended family has always been encouraging (and their patronage has lifted sales of my books, particularly in eastern and southwestern Ontario!). Alanson and Nora McDonell have curtailed their parental worries over my career path and been strong boosters. Likewise, my siblings and in-laws, Anne McDonell and John Travaglini, Carolyn McDonell and Ross Perrault, Marjorie and Larry MacIsaac, Kevin McDonell, Barbara and Ryan Vincent, Janet and Mike Palmer, Mary Gordon, Randy and Nancy Gordon, Chris Gordon and Eric and Eileen Gordon, have been generous in every possible way. Thank you for the sustaining love you give me, Sue and our children.

Valerie Varley Kenyon and Doug North frequently lent a sympathetic ear, as have so many of our friends from the London Waldorf School community. In particular, teachers Joanna Mickalski-Muma, Jim Reid, Sara Parsons and Dana Cole have given deeply of themselves to our family. Thank you all.

—*Chris McDonell*

CONTENTS

INTRODUCTION	10	HERB CAIN	40	DON EDWARDS	67
LEGENDS	13	JIM CAREY	40	PAT EGAN	67
		RANDY CARLYLE	41	BRIAN ENGBLOM	69
SID ABEL	15	LORNE CARR	41	PHIL ESPOSITO	69
TOM ANDERSON	15	WAYNE CASHMAN	42	TONY ESPOSITO	71
SYL APPS	16	LORNE CHABOT	43		
BARRY ASHBEE	17	ART CHAPMAN	43	SERGEI FEDOROV	71
LARRY AURIE	17	CHRIS CHELIOS	44	FERNIE FLAMAN	73
		REAL CHEVREFILS	45	THEOREN FLEURY	73
BILL BARBER	19	KING CLANCY	45	PETER FORSBERG	74
TOM BARRASSO	19	DIT CLAPPER	47	BOB FROESE	74
MARTY BARRY	21	BOBBY CLARKE	47	GRANT FUHR	76
ANDY BATHGATE	21	PAUL COFFEY	48		
BOBBY BAUER	22	NEIL COLVILLE	48	BILL GADSBY	76
ED BELFOUR	22	CHARLIE CONACHER	50	GERARD GALLANT	78
JEAN BELIVEAU	25	LIONEL CONACHER	51	CHUCK GARDINER	78
BRIAN BELLOWS	25	ROY CONACHER	51	DANNY GARE	81
DOUG BENTLEY	26	BILL COOK	52	BERNIE GEOFFRION	81
MAX BENTLEY	27	BUN COOK	52	ED GIACOMIN	82
PAUL BIBEAULT	28	ART COULTER	55	ROD GILBERT	82
ROB BLAKE	28	YVAN COURNOYER	55	CLARK GILLIES	84
TOE BLAKE	29	BILL COWLEY	57	BOB GOLDHAM	85
MIKE BOSSY	31	JACK CRAWFORD	57	EBBIE GOODFELLOW	85
BUTCH BOUCHARD	31	ROGER CROZIER	58	JOHNNY GOTTSELIG	86
FRANK BOUCHER	33	WILF CUDE	59	MICHEL GOULET	86
RAY BOURQUE	33			ADAM GRAVES	88
JOHNNY BOWER	34	BYRON DAFOE	59	TED GREEN	89
CARL BREWER	34	ALEX DELVECCHIO	60	WAYNE GRETZKY	90
FRANK BRIMSEK	35	ERIC DESJARDINS	61		
TURK BRODA	36	CECIL DILLON	61	VIC HADFIELD	90
MARTIN BRODEUR	37	MARCEL DIONNE	63	GLENN HALL	93
JOHNNY BUCYK	38	GORDIE DRILLON	63	GLEN HARMON	93
HY BULLER	38	KEN DRYDEN	65	TED HARRIS	94
PAVEL BURE	39	WOODY DUMART	65	DOUG HARVEY	94
		BILL DURNAN	66		

CONTENTS

DOMINIK HASEK 96
DALE HAWERCHUK 96
OTT HELLER 98
CAMILLE HENRY 98
SUGAR JIM HENRY 99
BRYAN HEXTALL SR. 99
RON HEXTALL 100
CHARLIE HODGE 100
KEN HODGE 101
FLASH HOLLETT 101
TIM HORTON 102
BRONCO HORVATH 102
PHIL HOUSLEY 105
GORDIE HOWE 105
MARK HOWE 106
SYD HOWE 106
HARRY HOWELL 108
BOBBY HULL 108
BRETT HULL 110
DENNIS HULL 111

AL IAFRATE 111

HARVEY JACKSON 113
JAROMIR JAGR 113
IVAN JOHNSON 114
TOM JOHNSON 115
AURELE JOLIAT 115

MIKE KARAKAS 117
PAUL KARIYA 117
RED KELLY 118
TED KENNEDY 118
DAVE KEON 121
DAVE KERR 121

TIM KERR 122
OLAF KOLZIG 123
VLADIMIR
   KONSTANTINOV 123
JARI KURRI 124

ELMER LACH 125
GUY LAFLEUR 126
PAT LaFONTAINE 126
ROD LANGWAY 128
JACQUES LAPERRIERE 128
GUY LAPOINTE 129
REGGIE LEACH 129
JOHN LeCLAIR 130
BRIAN LEETCH 131
MARIO LEMIEUX 132
MARIO LESSARD 132
TONY LESWICK 134
DANNY LEWICKI 134
NICKLAS LIDSTROM 135
PELLE LINDBERGH 137
ERIC LINDROS 137
TED LINDSAY 138
ED LITZENBERGER 138
MIKE LIUT 140
HAKAN LOOB 141
HARRY LUMLEY 141

AL MacINNIS 142
FLEMING MACKELL 142
FRANK MAHOVLICH 145
SYLVIO MANTHA 145
DON MARSHALL 147
RICK MARTIN 147
BRAD McCRIMMON 148
BUCKO McDONALD 148
LANNY McDONALD 149

JOHN McKENZIE 149
KIRK McLEAN 150
GERRY McNEIL 151
ROLLIE MELANSON 151
MARK MESSIER 153
RICK MIDDLETON 153
STAN MIKITA 155
MIKE MODANO 155
ALEXANDER MOGILNY 157
DICKIE MOORE 157
HOWIE MORENZ 158
GUS MORTSON 158
KEN MOSDELL 160
BILL MOSIENKO 161
JOHNNY MOWERS 161
JOE MULLEN 162
LARRY MURPHY 162

MATS NASLUND 165
CAM NEELY 165
JIM NEILSON 167
SCOTT NIEDERMAYER 167
BALDY NORTHCOTT 168

ADAM OATES 168
BUDDY O'CONNOR 169
JOHN OGRODNICK 169
BERT OLMSTEAD 170
BOBBY ORR 170
CHRIS OSGOOD 172
SANDIS OZOLINSH 172

BERNIE PARENT	174	BORJE SALMING	203	BILL THOMS	229
BRAD PARK	175	ED SANDFORD	203	JIMMY THOMSON	229
LYNN PATRICK	176	DENIS SAVARD	204	KEITH TKACHUK	230
PETE PEETERS	176	SERGE SAVARD	205	JOHN TONELLI	230
GILBERT PERREAULT	177	TERRY SAWCHUK	206	J.C. TREMBLAY	232
PIERRE PILOTE	178	MILT SCHMIDT	207	BRYAN TROTTIER	232
JACQUES PLANTE	179	JIM SCHOENFELD	208	ROMAN TUREK	234
BUD POILE	181	SWEENEY SCHRINER	208		
DENIS POTVIN	181	EARL SEIBERT	209	NORM ULLMAN	234
BABE PRATT	182	TEEMU SELANNE	210		
DEAN PRENTICE	182	BRENDAN SHANAHAN	210	ROGIE VACHON	235
JOE PRIMEAU	183	EDDIE SHORE	212	JOHN	
CHRIS PRONGER	183	STEVE SHUTT	213	VANBIESBROUCK	237
MARCEL PRONOVOST	184	BABE SIEBERT	214	ELMER VASKO	237
CLAUDE PROVOST	185	CHARLIE SIMMER	214	MIKE VERNON	238
DAREN PUPPA	185	DARRYL SITTLER	215	STEVE VICKERS	239
		TOD SLOAN	216		
BILL QUACKENBUSH	186	BILLY SMITH	216	PHIL WATSON	239
		HOOLEY SMITH	218	COONEY WEILAND	240
JEAN RATELLE	186	NORMIE SMITH	218	CY WENTWORTH	240
CHUCK RAYNER	188	SID SMITH	219	KENNY WHARRAM	241
KEN REARDON	189	ALLAN STANLEY	220	BILL WHITE	243
MARK RECCHI	190	WALLY STANOWSKI	220	DOUG WILSON	243
MICKEY REDMOND	190	PAT STAPLETON	221	GUMP WORSLEY	244
LEO REISE JR.	191	KEVIN STEVENS	222	ROY WORTERS	245
CHICO RESCH	192	SCOTT STEVENS	223		
HENRI RICHARD	192	GAYE STEWART	224	ALEXEI YASHIN	246
MAURICE RICHARD	194	JACK STEWART	224	STEVE YZERMAN	247
PAT RIGGIN	194	GARY SUTER	226		
JOHN ROSS ROACH	196			ALEXEI ZHAMNOV	248
RENE ROBERT	197	JEAN-GUY TALBOT	226		
EARL ROBERTSON	197	DAVE TAYLOR	227	FIRST AND SECOND	
LARRY ROBINSON	198	PAUL THOMPSON	227	ALL-STAR TEAMS	
LUC ROBITAILLE	199	TINY THOMPSON	228	BY SEASON	249
BOBBY ROUSSEAU	201			SOURCES	253
PATRICK ROY	201			PHOTO CREDITS	255

A t the close of every season, the National Hockey League pays tribute to its most brilliant performers by naming them "All-Stars." Only 12 players have the honor bestowed upon them each year. The First All-Star Team comprises a left wing, a center, a right wing, two defensemen and a goaltender. Six corresponding players make up the Second All-Star Team. The same simple criterion for selection has been in place since the inaugural NHL All-Stars were chosen after the 1930-31 campaign: whoever played his position best. At the conclusion of the regular season, the members of the Professional Hockey Writers' Association cast their votes by secret ballot.

It didn't take long, however, for the NHL to muddle the "All-Star" designation. When major-league baseball played its first All-Star Game in the summer of 1933, the NHL followed suit on Valentine's Day 1934, pitting a squad of unofficial league "All-Stars" against the Toronto Maple Leafs in a benefit game for injured Leaf Ace Bailey. While the contest featured bona fide stars, First All-Star Team members Frank Boucher and John Ross Roach were absent. Second All-Star Team constituents King Clancy, Charlie Conacher and Harvey Jackson played for Toronto. In addition, the "All-Star" lineup was salted with other players such as Nels "Old Poison" Stewart, a dazzling scorer who never made an official All-Star Team. Montreal hosted a Howie Morenz Memorial Game in 1937 and the Babe Siebert Memorial Benefit in 1939 before the NHL instituted an annual All-Star Game in 1947. As a result, "All-Star" references were—and are—confusing.

To be clear from the outset, then, *Hockey All-Stars: The NHL Honor Roll* does not concern itself with the All-Star Game. That entertaining exhibition match frequently includes participants selected for partisan, sentimental or geographic reasons. Instead, *Hockey All-Stars* is a comprehensive accounting of every member of every First and Second All-Star Team from 1930-31 to 1999-2000. Each player who appears here has been officially designated an All-Star by the NHL because of his feats that particular season.

In a perfect world, all the best players of the past 70 years would warrant All-Star status. Yet excellent performances are no guarantee of earning a berth on the First or Second All-Star Team. Pity the right-wingers who simultaneously competed for honors against both Maurice Richard and Gordie Howe. Center Steve Yzerman notched 155 points in 1988-89; unfortunately for Yzerman, the only men ever to tally more points, fellow pivots Mario Lemieux and Wayne Gretzky, scored 199 and 168 points, respectively, that season and took the First and Second All-Star Team spots. It wasn't until 2000, after Yzerman had transformed himself from an offensive juggernaut to the league's top defensive forward, that "Stevie Y" was named to an All-Star Team. For most, including many of the NHL's most distinguished players, making an All-Star Team has been a rare achievement. For some, their All-Star selection marks a career highlight.

As much as possible, *Hockey All-Stars* attempts to summarize just why these players were voted All-Stars, augmenting the statistical proof with the recollections of eyewitnesses. The results are testaments to greatness, but the peaks and valleys of an NHL hockey career become obvious as well. The high points—the All-Star seasons—are easy to identify, as is the length of time a player remained at the top of his game. While it is not an absolute test, the All-Star designation is one way to measure accomplishment, and it leads to inevitable comparisons. Evaluating athletes of different seasons is a difficult task, however, because there

DREAM TEAM 1933 (FROM TOP): FRANK BOUCHER, BALDY NORTHCOTT, BILL COOK, EDDIE SHORE, IVAN JOHNSON AND JOHN ROSS ROACH

are so many variables in the equation. Assorted styles of play have dominated dissimilar eras; war, league expansion and globalization have both enlarged and diffused the talent pool; and the vagaries of memory influence how strongly players and events take hold in our imaginations. "I seen 'em all score goals," reminisced four-time All-Star King Clancy. "Gordie Howe, wicked and deft, knocking everybody on their ass with his windshield-wiper elbows; Rocket Richard, coming mad, guys climbing all over him; Bobby Hull, booming a slap shot like a WWII cannon; Wayne Gretzky, mesmerizing the defense as he waltzes across the blue line, then wafting a feathery pass to a fast-coming winger…But I never saw anybody—nobody—score like Howie Morenz on a furious charge down center." Of course, facing Morenz man-to-man on the ice, as Clancy did for most of his playing career, would have a stronger effect than would watching a player from the sidelines in street clothes. Similarly, we all bring to the sport our own memories, experiences and biases. So while it may fuel some arguments or end some debates, *Hockey All-Stars* is above all a tribute to the All-Stars and their amazing talents.

Familiar names, such as the litany of greats in Clancy's recollection, abound in the list of All-Stars. Yet the old storytellers grow fewer every year, new idols arise, and as a result, many of yesteryear's heroes have faded into obscurity. Goaltender Mike Karakas, the first hockey player to appear on a Wheaties cereal box, is a case in point. Wearing a custom-made skate to protect a broken toe, Karakas backstopped the Chicago Blackhawks to the 1938 Stanley Cup. He made the 1946 Second All-Star Team, but when Chicago finally won its next Stanley Cup, in 1961, not even Hawks goalie Glenn Hall recognized Karakas when he entered the dressing room to offer his congratulations. The name of

8-time All-Star Eddie Shore is rightly recalled by many hockey fans, although he played in the 1930s, but his contemporary—10-time All-Star Earl Seibert— is almost unknown. *Hockey All-Stars* acknowledges the pantheon of NHL legends as well as all the current All-Stars, such as Jaromir Jagr, Paul Kariya and Pavel Bure. Just as important, though, this book describes illustrious players whom many readers will be discovering for the first time. "Iron Mike" Karakas, Seibert and dozens of other oft-forgotten greats, such as Sweeney Schriner, Ebbie Goodfellow and Flash Hollett, bask in the spotlight too.

Hockey All-Stars is arranged alphabetically, but a chronological list of every First and Second All-Star Team is also included. While these "dream teams" never took to the ice together, it is fascinating to look at the amazing combinations. What coach or appreciative fan doesn't salivate at the thought of Mario Lemieux centering Ducks Paul Kariya and Teemu Selanne, the 1997 First All-Star Team forwards, or of the 1970s defense tandem of Bobby Orr and Brad Park backstopped by goalie Tony Esposito? It's worthwhile noting, however, that similar feelings would have arisen in 1933 at the thought of Frank Boucher lining up between Baldy Northcott and Bill Cook, with blue-liners Eddie Shore and Ivan Johnson in front of netminder John Ross Roach. The NHL represents hockey at its highest level, and an appreciation of its past is important for understanding its present and its future. In raising their own game so high, these All-Stars, the dominant players of their day, have likewise elevated the sport. Celebrating their exploits raises the hope —and expectation—of continued excellence.

1997 FIRST ALL-STAR TEAM FORWARDS (FROM TOP):
MARIO LEMIEUX, PAUL KARIYA AND TEEMU SELANNE
THE DREAM DEFENSE, 1970S-STYLE: BOBBY ORR, BRAD PARK AND TONY ESPOSITO

Statistics are current as of June 30, 2000.

Calder: The Calder Memorial Trophy, inaugurated in 1933 as the rookie-of-the-year award and named the Calder in 1937, is an annual award presented to "the player selected as the most proficient in his first year of competition in the NHL," as chosen by the Professional Hockey Writers' Association.

Ross: The Art Ross Trophy, inaugurated in 1948, is an annual award presented to "the player who leads the league in scoring points at the end of the regular season." In this book, the scoring leaders from earlier seasons have also been given this designation.

Richard: The Maurice "Rocket" Richard Trophy, inaugurated in 1999, is an annual award presented to "the player who leads the league in goals scored at the end of the regular season."

Hart: The Hart Memorial Trophy, inaugurated in 1924, is an annual award presented to "the player adjudged to be the most valuable to his team," as selected by the Professional Hockey Writers' Association.

Jennings: The William M. Jennings Trophy, inaugurated in 1982, is an annual award presented to "the goalkeeper(s) having played a minimum of 25 games for the team with the fewest goals scored against it." (The winners of this award formerly earned the Vezina Trophy.)

Vezina: The Vezina Trophy, inaugurated in 1927, is an annual award presented to "the goalkeeper adjudged to be the best at his position," as selected by the general managers of the NHL clubs. Until 1982, this award went to "the goalkeeper(s) of the team with the fewest goals scored against it."

Byng: The Lady Byng Memorial Trophy, inaugurated in 1925, is an annual award presented to "the player adjudged to have exhibited the best type of sportsmanship and gentlemanly conduct combined with a high standard of playing ability," as selected by the Professional Hockey Writers' Association.

Pearson: The Lester B. Pearson Award, inaugurated in 1971, is an annual award presented to "the NHL's outstanding player," as selected by the National Hockey League Players' Association.

Norris: The James Norris Memorial Trophy, inaugurated in 1954, is an annual award presented to "the defense player who demonstrates throughout the season the greatest all-round ability in the position," as selected by the Professional Hockey Writers' Association.

Selke: The Frank J. Selke Trophy, inaugurated in 1978, is an annual award presented to "the forward who best excels in the defensive aspects of the game," as selected by the Professional Hockey Writers' Association.

Masterton: The Bill Masterton Memorial Trophy, inaugurated in 1968, is an annual award presented to "the player who best exemplifies the qualities of perseverance, sportsmanship and dedication to hockey," as selected by the Professional Hockey Writers' Association.

Clancy: The King Clancy Memorial Trophy, inaugurated in 1988, is an annual award presented to "the player who best exemplifies leadership qualities on and off the ice and has made a noteworthy humanitarian contribution in his community," as selected by the Professional Hockey Writers' Association.

Smythe: The Conn Smythe Trophy, inaugurated in 1965, is an annual award presented to "the most valuable player for his team in the playoffs," as selected by the Professional Hockey Writers' Association.

A-S Game: Three unofficial NHL All-Star Game benefits were played in the 1930s. In 1947, the NHL began organizing an official All-Star exhibition game, which has been played annually since, except in 1966, 1979, 1987 and 1995. Participants in the All-Star Game are not representative of the First and Second All-Star Teams featured in this book.

HOF: Honored member of the Hockey Hall of Fame. The year of induction follows.

RS: regular season
PO: playoffs
FOR FORWARDS AND DEFENSEMEN:
GP: games played; **G:** goals; **A:** assists;
P: total points; **PIM:** penalties in minutes
FOR GOALTENDERS:
GP: games played; **M:** minutes;
GA: goals against; **SO:** shutouts;
AVE: goals against per game average

LEGEND

The headline bars featuring the players' names are color-coded to indicate the span of a player's career.

The red and blue stars signify the player's membership on the First or Second All-Star Team.

1 9 3 0

1 9 4 0

1 9 5 0

1 9 6 0

1 9 7 0

1 9 8 0

1 9 9 0

2 0 0 0

SID ABEL

LEFT WING
CENTER

★2 1942
★ 1949, 1950 ★2 1951

Sid Abel cracked the Detroit Red Wings' lineup during the 1938-39 season, but he didn't have his first full NHL campaign until 1940-41. His aggressive play earned him the left-wing spot on the team's scoring line. Alongside Don Grosso and Eddie Wares, who had career years, Abel came fifth in 1941-42 league scoring and made the Second All-Star Team. Named team captain for 1942-43, Abel made his third consecutive trip to the Stanley Cup finals, where Detroit was victorious. Soon after, however, Abel registered for military duty. He would not return to Detroit until late in the 1945-46 season, when he was immediately restored as captain.

Abel first centered young wingers Ted Lindsay and Gordie Howe during the 1946-47 campaign. Within a couple of years, they were Detroit's "Production Line." Although Lindsay and Howe

missed a number of games in 1948-49, "Old Bootnose" Abel persevered with Pete Horeck and Gerry Couture and won the Hart Trophy. With an NHL-leading 28 goals, Abel also made the First All-Star Team. He retained his All-Star ranking in 1949-50, with a career-high 34 goals and 69 points. Second in scoring behind Lindsay and just ahead of Howe, Abel added 6 goals in 14 playoff games to help the Wings win the Stanley Cup.

Notching 61 points in 1950-51, Abel tied for fourth spot in scoring with Milt Schmidt and Ted Kennedy. He and Kennedy both made the Second All-Star Team. Although Abel slipped only to seventh place the following season and captained Detroit to another Stanley Cup, his playing career was coming to an end. With his agreement, the "greatest competitor and inspirational force the Red Wings ever had," in hockey his-

torian Ed Fitkin's opinion, was sold to Chicago to become a player/coach. There, Abel helped lift the Blackhawks into the 1952-53 playoffs, although he played only three games the following season before taking off his skates for good. The Red Wings retired his number 12, and he later served Detroit for many years as a coach and general manager.

SID ABEL
Melville, Saskatchewan
February 22, 1918–February 8, 2000
NHL Career: 1938-43, 1945-54
Detroit, Chicago

	GP	G	A	P	PIM
RS	612	189	283	472	376
PO	97	28	30	58	79

Hart, Stanley Cup (3), A-S Game (3), HOF 1969

TOM ANDERSON

DEFENSE

★ 1942

Although Tom "Cowboy" Anderson spent only one NHL season on defense, he made it a banner year. Anderson, who was born in Scotland and raised in the Canadian West, played left wing for most of his career. After four seasons with the Philadelphia Arrows of the Can-Am League, he was traded to the Detroit Red Wings. He scored 5 goals in 27 games over the 1934-35 NHL schedule, failing to impress Jack Adams, and was sold to the New York Americans in October 1935. He didn't do much better with the Amerks until he got a premier centerman in 1936-37. Supplying some much-

needed speed for slow-footed sniper Nels Stewart, Anderson tallied 10 goals and 15 assists.

He played a prominent role in the Americans' 1938 semifinal appearance, but that marked the franchise's peak success. On a line with Murray Armstrong and Lorne Carr in 1938-39, Anderson came second in team scoring behind Sweeney Schriner, with 13 goals and 40 points. A year later, however, the team began to experience severe financial difficulties. The Amerks sold or traded the team's star players before making a desperate attempt to solidify a fan base in 1941-42. They continued to play all home games in Madison Square Garden, but Anderson and his teammates moved to Brooklyn. Even wealthy manager Red Dutton took a Flatbush apartment.

Moved back to defense, Anderson led all rearguards in scoring, with 12 goals and 29 assists. Although the Brooklyn Americans remained in last place, Anderson won the prestigious Hart Trophy for his efforts and made the First All-Star Team. The franchise then folded, but by then, Anderson had already enlisted in the Canadian Army. He served three years before resuming a professional-hockey career in 1945-46, his rights having been transferred to Chicago. Anderson retired after two minor-league seasons.

TOM ANDERSON
Edinburgh, Scotland
July 9, 1910–September 15, 1971
NHL Career: 1934-42
Detroit, NY Americans, Brooklyn

	GP	G	A	P	PIM
RS	319	62	127	189	190
PO	16	2	7	9	8

Hart, A-S Game

 1939, 1942  1938, 1941, 1943

Syl Apps, a tough competitor who retained the gentlemanly qualities of an older era, was almost too good to be true. He was a superb all-round athlete who excelled at hockey, football and baseball, shot in the low 70s in golf and finished sixth in the pole-vault competition at the 1936 Berlin Olympics.

When he joined the Toronto Maple Leafs for the 1936-37 season, Apps was an immediate sensation, leading the league with 29 assists in his rookie campaign and finishing second in total scoring. That year, he was also the inaugural winner of the Calder Trophy. In 1937-38, his league-high 29 helpers again lifted him to second in the scoring race, and Apps became an All-Star for the first of five times in six seasons.

In 1940-41, Apps became Toronto's captain. He tied for eighth in league scoring in 1941-42, recording a penalty-free campaign, and won the Lady Byng Trophy. "His stickhandling and speed made him special," said Apps' frequent linemate Bob Davidson. "He didn't go out knocking anybody down too much, but he would check them. He wouldn't deliberately go out and hurt a guy, but he played to win all the time." Apps concluded his remarkable season by helping the Leafs to a Stanley Cup victory after the team had been down three games to none in the finals.

Apps entered the Canadian Army in 1943, and when he returned for the 1945-46 season, he picked up pretty much where he had left off. After captaining the Leafs to two more Cups in 1947 and 1948, however, he decided to retire, despite efforts to convince him otherwise. Apps briefly entertained second thoughts about ending his career, but when he was told that Ted Kennedy had already been given the team's captaincy, his decision became final.

During the 1970s, his son, Syl Apps Jr., also played in the NHL. "I've had excitement in hockey, Stanley Cups, and so on," said Apps in 1975, "but I can't think of a bigger thrill than I got just this year, watching Sylvanus score two goals in the All-Star Game and win that car as the best player of the night." Unfortunately, Apps died before his grandson, Syl Apps III, got a 1999 tryout with the Maple Leafs.

SYLVANUS APPS
Paris, Ontario
January 18, 1915–December 24, 1998
NHL Career: 1936-43, 1945-48
Toronto

	GP	G	A	P	PIM
RS	423	201	231	432	56
PO	69	25	29	54	8

Calder, Byng, Stanley Cup (3),
A-S Game (2), HOF 1961

DEFENSE

 1974

After playing 14 games with Boston in 1965-66, Barry Ashbee resumed a lengthy minor-league career. When the Philadelphia Flyers bought his rights in May 1970, however, Ashbee got his big break. He soon established himself as a dependable "stay-at-home" NHL blue-liner. His physical style resulted in his sustaining many injuries, and he often wore a "horse collar" neck support even when he was on the ice. But Ashbee endeared himself to his teammates by frequently playing through obvious pain.

Even though he accumulated a career-high 106 penalty minutes in 1972-73, Ashbee wasn't a stereotypical "Broad Street Bully." He tallied only 52 penalty minutes in 1973-74 and made the Second All-Star Team. Then, in the playoff semifinals, disaster struck. New York Ranger Dale Rolfe took a slap shot that struck Ashbee in the eye, causing profuse bleeding and permanent damage. Although Ashbee never played again, the Flyers triumphed a few weeks later. "I'm just happy I was able to get my name on the Stanley Cup," said Ashbee. "These things happen, and you have to accept them."

His teammates were less stoic. "I'm only sorry the old man wasn't there with me on this day," said Moose Dupont, fighting back tears. "I owe Barry so much."

Ashbee soon returned to the Flyers as an assistant coach but was diagnosed with leukemia in 1977. "Look, I don't want this written up as a 'Win One for the Gipper' story," he said from his hospital bed. "The players know I'm sick, and I'm going to get better, that's all." He died a month later.

Although his life and NHL career were tragically short, Ashbee had made his mark. "He was the strongest guy mentally I've ever seen," recalled Bobby Clarke. The Barry Ashbee Trophy has gone to the Flyers' outstanding defenseman annually since 1975, while the best defenseman on Philadelphia's minor-league affiliate receives the Barry Ashbee Award.

BARRY ASHBEE
Weston, Ontario
July 28, 1939–May 12, 1977
NHL Career: 1965-66, 1970-74
Boston, Philadelphia

	GP	G	A	P	PIM
RS	284	15	70	85	291
PO	17	0	4	4	22

Stanley Cup

RIGHT WING

 1937

The Detroit Red Wings retired Larry Aurie's sweater-number 6, but inexplicably, it does not hang from the rafters of the Joe Louis Arena with the franchise's other honored numbers. Perhaps Aurie's contributions have been forgotten.

In his rookie year with the Detroit Cougars, the five-foot-six right-winger scored 13 goals over the 44-game schedule. In 1930-31, the Cougars became the Falcons, and when the Falcons became the Red Wings in 1932-33, Aurie was named team captain. The following season, Detroit acquired Cooney Weiland and put him at center between Aurie and Herbie Lewis. The three of them weighed in at about 150 pounds each, but together, they carried the Wings to the top of the American Division. Aurie led the team with 16 goals and 19 assists. He added 10 points in nine playoff matches before Chicago won the clinching Stanley Cup game in double overtime.

Aurie finished third in 1934-35 scoring with 17 goals and a career-high 46 points. The Wings traded for Marty Barry to center Aurie and Lewis the following season, and Detroit won its first Cup. Aurie led the league with 23 goals in 1936-37, a personal best. He finished fourth overall with 43 points, one behind Barry. Both players made the First All-Star Team, but Aurie broke his ankle just before the playoffs started and missed the postseason entirely. Detroit successfully defended the Cup, but Aurie never completely recovered. He scored only 10 goals and 9 assists in 1937-38 and was out of the league after playing a single game the following season. The Pittsburgh Hornets were glad to have him, however, and Aurie made the AHL's Second All-Star Team of 1939.

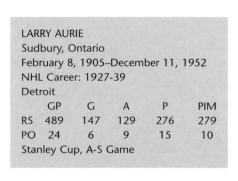

LARRY AURIE
Sudbury, Ontario
February 8, 1905–December 11, 1952
NHL Career: 1927-39
Detroit

	GP	G	A	P	PIM
RS	489	147	129	276	279
PO	24	6	9	15	10

Stanley Cup, A-S Game

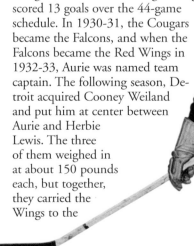

BILL BARBER

 1976  1979, 1981

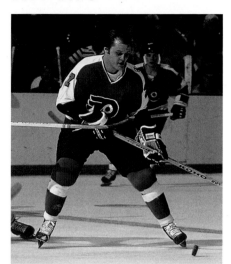

Coach Fred Shero deserves some of the credit for Bill Barber's Hall of Fame career. When Barber was selected by Philadelphia in the first round of the 1972 entry draft, he had tallied over 100 points in each of his last two junior seasons as a center, but Shero converted him to a winger. Barber scored 30 goals and 34 assists and finished runner-up behind Steve Vickers for 1972-73 rookie-of-the-year honors. One of the "skill" players on

the "Broad Street Bullies," Barber was a key to Philadelphia's Stanley Cup wins in the next two seasons.

"They had that line of [Bobby] Clarke, Bill Barber and Reggie Leach," recalled Scotty Bowman, who coached the Montreal Canadiens throughout most of the 1970s. "I think that was about the best line in history. One year, they were only on the ice for 28 goals against. When they won their Cups [in 1974 and 1975], we tried to match power against power, and it didn't work. They were the first defensive guys who could play two ways." Barber also became one of the most notorious but effective "divers" in the league, drawing numerous penalties for opposing players by embellishing a light hook or grab. About a quarter of his 420 career goals, still a franchise record, came on the power play.

Barber made the First All-Star Team when he erupted for his only 50-goal campaign in 1975-76. His 62 assists were also a career-high, and he finished fourth in league scoring. Bowman and the Canadiens found a way to counter the Flyers, however, rotating three different units against the Barber/Clarke/Leach

line, and the Flyers were swept in the Stanley Cup finals that year. Barber was frequently underrated by many, but in 1977-78, he led his team with 41 goals. In 1978-79, he made the Second All-Star Team with his team-leading 34 goals and 80 points. Philadelphia returned to the Stanley Cup finals the following season, but while Barber led the Flyers with 21 playoff points, the New York Islanders prevailed.

Barber's 45 goals and 85 points were again tops in Philadelphia in 1980-81, his last All-Star season. Knee surgery in 1984 brought an early end to his career, and his number 7 was officially retired on March 6, 1986.

BILL BARBER
Callander, Ontario
July 11, 1952–
NHL Career: 1972-84
Philadelphia

	GP	G	A	P	PIM
RS	903	420	463	883	623
PO	129	53	55	108	109

Stanley Cup (2), A-S Game (6), HOF 1990

TOM BARRASSO

 1984  1985, 1993

Like Frank Brimsek and Tony Esposito, Tom Barrasso won rookie-of-the-year honors, the Vezina Trophy and a spot on the First All-Star Team in the same season. Barrasso's stunning 1983-84 rise to the top, however, was unprecedented. The Buffalo Sabres gave Barrasso their starting job straight out of high school, whereas both Brimsek and Esposito had had minor-league or college experience.

Barrasso was still a teenager when he competed for the United States in the Canada Cup tournament in September 1984. Buffalo sent him to its AHL affiliate later that fall for a tune-up, but Barrasso quickly returned to the NHL. In February, he earned the starting position in the All-Star Game. At season's end, he led the league with five shutouts and

made the Second All-Star Team. He also shared the William M. Jennings Trophy with teammate Bob Sauve and finished runner-up for the Vezina.

In 1987-88, Barrasso again finished second in Vezina voting, but Buffalo traded him to Pittsburgh early the following season. He missed most of the 1989-90 campaign due to a broken wrist and a leave of absence he took during his young daughter's successful fight against cancer, but he rebounded strongly. Barrasso backstopped the Penguins to consecutive Stanley Cup victories in 1991 and 1992. He made the 1992-93 Second All-Star Team with an NHL-high 43 victories and came second for the Vezina.

Although Barrasso missed almost the entire 1994-95 and 1996-97 seasons

with injuries, he made an impressive recovery and earned a nomination for the 1997-98 Vezina. Traded to Ottawa in March 2000, Barrasso continued to add to his record for the most career wins by an American-born goaltender.

TOM BARRASSO
Boston, Massachusetts
March 31, 1965–
NHL Career: 1983-
Buffalo, Pittsburgh, Ottawa

	GP	M	GA	SO	AVE
RS	733	41727	2276	35	3.27
PO	119	6952	349	6	3.01

Calder, Jennings, Vezina, Stanley Cup (2), A-S Game

MARTY BARRY

  ★ 1937

Marty Barry lasted only nine games with the cellar-dwelling New York Americans in 1927-28. Fortunately, Boston took note of his subsequent scoring title in the Can-Am League and picked him up for the 1929-30 campaign. In 1931-32, the speedy center led the Bruins with 21 goals, then topped his teammates in points while finishing in the league's top-10 scorers over each of the next three seasons. However, the ultimate team success eluded Boston.

"If I had Cooney Weiland, my club would be here," said Bruins coach Frank Patrick during the 1935 Cup finals.

"If I had Marty Barry," retorted his Detroit counterpart Jack Adams, "we'd win the Cup." The deal was soon done. Placed between Herbie Lewis and Larry Aurie, "Goal-a-Game" Barry scored 21 goals and 19 assists in 1935-36, tying Paul Thompson for second spot in league scoring. In the playoffs against the Montreal Maroons, Barry played in the NHL's longest game on record. "The rink seemed like it was miles long along about 10 minutes to 2 o'clock in the morning," he told writer Ace Foley.

"Players of both teams were praying for somebody to score before we all fell from exhaustion." In the sixth overtime period, Detroit's Mud Bruneteau finally iced a 1–0 victory. The Red Wings went on to defeat Toronto for their first Stanley Cup.

Barry's strong 1936-37 season, with only six penalty minutes, earned him the Lady Byng Trophy. His 17 goals and 27 assists, good for third in the scoring race, also lifted him to the First All-Star Team. He then led the postseason with 11 points. Barry staved off defeat with the only goal in the fourth game of the Stanley Cup finals, tying the series against the New York Rangers. In the deciding game, he put in the Cup-winner late in the first period and added the final insurance goal in a 3–0 win.

Noting his dexterity and determination, Adams once described Barry as "an artist with the puck." But although he tied for fourth in league scoring in 1938-39, Adams released him. Barry finished out his NHL career the following season with the Montreal Canadiens.

MARTY BARRY
Quebec City, Quebec
December 8, 1905–August 20, 1969
NHL Career: 1927-28, 1929-40
NY Americans, Boston, Detroit, Montreal

	GP	G	A	P	PIM
RS	509	195	192	387	231
PO	43	15	18	33	34

Byng, Stanley Cup (2), A-S Game,
HOF 1965

ANDY BATHGATE

  ★ 1959, 1962 ★2 1958, 1963

Andy Bathgate was a generous playmaker, but he also had a blistering shot. In the late 1950s, he sent the glove of Boston goaltender Harry Lumley into the net with the puck in it. "It was like trying to catch a brick," recalled Lumley. When he broke Jacques Plante's nose with a devastating backhand, Bathgate helped usher in the use of the goalie mask.

When he was still playing junior hockey, Bathgate had had a steel plate inserted in his knee. The brace he wore continued to bother him, and he had two other handicaps: He played for the lowly Rangers, and he competed with Gordie Howe and Rocket Richard for league honors. Although Bathgate finished in a fifth-place tie in 1955-56 scoring and came fourth the following season, it took his third-place finish in

1957-58 to put him on the Second All-Star Team. Bathgate notched his only 40-goal campaign and a career-high 88 points in 1958-59 to earn a First All-Star Team berth. Most satisfying, he outscored Howe 133 to 60 in Hart Trophy voting.

When he tied for the league lead with 84 points, Bathgate made the 1961-62 First All-Star Team, but having fewer goals, he lost the Art Ross Trophy to Bobby Hull. He finished second in scoring again the following season, just behind Howe, and once more made the Second Team. Traded to Toronto late in the 1963-64 campaign, Bathgate finished fourth in NHL scoring, leading the league with 48 assists and helping the Leafs win the 1964 Stanley Cup. The outspoken Bathgate was dealt to Detroit a year later.

Left unprotected in the 1967 expan-

sion draft, Bathgate finished out his NHL career with the Pittsburgh Penguins. "Andy's legs weren't what they once were," said Pittsburgh coach Red Sullivan, a former teammate. "But he had that shot and that head of his. And that's more than most people have."

ANDY BATHGATE
Winnipeg, Manitoba
August 28, 1932–
NHL Career: 1952-68, 1970-71
NY Rangers, Toronto, Detroit, Pittsburgh

	GP	G	A	P	PIM
RS	1069	349	624	973	624
PO	54	21	14	35	76

Hart, Stanley Cup, A-S Game (8),
HOF 1978

BOBBY BAUER

RIGHT WING

Although older than Milt Schmidt and Woody Dumart, Bobby Bauer was the last of the renowned "Kraut Line" to join the NHL. He was also the last of the three childhood friends to receive hockey's highest honor. "I always maintained Bobby was the brains of our line," said Schmidt at Bauer's posthumous 1996 induction into the Hockey Hall of Fame. "It's like winning the Stanley Cup all

over again to have all three of us in here."

Called up to the Boston Bruins for the last game of the 1936-37 season, Bauer managed to score. The following season, he led the team with 20 goals. In 1938-39, he made the Second All-Star Team for the first of three consecutive seasons, and the Bruins took the Stanley Cup. "He had a knack of getting between the boards and the opposing winger and making a play," recalled Dumart. "He had a good shot, was a good skater and stickhandler and had a way of finding holes. He and Milt would pass the puck back and forth. I got the garbage goals." Bauer tied Dumart for second place in NHL points in 1939-40, right behind Schmidt.

Only five-foot-six and 150 pounds, Bauer also won the Lady Byng Trophy in 1940 and 1941 with just two penalty minutes in each season. He scored the Cup-clinching goal in the 1941 playoffs, but late in the 1941-42 season, Bauer's NHL career was put on hold when he, Dumart and Schmidt joined the Royal Canadian Air Force. The trio didn't return to the Bruins until the 1945-46 season, but Bauer began to talk about retirement soon afterward.

Persuaded by the Bruins to return for one last season, Bauer finished seventh in league scoring. His 30 goals and 54 points were both career-highs, and he picked up his third Lady Byng Trophy and fourth All-Star selection. His ambition, however, was to play hockey in Kitchener, where he could also help with the family sporting-goods business. On March 18, 1952, a Schmidt/Dumart tribute night in Boston, the "Kraut Line" was reunited with a noticeably heavier Bauer on right wing. Not only did he score, but he assisted on Schmidt's 200th career goal. "Bobby was our team," said Schmidt years later, "my right arm."

BOBBY BAUER
Waterloo, Ontario
February 16, 1915–September 16, 1964
NHL Career: 1936-42, 1945-47, 1951-52
Boston

	GP	G	A	P	PIM
RS	327	123	137	260	36
PO	48	11	8	19	6

Byng (3), Stanley Cup (2), A-S Game (2), HOF 1996

ED BELFOUR

GOALTENDER

Ed Belfour joined Chicago for 23 games in 1988-89, but his 3.87 goals-against average failed to impress management—he didn't play for the Blackhawks again until the 1990 play-offs. As the Hawks' starter for 1990-91, he was assigned Soviet great Vladislav Tretiak as his tutor (he later adopted Tretiak's number 20 as his own). Officially still a rookie, Belfour then took the Calder Trophy with a spectacular First All-Star Team campaign. He played a franchise-record 74 games and won both the Vezina and the William M. Jennings trophies with a 2.47 average.

Belfour posted the most shutouts in the league over each of the next four seasons. Runner-up for the 1991-92 Jennings, he backstopped Chicago to the Stanley Cup

finals. He rejoined the First All-Star Team again the following season with a career-high seven shutouts, winning his second Vezina and Jennings. Yet "Eddie the Eagle" heard whispers that he couldn't win the big game. Of course, his abrasive nature and high penalty totals—he tallied 61 minutes in 1993-94—didn't endear him to anyone but Chicago fans. In 1994-95, he made the Second All-Star Team with another Jennings-winning season and finished runner-up for the Vezina. It took a trade to get Belfour more respect.

Chicago dealt him to the San Jose Sharks in January 1997, anticipating his free-agent status the following summer. Belfour signed with the Dallas Stars for 1997-98 and posted the league's lowest average in the regular season and in the

playoffs. In 1998-99, he shared the Jennings with Roman Turek and out-dueled Dominik Hasek in the championship finals. "The Stanley Cup was the lifelong dream for me," said Belfour. "Now I can relax and have a little fun."

ED BELFOUR
Carman, Manitoba
April 21, 1965–
NHL Career: 1988-
Chicago, San Jose, Dallas

	GP	M	GA	SO	AVE
RS	612	35173	1446	49	2.47
PO	131	7968	283	11	2.13

Calder, Jennings (4), Vezina (2), Stanley Cup, A-S Game (5)

JEAN BELIVEAU

CENTER   1955, 1956, 1957, 1959, 1960, 1961   ⭐2 1958, 1964, 1966, 1969

The Montreal Canadiens eagerly awaited the start of Jean Beliveau's NHL career, and their appetite was further whetted when the young player racked up a goal and an assist during a two-game call-up in 1950-51 and 5 goals in a three-game appearance in 1952-53. But it took an extraordinary effort to pry him from the Quebec Aces of the Quebec Hockey League. Ostensibly an amateur, Beliveau earned more than most NHL players of the day. He had signed a contract with Montreal stating that he would play for the Canadiens when he turned professional. To speed up the process, Montreal bought the entire Quebec Hockey League and put an end to its amateur status.

Although Beliveau battled through injuries in his 1953-54 rookie campaign, his sharp passing, hard shot and elegant leadership lifted him into the NHL elite for the rest of his career. He made the First All-Star Team as a sophomore, finishing third in NHL scoring. The following season, he played a rougher game and won the Art Ross and Hart trophies with 47 goals and 41 assists. Gradually, Beliveau settled into the cleaner style that was his trademark, but he remained near the top of the scoring charts while the Habs owned the Cup for five straight seasons.

In 1960-61, the Canadiens were finally dethroned as champions, although Beliveau notched a record-breaking 58 assists. The following season, his teammates voted him captain, a position that he held until his retirement. Beliveau won his second Hart Trophy in 1963-64, and with 8 goals and 8 assists in 13 games in the 1965 playoffs, he was the inaugural winner of the Conn Smythe Trophy.

"Although we are very well paid by the Canadiens, money is not the incentive," he claimed in the late 1960s. "We think the Stanley Cup is the important thing. We feel we are representing French Canada, and winning the Cup for our supporters is the main objective." Beliveau lifted the Cup for the tenth time in 1971 and retired a winner. His 176 career playoff points survived as a league record until Wayne Gretzky passed him in 1987.

JEAN BELIVEAU				
Trois-Rivières, Quebec				
August 31, 1931–				
NHL Career: 1950-51, 1952-71				
Montreal				
GP	G	A	P	PIM
RS 1125	507	712	1219	1029
PO 162	79	97	176	211
Ross, Hart (2), Smythe, Stanley Cup (10),				
A-S Game (13), HOF 1972				

BRIAN BELLOWS

LEFT WING   ⭐2 1990

Minnesota general manager Lou Nanne insisted on giving Brian Bellows, the North Stars' 1982 number-two draft pick, his former sweater-number 23. "There's certainly got to

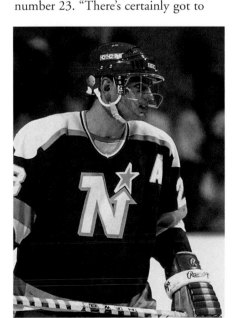

be a lot of goals left in that old jersey," joked Nanne. "I know I didn't use them all up when I played."

Bellows averaged more than 30 goals over his first seven seasons, but he wasn't content. When he complained about the quality of his linemates, coach Pierre Page united Bellows with playmaking center Neal Broten and sniper Mike Gartner in 1989-90. "I know he wants to win," said Page, "and if that remains his top priority, we'll get along just fine. Last year, I wanted things done my way and he wanted things done his way. Now, it's not my way or his way; it's midway." Bellows responded by making the Second All-Star Team, finishing the season with 55 goals and 99 points.

He notched 29 playoff points during Minnesota's surprising trip to the 1991 Stanley Cup finals, but in the summer of 1992, the trade winds blew Bellows to Montreal. He led the Canadiens with 40 goals in 1992-93 and earned a Cup ring with 15 playoff points. Traded to Tampa Bay in June 1995, he then became a

Mighty Duck in November 1996. After Bellows spent most of the next season playing in Germany, the Washington Capitals signed him in March 1998. "When I played with him, I couldn't stand him, but as a coach, I love him," said Ron Wilson, a former North Star who also coached Bellows in Anaheim. "He has lost a step or two over the years, but he's still the original bull in the china shop. He's all legs driving to the net." Bellows helped the Caps to the 1998 Cup finals and retired a year later.

BRIAN BELLOWS				
St. Catharines, Ontario				
September 1, 1964–				
NHL Career: 1982-99				
Minnesota, Montreal, Tampa Bay,				
Anaheim, Washington				
GP	G	A	P	PIM
RS 1188	485	537	1022	718
PO 143	51	71	122	143
Stanley Cup, A-S Game (3)				

DOUG BENTLEY

LEFT WING
CENTER

★ 1943, 1944, 1947
2 1949

The first of three Bentleys to play in the NHL, Doug Bentley made the Chicago Blackhawks in 1939-40. His younger brother Max followed him in 1940-41, and his older brother Reggie joined the team in 1942-43. Although Reggie played only 11 games that campaign—the sum of his major-league career—Doug became the First All-Star Team left wing and top goal scorer both that season and the next. He won the 1943 scoring title with a record-tying 73 points and finished runner-up to scoring champion Herb Cain of Boston in 1943-44.

A rarely invoked wartime travel ban prevented Bentley from leaving Canada, and he missed the entire 1944-45 NHL campaign. When he returned to Chicago, the famed "Pony Line"—so called because of the slight stature of all three players—was formed. At five-foot-eight and 145 pounds, Bentley was the smallest. His centerman, brother Max, stood five-foot-ten and weighed 155 pounds, while five-foot-eight, 155-pound Bill Mosienko played the right wing. But the "Pony Line" had tremendous speed, playmaking ability and determination. Bentley made the 1947 First All-Star Team with his sixth-place finish in points, and his brother won the scoring crown. Then, in a stunning trade early the next season, Max was sent to Toronto.

In an impressive transition, Bentley then centered Mosienko and newcomer Roy Conacher, finishing third in 1947-48 NHL scoring with a league-high 37 assists. His 43 assists the following season pulled him to second place, behind Conacher, and onto the Second All-Star

Team. In 1950, a Chicago newspaper named Bentley the greatest player in Chicago Blackhawk history, but he played only eight games of the 1951-52 season before returning to Saskatchewan. He had one final NHL turn when the New York Rangers reunited him with his brother Max for the last half of the 1953-54 campaign.

DOUG BENTLEY
Delisle, Saskatchewan
September 3, 1916–November 24, 1972
NHL Career: 1939-44, 1945-52, 1953-54
Chicago, NY Rangers

	GP	G	A	P	PIM
RS	566	219	324	543	217
PO	23	9	8	17	8

Ross, A-S Game (5), HOF 1964

MAX BENTLEY

CENTER

Artful playmaker Max Bentley, the "Dipsy-Doodle-Dandy of Delisle," also had a hard shot. "My dad has had eight cows on the farm back in Delisle ever since I can remember," he told Herb Goren of *The New York Sun*. "I milked those cows every day—two hours in the morning and two hours at night. That's a lot of milking, but it gives a guy strong wrists." Deemed too frail by Montreal, Bentley joined his older brother Doug in Chicago in 1940-41, where they both exploded onto the NHL scoring charts in 1942-43. Doug's 73 points led the league, while Max—the Lady Byng Trophy-winner with only two penalty minutes—came third with 26 goals and 44 assists. He spent the next two seasons in the Canadian Army.

The "Pony Line" was formed in 1945-46, with five-foot-ten, 155-pound Bentley centering his brother Doug and Bill Mosienko, who were also small in stature. Their nifty passing and quick speed, however, more than compensated for their lack of size. Bentley handily won the 1945-46 scoring crown, was awarded the Hart Trophy and made the First All-Star Team. He won his second scoring title and a Second Team berth the following season.

A blockbuster trade saw Bentley and Cy Thomas go to Toronto for Gus Bodnar, Bud Poile, Gaye Stewart, Bob Goldham and Ernie Dickens on November 2, 1947. While saddened to leave his brother, Bentley tied for fifth in 1947-48 league scoring and helped the Leafs successfully defend the Stanley Cup that spring and the next.

Bentley came third in 1950-51 regular-season scoring and tied Maurice Richard with 13 points in the play-offs. Toronto took the Cup again, but two seasons later, Bentley was sold to the New York Rangers. There, he was reunited with his brother Doug, although both men retired at season's end to play and coach back home in Saskatchewan.

MAX BENTLEY
Delisle, Saskatchewan
March 1, 1920–January 19, 1984
NHL Career: 1940-43, 1945-54
Chicago, Toronto, NY Rangers

	GP	G	A	P	PIM
RS	646	245	299	544	179
PO	51	18	27	45	14

Ross (2), Hart, Byng, Stanley Cup (3), A-S Game (4), HOF 1966

PAUL BIBEAULT

GOALTENDER

On March 15, 1941, Montreal coach Dick Irvin alternated rookie goalie Paul Bibeault with Bert Gardiner at seven-minute intervals. The ensuing 6–0 victory over the New York Americans marked the first shared shutout in NHL history. Irvin went with Gardiner in the 1941 playoffs, but Bibeault played most of 1941-42 and every minute of the following season. He became especially popular with the Francophone fans, but when Bill Durnan signed a contract with the Habs on the eve of the 1943-44 season, Bibeault was out of a job.

Just before Christmas 1943, Montreal loaned Bibeault to the Leafs. Toronto's regular goalie, Turk Broda, had been drafted onto an army team, while Bibeault, five years his junior, was only in the army reserve. He played the last 29 games of the NHL season for the Leafs, notched a league-high five shutouts and was elected to the Second All-Star Team. During the playoffs, however, his average ballooned to 4.60 in a first-round loss to Detroit. Toronto decided that it had no further need of Bibeault's services.

Bruins goalie Frank Brimsek was serving in the U.S. Coast Guard when Boston borrowed Bibeault on December 27, 1944. Montreal didn't call him back until January 6, 1946. While Habs goaltender Durnan nursed an injury, Bibeault played 10 games for the Canadiens. Meanwhile, Brimsek returned to Boston. Bibeault sat out the rest of the season and was traded to Chicago just before the 1946-47 campaign began. He had played 41 games for the last-place Blackhawks when Montreal invoked a right of recall, and Bibeault returned to the Canadiens. Although the Montreal fans chanted his name whenever they were unhappy with Durnan, Bibeault never played in the NHL again.

PAUL BIBEAULT
Montreal, Quebec
April 13, 1919–August 2, 1970
NHL Career: 1940-47
Montreal, Toronto, Boston, Chicago

	GP	M	GA	SO	AVE
RS	214	12890	785	10	3.65
PO	20	1237	71	2	3.44

ROB BLAKE

DEFENSE

Rob Blake joined Los Angeles late in the 1989-90 campaign but still qualified as a rookie the following season. He led all first-year rearguards in scoring with 46 points and made the All-Rookie Team. Blake also won his team's outstanding defenseman award for the first of four straight seasons. "He looks like Bobby Orr out there," said his first coach Tom Webster. "Some nights, however, he looks like iron ore." But Blake continued to improve and started to get notices as a future Norris Trophy-winner.

He helped the Kings to their first Stanley Cup finals in 1993. Six-foot-two and 220 pounds, with a bit of a mean streak, Blake played a hard-hitting defensive game while contributing offensively. He tallied a career-high 48 assists and 68 points in 1993-94. Because of injuries, however, he was able to play only 30 games over the next two seasons.

Although he missed 18 matches in 1996-97, Blake still led the Kings' blue-line corps in scoring. Fully healed for 1997-98, Blake was a finalist for the Bill Masterton Trophy. He led all NHL defensemen with 23 goals and made the First All-Star Team; he also won the Norris. "I think it lifts a huge, huge load off his shoulders," said coach Larry Robinson, a former Norris-winner himself.

Blake agreed completely. "It was really tough being tagged as a potential winner so early in my career, but [that] helps make it so exciting, to finally win it and to be considered at that level. It's somewhere I want to get back to each year now." Team captain since Wayne Gretzky's trade in 1995-96, Blake became the top-scoring defenseman in Los Angeles King history in 1998-99.

ROB BLAKE
Simcoe, Ontario
December 10, 1969–
NHL Career: 1989-
Los Angeles

	GP	G	A	P	PIM
RS	608	121	259	380	982
PO	57	8	16	24	98

Norris, A-S Game (3)

LEFT WING

 1939, 1940, 1945 ⭐ 1938, 1946

For most fans, Toe Blake was the man with the fedora, the legendary coach of the Montreal Canadiens. But Blake also had a stellar playing career and was one of three Montreal Maroons sent to the Canadiens in exchange for Lorne Chabot in February 1936. Toe, a childhood nickname that stuck when a younger sibling called him "Hec-toe," soon became

known as "The Lamplighter" for turning on the red light behind the net so often. He made the 1937-38 Second All-Star Team with 33 points. The following season, he made the First Team, won the Hart Trophy and led the league with 47 points over the 48-game schedule.

Blake tied for ninth in 1939-40 league scoring and was named to the First All-

Star Team, but the team success he coveted didn't come his way until 1943-44, when he, Maurice Richard and Elmer Lach formed the "Punch Line." Blake notched a record 18 playoff points that season, including the overtime winner in the clinching game, to help the Canadiens win the 1944 Stanley Cup. In 1944-45, Lach, Richard and Blake finished 1–2–3, respectively, in league scoring. Blake's 29 goals and 38 assists were career-highs, and the "Punch Line" made the First All-Star Team.

In 1945-46, Blake made the Second Team with a team-leading 50 points and, with only two penalty minutes, was also awarded the Lady Byng Trophy. "A former free-swinging ice warrior," wrote A.W. O'Brien in *The Montreal Standard*, "he conquered his temper by sheer willpower."

In the 1946 finals, "The Lamplighter" clinched another Cup. "Blake, hobbled by a spine injury and playing on nerve alone, pelted the puck past Brimsek to break a 3–3 deadlock," wrote Dink Carroll in *The Gazette*. Midway through the 1947-48 season, however, Blake's NHL playing career ended when he broke his leg.

In 1955-56, Blake moved behind the Hab bench and guided the team to five consecutive victories. "We all admired Toe," said Jean Beliveau. "We found that even if he was very strict, he was very honest, and he would stand behind us if somebody attacked one of the players. I was captain for 10 years, so I was very close to Toe. I saw him cry after winning, and I saw him cry after losing." Blake certainly won more than he lost, though, and retired after coaching his eighth Cup-winner in 1968.

HECTOR "TOE" BLAKE
Victoria Mines, Ontario
August 21, 1912–May 17, 1995
NHL Career: 1934-48
Montreal Maroons, Montreal

	GP	G	A	P	PIM
RS	577	235	292	527	272
PO	58	25	37	62	23

Ross, Hart, Byng, Stanley Cup (2),
A-S Game (2), HOF 1966

MIKE BOSSY

RIGHT WING
★ 1981, 1982, 1983, 1984, 1986 ★ 1978, 1979, 1985

Perennial All-Star Mike Bossy was as pure a goal scorer as the NHL has ever seen. His 53-goal, 38-assist rookie-of-the-year campaign put him sixth in league scoring. His doubters, who had looked disparagingly at his scoring history in junior hockey, were forever silenced. Bossy also proved to be more than a one-dimensional player. "He's a hell of a skater, plays his position well and never has his back to the play," noted scout and former NHL goalie Ed Chadwick midway through Bossy's 1978-79 season. Bossy led the league with a career-high 69 goals that year.

Despite scoring 51 goals, Bossy missed being named to an All-Star Team in 1979-80, but he was a key to the New York Islanders' Stanley Cup win

that spring, the first of four consecutive championships. In 1980-81, goals 49 and 50 came during the last five minutes of Bossy's 50th game, matching Rocket Richard's 1944-45 campaign. "I felt like someone [had] lifted 1,000 pounds off me," he said. Bossy's charge at the record was intense, and he barely slackened his pace. By the end of the season, he had tallied a league-high 68 goals. He then led all 1981 playoff performers with 17 goals and 18 assists in 18 games. The following season, Bossy won the Conn Smythe Trophy, again the leading post-season scorer with 17 goals.

Refusing to retaliate against fouls or to be drawn into fisticuffs, Bossy was runner-up for the 1982 Lady Byng Trophy. He won the award three out of the

next four seasons. But the abuse he suffered on the ice exacted a price. Hobbled with back problems throughout much of the 1986-87 season, Bossy scored "only" 38 goals, his sole campaign with fewer than 50, then retired.

MIKE BOSSY
Montreal, Quebec
January 22, 1957–
NHL Career: 1977-87
NY Islanders

	GP	G	A	P	PIM
RS	752	573	553	1126	210
PO	129	85	75	160	38

Calder, Byng (3), Smythe, Stanley Cup (4), A-S Game (7), HOF 1991

BUTCH BOUCHARD

DEFENSE
★ 1945, 1946, 1947 ★ 1944

It is an honor to receive the Emile "Butch" Bouchard Trophy, presented annually to the best defenseman in the Quebec Major Junior Hockey League. At the age of 21, Butch Bouchard cracked Montreal's 1941-42 roster with just the right blend of strength and aggression. In 1943-44, he made the Second All-Star Team and helped the Habs win the Stanley Cup. "If he happened to get you along the fence, well, you were going to come out second best," said Toronto's Ted Kennedy. "But he wouldn't be one of these guys who would run you into the fence to hurt you. He'd rub you out, that's all."

With a career-high 11 goals and 23 assists, Bouchard joined the First All-Star Team in 1944-45. He remained an All-Star for two more seasons and was on another Cup-winner in 1946. In 1949-50, his teammates unanimously voted him team captain. "That made me happy," said Bouchard, "because, to tell you the truth, I don't agree with management nominating you. I can respond to the players, not be a yes-man for the proprietor."

Bouchard, whose nickname "Butch"

indicated toughness, remained one of the strongest NHL players for most of his career. "When I first saw his body, I couldn't believe it," recalled Dickie Moore, who joined the team in 1952. "It was like he was chiseled out of stone. He had the biggest shoulders and the smallest waist I had ever seen." Bouchard captained the Habs to another Cup in 1953, but by 1955-56, the game had started to take its toll. Dressed for only 36 games, he didn't record a point. He made one brief playoff appearance in Montreal's 1956 Cup-clinching game, then retired. In 1970-71, his son Pierre began an 11-season NHL career with Montreal and Washington.

EMILE "BUTCH" BOUCHARD
Montreal, Quebec
September 11, 1920–
NHL Career: 1941-56
Montreal

	GP	G	A	P	PIM
RS	785	49	144	193	863
PO	113	11	21	32	121

Stanley Cup (4), A-S Game (6), HOF 1966

FRANK BOUCHER

CENTER

★ 1933, 1934, 1935 ★2 1931

Frank Boucher played the 1921-22 season for the Ottawa Senators before being traded to the Vancouver Maroons of the Pacific Coast Hockey Association. In 1926, the New York Rangers paid the Maroons a hefty $15,000 for Boucher, and he became center of the "A" Line between brothers Bill and Bun Cook. "No unit ever had better puck control," claimed *Toronto Star* reporter Baz O'Meara in 1962. "Boucher owed his eminence to his great passing ability. He feathered the puck in caressing fashion, and he and the Cooks had worked out a precision passing program which was the delight of the fans."

Perhaps hockey's greatest gentleman, Boucher won the Lady Byng Trophy in 1927-28, the first of a record seven wins over the next eight years. He also led all playoff scorers in goals and points as the Rangers won their first Stanley Cup. Arthur Daley of *The New York Times* recalled Boucher's Cup-winning goal as "a stark demonstration of the Boucher artistry. Frank flashed down the ice with the puck on his stick, heading straight for Red Dutton, brawny Montreal [Maroons] defenseman. Dutton braced, but Boucher gently pushed the disk between the redhead's skates. While Dutton looked down to find the rubber, Frank had swooped around him to regain the puck and hammer in the goal."

Boucher earned a Second Team berth when All-Star selections commenced in 1930-31. He led the league in assists in 1932-33, and the Rangers won their second Stanley Cup. The "diminutive whirlwind" took the centerman's spot on the First All-Star Team for three consecutive seasons, and he also won the Byng simultaneously. After the 1934-35 campaign, the NHL decided to award Boucher the original Byng Trophy permanently, and a new trophy was created for subsequent winners.

Boucher became the first player in the NHL to reach 250 assists before retiring after the 1937-38 season. He coached the Rangers to a Stanley Cup victory in 1939-40, but his final hurrah came in 1943-44. With the Second World War thinning his roster, Boucher went back on the ice for 15 games and notched 4 goals and 10 assists.

FRANK BOUCHER
Ottawa, Ontario
October 7, 1901–December 12, 1977
NHL Career: 1921-22, 1926-38, 1943-44
Ottawa, NY Rangers

	GP	G	A	P	PIM
RS	557	160	263	423	119
PO	55	16	18	34	12

Byng (7), Stanley Cup (2), A-S Game, HOF 1958

RAY BOURQUE

DEFENSE

★ 1980, 1982, 1984, 1985, 1987, 1988, 1990, 1991, 1992, 1993, 1994, 1996
★2 1981, 1983, 1986, 1989, 1995, 1999

Ray Bourque, already 18 times an All-Star, gives every indication that he can compete for years to come. The Boston Bruins selected him in the first round of the 1979 entry draft with a pick they got from Los Angeles in exchange for goaltender Ron Grahame. Ironically, Grahame's son John became Bourque's teammate in 1999. Rookie Bourque not only won the Calder Trophy but made the First All-Star Team. "There's no doubt in my mind that he's going to make one heck of a mark on the game," teammate Brad Park accurately predicted. "He's the finest rookie defenseman I've ever seen come into the league."

Like his Bruins predecessor Bobby Orr, Bourque has been explosive on the rush, hard and accurate from the point and steady on the blue line. Unlike Orr, he has avoided serious injury and still plays about half of every game. In the heart of his career, between 1987 and 1994, Bourque won the Norris Trophy five times. He tallied personal bests in 1983-84 with 31 goals and 96 points but has been a model of consistency. With at least 10 goals and 40 points every season, Bourque became Boston's all-time scoring leader on February 1, 1997.

"Every day, you've got to prove yourself," he said, "and that's how I've played this game my entire career." Bourque shared the captaincy with Rick Middleton for three seasons, beginning in 1985-86, and wore the Bruins' "C" until his trade to Colorado in March 2000. He asked to be dealt in order to get the one thing missing in his career: a Stanley Cup ring. The Bruins had won only one game during Bourque's two trips to the Cup finals, in 1988 and 1990.

Bourque, still demonstrating an unflagging commitment to excellence, seemed to become rejuvenated with the Avalanche, who were likewise inspired by his mission. Colorado went on a late-season tear but lost the Western Conference finals. Bourque re-signed with Colorado for 2000-01.

RAYMOND BOURQUE
Montreal, Quebec
December 28, 1960–
NHL Career: 1979-
Boston, Colorado

	GP	G	A	P	PIM
RS	1532	403	1117	1520	1093
PO	193	37	133	170	159

Calder, Norris (5), Clancy, A-S Game (19)

GOALTENDER   ★ 1961

Johnny Bower was old enough to retire when he joined the Toronto Maple Leafs in the fall of 1958. He'd already been a professional goalie for 14 seasons, having had his first taste of the big time in 1953-54, when he put in a full and solid season for the New York Rangers. Nevertheless, Bower was back in the minors when Toronto general manager and coach Punch Imlach resurrected his NHL career.

Bower won the 1960-61 Vezina Trophy with a 2.50 goals-against average, but Detroit upset the Leafs in the playoffs. The next three seasons had a better finish. Although Bower missed the last two games of the 1962 Stanley Cup finals because of an injury, the Leafs won the championship in large part due to his playoff-leading 2.28 average. Bower led all goalies in the postseason in 1963 and 1964 as well. "Anytime you win the Stanley Cup, the goaltender is the big

reason," asserted Imlach. "We've got a lot of good hockey players on our team, but they're not worth a darn unless the old guy is making the big saves."

Bower celebrated his fortieth birthday and the Leafs finally relinquished the Cup in 1964-65, but he wasn't finished yet. "Bower is the most remarkable athlete in professional sport," said Imlach. "Show me any other man his age who fills a

job half as tough as playing goal in the NHL. I don't think you can find one."

"I don't care how long I've played," said Bower. "I still can improve on things like cutting down the shooter's angles and clearing the puck around the boards." Once again, in 1966-67, the ageless goalie helped the Leafs to a Stanley Cup win. Concluded Bower: "Too many guys quit too soon."

JOHNNY BOWER
Prince Albert, Saskatchewan
November 8, 1924–
NHL Career: 1953-55, 1956-57, 1958-70
NY Rangers, Toronto

	GP	M	GA	SO	AVE
RS	552	32016	1347	37	2.52
PO	74	4378	184	5	2.52

Vezina (2), Stanley Cup (4),
A-S Game (4), HOF 1976

DEFENSE   ★ 1963   ★ 1962, 1965, 1970

Carl Brewer, arguably the most obstinate free spirit ever to skate in the NHL, was an integral part of the league's strongest blue-line corps of the 1960s. He skated and stickhandled well but concentrated on the defensive side of the game. Brewer led the league with 150 penalty minutes in 1959-60 and made the Second All-Star Team in 1962. The following season, he

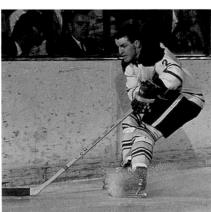

graduated to the First All-Star Team.

Brewer frequently butted heads with general manager and coach Punch Imlach, but his contract dispute prior to the 1963-64 season became quite theatrical. Brewer had enrolled at Hamilton's McMaster University and had even tried out for the football team before finally agreeing to terms and helping the Leafs win their third straight Stanley Cup. With a league-leading 177 penalty minutes, Brewer made the Second All-Star Team in 1964-65. But he and the Leafs then parted ways, reportedly because of Imlach's criticism of Brewer's friendship with NHL Players' Association chief Alan Eagleson.

After four years, which included a season with the Canadian national team and a year coaching in Finland, Brewer returned to the NHL for the 1969-70 season. He tallied a career-high 37 assists and 39 points for Detroit and made the Second All-Star Team. He played the next two seasons for St. Louis,

then hung up his skates once more. Besides his 1973-74 campaign with the WHA's Toronto Toros, Brewer didn't play again until 1979-80, when Imlach, trying to re-create a bygone era, brought him to Toronto for 20 games. The rest of the Leafs, however, resented Brewer's presence, seeing him as Imlach's puppet. Brewer's relationship with Eagleson also came full circle, and he prodded the investigation into Eagleson's conflicts of interest, which ultimately led to his former friend's disgrace and imprisonment.

CARL BREWER
Toronto, Ontario
October 21, 1938–
NHL Career: 1957-65, 1969-72, 1979-80
Toronto, Detroit, St. Louis

	GP	G	A	P	PIM
RS	604	25	198	223	1037
PO	72	3	17	20	146

Stanley Cup (3), A-S Game (3)

FRANK BRIMSEK

GOALTENDER ★ 1939, 1942 ★ 1940, 1941, 1943, 1946, 1947, 1948

Frank Brimsek launched his NHL career in spectacular fashion. Despite the pressure of replacing the Bruins' legendary Tiny Thompson, Brimsek notched six shutouts in his first 10 appearances in the 1938-39 season. Soon christened "Mr. Zero," Brimsek finished his rookie-of-the-year campaign with a league-leading 10 shutouts. He earned the Vezina Trophy with a 1.56 goals-against average and made the First All-Star Team. To cap his sparkling debut, Brimsek knocked his playoff average down to 1.25 on the way to Stanley Cup victory.

One of the first American-born stars of the NHL, Brimsek had set high marks in his rookie year that he never duplicated. Nonetheless, over his next four All-Star seasons, he missed only a single game, helping Boston win another Stanley Cup in 1941 and picking up his second Vezina in 1942. Writer Bill Roche

carried vivid memories of Brimsek's "cold efficiency" and, in 1953, rated him the best he had ever seen. "With his coordination of reflexes and lightninglike moves with hands, skates and stick," recalled Roche, "he had would-be snipers cursing him all around the NHL." Unfortunately, the Second World War was picking up steam at the same time.

"You just get established in a business like hockey, and you have to give it all up," complained Brimsek. "A damned war comes along." Brimsek stayed long enough to backstop the Bruins to the 1943 Stanley Cup finals before he enlisted. He played the 1943-44 season with the U.S. Coast Guard Cutters, a Baltimore-based hockey club conceived as a community morale booster. The team felt a backlash from the patriotic public, however, and Brimsek finished his military duty on a patrol boat in the South Pacific.

When he returned to the NHL for the latter half of the 1945-46 season, Brimsek felt "jumpy" and had lost some of his edge, but he made the Second All-Star Team three more times. He was growing tired, though, and the end of his career was in sight. At his insistence, Brimsek was dealt to Chicago for the 1949-50 season so that he could initiate business contacts just before he retired.

FRANK BRIMSEK
Eveleth, Minnesota
September 26, 1915–November 11, 1998
NHL Career: 1938-43, 1945-50
Boston, Chicago

	GP	M	GA	SO	AVE
RS	514	31210	1404	40	2.70
PO	68	4394	186	2	2.54

Calder, Vezina (2), Stanley Cup (2),
A-S Game (3), HOF 1966

GOALTENDER ⭐ 1941, 1948 ⭐2 1942

Turk Broda arrived in Toronto in the autumn of 1936. Before long, coach Dick Irvin declared, "He's the man who holds the Maple Leafs together." Irvin had departed by 1940, but Broda was just starting to peak. In 1940-41, he became the first Toronto netminder to win an All-Star selection or a Vezina Trophy. In 1941-42, he made the Second All-Star Team, but more memorably, he helped the Leafs complete an unprecedented comeback from a 3–0 deficit in games to defeat Detroit in the Stanley Cup finals. Broda shut out the Red Wings in the sixth match and allowed only a single goal in the deciding game.

He missed almost three entire NHL seasons because of military service but returned late in the 1945-46 campaign.

The Leafs failed to make the playoffs, but Broda sparkled in three consecutive Stanley Cup victories before the decade was out. Unfortunately, he didn't always get his due respect. "Every time the Leafs fall into a prolonged losing streak and the going is rough," commented author Ron McAllister in 1950, "it's an old Toronto custom to level abuse at the short, balding Polish-Canadian standing in the breach." Broda had just withstood his personal "Battle of the Bulge"—an enforced weight-loss exercise-cum-publicity-stunt that had garnered copious press coverage—with Leafs owner/manager Conn Smythe. "Turk Broda has learned to hold both his tongue and his temper in check," said McAllister, "and to fight on and

hope that courage and nerve and the breaks of the game will bring him out again on top." Fortunately, that came to pass. In the spring of 1951, Broda backstopped the Leafs to another Stanley Cup victory.

WALTER "TURK" BRODA
Brandon, Manitoba
May 15, 1914–October 17, 1972
NHL Career: 1936-43, 1945-52
Toronto

	GP	M	GA	SO	AVE
RS	629	38167	1609	62	2.53
PO	101	6406	211	12	1.98

Vezina (2), Stanley Cup (5),
A-S Game (4), HOF 1967

MARTIN BRODEUR

GOALTENDER

 1997, 1998

Teenager Martin Brodeur joined the New Jersey Devils for five games in 1991-92. A year of minor-league seasoning served him well for the 1993-94 campaign. "It was a surprise the way the kid came along at the start," admitted former coach Jacques Lemaire. "We gave him a chance to prove himself, and he did." Brodeur won the 1994 Calder Trophy with a 2.40 goals-against average and backstopped New Jersey to the Eastern Conference finals. The following season, he took the Devils all the way, winning a Stanley Cup ring after leading the playoffs with three shutouts and a 1.67 average.

Brodeur set an NHL record by playing 4,433 minutes in 1995-96, the longest season for any goalie. His partner Mike Dunham got more work the following year and shared Brodeur's 1997 William M. Jennings Trophy. That same campaign, Brodeur made the Second All-Star Team with a league-leading 10 shutouts. His sparkling 1.88 goals-against average was the NHL's lowest since Tony Esposito's in 1970-71. Brodeur had another highlight during the ensuing playoffs. Strong with his stick and a good playmaker, he fired a puck into the Montreal net after the Canadiens had pulled their goalie.

Brodeur returned to the Second All-Star Team in 1997-98, again blanking the opposition 10 times. He won the 1998 Jennings with a 1.89 average, but for the second consecutive season, he finished runner-up to Dominik Hasek in Vezina Trophy voting. While admitting that competition with his peers is a motivator, Brodeur keeps his primary focus on the team's success. "I want the people in front of me to feel confident, to know that I can make the big save at the right time or steal a game," he said. "I always want to give them a chance to win."

MARTIN BRODEUR
Montreal, Quebec
May 6, 1972–
NHL Career: 1991-92, 1993-
New Jersey

	GP	M	GA	SO	AVE
RS	447	25939	950	42	2.20
PO	84	5325	165	8	1.86

Calder, Jennings (2), Stanley Cup (2), A-S Game (5)

JOHNNY BUCYK

LEFT WING

★ 1971   ★ 1968

In six different seasons, Johnny Bucyk came first or second in Lady Byng Trophy voting. Yet despite his gentlemanly demeanor, Bucyk was also an important member of the "Big, Bad Bruins." Veteran defenseman Allan Stanley saw the left-winger's other side. "The guy is deceptive," he said. "He's much heavier than he looks, and he hits low, with his hip. Whenever he's on the ice, you can never afford to stand admiring your passes. Not the way Bucyk hits."

Bucyk cracked the Detroit lineup in 1955-56, although he didn't see much ice time. In the summer of 1957, the Red Wings traded him to Boston for Terry Sawchuk, who had fallen apart as a Bruin. Bucyk was delighted. Not only would he now get a regular shift, but the Bruins had also picked up Bronco Horvath from Montreal. Boston's two latest additions were reunited with Vic Stasiuk, their junior hockeymate in Edmonton. Dubbed the "Uke Line," because of

Bucyk and Stasiuk's Ukrainian heritage, the trio led Boston to the Stanley Cup finals in 1958 and 1959.

Bucyk was named team captain for 1966-67, but after one season, he requested an "A" for assistant captain instead of the "C." However, there was never any doubt that "the Chief" was a team leader. "Bucyk has been Boston's most talented individual over the past decade," wrote Dan Proudfoot in *The Canadian Magazine*, "even though he's never been voted a season's All-Star and he's never won a league trophy." That soon changed. Bucyk notched his first 30-goal season in 1967-68 and added 39 assists to join the top-10 league scorers. He placed second in Lady Byng Trophy voting and made the Second All-Star Team.

"I always knew the wheel had to turn sometime," said Bucyk. "I knew we'd start winning one of these seasons."

Bucyk hoisted the Stanley Cup in 1970 and 1972, sandwiching a 50-goal season in between in 1970-71, only the fifth player to do so. That year, he came third in league scoring, made the First All-Star Team and won the Byng with only eight penalty minutes. Bucyk became captain again in 1973-74 and picked up his second Byng Trophy. He retired in 1978, fourth in all-time NHL scoring.

JOHNNY BUCYK				
Edmonton, Alberta				
May 12, 1935–				
NHL Career: 1955-78				
Detroit, Boston				
GP	G	A	P	PIM
RS 1540	556	813	1369	497
PO 124	41	62	103	42
Byng (2), Stanley Cup (2), A-S Game (7),				
HOF 1981				

HY BULLER

DEFENSE

★ 1952

Although Hy Buller had played nine games for the Detroit Red Wings between 1943 and 1945, it looked as if he might spend the rest of his career in the minor leagues. He was a two-time AHL First All-Star with Cleveland, a club that was reluctant to trade him until it ran short of funds after the 1950-51

campaign. The New York Rangers sent cash and players, and Buller had a smashing Broadway debut in 1951-52.

He benefited by playing with Allan Stanley, and after scoring the tying goals in two December weekend games, Buller earned "Player of the Week" honors from *The Hockey News*. Rangers coach Frank Boucher likened him to Boston's All-Star rearguard. "Sure, I'd like to see him crack them [the opposition]," admitted Boucher. "But you can't have everything. Bill Quackenbush doesn't hit them either, and he's quite a defenseman. They're [both] exceptional stick checkers, fine stickhandlers and rushers. Buller, like Quackenbush, is very good on point in power plays. He has our best shot from the blue line and can get it away without a windup. The most noticeable thing about Buller is his coolness and quick thinking under fire. He'll adapt himself in any situation."

At season's end, Buller had 12 goals and 23 assists, and the Rangers nomi-

nated him for the Calder Trophy. He finished a close second behind Boom-Boom Geoffrion. When he was nominated to the Second Team, Buller became only the third rookie ever to make an All-Star Team (goalies Frank Brimsek and Terry Sawchuk were the others). Unfortunately, his time in the limelight was short-lived. Midway through the 1953-54 season, he was back in the minors. In June 1954, New York traded him to Montreal, but Buller never played another NHL game.

HYMAN BULLER				
Montreal, Quebec				
March 15, 1926–deceased				
NHL Career: 1943-45, 1951-54				
Detroit, NY Rangers				
GP	G	A	P	PIM
RS 188	22	58	80	215
PO 0	0	0	0	0
A-S Game				

PAVEL BURE

RIGHT WING

★ 1994 ★ 2000

Pavel Bure's creativity and explosive speed have made him the "Russian Rocket." He won the Calder Trophy with 34 goals and 60 points in 1991-92 and followed up with an electrifying 60-goal, 110-point campaign in 1992-93. "I've played with and against a lot of great players," said Rick Ley, who coached Bure for several seasons, "but I've never seen a player like him, where you stand behind the bench, watch him and just say, 'Wow.'"

Bure's second 60-goal campaign the following season led the league and lifted him onto the First All-Star Team. He finished fifth in overall scoring with 107 points and kept up his torrid pace in the playoffs. Bure led Vancouver with 31 points, including a postseason-high

16 goals, before the Canucks lost game seven of the Cup finals to the New York Rangers. He led his team with 20 goals and 43 points over the lockout-shortened 1994-95 schedule. Unfortunately, early the next season, Bure had major knee surgery. After a mediocre 1996-97 campaign, he notched 51 goals and a third-place finish in 1997-98 scoring. His days with the Canucks, however, were over.

Bure soon confessed that he had requested a trade several times, and after a prolonged holdout, he joined the Florida Panthers in February 1999. He scored 13 goals in his first 11 games with the Panthers before reinjuring his knee. "I know what kind of player I am," he said. "Instead of crying about how unlucky I was, I set my mind to-

ward returning." After surgery and another long rehabilitation, he made an impressive comeback in 1999-2000, winning the Maurice "Rocket" Richard Trophy with 58 goals, finishing just behind Jaromir Jagr in total scoring and making the Second All-Star Team.

PAVEL BURE				
Moscow, U.S.S.R.				
March 31, 1971–				
NHL Career: 1991-				
Vancouver, Florida				
GP	G	A	P	PIM
RS 513	325	263	588	348
PO 64	35	35	70	74
Calder, Richard, A-S Game (5)				

LEFT WING ⭐ 1944

Herb Cain completed a respectable NHL career but did not receive his full due. When he won the 1943-44 scoring championship, his 36 goals and 46 assists shattered the previous record of 73 points in a season. Unfortunately, because he played almost half of the 50-game season on the right wing, the All-Star votes cast for him were split between two positions. Cain was relegated to the Second Team. It's less clear why Chicago's Clint Smith, fifth in league scoring, outpointed him in voting for the Lady Byng Trophy. Both players spent a mere four minutes apiece in the sin bin, yet Cain was only the runner-up.

Cain broke into the NHL with the Montreal Maroons in 1933-34 and led the team with 20 goals the following season. The Maroons won the 1935 Stanley Cup, but in the autumn of 1938, the franchise liquidated its assets and folded. Cain spent 1938-39 with the Montreal Canadiens but was traded to Boston the following season. He notched his second 20-goal campaign playing on a line with Bill Cowley and Mel "Sudden Death" Hill. Although Cain scored only eight times in 1940-41, he added three important playoff goals to help Boston win the Stanley Cup.

With the "Kraut

Line" in the military, Cain was on Boston's top line during his surprising All-Star campaign, and he notched 32 goals in 1944-45. After one more NHL season, though, he was demoted to the AHL's Hershey Bears, where he spent the next four years. Cain eventually earned a footnote in NHL history as the last of the old Maroons to retire.

HERB CAIN
Newmarket, Ontario
December 24, 1912–February 15, 1982
NHL Career: 1933-46
Montreal Maroons, Montreal, Boston

	GP	G	A	P	PIM
RS	570	206	194	400	178
PO	67	16	13	29	13

Ross, Stanley Cup (2)

GOALTENDER ⭐ 1996

Jim Carey's quick slide out of the game mirrored his meteoric rise to the pinnacle of his profession. The Washington Capitals drafted Carey right

out of high school in 1992. After a couple of seasons of college hockey, he won the AHL's top rookie and goaltending honors for 1994-95. When the NHL lockout ended in January 1995, however, the Capitals called Carey up to the big leagues. He notched four shutouts in 28 games, lost only six times and finished runner-up for the Calder Trophy and third in Vezina Trophy voting.

The following season, Carey made the First All-Star Team and won the Vezina. Leading the league with nine shutouts, he notched a 2.26 goals-against average. The playoffs, unfortunately, were another matter, and he got the hook several times. "Hopefully," said Carey, "more games under my belt will pay dividends," but he never saw post-season action again. Washington traded him to Boston on March 1, 1997. The Bruins, already in the midst of a lackluster season, finished out of the play-offs for the first time in 30 years.

Although he posted two shutouts in his first 10 games of the 1997-98 campaign, Carey was sent to the minors,

and the Bruins went with Byron Dafoe. Unable to get back to the NHL with Boston, Carey accepted a contract buy-out in March 1999. Although the move cost him about $2 million in future earnings, Carey wanted to sign with the St. Louis Blues. "There's nothing like playing in the NHL," said Carey, "and if you feel you belong there, money is not an issue." However, after only four appearances in the St. Louis net, Carey was demoted to the minors. He decided, instead, to take his life in another direction and, at only 25 years of age, retired from professional hockey.

JIM CAREY
Dorchester, Massachusetts
May 31, 1974–
NHL Career: 1994-99
Washington, Boston, St. Louis

	GP	M	GA	SO	AVE
RS	172	9668	416	16	2.58
PO	10	455	35	0	4.62

Vezina

RANDY CARLYLE

DEFENSE

Randy Carlyle reportedly had a deal with the WHA's Cincinnati Stingers, but when the Maple Leafs got a tip that he had only signed a letter of intent, they gleefully used their first pick in the 1976 amateur draft to get Carlyle under contract. After two disappointing seasons, however, Toronto traded him to Pittsburgh for 1978-79. Eddie Johnston became the Penguins coach in 1980-81 and brought his former teammate Bobby Orr to training camp. Carlyle got more ice time, found his first consistent partner in Mario Faubert and blossomed. "We seem to know what each other is thinking out there, what's going on and what we plan on doing in different situations," Carlyle told Chuck Moody of *The Hockey News*. After notching a career-high 67 assists and 83 points in 1980-81, Carlyle made the First All-Star Team and won the Norris Trophy. The Penguins appointed him captain for the following season.

When he was cut from the 1981 Canada Cup squad, an angry Carlyle became a man with a mission. "He

wants to prove why he was the best defenseman in the league last year," said Johnston. "He's right back to where he was last year. He's very offensive-minded; he's good with the puck. He

goes into the holes and can maneuver to set up shots. He always makes the big plays." Carlyle scored 75 points in 73 games and anchored the Penguins' blue line until March 1984.

The Winnipeg Jets traded a first-round draft pick and future considerations and welcomed Carlyle with open arms. "Randy has an air about him that creates an atmosphere of confidence that spreads from the dressing room to the ice," said Doug Smail. Nine seasons later, the NHL honored Carlyle with an invitation to the 1993 All-Star Game in February. He retired later that spring.

RANDY CARLYLE
Sudbury, Ontario
April 19, 1956–
NHL Career: 1976-93
Toronto, Pittsburgh, Winnipeg

	GP	G	A	P	PIM
RS	1055	148	499	647	1400
PO	69	9	24	33	120

Norris, A-S Game (4)

LORNE CARR

RIGHT WING

Although Lorne Carr dressed for 14 games for the New York Rangers in 1933-34, he never stepped onto the ice. He spent the latter part of the season in the minors and joined the New York Americans for 1934-35. Carr, only five-foot-eight and 160 pounds, tallied 17 goals and 14 assists in his first full campaign, earning a spot on the Amerks' top line with Art Chapman and two-time scoring-leader Sweeney Schriner.

Carr's overtime goal 40 seconds into the third overtime period on March 27, 1938, knocked his former club out of the playoffs. "That was the greatest thrill I ever

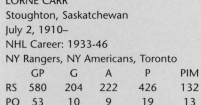

got in hockey," said Red Dutton, player/coach of the Amerks. "The Rangers had a high-priced team then, and beating them was like winning the Stanley Cup to us."

That did, indeed, prove to be the closest the New York club got to a championship. Carr joined the top-10 league scorers in 1938-39, but after 1940-41, in an effort to save cash, the Americans dealt Carr to Toronto for the loan of three fringe NHL players.

Rejoining Schriner on a line centered by Billy Taylor, Carr flourished with the Maple Leafs and helped Toronto win the 1942 Stanley Cup. With a team-leading 27 goals, Carr made the 1943 First All-Star Team and tied Taylor for fifth in league scoring.

He finished third overall and was voted an All-Star again the following season with a career-high 36 goals and 38 assists. Carr scored 21 goals and 25 helpers in his last Cup-winning campaign of 1944-45. Although the Leafs then went into a slump and failed to make the 1946 playoffs, Carr noted his less-than-impressive 13-point season and retired.

LORNE CARR
Stoughton, Saskatchewan
July 2, 1910–
NHL Career: 1933-46
NY Rangers, NY Americans, Toronto

	GP	G	A	P	PIM
RS	580	204	222	426	132
PO	53	10	9	19	13

Stanley Cup (2)

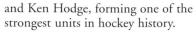
Wayne Cashman personified the "Big, Bad Bruins." In 1964-65, he played a single game for Boston, then returned to junior hockey for another season. The Bruins were determined to establish a bigger, tougher physical presence, however, and Cashman filled the bill perfectly. After spending some time going back and forth to the minors, he eventually latched onto a full-time NHL job late in the 1968-69 campaign. The following season, Cashman supplanted Ron Murphy on a line with Phil Esposito and Ken Hodge, forming one of the strongest units in hockey history.

Cashman's greatest contribution was made in the corners. His rough and fearless approach forced innumerable turnovers, and he could handle the puck when he got it. During the Bruins' 1970 playoff run, Cashman had 5 goals (two of them shorthanded), 4 assists and 50 penalty minutes—an integral part of Boston's Stanley Cup win. "Cash" broke into the top-10 NHL scorers for the first time in 1970-71, finishing seventh with 21 goals and 58 assists. He helped the Bruins win the Cup again in 1972, with 4 goals and 7 assists in 15 playoff games.

Cashman played in Team Canada's home-ice win and tie in the 1972 Summit Series against the Soviet Union, assisting on two goals. Drawing 14 penalty minutes, he sat out the last game in Canada and was knocked right out of the lineup in Sweden. When Canada played a couple of European "tune-up" games against Sweden before traveling to Moscow, Cashman took a spear to the mouth that almost severed his tongue.

In the 1973-74 NHL season, Cashman tallied career-highs with 30 goals and 59 assists, finishing fourth in league scoring behind teammates Esposito, Bobby Orr and Hodge. His selection to the Second All-Star Team that season proved to be his single league honor, although as time passed, his stature in the game scarcely faded. Representing both Boston's present and the values of a bygone era, Cashman captained the Bruins from 1977-78 until his retirement in 1983. By then, he was the last remaining NHL player from the preexpansion days.

WAYNE CASHMAN				
Kingston, Ontario				
June 24, 1945–				
NHL Career: 1964-65, 1967-83				
Boston				
	GP	G	A	P	PIM
RS	1027	277	516	793	1041
PO	145	31	57	88	250
Stanley Cup (2), A-S Game				

LORNE CHABOT

GOALTENDER

The New York Rangers' first goalie, Lorne Chabot was known as "Chabotsky" for a time, as manager/coach Lester Patrick tried to draw the city's Jewish community to games. Chabot played two strong seasons for the Rangers. Midway through the 1928 playoffs, Montreal Maroons sniper Nels Stewart felled Chabot with a backhand to the face. In the stuff of legend, the Rangers went on to win the Stanley Cup, with Patrick substituting for Chabot before Joe Miller of the New York Americans came in for the remaining games.

Traded to Toronto, Chabot helped the Leafs win the 1932 Stanley Cup, then wore out his welcome protesting a league-imposed salary cap. Toronto dealt him to the Montreal Canadiens, but Chicago's great netminder Chuck Gardiner died suddenly after the 1933-34 season, and Chabot, along with

Howie Morenz, became a Blackhawk.

"Lorne stepped into the toughest spot any goaler ever walked into last fall," said Blackhawks owner Major Frederic McLaughlin, "and he ended up by winning the Vezina Trophy. Wasn't he grand out there tonight?" The date was March 23, 1935, and Chabot had just blanked the Montreal Maroons in an unusual 0–0 playoff tie, the first match in a two-game, total-goals series.

"The titanic battle was tossed into the hands of the rival goaltenders," *The Gazette* reported, "tall and rangy Chabot, the mercurial goaler of the Hawks, and small, pale-faced [Alex] Connell, the imperturbable." It wasn't until overtime in the final game that Montreal's Baldy Northcott found the net for the only goal of the series. Chabot retired, then joined the Montreal Maroons in February 1936. He finished his career a year later with the New York Americans.

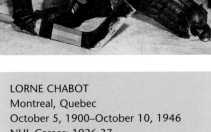

LORNE CHABOT
Montreal, Quebec
October 5, 1900–October 10, 1946
NHL Career: 1926-37
NY Rangers, Toronto, Montreal, Chicago,
Montreal Maroons, NY Americans

	GP	M	GA	SO	AVE
RS	411	25307	860	73	2.04
PO	37	2498	64	5	1.54

Vezina, Stanley Cup (2)

ART CHAPMAN

CENTER

When traded from a perennially strong Boston club to the lowly New York Americans, Art Chapman never looked back. The Bruins had drafted the 1929-30 Can-Am League's leading goal scorer, but his 11 goals and 14 assists in 1931-32 were his best totals in Beantown. Midway through the 1933-34 campaign, Chapman joined the Amerks and emerged as an elite playmaker. He was soon centering a powerful line between wingers Sweeney Schriner and Lorne Carr.

In his first full season in New York, Chapman led the NHL with 34 assists, finishing in a tie for sixth in total scoring. His 28 helpers were league-high again in the 1935-36 season, when he finished the scoring race in

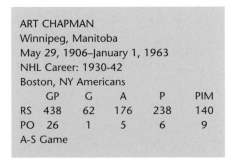

a tie for fourth. Today, Chapman's 1936-37 All-Star season looks curious. He competed aggressively, earning two misconducts in three February games by arguing with referees, but his numbers slipped a bit. Chapman's 8 goals and 23 assists placed him below several other centers in scoring. Perhaps a sympathy vote came into play.

"Art Chapman, clever center of the New York Americans, may be out for the rest of the season," reported *The Gazette* on March 3, 1937. "He will enter hospital here [Montreal] to have his broken nose repaired. Chapman suffered the injury in a game at Toronto over a week ago but gamely tried to finish the campaign. He could barely breathe through

the proboscis that is knocked askew."

Chapman returned to action in 1937-38 and picked up much where he had left off. His production slowed during the 1939-40 season, however, and he became his team's last coach. He was still behind the bench when the Americans adopted Brooklyn as their home base in 1941-42, but the effort to solidify a fan base failed. When the franchise folded, Chapman resumed his career in the AHL in 1942-43. After playing a single game the following season, he retired for the last time.

ART CHAPMAN
Winnipeg, Manitoba
May 29, 1906–January 1, 1963
NHL Career: 1930-42
Boston, NY Americans

	GP	G	A	P	PIM
RS	438	62	176	238	140
PO	26	1	5	6	9

A-S Game

DEFENSE   ★ 1989, 1993, 1995, 1996   ★ 1991, 1997

American Olympian Chris Chelios joined the Montreal Canadiens late in the 1983-84 campaign. He made the NHL All-Rookie Team the following season, leading Montreal with 55 assists, and won a Stanley Cup ring in 1986. A tough, oftentimes dirty player, Chelios matured into a premier blue-liner. Effective in his own end and strong offensively, Chelios captained the Habs for most of the 1988-89 campaign. With a team-leading 58 assists and 73 points, he earned his first All-Star berth and Norris Trophy. But Montreal swapped him for Chicago's top scorer, Denis Savard, in the summer of 1990.

Chelios reveled in playing for his hometown Blackhawks. He became an All-Star in five of the next seven seasons and helped the Hawks to the 1992 Stanley Cup finals. He matched his career-high 73 points in 1992-93 and won his second Norris. In 1995-96, Chelios became team captain, the first Blackhawk defenseman to lead his team in scoring, and picked up the Norris again. He even managed to curb his penalty minutes.

Yet when he sought a contract extension in 1998-99, Chicago wouldn't give it, so in March 1999, Chelios joined the Detroit Red Wings. "He competes every night and never takes a shift off," said Wings associate coach Dave Lewis.

Former Chicago coach Craig Hartsburg agreed: "He plays every shift like it could be his last. He's a warrior."

The former Blackhawks hero must now face boos whenever he plays in Chicago. "That's just the way it is," Chelios told *The Chicago Tribune.* "There's a big rivalry there. It's nothing I didn't expect."

CHRIS CHELIOS
Chicago, Illinois
January 25, 1962–
NHL Career: 1983-
Montreal, Chicago, Detroit

	GP	G	A	P	PIM
RS	1157	168	644	832	2385
PO	182	28	93	121	341

Norris (3), Stanley Cup, A-S Game (10)

REAL CHEVREFILS

 1957

Real Chevrefils joined the Boston Bruins in January 1952. " 'Chevvy' is the best left-wing prospect to come to the Bruins in the last 10 years," enthused coach Lynn Patrick to *The Hockey News* that spring. "Right now, regardless of his lack of experience, he is the best left wing on our team. Within three years, he will be the best left wing in the league, an All-Star. He has all the assets of a great player."

Unfortunately, Chevrefils had developed a drinking problem that some characterized simply as high living. "I was so lonely, it wasn't even funny," he later said. "I didn't know what to do with myself."

Chevrefils scored 19 goals in 1952-53. Although a broken leg cost him most of the following season, he rebounded with 18 goals and 40 points in 1954-55. Traded to Detroit in the summer of 1955 as part of the deal that sent Terry Sawchuk to Boston, Chevrefils proved too hard for the Red Wings to manage. Since he had scored only 3 goals in 38 games, Detroit flipped him back to the Bruins in January 1956. Chevrefils continued to get into trouble in Boston but managed a strong 1956-57 campaign. He made the Second All-Star Team with 48 points, including a team-leading 31 goals.

Over the next two seasons, however, Chevrefils spent stints in the minors, and the Bruins finally cut the ties. "When a man doesn't produce on the ice and his conduct off the ice suggests a reason," said Patrick, "that's grounds for getting rid of him. Keeping him under those conditions isn't fair to the team." Chevrefils bounced around various minor leagues until 1964, when he qualified for a disability pension because of alcohol-related diseases. He died in a car accident in 1981.

REAL CHEVREFILS
Timmins, Ontario
May 2, 1932–January 8, 1981
NHL Career: 1951-59
Boston, Detroit

	GP	G	A	P	PIM
RS	387	104	97	201	185
PO	30	5	4	9	20

A-S Game (2)

KING CLANCY

⭐ 1931, 1934   ⭐ 1932, 1933

Ottawa Senators' star King Clancy led the league in assists in 1923-24 and set a career-high with 17 goals and 23 assists in 1929-30. "He was always a damned nuisance [too]," recalled Aurele Joliat. "He could really get people worked up with that mouth of his." Just before the 1930-31 season began, Toronto Maple Leafs owner Conn Smythe traded two players and an un-precedented $35,000 to Ottawa for the five-foot-seven rapscallion.

"There were few defensemen in NHL history as small as he," recalled *Globe and Mail* writer Trent Frayne in 1986, "or with a heart as big. His play was inspirational. He'd get the puck in his own end, and he'd run five, seven, eight quick little strides to accelerate, and then he'd be whirling down center, eyes wide, eyebrows halfway to his hairline." Clancy made the inaugural First All-Star Team in 1930-31, then helped Toronto to its highest achievement the following season.

"That battling gamecock King Clancy dug up a new lease on life from somewhere," wrote *Toronto Daily Star* columnist Lou Marsh in March 1932 after Clancy helped the Leafs defeat Chicago to advance to the Stanley Cup finals. "The boy is worn to a shadow from an unselfish season's work. He was in the forefront of all the early battling and took some terrific punishment at both ends of the ice, but he was still fighting when they finished."

The Leafs went on to sweep the Rangers in three games to win their first title.

Clancy posted two more All-Star years before he decided to retire early in the 1936-37 season. " 'The King' was a great player, a spirited rusher and a grand blocker," read the announcement of his retirement, "but his effectiveness did not end there. Clancy's quick thinking won many games." With the same vivid color he'd displayed as a player, Clancy went on to lengthy careers as a referee, a coach and Toronto's hockey ambassador.

FRANK "KING" CLANCY
Ottawa, Ontario
February 25, 1903–November 10, 1986
NHL Career: 1921-37
Ottawa, Toronto

	GP	G	A	P	PIM
RS	592	137	144	281	906
PO	61	9	8	17	92

Stanley Cup (3), A-S Game (2), HOF 1958

DIT CLAPPER

RIGHT WING
DEFENSE

"Dit Clapper, coasting with apparent ease through his 20th big-league season," noted *The Toronto Star* in December 1946, "has few, if any, peers, physically or mentally, in the long history of hockey." While Clapper's longevity was unheard of, it hadn't come without hard work. Besides "clean living and rest aplenty," Clapper himself noted that "the most important thing is to stay in condition 12 months of the year."

Clapper got his nickname when a childhood lisp twisted "Vic" into "Dit." In 1927-28, he broke into the NHL on right wing, and Boston's "Dynamite Line" was soon formed. With Dutch Gainor at center and Cooney Weiland on left wing, the trio was aptly named. In 1929-30, Clapper exploded with 41 goals, while Weiland blasted home 43. Clapper made the inaugural Second

All-Star Team the following season and again in 1934-35. Yet despite his success and established reputation as a "clutch" goal scorer, Clapper dropped back to defense in 1937-38.

"Clapper diagnosed the plays like a great infielder in baseball," explained Bruins goalie Tiny Thompson, "and put himself where he knew the puck had to come."

Dink Carroll of Montreal's *Gazette* described defenseman Clapper as "an ice general back of the blue line, an organizer who rallied his mates when they were behind and held them together in the tight spots." The Bruins won the Stanley Cup in 1938-39 and 1940-41, while Clapper was garnering First All-Star status.

In 1948, *The Hockey News* summed up Clapper's approach: "Clapper had a simple creed—he fought his heart out, bounced players around and took the

same kind of punishment he dished out. Once the game was over, however, he forgot it all and never held a grudge. That's what made him so popular with other players and fans throughout the entire NHL circuit." Clapper finished his career as Boston's player/coach and was inducted into the Hockey Hall of Fame the day after he retired.

VICTOR "DIT" CLAPPER
Newmarket, Ontario
February 9, 1907–January 21, 1978
NHL Career: 1927-47
Boston

	GP	G	A	P	PIM
RS	833	228	246	474	462
PO	82	13	17	30	50

Stanley Cup (3), A-S Game (2), HOF 1947

BOBBY CLARKE

CENTER

Bobby Clarke had loads of talent, but it was his grit and determination that made him a four-time All-Star. "All I ever wanted to do was play hockey," he said, "and I just played it the way I thought it had to be played." Despite the onset of diabetes, Clarke won west-

ern Canada's junior scoring championship two years running, yet he wasn't selected by Philadelphia until the second round of the 1969 amateur draft.

"He sure does a lot of things well," observed veteran tough-guy Reggie Fleming in the fall of 1969. "I especially like the way he forechecks. You don't see that in kids who just turned pro." Clarke won the 1972 Bill Masterton Trophy for his perseverance after cracking the top-10 scoring list for the first of seven consecutive times. Midway through the 1972-73 campaign, he became Philadelphia's team captain. Clarke finished second in league scoring that season with a career-high 37 goals, earning both the Pearson Award and the Hart Trophy.

Boston won the opener of the 1974 Stanley Cup finals, but Clarke turned the series around by scoring an overtime goal in game two. "If we'd lost this one, we would have been tired going home," he said. "Now we're fresh as daisies." Philadelphia won the series 4–2. Clarke led the league with 89 assists the follow-

ing season, winning his second Hart Trophy. He also contributed a playoff-high 12 assists toward another Stanley Cup victory.

Clarke won his third Hart after tallying a career-best 119 points in 1975-76 and finished second overall. Although Montreal swept Philly in the finals, Clarke remained a consistently strong two-way player throughout his entire career. He took the Flyers to the Cup finals again in 1979-80 and won the 1983 Frank Selke Trophy.

BOBBY CLARKE
Flin Flon, Manitoba
August 13, 1949–
NHL Career: 1969-84
Philadelphia

	GP	G	A	P	PIM
RS	1144	358	852	1210	1453
PO	136	42	77	119	152

Hart (3), Pearson, Selke, Masterton, Stanley Cup (2), A-S Game (8), HOF 1987

PAUL COFFEY

DEFENSE

 1985, 1986, 1989, 1995 ⭐ 1982, 1983, 1984, 1990

Blue-line dynamo Paul Coffey scored 29 goals and 60 assists in 1981-82, his first of eight All-Star campaigns. He notched 96 points the following season, then leapt to second in 1983-84 league scoring. Coffey tallied 40 goals and 86 assists, was runner-up for the Norris Trophy, then contributed 22 playoff points toward Edmonton's first Cup win. He won the Norris and finished fifth in 1984-85 scoring with 121 points, adding 44 more in a successful title defense. In the 1985-86 campaign, Coffey broke Bobby Orr's record for defensemen with 48 goals, scored a career-high 90 assists, finished third in NHL scoring and won another Norris. Coffey earned his third Cup ring in 1986-87, but he felt unappreciated and demanded a trade. He joined Pittsburgh in November 1987.

Coffey came second for the Norris in 1988-89, finishing among the top-10 scorers both that season and the next. An elegant skater, he also proved himself the league's fastest at the 1991 NHL Skills Competition. He helped the Penguins win the 1991 Stanley Cup, but Pittsburgh dealt Coffey to Los Angeles in February 1992, and he bounced to Detroit a year later. Coffey won his final All-Star berth in 1994-95. The first rearguard to lead the Red Wings in scoring, he picked up his third Norris. After his trade to the Hartford Whalers in October 1996, however, Coffey's career started to unravel.

He spent short, unsuccessful stints with Hartford, Philadelphia, Chicago and Carolina before rebounding with a stronger 1999-2000 campaign for the Hurricanes. With Ray Bourque a close second, Coffey is still the highest-scoring defenseman in NHL history. "What you see from him now is probably 80 percent of what he was," observed Grant Fuhr, "but that's still pretty darn good." In July 2000, Boston signed Coffey to a two-year contract.

PAUL COFFEY
Weston, Ontario
June 1, 1961–
NHL Career: 1980-
Edmonton, Pittsburgh, Los Angeles, Detroit, Hartford, Philadelphia, Chicago, Carolina, Boston

	GP	G	A	P	PIM
RS	1391	396	1131	1527	1772
PO	194	59	137	196	264

Norris (3), Stanley Cup (4), A-S Game (14)

NEIL COLVILLE

CENTER
DEFENSE

2️⃣ 1939, 1940 ⭐ 1948

Breadlines were a harsh reality during the Great Depression, but the New York Rangers' "Bread Line" was an entertaining and productive trio. Neil

Colville, his younger brother Mac and Alex Shibicky all graduated from the Philadelphia Ramblers of the Can-Am League during the 1935-36 season. They quickly emerged as the team's bread and butter, hence the nickname. Colville centered the youngsters and collected the most points. After breaking his jaw in the first game of the 1937 playoffs, the resilient Colville wore a brace and didn't miss a game. He led his team in scoring to within one game of the Stanley Cup championship.

Colville cracked the NHL's top-10 scorers in 1937-38 for the first of four consecutive campaigns. His 37 points in 1938-39 earned him a spot on the Second All-Star Team, and he repeated the feat the following season with a career-high 19 goals. Even more significant, however, were his league-leading 7 assists and 9 points in the playoffs, helping the Rangers take the 1940 Stanley Cup.

In 1940-41, Colville hit personal bests with 28 assists and 42 points, but a year later, he signed on with the Cana-

dian military. He and his brother helped the Ottawa Commandos win the 1943 Allan Cup, and Colville didn't return to New York until late in the 1944-45 season. He had lost much of his jump, however. Known as "Frosty" for his gray hair, he became team captain in 1945-46 but moved back to defense. The transition was a smooth one, and blue-liner Colville made the Second All-Star Team in 1947-48 with 16 points. He left the Rangers 14 games into the following campaign, although he returned to coach in 1950-51.

NEIL COLVILLE
Edmonton, Alberta
August 4, 1914–December 26, 1987
NHL Career: 1935-42, 1944-49
NY Rangers

	GP	G	A	P	PIM
RS	464	99	166	265	213
PO	46	7	19	26	32

Stanley Cup, A-S Game (2), HOF 1967

RIGHT WING

 1934, 1935, 1936 ⭐ 1932, 1933

When Charlie Conacher broke into the NHL in 1929-30, Toronto's "Kid Line" was formed, with Joe Primeau at center and Harvey "Busher" Jackson on left wing. Conacher became known as "The Big Bomber" because of the heavy wrist shot he had honed. "Even when I made the Maple Leafs, I kept at it," recalled Conacher. "I practiced with Lorne Chabot, the Leaf goaltender. Poor Chabot—how I used to black-and-blue him."

The opposition goalies weren't much better off. "I stopped that shot with my pads," said Chicago's Chuck Gardiner, "but it still hurt. No one has ever driven a shot as hard as that at me before." In 1930-31, Conacher led the NHL in goals scored, and the following season, he tied fellow right-winger Bill Cook for the league lead with 34 goals, assisted by the 5 tallies he put behind Shrimp Worters of the New York Americans in an 11–3 victory on January 19, 1932. The Leafs finished the season by winning the Stanley Cup, with Conacher the leading playoff goal scorer.

Although his production slipped in 1932-33, Conacher still made the Second All-Star Team before going on to win his first scoring championship the following season. He retained his title in 1934-35, scoring a career-high 36 goals and a league-record 57 points. "King Clancy and Syl Apps were great because they could rally a team," recalled Dick Irvin, who coached the Leafs throughout most of the 1930s. "But Charlie Conacher was the guy who could score the big goal for you, and he could score in more different ways than anyone I ever saw until 'The Rocket' came along." Conacher led NHL goal scorers for a fifth time in 1935-36 before injuries reduced his ice time and effectiveness. In October 1938, Toronto sold Conacher to Detroit. He finished out his playing career with the New York Americans. In 1947-48, he returned to the NHL as a coach. His brother Roy took the 1948-49 scoring crown, but that was about all the Hawks won. Conacher was fired in the summer of 1950.

CHARLIE CONACHER
Toronto, Ontario
December 20, 1909–December 30, 1967
NHL Career: 1929-41
Toronto, Detroit, NY Americans

	GP	G	A	P	PIM
RS	459	225	173	398	523
PO	49	17	18	35	49

Ross (2), Stanley Cup, A-S Game (2), HOF 1961

LIONEL CONACHER

DEFENSE

 ★ 1934 ★2 1933, 1937

Voted Canada's male athlete of the half-century in 1950, Lionel Conacher was an awesome competitor in every sport to which he turned his hand. He didn't start skating seriously until he was 16 years old and was never more than determined and plodding on ice. At 19, however, he was on a Memorial Cup-winning junior team. Yet it was on the football field that he earned his nickname "The Big Train." With a fearsome running style, he churned up the yardage, his knees pumping high. In 1921, he led the Toronto Argonauts to Grey Cup victory, but he was also an outstanding baseball and lacrosse player, wrestler and fighter. Conacher even took on heavyweight boxer Jack Dempsey in an exhibition bout in 1922.

In 1923, Conacher turned down professional hockey offers in favor of a football scholarship to Pittsburgh's Duquesne University. While there, he also captained the Pittsburgh Yellow Jackets to two U.S. amateur hockey titles. Conacher finally turned pro when Pittsburgh was granted an NHL franchise for 1925-26. He was

traded to the New York Americans in December 1926, and by 1929-30, Conacher was the Amerks' player/coach. The Montreal Maroons bought his services for the following season.

Conacher's 28 points in 1932-33 represented a career-high, and he joined his younger brother Charlie on the 1933 Second All-Star Team. He was traded yet again, this time to Chicago. Conacher came second in Hart Trophy voting and led the Blackhawks to the 1934 Stanley Cup. The Maroons quickly reacquired "The Big Train," and Conacher's grit helped them secure the 1935 championship. He was still at his peak in 1936-37. "[The] Maroons were gloriously led to victory by Lionel Conacher," wrote *The Toronto Star*'s Andy Lytle, as Montreal knocked the Boston Bruins out of the 1937 playoffs. "The big fellow played

defense [and] secondary goal and inspired the attack each time it threatened to waver. Conacher was everywhere, a raging, tearing torrent of skill and fighting strength." The Maroons failed to advance further, however, and Conacher retired from the game. Although he spent the rest of his life in politics, he died on the playing field. Moments after hitting a triple in a 1954 exhibition softball game in Ottawa, Conacher suffered a heart attack and collapsed on third base.

LIONEL CONACHER
Toronto, Ontario
May 24, 1901–May 26, 1954
NHL Career: 1925-37
Pittsburgh, NY Americans,
Montreal Maroons, Chicago

	GP	G	A	P	PIM
RS	498	80	105	185	882
PO	35	2	2	4	34

Stanley Cup (2), A-S Game, HOF 1994

ROY CONACHER

LEFT WING

★ 1949

Although he never matched the accomplishments of his older brothers Charlie and Lionel, Roy Conacher eventually joined them in the Hockey Hall of Fame. He made an exciting NHL debut with Boston in 1938-39 and finished runner-up for the Calder Trophy behind teammate Frank Brimsek. Conacher's league-leading 26 goals lifted him into a four-way tie for tenth in league scoring. In the playoffs, he helped the Bruins win the Stanley Cup with 6 goals and 4 assists in 12 games.

He tied for tenth in NHL scoring again in 1940-41, and the Bruins reclaimed the Cup. Swift-skating Conacher led his team with 24 goals the following season, then enlisted in the Royal

Canadian Air Force. He didn't return to the Bruins until the tail end of the 1945-46 campaign. Traded to Detroit for the following season, Conacher tallied 30 goals and a team-leading 54 points. He couldn't come to contract terms for 1947-48, however, so Detroit manager Jack Adams traded him to the New York Rangers. When Conacher refused to report and decided to retire instead, Adams struck an alternative deal, and Conacher became a Blackhawk eight games into the season.

Chicago hired his brother Charlie to coach later in the season, and again, Conacher finished tenth in league scoring. He vaulted to first in 1948-49—and onto the First All-Star Team. Playing on the high-flying "Boilermaker Line"

with Doug Bentley and Bill Mosienko, Conacher tallied 26 goals, 42 assists and only 8 penalty minutes. He finished sixth in the league in 1949-50 and led in Hawks' scoring three consecutive times, but Conacher had had enough. He announced his retirement 12 games into the 1951-52 campaign.

ROY CONACHER
Toronto, Ontario
October 5, 1916–December 29, 1984
NHL Career: 1938-42, 1945-52
Boston, Detroit, Chicago

	GP	G	A	P	PIM
RS	490	226	200	426	90
PO	42	15	15	30	14

Ross, Stanley Cup (2), A-S Game, HOF 1998

BILL COOK

★ 1931, 1932, 1933 ★ 1934

Bill Cook's first NHL score, in 1926, was the first winning goal in New York Rangers' franchise history and was "a brilliant sally down the ice," according to *The New York Times*. Manager Lester Patrick's purchase of the Western Hockey League All-Star paid further quick dividends when Cook won the NHL scoring race in that 1926-27 season, then scored the Stanley Cup-winning goal in overtime the following season. "I look for the leaders," explained Patrick in an interview with Daniel Mahoney years later. "Then I let them lead. The placid player can be depended on for a safe, steady game, but for the kind of inspired hockey needed to win championships, I need the Bill Cooks. The other players, when it comes right down to the crunch, will follow the Bill Cooks."

"He's got fire in his belly," said Toronto's Joe Primeau. "You didn't fool around with Bill Cook. He was tough. I always based any right-wingers against Charlie Conacher, my linemate on the Leafs. Bill was the best we ever played against." As the strongest sniper on the "A" Line, which also featured his brother Bun and center Frank Boucher, Cook finished a point behind Conacher in the 1930-31 scoring race but still took First All-Star Team honors. He retained his ranking with a league-leading 34 goals in 1931-32 and won the 1932-33 scoring race and his second Stanley Cup ring.

In 1951, *The Winnipeg Tribune* maintained that Cook had been as good a player as Rocket Richard, comparing the ability of each "to get off a shot from any angle, whether skating backwards or forwards…[Cook] was that rare type of athlete who instinctively did the right thing, who thought and acted simultaneously. One little mistake by an opposing defenseman or a lapse of vigilance by the goalie, and *bingo*, the puck was in the net."

BILL COOK
Brantford, Ontario
October 9, 1896–April 6, 1986
NHL Career: 1926-37
NY Rangers

	GP	G	A	P	PIM
RS	474	229	138	367	386
PO	46	13	11	24	68

Ross (2), Stanley Cup (2), A-S Game, HOF 1952

BUN COOK

★ 1931

"**W**hen Bun Cook is hot, he is one of the most amazing players in hockey," wrote *New York Graphic* entertainment columnist Ed Sullivan. "At such moments, he attempts plays that stagger the imagination." Cook peaked offensively in 1929-30, when he scored 24 goals and 18 assists, and he earned his sole All-Star selection with a tenth-place finish in the 1930-31 scoring race. Yet Cook was an innovator and was even known to pick a rolling puck up on his stick blade and try to carry it through the opposing team.

Although he lacked his linemate brother Bill's consistency, Cook was a key member of the New York Rangers' "A" Line, with Bill and center Frank Boucher. Frank Selke, in a letter petitioning for Cook's posthumous nomination to the Hockey Hall of Fame, described the least spectacular member of the famous trio as a "safety-valve trailer and defensive specialist," although "men who would know credit Bunny Cook with the introduction of the passing attack." More often, Cook is credited with the invention of the drop pass.

"I had a dream about the drop pass one night," said Cook, "and at our next practice, I told Frank and Bill about it. They thought I was crazy, but they decided to humor me. By gosh, it worked. I'd cross over from left wing to center as I moved in on the defense. I'd fake a shot and leave the puck behind and skate away from it, with Frank or Bill picking it up. We got a lot of goals off the crisscross and drop pass." Traded to the Boston Bruins for the 1936-37 campaign, Cook became player/coach for the Providence Reds the following season, beginning a highly successful AHL coaching career.

FRED "BUN" COOK
Kingston, Ontario
September 18, 1903–March 19, 1988
NHL Career: 1926-37
NY Rangers, Boston

	GP	G	A	P	PIM
RS	473	158	144	302	444
PO	46	15	3	18	50

Stanley Cup (2), HOF 1995

ART COULTER

⭐2 1935, 1938, 1939, 1940

Art Coulter was a tireless and exceptionally strong defenseman, with a fierce commitment to teamwork. He broke into the NHL with the Chicago Blackhawks late in the 1931-32 season. By 1933-34, he had established himself as a defensive rock. Partnered with the beefy Taffy Abel, Coulter helped the Blackhawks win the 1934 Stanley Cup. He made the Second All-Star Team the following season but was involved in a surprising trade halfway through the 1935-36 campaign. The Hawks and the New York Rangers swapped All-Star blue-liners, and Coulter replaced Earl Seibert on Broadway. It wasn't long before he was an integral part of his new club.

Named captain for the 1937-38 season—a job he held until his retirement—Coulter began three consecutive seasons on the Second All-Star Team. His rugged play led to a career-high 90 minutes in penalties, but he went down with an injury and missed the 1938 playoffs. The Rangers were upset 2–0 by the Americans in the opening round, and in 1938-39, it looked as if the Rangers might make another quick exit. Facing the runaway regular-season champion Boston Bruins, the Rangers lost the first three games.

Coulter sent each of his teammates an inspirational telegram: "Determination was dominating quality of last Stanley

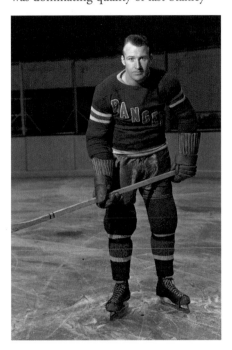

Cup-winners [Chicago]…We have it too…Let's go…the Trapper." The Rangers made a remarkable rally and forced a seventh game. Unfortunately, New York's season ended when Mel "Sudden Death" Hill scored for Boston in the third overtime period.

The next season took a better turn. Coulter scored one of his rare playoff goals and helped the Rangers defeat Boston and Toronto for his second Stanley Cup ring. He was a steady force over the following two seasons, his most productive, with 19 points in 1940-41 and 17 in 1941-42. Coulter then enlisted in the U.S. Coast Guard, which marked the end of his NHL career.

ARTHUR COULTER
Winnipeg, Manitoba
May 31, 1909–deceased
NHL Career: 1931-42
Chicago, NY Rangers

	GP	G	A	P	PIM
RS	465	30	82	112	543
PO	49	4	5	9	61

Stanley Cup (2), A-S Game, HOF 1974

YVAN COURNOYER

⭐2 1969, 1971, 1972, 1973

He was "The Roadrunner," constantly flirting with danger but able to avoid it with marvelous speed. "You have to be fast when you are my size," noted five-foot-seven Yvan Cournoyer. "Otherwise, those big guys will catch up with you." He made his first appearance with the Montreal Canadiens as a teenager in 1963-64. Although he possessed a heavy shot and displayed strong stickhandling skills in addition to his quickness, Cournoyer took several seasons to establish himself as a regular. The Habs used him only as a power-play specialist, but he gradually developed into a complete player. Meanwhile, he helped Montreal win several Stanley Cups.

Cournoyer exploded offensively in 1968-69 and scored 43 goals. He finished sixth in the league with a career-high 87 points, making the Second All-Star Team for the first of four times in five seasons. Cournoyer found the net 37 times in 1970-71, and in the following campaign, he scored 47 goals, his personal best. He began his most satisfying season by helping Canada defeat the Soviet Union in the Summit Series in September 1972. In the NHL, he tallied 40 goals and set a scoring record with 15 playoff goals. "The best part of that 15th goal was that it was the winning goal of the last game," he said, smiling. Cournoyer won the Conn Smythe Trophy and his sixth Stanley Cup ring.

In 1975-76, Cournoyer became team captain and led the Canadiens to four consecutive Cup wins. A nagging back injury finally forced him to hang up his skates in 1979. "The best day of my life was when I made the Montreal Canadiens," recalled Cournoyer. "The worst day of my life was when I retired."

YVAN COURNOYER
Drummondville, Quebec
November 22, 1943–
NHL Career: 1963-79
Montreal

	GP	G	A	P	PIM
RS	968	428	435	863	255
PO	147	64	63	127	47

Smythe, Stanley Cup (10), A-S Game (6), HOF 1982

BILL COWLEY

CENTER

Shortly before the start of the 1935-36 season, the NHL divvied up the assets of the defunct St. Louis Eagles, and Bill Cowley became a Boston Bruin. Although he soon earned a reputation as one of the premier playmakers of his day, Cowley centered Boston's second line, behind Milt Schmidt's "Kraut Line," for most of his career. "Cowley is the player who glorified the assist," wrote Frank Duggan in a vintage profile. "It is an old axiom that the pen is mightier than the sword. With Cowley, the assist is mightier than the goal. Cowley provides the ammunition; his wings do the firing."

In 1938-39, Cowley led the NHL in assists and added 14 playoff points. He made Mel "Sudden Death" Hill famous, feeding the rookie three glorious passes in overtime. He also had the helper on the Stanley Cup-winning goal. "I was in the corner and got the puck," he recalled. "[Roy] Conacher broke from the blue line. I passed the puck back and laid it on his stick. He was coming at full speed and picked the top corner." In a manner not repeated until Wayne Gretzky came along, Cowley dominated the 1940-41 points race. His record-breaking 45 assists alone were enough to win the scoring crown, and he added 17 goals. Cowley took home the Hart Trophy, and Boston won its second championship in three years.

Cowley missed almost half of the 1941-42 campaign with a broken jaw but reclaimed the Hart Trophy in 1943, tallying another 45 assists. In 1943-44, he had 71 points and was well on his way to shattering the single-season record of 73 before he was knocked out of the lineup with six weeks left in the season. He recovered and posted a strong 1944-45 campaign. "He comes at you like a bulldog, then he slips a pass right under your guard," praised Canadiens defenseman Butch Bouchard, "and he's always ready for a return play." Cowley retired after the 1946-47 season as the NHL's all-time leader in both assists and total points.

BILL COWLEY				
Bristol, Quebec				
June 12, 1912–December 31, 1993				
NHL Career: 1934-47				
St. Louis, Boston				
	GP	G	A	P	PIM
RS	549	195	353	548	143
PO	64	12	34	46	22
Ross, Hart (2), Stanley Cup (2), HOF 1968				

JACK CRAWFORD

DEFENSE

Wearing a helmet made Jack Crawford an NHL rarity in his time. Eddie Shore had worn one regularly after seeing Ace Bailey's career cut short because of a fractured skull in 1933, but Crawford used his for more than safety. As a boy, he had suffered from a terrible infection that had been caused by the paint on a football helmet. As a result, he lost most of his hair, and his hockey headgear offered him a dignified cover-up.

Crawford broke into the Boston Bruins' lineup for two games in 1937-38 and drew comparisons to his teammate Shore for more than sartorial reasons. Although Crawford's numbers never approached Shore's, his strong puck-rushing and body-checking skills earned him a regular spot in the 1938-39 Boston lineup. Partnered with Flash Hollett, he helped the Bruins to Stanley Cup victory that spring. Still improving, Crawford was on his second, and last, Cup-winning team in 1941.

In 1942-43, Crawford increased his offensive production, scoring 5 goals and 18 assists, and both he and Hollett made the Second All-Star Team. When Hollett was traded to Detroit midway through the following season, Crawford was paired with Boston captain Dit Clapper. Crawford posted a career-high 24 points in 1944-45, and the following season, he graduated to the First All-Star Team, with 7 goals and 9 assists.

A respected team leader, Crawford was handed the Boston captaincy when Clapper retired to coach full-time early in the 1946-47 season. One scribe of the time called Crawford the team comedian. Seeing former teammate Ray Getliffe, then an NHL linesman, one Saturday afternoon in March 1947, Crawford asked for a little favor: "Hit a few of those guys, will you? You don't have to hit 'em—just tip 'em and make it look like an accident. I need some help out there." But Crawford played remarkably consistent hockey. He remained team captain in Boston throughout the 1949-50 campaign, then moved down to the AHL's Hershey Bears, where he picked up a coaching career.

JOHN (JACK) CRAWFORD				
Dublin, Ontario				
October 26, 1916–January 17, 1979				
NHL Career: 1937-50				
Boston				
	GP	G	A	P	PIM
RS	548	38	140	178	202
PO	66	4	13	17	36
Stanley Cup (2)				

GOALTENDER ★ 1965

Roger Crozier won the AHL's 1963-64 rookie-of-the-year award, but his big break came when Detroit's veteran goalie Terry Sawchuk was injured the same season. With an acrobatic butterfly style, Crozier posted two shutouts for the Wings in 15 games. Although Sawchuk backstopped Detroit to a seventh game in the Stanley Cup finals, Detroit went with Crozier the following season. Crozier's league-leading six shutouts helped him to the First All-Star Team, and he won the Calder Trophy. He almost added the Vezina Trophy as well, finishing second by two goals to Sawchuk and Johnny Bower of Toronto.

Crozier missed the first six games in 1965-66 with pancreatitis, an illness that knocked him out of the lineup from time to time for the rest of his career. Once he was healthy again (and with his right-hand catching glove still confusing many shooters), his seven shutouts led the league that season. Crozier helped stake the underdog Red Wings to two victories in the Montreal Forum before the Stanley Cup finals moved to Detroit. "I still do not believe it," said Jean Beliveau after game two. "I don't think I ever shot a puck harder. I put everything into it. It was streaking for the upper right-hand corner, but Crozier threw out his hand, made a perfect catch and tossed the puck away. How did he stop it?" Even though Montreal won the next four games and the Cup, Crozier tumbled and sprawled his way to the Conn Smythe Trophy.

In the summer of 1970, Detroit sold Crozier to the expansion team in Buffalo. He starred for the Sabres for several seasons but played only a backup role when Buffalo made the 1975 Cup finals. Crozier completed his career with three games for Washington in 1976-77.

ROGER CROZIER
Bracebridge, Ontario
March 16, 1942–January 11, 1996
NHL Career: 1963-77
Detroit, Buffalo, Washington

	GP	M	GA	SO	AVE
RS	518	28567	1446	30	3.04
PO	32	1789	82	1	2.75

Calder, Smythe

WILF CUDE

 1936, 1937

Wilf Cude spent his 1930-31 rookie season deep in the NHL basement with the Philadelphia Quakers before accepting an unusual job. When the Quakers folded, the NHL hired Cude as a utility backup goaltender. He played two games for Boston and one for Chicago in 1931-32 before joining the Can-Am League. Montreal bought his rights, but Cude played only one game for the Canadiens in 1933-34 (earning a shutout) before being "loaned" to the Detroit Red Wings for the rest of the season.

Cude's 1.52 goals-against average was the league's lowest, and he helped Detroit to its best finish ever. He even took a hero's turn in game three of the Stanley Cup finals that year. Knocked unconscious when he was accidentally clipped by a stick, Cude was carried off the ice, only to return 10 minutes later. Bloody, with his right eye almost swollen shut, he finished the game, Detroit's only victory. Although Chicago won the Cup in game four, it took the Blackhawks 90 minutes to put the first puck past the young goalie.

Returning to the Canadiens in 1934-35, Cude notched 10 shutouts the following season to earn a spot on the Second All-Star Team. According to *The Gazette*, Detroit's Jack Adams declared that he would trade his goaltender Normie Smith for Cude, although not for the usual reasons. "When Cude was with the Red Wings two years ago," explained Adams, "the little Welshman received more fan mail than any other man on the club." But Adams was unsuccessful in prying his potential drawing card from the Canadiens. Cude, who finished just behind Smith in 1936-37 All-Star voting, completed his career in Montreal.

WILF CUDE				
Barry, South Wales				
July 4, 1910–April 5, 1968				
NHL Career: 1930-32, 1933-41				
Philadelphia, Boston, Chicago,				
Montreal, Detroit				
	GP	M	GA	SO	AVE
RS	282	17586	798	24	2.72
PO	19	1257	51	1	2.43
A-S Game (2)				

BYRON DAFOE

GOALTENDER

 1999

Born in Britain but raised in Canada, Byron Dafoe was picked by the Washington Capitals in the second round of the 1989 draft. He played one minute in the Washington net in 1992-93 and appeared in only nine games over

the following two seasons. "It's been a tough climb for me to get to the NHL," said Dafoe in 1998. "I've definitely paid my dues." The Capitals traded Dafoe to Los Angeles in the summer of 1995. He played about half of the team's games over two seasons and won the Kings' 1996-97 Unsung Hero award. Yet L.A. traded him to Boston in August 1997.

Dafoe responded with an acrobatic and enthusiastic 1997-98 campaign for the Bruins. "I've had these good stretches before, but I've never had this kind of stinginess, with a goals-against so low," he said in November. "A lot of that is a reflection of the team defense. It's never been this much fun for me to go to the rink every day." By season's end, he had six shutouts in 65 games with a 2.24 goals-against average.

"Lord Byron" sparkled even more in 1998-99, notching a league-high 10 shutouts. "He has been the Bruins' rock all year with his determined, passionate play," noted ESPN's Darren Pang. A finalist for the Vezina Trophy, Dafoe made the Second All-Star Team with a 1.99 average and posted similar numbers in the playoffs for the second straight season.

Sitting out the first weeks of 1999-2000 in a contract stalemate, Dafoe proved he could be just as aggressive and bold off the ice as he is on. He fired his agent, met with general manager Harry Sinden for 40 minutes and inked a three-year $9.45 million deal.

BYRON DAFOE				
Sussex, England				
February 25, 1971–				
NHL Career: 1992–				
Washington, Los Angeles, Boston				
	GP	M	GA	SO	AVE
RS	271	15247	693	20	2.73
PO	21	1328	46	3	2.08

ALEX DELVECCHIO

CENTER
LEFT WING

★2 1953
★2 1959

With his size and elegant skating, the six-foot, 195-pound rookie Alex Delvecchio made a strong first impression. He helped the Detroit Red Wings win the 1952 Stanley Cup, and when Sid Abel departed the following season, Delvecchio centered the "Production Line." He proved himself an excellent center for wingers Gordie Howe and Ted Lindsay, who finished the 1952-53 campaign 1–2 in league scoring. Delvecchio tied for fourth with 16 assists and 43 helpers and made the Second All-Star Team.

Although he helped the Wings win the Cup in 1954 and 1955 and cracked the NHL's top-10 scoring list twice after that, Delvecchio switched positions for 1958-59. Norm Ullman had established himself as a strong center, so Delvecchio hopped over to left wing, opposite Howe on Ullman's right, thereby joining the select group of players who have made an All-Star Team at two different positions. He also won the 1959 Lady Byng Trophy after taking only six minutes in penalties.

Nicknamed "Fats" because of his round face, Delvecchio became team captain in 1962-63. He retained the position until his retirement and was the longest-serving captain in league history until Steve Yzerman surpassed his record in October 1997. The "Production Line" reunited for a season when Lindsay came out of retirement for 1964-65. Delvecchio finished fifth in the scoring race and was runner-up for the Byng. Although he dropped to seventh in scoring the following season, he picked up his second sportsmanship award. A third Byng came in 1968-69, when Delvecchio centered the "Production Line II," between Howe and Frank Mahovlich.

Delvecchio retired during the 1973-74 season in sixth place on the all-time goal-scoring list and second in assists and points. To date, he remains second only to Howe in seasons played.

ALEX DELVECCHIO
Fort William, Ontario
December 4, 1932–
NHL Career: 1950-74
Detroit

	GP	G	A	P	PIM
RS	1549	456	825	1281	383
PO	121	35	69	104	29

Byng (3), Stanley Cup (3),
A-S Game (13), HOF 1977

DEFENSE

 1999, 2000

Philadelphia made a shocking move in March 2000 by stripping the "C" from Eric Lindros, who was out with a concussion, and naming Eric Desjardins captain. Some felt the change lacked class, but the Flyers' players seemed pleased to see Desjardins get the job. "He's well respected in this room," said John LeClair, "and he's a leader of the guys we have in here right now."

"He's been a great leader of this team for a long time," echoed Keith Jones. "There was no one here more deserving."

Desjardins made his NHL debut in 1988-89 with the Montreal Canadiens. In 1992-93, he scored 13 goals and 32 assists and helped Montreal make a surprisingly successful run for the Stanley Cup. In game two of the finals against Los Angeles, he scored all three goals in Montreal's 3–2 overtime victory, becoming the first defenseman to notch a hat trick in the Stanley Cup finals. Desjardins' career took a major turn when Montreal traded him to Philadelphia in February 1995. He took off with the Flyers, notching 5 goals and 18 assists in 34 games and topping all Philadelphia rearguards in points that season and every season since. In 1998-99, Desjardins set career records with 15 goals and 51 points and made the Second All-Star Team.

General manager Bob Clarke successfully lobbied for an invitation to the midseason 2000 All-Star Game. "He's having a Norris Trophy year," Clarke told *The Philadelphia Daily News*. "Everybody in our organization knows how good he is, how important he is to a team, what a good person he is. He has real brains, great hockey intelligence, instincts. He's very competitive." At season's end, Desjardins picked up his sixth consecutive Barry Ashbee Trophy as the Flyers' top defenseman and made the Second All-Star Team for the second time. He led the Flyers to the Eastern Conference finals, but after being up three games to one, Philadelphia fell to New Jersey.

ERIC DESJARDINS
Rouyn, Quebec
June 14, 1969–
NHL Career: 1988-
Montreal, Philadelphia

	GP	G	A	P	PIM
RS	827	102	332	434	564
PO	146	19	51	70	85

Stanley Cup, A-S Game (3)

RIGHT WING

 1938  1936, 1937

New York Rangers manager Lester Patrick made an astute purchase when he bought Cecil Dillon from the Springfield Indians on January 1, 1931. The left-handed shooter potted 23 goals in the 1931-32 season, a remarkable total considering that his teammate Bill Cook played right wing on the first line. Although the Rangers lost to Toronto in the Stanley Cup finals that spring, they took the Cup from the Leafs the following year. Dillon's 8 goals and 10 points led all play-off scorers.

With 13 goals and 39 points in 1933-34, Dillon came fifth in league scoring, and he hit the net 25 times the following season, a career-high. Meanwhile, Cook, his brother Bun and their centerman Frank Boucher were starting to slow down. Patrick juggled the lines for the 1935-36 campaign, and Dillon led the team in scoring for the next three seasons. He hit 39 points again in 1937-38, once more finishing fifth in the scoring race, and tied Toronto's Gordie Drillon in All-Star voting. For the first time, two players made the First All-Star Team in the same position. In 1936,

Patrick called Dillon "the perfect hockey player," but three years later, he deemed him expendable. Dillon was sold to the Detroit Red Wings on May 17, 1939, played only one season in Motown and was out of the NHL. He played two more years in the American Hockey League before retiring.

CECIL DILLON
Toledo, Ohio
April 26, 1908–November 14, 1969
NHL Career: 1931-40
NY Rangers, Detroit

	GP	G	A	P	PIM
RS	453	167	131	298	105
PO	43	14	9	23	14

Stanley Cup, A-S Game

MARCEL DIONNE

CENTER

Although he retired behind only Gordie Howe in NHL goals and points scored, Marcel Dionne had trouble garnering the respect he deserved. Nicknamed "L'il Beaver" by Howe, five-foot-nine Dionne set a rookie scoring record with 77 points for Detroit in 1971-72, yet he finished third in Calder Trophy voting. He finished third in 1974-75 scoring with 47 goals and 74 assists but won only the Lady Byng Trophy. Unhappy in Detroit, Dionne moved to Los Angeles the following summer.

Initially, Dionne had a tough time adjusting to the Kings' more defensive style. "The little things meant more—holding your man, just standing in front of him—things that the average fan doesn't notice," he said. "They never mattered in Detroit." Yet he scored 94 points in 1975-76 and vaulted to second in NHL scoring in 1976-77. Dionne picked up his second Byng, but his selection to the First All-Star Team at center showed that the voters hadn't watched him closely—he had spent most of the season on right wing.

Dionne was back at center the next season, however, between Charlie Simmer and Dave Taylor. The "Triple Crown Line" started to tear up the league, and Dionne, second in NHL scoring, made the 1979 Second All-Star Team. The players voted him the Pearson Award both that season and the next. Dionne's 53 goals and 137 points earned him the 1980 Art Ross Trophy and another berth on the First All-Star Team. He finished second in 1980-81 scoring in his last All-Star season.

Dionne continued to rack up points, but his milestone 700th career goal came late in the 1986-87 season with a new team. Even though he finished out his career two seasons later with the New York Rangers, the Kings retired Dionne's number 16 in 1990.

MARCEL DIONNE
Drummondville, Quebec
August 3, 1951–
NHL Career: 1971-89
Detroit, Los Angeles, NY Rangers

	GP	G	A	P	PIM
RS	1348	731	1040	1771	600
PO	49	21	24	45	17

Ross, Byng (2), Pearson (2),
A-S Game (8), HOF 1992

GORDIE DRILLON

RIGHT WING

Gordie Drillon's NHL career was brief but brilliant. Brought in as a temporary replacement for Toronto's Charlie Conacher early in the 1936-37 season, the lanky six-foot-two, 178-pound winger made an immediate impression. Drillon finished his rookie season with 33 points and only two penalty minutes, runner-up to linemate Syl Apps in Calder Trophy voting and to Detroit's Marty Barry for the Lady Byng.

In 1937-38, Drillon's 26 goals led the league, as did his 52 points. (To date, he remains the last Toronto Maple Leaf to win an NHL scoring championship.) He also won the Lady Byng Trophy, with a paltry four minutes in penalties. The All-Star voting for right wing was tied, so Drillon joined his longtime idol Cecil Dillon on the First Team.

Drillon led all 1938 playoff scorers, with 7 goals, but the Leafs lost the Stanley Cup to Chicago three games to one. He retained his First All-Star status in 1939 with 34 points in 40 games, and his 18 goals led the Leafs for the second time. Once again, his 7 playoff goals were a league-high, but the Leafs fell to Boston in the finals. Although Drillon led Toronto in goals, assists and points in the 1939-40 regular season, he tallied only four playoff points before the runner-up Leafs bowed to the New York Rangers.

For the next two seasons, Drillon was once again the Leafs' top point-getter, coming second in Lady Byng Trophy vot-

ing. His 23 goals and 18 assists in 1941-42 were good for eighth in league scoring. He was selected to the Second All-Star Team, but that marked his final honor in Toronto. When the Leafs dropped the first three games of the 1942 Cup finals to Detroit, Drillon—in a seven-game scoring drought—was benched for the rest of the playoffs. Toronto made a miraculous recovery, winning the Cup in game seven, but Drillon was sold to the Montreal Canadiens days later. His 28 goals in 1942-43 were a career-best, but he entered military service and never played in the NHL again.

GORDIE DRILLON
Moncton, New Brunswick
October 23, 1914–October 22, 1986
NHL Career: 1936-43
Toronto, Montreal

	GP	G	A	P	PIM
RS	311	155	139	294	56
PO	50	26	15	41	10

Ross, Byng, Stanley Cup, A-S Game,
HOF 1975

KEN DRYDEN

GOALTENDER ⭐ 1973, 1976, 1977, 1978, 1979   ⭐ 1972

At six-foot-four and over 200 pounds, Ken Dryden didn't look or behave like the average goaltender. His approach, personified by his famous resting pose—his stick stabbing upright into the ice, his gloves stacked on top—combined cerebral coolness with remarkable athleticism. Dryden was drafted by Boston in 1964, but Montreal quickly acquired his rights. After pursuing a law degree through three All-American years at Cornell University, a season with the Canadian national team and an apprenticeship in the AHL, Dryden followed his older brother Dave's footsteps into the NHL for the last six games of 1970-71. With surprising success, he started the playoffs against the defending-champion Bruins. "That was the greatest save that's ever been made off me in my life," said Phil Esposito after game four. "My God, he's got arms like a giraffe." Montreal defeated Boston in seven games.

"In my opinion, we beat them in every phase of the game," recalled Bobby Orr, "except that Dryden stood on his head, and we couldn't get the puck past him." The Canadiens went on to win the Stanley Cup, and Dryden took home the Conn Smythe Trophy. He then led all NHL netminders with 64 appearances in 1971-72, was awarded the Calder Trophy and made the Second All-Star Team.

In 1972-73, Dryden earned his first Vezina Trophy, a spot on the First All-Star Team and a second Stanley Cup ring. Unhappy with Montreal's contract offer, however, he stunned the hockey world by articling with a Toronto law firm for the 1973-74 season. The Habs lured him back with a considerable raise, and Dryden became the backbone of a dynastic club. His subsequent All-Star seasons, when he either won the Vezina Trophy outright or shared it with teammate Bunny Larocque, were spent on Stanley Cup-winners. "Any time you were fortunate enough to catch Montreal playing badly," said Boston general manager Harry Sinden, "Dryden stopped you anyway."

Dryden's back was bothering him and so, too, was his belief that he had little more to accomplish as a hockey player. He retired in 1979 and became an acclaimed writer and broadcaster, returning to the NHL in 1997 as president of the Toronto Maple Leafs.

KEN DRYDEN
Hamilton, Ontario
August 8, 1947–
NHL Career: 1970-73, 1974-79
Montreal

	GP	M	GA	SO	AVE
RS	397	23352	870	46	2.24
PO	112	6846	274	10	2.40

Calder, Vezina (5), Smythe, Stanley Cup (6), A-S Game (5), HOF 1983

WOODY DUMART

LEFT WING ⭐ 1940, 1941, 1947

Woody Dumart joined the Boston Bruins for a single game in the 1935-36 season, the first of the famous "Kraut Line" to play an NHL game. Midway through the following campaign, he became a Boston regular with the other "Krauts," his childhood friends Bobby Bauer and Milt Schmidt. All three shared a German heritage. Their strong commitment to two-way hockey helped the Bruins win the 1939 Stanley Cup. Dumart finished the 1939-40 season with 22 goals and 21 assists, tying with Bauer as runner-up to Schmidt in league scoring. Elected to the Second All-Star Team, Dumart retained that honor in 1940-41, when the Bruins were again Cup-winners.

In February 1942, Dumart, Schmidt and Bauer enlisted in the Royal Canadian Air Force. Their main business continued to be hockey, however. Skating 19 games for the Ottawa RCAF team, Dumart led all playoff performers with 21 goals and 35 assists in the 1942 battle for the Allan Cup, Canada's senior league championship. Three years later, the "Kraut Line" was back in Boston for the opening of the 1945-46 NHL season. Although somewhat slower then—and known to some as "Porky" for his girth—Dumart scored 22 goals. In

1946-47, the famed trio's last season together before Bauer retired, Dumart reached his offensive highs. He tallied 24 goals, 28 assists and 52 points, good for ninth in the league and a spot on the Second All-Star Team.

An exceptionally clean player, Dumart went penalty-free through 10 of his 13 playoff campaigns. He posted his fifth 20-goal season in 1950-51 and was runner-up for the Lady Byng Trophy. Slipping more and more into a checking role, Dumart covered Gordie Howe so effectively in the 1953 playoffs that the Bruins were able to eliminate the defending-champion Detroit Red Wings. Boston lost the finals to Montreal, though, and Dumart retired after the 1953-54 season.

WOODROW "WOODY" DUMART
Kitchener, Ontario
December 23, 1916–
NHL Career: 1935-42, 1945-54
Boston

	GP	G	A	P	PIM
RS	772	211	218	429	99
PO	88	12	15	27	23

Stanley Cup (2), A-S Game (2), HOF 1992

BILL DURNAN

 1944, 1945, 1946, 1947, 1949, 1950

Although Bill Durnan wasn't eager to begin an NHL career, his success was immediate, consistent and legendary. He was runner-up for 1943-44 rookie-of-the-year honors, and the Canadiens took the Stanley Cup. In earning both the Vezina Trophy and First All-Star Team status that same year, Durnan set a pattern that lasted for most of the decade.

Much of Durnan's mastery was due to his ambidexterity. He wore specially fingered trappers that allowed him to hold his stick or catch the puck with either hand, and he could make the switch at lightning speed. "Durnan was toughest for me," recalled Boston's Milt Schmidt. "I could never do much with the guy. At the outset, he troubled me, and it got to be a complex, I guess. It got to the point where I'd break through on him

and have the feeling he had me beaten anyway." Durnan's ever-changing stance wasn't his only weapon. "Durnan had an uncanny way of cutting off all the angles," said Schmidt, "and waiting patiently for you to commit yourself."

The Canadiens won the 1946 Stanley Cup, and Durnan never faltered until 1947-48. When Montreal failed to make the playoffs, Durnan received sustained booing for the first time, and he couldn't stand the pressure. "It got so bad," he later recalled, "that I couldn't sleep the night before a game or the night afterwards, either. Nothing is worth that kind of agony." The Canadiens talked him out of quitting, though, and Durnan posted career-highs in 1948-49, with 10 shutouts and a 2.10 goals-against average. His next season went almost as well, until the playoffs.

The underdog New York Rangers took the first three games of the 1950 semifinals, and Durnan lost the last remnant of his fragile confidence. He stunned everyone when he announced his retirement before the series was even over. True to his word, Durnan never played another game.

BILL DURNAN
Toronto, Ontario
January 22, 1916–October 31, 1972
NHL Career: 1943-50
Montreal

	GP	M	GA	SO	AVE
RS	383	22945	901	34	2.36
PO	45	2871	99	2	2.07

Vezina (6), Stanley Cup (2),
A-S Game (3), HOF 1964

DON EDWARDS

GOALTENDER

His uncle Roy wound up a seven-season NHL netminding career in 1973-74—the same season Don Edwards became a junior OHA All-Star. The younger Edwards joined the Buffalo Sabres for 25 games in the latter part of the 1976-77 campaign, where he posted an excellent 2.51 goals-against average and made a huge impression on general manager Punch Imlach, who effectively controlled the Sabres' lineup. "You can see quick hands and feet. You can't see desire to play and will to win," noted Imlach. "Don has it all."

Although 1977-78 was Edwards' official rookie season, Imlach ensured that he started a league-high 72 games. "Goalies used to do it all the time," said Imlach, "and there's no reason they can't do it in these times."

Edwards agreed completely, maintaining that he could relax enough between games to avoid fatigue. "I think I could play all the time," he said. "I hate a game when I don't play." He backed up his claim with five shutouts and an

NHL-best 38 wins. Edwards made the Second All-Star Team and finished third in Calder Trophy voting.

He split more of the load with Bob Sauve in 1978-79, playing 54 games. The following season, the two reverted

to a traditional two-goalie rotation. They shared the 1980 Vezina Trophy, while Edwards returned to the Second All-Star Team. When his average crept up over the next two campaigns, the Sabres traded Edwards to Calgary in May 1982. He never regained his All-Star form. He served behind Reggie Lemelin for three seasons, consistently letting in an average four goals per game. The Flames traded Edwards to Toronto for 1985-86, where he concluded his NHL career with a 4.78 average in 38 appearances.

DON EDWARDS
Hamilton, Ontario
September 28, 1955–
NHL Career: 1976-86
Buffalo, Calgary, Toronto

	GP	M	GA	SO	AVE
RS	459	26181	1449	16	3.32
PO	42	2302	132	1	3.44

Vezina, A-S Game (2)

PAT EGAN

DEFENSE

At five-foot-ten and 195 pounds, Pat Egan became known as "The Skating Boxcar." But his first nickname came to him when he was a baby. Friends teased his father about being too proud of his Irish heritage and tagged little Martin Egan "Pat."

Egan joined the New York Americans during the 1939-40 season. In 1951, Andy O'Brien of *The Montreal Standard* recalled a dressing-down that manager Red Dutton had given his young defenseman, concluding a seven-minute blast with: "And I suppose you think you are really a big-league player?"

Egan smilingly retorted: "If I was a big-leaguer, I wouldn't be working for you for a crummy $3,500." Dutton couldn't help laughing.

In 1941-42, the team took to the ice as the Brooklyn Americans. Egan made the Second All-Star Team with 28 points and a league-leading 124 penalty minutes, but his club folded soon afterward. Detroit acquired his rights, but Egan signed up for the Canadian Army and didn't join the Red Wings until the 1943-44 campaign. Midway through the season, he was on the move again. Traded for Flash Hollett, he joined the Boston Bruins and erupted for 11 goals and 13 assists in only 25 games, giving him a hefty season total of 43 points.

Egan's 86 minutes in the sin bin were tops in 1944-45, and the next season, he helped the Bruins get to the Stanley Cup finals. "Egan today rates

as the hardest shot in hockey," noted *The Montreal Herald*, describing the "rifle-ball drive" he put past the Montreal netminder. Back to the finals in 1950 as a member of the New York Rangers, Egan was traded to the AHL's Providence Reds after the 1950-51 season. He hung up his skates in 1959, then turned his attention to a successful coaching career.

MARTIN "PAT" EGAN
Blackie, Alberta
March 25, 1918–
NHL Career: 1939-42, 1943-51
NY Americans, Brooklyn, Detroit, Boston, NY Rangers

	GP	G	A	P	PIM
RS	554	77	153	230	776
PO	44	9	4	13	44

A-S Game

BRIAN ENGBLOM

DEFENSE   ⭐2 1982

Brian Engblom won the Eddie Shore Award in 1977 as the AHL's outstanding defenseman. He got his first call-up to the Montreal Canadiens in the playoffs that spring. Although he dressed for only two games, Engblom had his name inscribed on the Stanley Cup. He enjoyed a little more ice time the following season and earned a second Cup ring. In 1978-79, Engblom took a regular

turn and helped the Habs to another title.

At six-foot-two and 200 pounds, Engblom looked like a natural successor to one of "The Big Three" rearguards: Larry Robinson, Serge Savard and Guy Lapointe. Engblom couldn't have had better tutors, and he improved steadily. He even led the NHL in the 1980-81 plus/minus statistics. Although a strictly defensive defenseman, Engblom also increased his offensive output incrementally every season. He peaked with 29 assists and 33 points in 1981-82, while also anchoring the NHL's stingiest defense and making the Second All-Star Team. However, Engblom was included in a multiplayer trade that Montreal made with Washington in September 1982.

Engblom helped the Capitals to their first playoffs in 1982-83, but he moved again in October 1983. Traded with winger Ken Houston for the more offensive-minded defenseman Larry Murphy, Engblom became a Los Angeles King

for 2½ seasons. He played the latter half of the 1985-86 campaign for Buffalo before finishing his NHL career with Calgary. Engblom suffered a serious neck injury during the 1986-87 season. In a delicate operation to avoid possible paralysis, a surgeon removed bone spurs from Engblom's spinal column and fused a bone from his hip to several vertebrae. Engblom moved into the broadcast booth in 1991 and has worked for ESPN since 1993.

BRIAN ENGBLOM
Winnipeg, Manitoba
January 27, 1957–
NHL Career: 1976-87
Montreal, Washington, Los Angeles,
Buffalo, Calgary

	GP	G	A	P	PIM
RS	659	29	177	206	599
PO	48	3	9	12	43

Stanley Cup (3)

PHIL ESPOSITO

CENTER   ⭐ 1969, 1970, 1971, 1972, 1973, 1974   ⭐2 1968, 1975

Lumbering Phil Esposito never found the spotlight in Chicago. "When you're on a line with Bobby Hull, it's only logical to give him the puck in the offensive zone," said Esposito. "He's the greatest scorer in hockey." But a May 1967 trade to Boston gave "Espo" the chance to be an All-Star himself. Initially, Bruins general manager Milt Schmidt was criticized for the deal, but as time passed, he began to look like a cunning thief.

"This is a team that will learn how to win," said Esposito. "This year [1967-68], we'll make the playoffs for sure. Next year, we'll be second or third. The third year, we'll win the whole thing, Stanley Cup and all." Esposito helped ensure that his forecast was completely accurate. Averaging 35 to 40 minutes of ice time per game, he led the league in 1967-68 with 49 assists. During the following campaign, he broke the assists record with 77 and added 49 goals,

becoming the first player to tally more than 100 points in a season. Esposito won the Hart Trophy and his first of five scoring championships.

In the spring of 1970, Esposito led all playoff scorers with 13 goals and 14 assists and supped from the Stanley Cup for the first time. In 1970-71, he shattered records with a 76-goal, 76-assist campaign. He won his second Art Ross Trophy and the Pearson Award, but the Bruins were upset in the playoffs. The next season, Esposito exacted his revenge. Once again, he led the league in points over the regular season and the playoffs, and Boston reclaimed the Cup.

As Canada's inspirational leader in the grueling Summit Series against the Soviet Union in September 1972, Esposito seemed almost larger than life. He remained the NHL's top scorer until 1974-75, when he finished second to teammate Bobby Orr. Yet early in the 1975-76

season, Boston coach Don Cherry told Esposito he'd been traded again. "Tell me I'm not going to New York, Don," pleaded Esposito, but he had been dealt to the Bruins' archrival. While he never lit up on Broadway quite the way he had in Beantown, Esposito did lead the Rangers to the 1979 Stanley Cup finals. When he retired in 1981, he was second only to Gordie Howe in goals and points scored.

PHIL ESPOSITO
Sault Ste. Marie, Ontario
February 20, 1942–
NHL Career: 1964-81
Chicago, Boston, NY Rangers

	GP	G	A	P	PIM
RS	1282	717	873	1590	910
PO	130	61	76	137	138

Ross (5), Hart (2), Pearson (2), Stanley Cup (2), A-S Game (10), HOF 1984

TONY ESPOSITO

GOALTENDER

Tony Esposito's older brother Phil played for the Chicago Blackhawks, which gave Tony the opportunity to talk shop with goalie Glenn Hall. "I tried to copy his style," said Esposito. In 1968-69, Esposito played 13 games for the Montreal Canadiens and earned a Stanley Cup ring as a backup. But that summer, he was drafted by the Blackhawks. By then, Phil was in Boston and Hall in St. Louis, but Esposito posted a stunning rookie season in Chicago. His 15 shutouts put him on the First All-Star Team and set the modern-day record. In addition, he took both the Calder and Vezina trophies. "He'll even open up his pads for a shot through the middle," said Bobby Orr, commenting on Esposito's exaggerated "butterfly" style. "But he's so quick with his arms and legs that he'll close up the opening before you can get the puck through."

Esposito was runner-up for the Vezina in 1970-71 and shared it with teammate Gary Smith in 1971-72 and with Philadelphia's Bernie Parent in 1973-74. His Team Canada play was outstanding in the famed 1972 Summit Series. Although Esposito backed Chicago to the Cup finals in 1971 and 1973, the Hawks had only middling playoff success in subsequent years. Yet "Tony O" remained remarkably consistent. He was an All-Star again in 1979-80 when he led the league with six shutouts.

By the time he retired at age 41, Esposito held most Chicago goaltending records. "The older you get, the more afraid you get," he once said. "But to be playing well as a goalie, you have to be afraid. Not afraid they'll hurt you, but afraid they'll score on you. Every time they come down the ice with the puck, I'm afraid it's going to go in."

TONY ESPOSITO
Sault Ste. Marie, Ontario
April 23, 1943–
NHL Career: 1968-84
Montreal, Chicago

	GP	M	GA	SO	AVE
RS	886	52585	2563	76	2.92
PO	99	6017	308	6	3.07

Calder, Vezina (3), Stanley Cup, A-S Game (6), HOF 1988

SERGEI FEDOROV

CENTER

Sergei Fedorov joined the Soviet national team at the age of 16, then defected to the Detroit Red Wings for the 1990-91 NHL campaign. With 31 goals and 48 assists, Fedorov led all rookie scorers and came second to goalie Ed Belfour in Calder Trophy voting. Over the next two seasons, he scored 86 and 87 points, respectively, but in 1993-94, he exploded with 56 goals and 120 points. Fedorov had proved himself the fastest skater at both the 1992 and 1994 NHL All-Star Game Skills Competition. In league action, he applied that speed to diligent two-way play. Although he finished second to Wayne Gretzky in scoring in 1993-94, he won the Hart Trophy, the Pearson Award, the Frank Selke Trophy and a spot on the First All-Star Team.

Fedorov led the 1995 playoffs with 17 assists and 24 points. He tied for ninth in 1995-96 scoring with 39 goals and 68 assists and won his second Selke. His 18 helpers in the 1996 postseason were another league-high. "The goals don't mean anything to me now," said Fedorov. "It doesn't matter who scores, as long as someone does." Despite Fedorov's willingness to fill in on defense and the wing, some wondered about his commitment. He responded by helping the Wings win the 1997 Stanley Cup, scoring 20 playoff points.

After sitting out three-quarters of 1997-98, restricted free-agent Fedorov got a front-loaded, six-year $38 million offer from Carolina. Detroit invoked its right to match the offer and, aided by Fedorov's playoff-leading 10 goals, successfully defended the Cup. "For those who questioned the wisdom of signing Sergei Fedorov," said Detroit mayor Dennis Archer at the downtown victory celebration, "I think they [now] clearly understand his value to the team."

SERGEI FEDOROV
Pskov, U.S.S.R.
December 13, 1969–
NHL Career: 1990-
Detroit

	GP	G	A	P	PIM
RS	672	301	433	734	459
PO	129	42	92	134	93

Hart, Pearson, Selke (2), Stanley Cup (2), A-S Game (3)

FERNIE FLAMAN

DEFENSE

Gordie Howe once called Fernie Flaman "the toughest defenseman I ever played against." After playing a single NHL game in each of the 1944-45 and 1945-46 seasons, Flaman joined the Boston Bruins full-time midway through the 1946-47 campaign. Admired as a fighter by coach Dit Clapper, Flaman took several seasons to establish himself as a dependable blue-liner.

Flaman was dealt to the Maple Leafs early in the 1950-51 season—it was probably his 122 penalty minutes in 1949-50 that had attracted Toronto's interest. Although Flaman helped the Leafs win the Stanley Cup later that spring, his "stay-at-home" style led to only two goals over the next three seasons. His real strength was as a body checker and shot-blocker, and he defended the front of his own net aggres-

sively and effectively. In the summer of 1954, the Bruins traded 20-goal-scorer Dave Creighton to Toronto to get Flaman back in a Boston uniform. Heavy-hitting Leo Boivin soon joined Flaman in Beantown—the two had frequently been paired together with the Leafs—forming a devastating tandem.

Flaman made the Second All-Star Team in three of the next four seasons and led the league with a career-high 150 penalty minutes in 1954-55. The following season, he became team captain, a position that he held until his retirement. Flaman hit his offensive peak in 1956-57, with 6 goals and 25 assists, and he steered the Bruins to both the 1957 and the 1958 Stanley Cup finals.

He retired from the NHL after the 1960-61 season, but Flaman didn't leave the game. Instead, he took the job of

player/coach with the AHL's Providence Reds, adding general-manager duties during the team's 1963-64 championship season, before turning solely to coaching. In 1970, Flaman went behind the bench of Boston's Northeastern University Huskies. After winning four U.S. collegiate titles, he finally retired from hockey in 1989.

FERDINAND FLAMAN
Dysart, Saskatchewan
January 25, 1927–
NHL Career: 1944-61
Boston, Toronto

	GP	G	A	P	PIM
RS	910	34	174	208	1370
PO	63	4	8	12	93

Stanley Cup, A-S Game (6), HOF 1990

THEOREN FLEURY

RIGHT WING

Although Theoren Fleury has fought Crohn's disease, a painful bowel disorder, since 1995, he's missed only a handful of games. The five-foot-six, 160-pound NHL All-Star got used to fighting adversity by overcoming years of prejudice against his size. "I don't think of myself as small," he said. "I don't play small. I don't act small. Small is just a word." Fleury's rambunctious style, combined with his cocky attitude and strong skills, encouraged the Calgary Flames to give him a chance midway through the 1988-89 season. He notched 34 points in 36 games. In the playoffs, Fleury added 5 goals and 6 assists to help Calgary win the Stanley Cup.

Eighth in 1990-91 scoring, Fleury set an NHL record with three

shorthanded goals on March 9 before finishing the campaign with a career-best 51 goals and 104 points. He tallied another 100 points in 1992-93 and notched 40 goals the following season. Tied for sixth place in scoring over the 48-game 1994-95 schedule, with 29 goals and 29 assists, Fleury made the Second All-Star Team. Calgary named him captain for 1995-96, a position he held for two seasons.

He had become Calgary's all-time leading scorer by 1997-98. Anticipating his pending free-agent status, however, the Flames traded him to Colorado in March 1999. Fleury enjoyed playing for a contender again

and went on a tear with the Avalanche. He added 10 goals and 14 assists in 15 games with Colorado, finishing the season tied for seventh in league scoring with 93 points.

Fleury signed with the New York Rangers for 1999-2000. He has experienced some frustration and has even heard some boos in Manhattan, but he remains confident. "I've taken a lot of bumps and bruises, [but] I've proven myself," he said. "I know if I just go out and play the way I've always played throughout my career, everything will take care of itself."

THEOREN FLEURY
Oxbow, Saskatchewan
June 29, 1968–
NHL Career: 1988-
Calgary, Colorado, NY Rangers

	GP	G	A	P	PIM
RS	886	389	529	918	1425
PO	77	34	45	79	116

Stanley Cup, A-S Game (6)

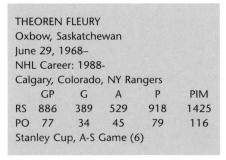

PETER FORSBERG

CENTER

⭐1 1998, 1999

The Philadelphia Flyers picked Peter Forsberg in the first round of the 1991 draft but included him in the package sent to the Quebec Nordiques for Eric Lindros in 1992. "I have not seen a player of Forsberg's calibre in a long time," said former NHL star Kent Nilsson, scouting the 1993 World Junior Championships. "If Quebec keeps him, they're going to be the team of the '90s." When he scored an overtime shootout goal to give Sweden the gold medal at the 1994 Olympic Games, Forsberg became a national hero. He remained in Sweden, however, until the NHL lockout of 1994-95 ended. He promptly won the Calder Trophy, notching 15 goals and 35 assists in 47 games for the Nordiques.

When the team transferred to Colorado for 1995-96, Forsberg jumped to fifth place in scoring with 30 goals and a career-high 86 assists. He added 10 goals and 21 points in the playoffs to help the Avalanche win the Stanley Cup. But Forsberg's game includes more than scoring ability. "You see some skill players who don't normally get involved physically," said general manager Pierre Lacroix. "Not Peter. He hits so hard, it is unbelievable." His bruising style sometimes results in injuries or penalties, but Forsberg came runner-up for the 1997 Frank Selke Trophy. He missed 17 games because of injuries but still led Colorado with 86 points.

Although he missed 10 games in 1997-98, Forsberg finished second in league scoring with 25 goals and 66 assists. He made the First All-Star Team, an honor he retained in 1998-99 with a 30-goal, 67-assist campaign. Although the Avalanche lost the Western Conference finals, Forsberg still led all postseason scorers with 24 points.

He suffered through an injury-riddled 1999-2000 campaign but still notched 51 points in 49 games. The opposition doesn't dare relax. "He's extremely patient and creative," said New Jersey goalie Martin Brodeur. "The way he calmly masters the situation, the way he continuously feeds his wingers and his defensemen, he makes everybody nervous. There are so many ways he can hurt you. A pass, a precise slap shot or a wrist shot upstairs, he does it all."

PETER FORSBERG
Örnsköldsvik, Sweden
July 20, 1973–
NHL Career: 1995-
Quebec, Colorado

	GP	G	A	P	PIM
RS	393	142	349	491	390
PO	84	38	56	94	87

Calder, Stanley Cup, A-S Game (3)

BOB FROESE

GOALTENDER

⭐2 1986

After three seasons in the IHL, Bob Froese signed a contract with the Philadelphia Flyers. He and fellow goaltending prospect Pelle Lindbergh then joined the Flyers' AHL affiliate in Maine for the 1981-82 campaign. Lindbergh made the jump to the NHL midseason, but it was another year before Froese made his big-league debut. Although relegated to the backup role, Froese nonetheless posted four NHL shutouts in 25 games in 1982-83. When Lindbergh struggled the following season, Froese became Philadelphia's starter. Coach Mike Keenan's hiring for 1984-85 changed all that.

Keenan handed the puck to Lindbergh at the beginning of the season, and Froese got only 17 starts. "We both played well," said Froese, "but Pelle had an outstanding year." Lindbergh won the Vezina Trophy and First All-Star Team honors. Unfortunately, he died in a tragic car accident only eight games into the 1985-86 campaign. Thrust un-

expectedly into the number-one position, Froese coolly backstopped the Flyers to the top of the Patrick Division. For insurance, Philadelphia picked up veteran netminder Chico Resch at the March trading deadline, but Froese kept his focus. "I never felt so young coming to the rink," he joked later. Elected to the Second All-Star Team, Froese led the league with five shutouts and a 2.55 goals-against average. He finished runner-up to New York Ranger John Vanbiesbrouck for the Vezina Trophy and shared the William M. Jennings Trophy with partner Darren Jensen.

Despite Froese's accomplishments, rookie goalie Ron Hextall managed to push him aside early in 1986-87. The Flyers traded Froese to the New York Rangers midseason. He played backup to Vanbiesbrouck until 1989-90. Rookie Mike Richter's arrival that season was an ominous sign, but it was a nagging shoulder injury that forced Froese to retire.

BOB FROESE
St. Catharines, Ontario
June 30, 1958–
NHL Career: 1982-90
Philadelphia, NY Rangers

	GP	M	GA	SO	AVE
RS	242	13451	694	13	3.10
PO	18	830	55	0	3.98

Jennings, A-S Game

GOALTENDER

 1988  1982

Most of Grant Fuhr's career numbers are average, yet he's destined for the Hockey Hall of Fame. "The only statistic that matters is winning," said Fuhr, the owner of five Stanley Cup rings.

"I rate him right up there among goalies of any era," said Glenn Hall. "He gave [Edmonton] the opportunity to play that run-and-gun style. Without a goalie like Fuhr, none of it works."

Fuhr had an auspicious NHL debut, making the Second All-Star Team and finishing runner-up for the Calder and Vezina trophies. Although he shared the regular-season goaltending duties with Andy Moog, Fuhr soon became Edmonton's playoff starter. He backstopped the Oilers to four Cup wins in five seasons, beginning in 1984. The latter win, in 1988, punctuated Fuhr's most brilliant campaign. He set a record by playing in 75 games and made the First All-Star Team. He also won the Vezina Trophy and finished second behind Mario Lemieux in Hart Trophy voting.

Fuhr's game began to unravel in 1989, reportedly because of cocaine abuse. Bill Ranford took the first-string position, and Fuhr sat on the bench while the Oilers won the 1990 Cup. After his problem came to light the following season, Fuhr served a 60-game suspension. Traded to Toronto in 1991-92, he lost his job to Felix Potvin. In Buffalo, he shared the 1993-94 William M. Jennings Trophy with Dominik Hasek but was traded to Los Angeles the next season. Fuhr signed a free-agent contract with St. Louis for 1995-96 and finally found himself with the right team at the right time once again. He broke his own record with 79 starts, although injuries slowed him down in his later seasons. Fuhr joined the Calgary Flames for 1999-2000, where he posted career-win number 400 before retiring at season's end.

GRANT FUHR
Spruce Grove, Alberta
September 28, 1962–
NHL Career: 1981-2000
Edmonton, Toronto, Buffalo, Los Angeles, St. Louis, Calgary

	GP	M	GA	SO	AVE
RS	868	48928	2756	25	3.38
PO	150	8819	430	6	2.93

Jennings, Vezina, Stanley Cup (5),
A-S Game (6)

BILL GADSBY

DEFENSE

 1956, 1958, 1959  1953, 1954, 1957, 1965

Completing 20 NHL seasons, Bill Gadsby became the first player to tie Dit Clapper's longevity record. The seven-time All-Star was a premier rusher and playmaker for most of his career. Gadsby scored 8 goals as a rookie with Chicago in 1946-47. Contracting the polio virus in training camp in 1952, he made a quick and full recovery and was named team captain in 1952-53. He and the Hawks then made their first and only trip to the playoffs together. Gadsby concluded his most productive campaign with Chicago the following season, notching 12 goals and 29 assists. But in November 1954, he and New York Ranger Allan Stanley were the key components of a multiplayer trade.

Gadsby was runner-up for the Norris Trophy during his three First All-Star Team seasons with the Rangers. His 9 goals and 42 assists in 1955-56 led all defensemen, and he tied for ninth in league scoring. Over the next three campaigns, he scored 41, 46 and 51 points, respectively, but New York never managed to get past the semifinals. In the middle of the 1959-60 season, the Rangers traded Gadsby and Eddie Shack to Detroit for Red Kelly and Billy McNeil. Kelly nixed the deal, however, by refusing to report, and it wasn't until June 1961 that Gadsby became a Red Wing.

In 1964-65, the only campaign in which he didn't score a goal, Gadsby made the Second All-Star Team for his defensive skills alone. Although he battled hard through three trips to the finals in his last five seasons, Gadsby never won a Stanley Cup ring. The grizzled veteran eventually retired with the record for most career points by a defenseman.

BILL GADSBY
Calgary, Alberta
August 8, 1927–
NHL Career: 1946-66
Chicago, NY Rangers, Detroit

	GP	G	A	P	PIM
RS	1248	130	438	568	1539
PO	67	4	23	27	92

A-S Game (8), HOF 1970

GERARD GALLANT

★ 1989

Gerard Gallant had a quiet NHL debut, notching 6 rookie goals after joining Detroit in January 1985. The following season, he began to

make his mark. "He's been our best forward," said coach Harry Neale in November 1986. "He's a hardworking guy with more talent than I thought he had."

General manager Jimmy Devellano agreed: "He's a gamer. He gives it second effort and determination. I'd like to have another three or four like Gerard Gallant."

Taking his feisty approach a step further, Gallant earned more than 200 penalty minutes in 1986-87 while tallying 38 goals and 72 points. "Some people might say I'm established, but I still have a long way to go," said Gallant. "I can do a lot more."

New coach Jacques Demers called him a franchise "untouchable," however, and former Detroit great Mickey Redmond was equally admiring. "Gerard's not overly big, and I don't think overly strong," he observed, "but he's fearless when he goes in front of the net. That's where he gets it done. Of the 38 goals he got last year, probably 20 of them were deflections or redirections directly in

front of the goaltenders. When you go in there, you're going to pay a price. Gallant is not afraid to pay it."

Gallant earned 73 points in 1987-88 and made the Second All-Star Team the following season. His 39 goals and 54 assists in 1988-89 both proved to be personal bests. He scored 36 times in 1989-90 before his production tailed off dramatically. Gallant signed a free-agent contract with the Tampa Bay Lightning for 1993-94 but scored only four times in 51 games. He played one NHL game the following season and finished out his pro career in the IHL.

GERARD GALLANT
Summerside, Prince Edward Island
September 2, 1963–
NHL Career: 1984-95
Detroit, Tampa Bay

	GP	G	A	P	PIM
RS	615	211	269	480	1674
PO	58	18	21	39	178

CHUCK GARDINER

★ 1931, 1932, 1934   1933

Chuck Gardiner fully came into his own during the 1930-31 NHL season, when he notched a league-high 12 shutouts. He helped the Blackhawks to the Stanley Cup finals that spring, and *The Toronto Star* commented on his remarkable play in the deciding fifth game: "Gardiner warded off shots with either hand, with his stick and with his broad pads, at times dropping his stick to catch the rubber in his gloved hands." Chicago failed to score, however, and the Montreal Canadiens eventually triumphed.

Scottish-born but Winnipeg-raised, Gardiner was known for his joking exchanges with rink-side fans. In a March 1932 column, *Toronto Star* reporter Lou Marsh described the goalie's indomitable nature. Gardiner, Chicago's only real star at the time, had won his first Vezina Trophy in that 1931-32 season, but the

Leafs had just eliminated the Hawks from the playoffs with a 6–1 victory. "Late in the last period," wrote Marsh, "an overenthusiastic fan threw his iron lid [a derby hat] out on the ice. Gardiner, as cool as a cucumber, skated over and picked up the christy-stiff and stuck it on his head, defying the Leafs to knock it off for the rest of the game. He wore it off the ice too."

But after two more stellar seasons, disaster struck. Named team captain for 1933-34, Gardiner had just put an exclamation mark on his fourth consecutive All-Star campaign by backing the Blackhawks to their first Stanley Cup victory, with a 1.33 playoff goals-against average. He had been suffering for some time from an excruciating tonsil infection, but he fought the pain through a double-overtime shutout victory in the deciding fourth game.

Only days after the win, however, the 29-year-old netminder suffered a massive brain hemorrhage and died two months later.

Toronto's *Mail and Empire* noted: "Gardiner's deft hands and lightning-fast feet, combined with uncommon craftiness, made him a standout...the greatest goaler in the game."

CHARLES "CHUCK" GARDINER
Edinburgh, Scotland
December 31, 1904–June 13, 1934
NHL Career: 1927-34
Chicago

	GP	M	GA	SO	AVE
RS	316	19687	664	42	2.02
PO	21	1472	35	5	1.43

Vezina (2), Stanley Cup, A-S Game,
HOF 1945

DANNY GARE

RIGHT WING

Only 18 seconds into his first NHL game, Danny Gare scored a goal, just three seconds shy of the rookie record set by Gus Bodnar in 1943. Short, at five-foot-nine, but stocky, feisty and quick, Gare finished his rookie season with 31 goals, then helped the Sabres get to the Stanley Cup finals. He followed up with a 50-goal 1975-76 campaign. Unfortunately, Gare hurt his back playing in the Canada Cup tournament in the fall of 1976. He counted only 11 goals in 35 games in 1976-77. Although Gare became team captain in 1977-78 and managed to score 39 goals, he battled injuries and ill health for two seasons.

"I [felt] I had something to prove this year," he said in March 1980. "I felt strong again. I felt like I could jump into the open spot again and could shoot the way I used to." Gare made the Second All-Star Team with 89 points, and his 56 goals tied for the NHL lead. He got off to a slow start for 1980-81, though. "It's kind of frustrating when the puck won't go in the net," he said in

November. "You just have to keep doing the other things you are supposed to do: forecheck, dig in the corners, go up and down your wing and keep shooting." His determination paid off. By season's end, Gare had 46 goals and 85 points.

Buffalo fans were shocked when the Sabres traded the popular winger to Detroit in December 1981. Gare played with the same intensity for the Red Wings but never neared the success he'd enjoyed previously. He signed with Edmonton as a free agent for 1986-87 but, with limited ice time, retired after scoring only once in 18 games.

DANNY GARE				
Nelson, British Columbia				
May 14, 1954–				
NHL Career: 1974-87				
Buffalo, Detroit, Edmonton				
	GP	G	A	P	PIM
RS	827	354	331	685	1285
PO	64	25	21	46	195
A-S Game (2)				

BERNIE GEOFFRION

RIGHT WING

Bernie Geoffrion ruled the right wing with his devastating slap shot, which was his invention. Geoffrion got his nickname "Boom-Boom" for the echoing sounds the puck made off the end boards. He joined the Montreal Canadiens for 18 games in 1950-51, intentionally preserving his rookie status in order to play a full roster of games the next season. Geoffrion's strategy worked when he played a 30-goal Calder Trophy-winning campaign, finishing sixth in league scoring. He led the 1953 postseason with 6 goals to help the Habs win the Stanley Cup. In 1953-54, he came fourth in the scoring race. Yet when Geoffrion won the 1955 Art Ross Trophy with a league-leading 38 goals and 75 points, the Montreal fans turned on him. He had passed Maurice Richard, who was sitting out

a suspension, by a single point. It took years for many of the fans to forgive him. That year, Geoffrion made the Second All-Star Team; Richard made the First Team.

Geoffrion played a large role in Montreal's five consecutive Stanley Cups. His 11 goals and 18 points were highs in the 1957 playoffs, as were his 10 assists and 12 points in 1960. He concluded his 1959-60 All-Star season in sixth place in league scoring but exploded to first in 1960-61. Geoffrion irked some Richard loyalists by becoming the second player to post a 50-goal season, and he added 45 assists and won both the Art Ross and Hart trophies. He also made the First All-Star Team.

Although Geoffrion turned to coaching in 1964-65, he made a surprising comeback in 1966-67. "I don't intend

to go out as a bum," he stated after New York picked him up on waivers. "If I can't keep scoring, I'll know when to quit." He retired after tallying 22 goals and 63 points over two seasons with the Rangers. Geoffrion went on to a colorful career as a coach and corporate pitchman.

BERNARD "BOOM-BOOM" GEOFFRION				
Montreal, Quebec				
February 14, 1931–				
NHL Career: 1950-64, 1966-68				
Montreal, NY Rangers				
	GP	G	A	P	PIM
RS	883	393	429	822	689
PO	132	58	60	118	88
Calder, Ross (2), Hart, Stanley Cup (6),				
A-S Game (11), HOF 1972				

ED GIACOMIN

GOALTENDER

"Eddie! Eddie! Eddie!" The chant breaks out in Madison Square Garden to this day. Yet it never rang forth as strongly or as often as it did on November 2, 1975, two days after Detroit had picked up Ed Giacomin on waivers. While he initially feared the New York crowd's reaction to seeing him in a Red Wings uniform—his family didn't dare attend—Giacomin later hailed the game as one of his fondest NHL memories.

"I've never been an emotional man, but I couldn't hold back the tears tonight," he said in a postgame interview. "When the people started cheering me at the beginning, the tears came down my face. A couple of times, I thought I would collapse from the emotion." Giacomin faced 46 shots in a 6–4 Detroit victory and received numerous standing ovations. One of his former teammates even apologized for scoring.

Giacomin had served a seven-season minor-league apprenticeship before moving up to the Rangers in 1965-66. While his NHL rookie year was uneven—he was sent down to Baltimore for seven games—Giacomin had a league-high nine shutouts in 1966-67 and was named to the First All-Star Team. An excellent puck-handler, Giacomin had great success ranging far from his net to corral pucks and feed them to his teammates. He actually hit the goalpost once in attempting to score on an empty opposition net, and he was the first netminder to record two assists in one game.

Wiry and acrobatic, Giacomin was the busiest NHL goalie from 1966-67 to 1969-70, frequently refusing respite even when visibly hurt and bleeding. With his prematurely silver hair, he always looked older than his years, and Giacomin refused to don a protective mask until 1970. In 1970-71, though, goaltender Gilles Villemure took on part of the load. Giacomin led the NHL in shutouts for the third time, compiling eight, and he and Villemure shared the Vezina Trophy that year.

ED GIACOMIN
Sudbury, Ontario
June 6, 1939–
NHL Career: 1965-78
NY Rangers, Detroit

	GP	M	GA	SO	AVE
RS	610	35693	1675	54	2.82
PO	65	3834	180	1	2.82

Vezina, A-S Game (6), HOF 1987

ROD GILBERT

RIGHT WING

Rod Gilbert, winner of the 1960-61 Ontario junior scoring championship, collected an assist and a penalty during his one-game call-up with the New York Rangers that season. When Gilbert skated over a piece of debris in his last junior game and broke his back, however, it looked as if that single game with the Rangers would summarize his NHL experience. He almost lost his leg when complications from a spinal fusion set in.

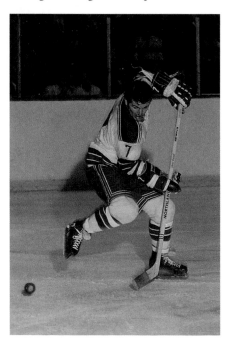

After an eight-month recovery, Gilbert resumed playing with a brace. In 1962-63, the Rangers brought him to New York to stay. "I think that never being able to take anything for granted made me a better player," noted Gilbert. Although only five-foot-nine, he established himself as a finesse player with speed. He finished seventh in 1964-65 NHL scoring, tallying 25 goals and 36 assists. When he was hit into the boards midway through the following season, however, his back snapped again. After another spinal fusion, Gilbert was back among the elite scorers in 1967-68. Finishing fifth, he was elected to the Second All-Star Team.

Gilbert played most of his career with Vic Hadfield and center Jean Ratelle, his childhood friend. When all three were on pace for 50 goals in 1971-72, they became known as New York's "GAG Line" (for "goal-a-game"). Gilbert made the First All-Star Team with a career-best 43 goals and 97 points. He lost his best chance at a Cup ring when Boston defeated the Rangers in the playoff finals but earned a coveted spot in the famed 1972 Summit Series.

"Playing for Team Canada in 1972 was like my Stanley Cup," said Gilbert. He received the Bill Masterton Trophy in 1976, an acknowledgment of his dedication to the game. Two seasons later, Gilbert retired, holder of 20 Rangers' scoring records.

ROD GILBERT
Montreal, Quebec
July 1, 1941–
NHL Career: 1960-78
NY Rangers

	GP	G	A	P	PIM
RS	1065	406	615	1021	508
PO	79	34	33	67	43

Masterton, A-S Game (9), HOF 1982

CLARK GILLIES

LEFT WING

The opposition's approach to Clark Gillies was to not antagonize him. His nickname "Jethro"—an allusion to the hulking man/child of television's *The Beverly Hillbillies*—was a joke. At six-foot-three and 215 pounds, Gillies became widely respected as a fighter. Yet he never tallied 100 penalty minutes in a season. A first-round draft pick, Gillies notched 25 rookie goals for the New York Islanders in 1974-75. He scored at least 33 over each of the next four seasons and became team captain midway through 1976-77, a position he held until 1979.

Gillies' career really took off in 1977-78, when Mike Bossy joined him and Bryan Trottier to form the NHL's top scoring line. Gillies tallied 35 goals and 85 points and made the First All-Star

Team. He was an All-Star again the following season, cracking the top-10 scorers with another 35-goal campaign and 91 points. Although he scored a record four consecutive playoff game-winners in 1977, further team success eluded him.

"We went through some real bitter defeats to get to the point where we weren't going to lose anymore," recalled Gillies. "We lost to Toronto in 1978 in the seventh game [of the quarter-finals]. In 1979, we finished first overall and lost to the Rangers in the semifinal. You've got to learn to hate losing before you learn to win." Gillies finished the 1980 postseason with 16 points and 63 penalty minutes after successfully battling Philadelphia for the Stanley Cup.

The Islanders won four consecutive

titles, but Gillies' production slipped dramatically in 1985-86. New York waived him to Buffalo, where he played for two seasons before leaving the game. He wasn't forgotten on Long Island, however. The Islanders retired Gillies' jersey number 9 in 1996.

CLARK GILLIES				
Moose Jaw, Saskatchewan				
April 7, 1954–				
NHL Career: 1974-88				
NY Islanders, Buffalo				
	GP	G	A	P	PIM
RS	958	319	378	697	1023
PO	164	47	47	94	287
Stanley Cup (4), A-S Game				

84

BOB GOLDHAM

DEFENSE

Bob Goldham began his career as an offensive defenseman. Although he spent most of the 19 games he played as a rookie on the Maple Leafs' bench, he notched 4 goals and 7 assists. Toronto coach Hap Day didn't give him a regular shift until the Leafs fell three games to none in the Stanley Cup finals. Goldham then scored 2 goals and 2 assists to help his team in the greatest comeback in hockey history. He drank champagne from the Cup that spring, then enlisted in the Canadian Navy.

Returning to Toronto for the 1945-46 campaign, Goldham notched 7 goals and 14 assists. He was injured the following season and played only 11 games. Assigned to Pittsburgh in the AHL for 1947-48, Goldham found himself en route to Chicago seven games later.

One of five players sent in exchange for Max Bentley, Goldham spent the better part of three seasons on the Blackhawks' blue line.

Another multiplayer trade in the summer of 1950 made Goldham a Red Wing. After posting a 23-point 1950-51 season, he became a different type of rearguard. "My transition to a defensive player began when they paired me off with Red Kelly," Goldham explained to George Gross of *The Toronto Sun*. "His forte was carrying the puck, and since the two of us couldn't take off at the same time, I decided to mind the store."

Goldham became a premier shot-blocker—"something I had seen Bucko McDonald do in the early 1940s." Detroit won three Stanley Cups between 1952 and 1955, and Goldham made the Second All-Star Team in the latter season. He retired a year later and became familiar to a new generation of fans in the 1960s and 1970s as an affable and insightful commentator for *Hockey Night in Canada*.

BOB GOLDHAM
Georgetown, Ontario
May 12, 1922–November 6, 1991
NHL Career: 1941-42, 1945-56
Toronto, Chicago, Detroit

	GP	G	A	P	PIM
RS	650	28	143	171	400
PO	66	3	14	17	53

Stanley Cup (4), A-S Game (6)

EBBIE GOODFELLOW

DEFENSE

Although he spent his entire NHL career in Detroit, Ebbie Goodfellow played on three different teams. He broke into the league in 1929-30 as a center with the Detroit Cougars and scored an excellent 17 goals and 17 assists as a rookie. The team became the Falcons the following season, and Goodfellow finished second only to veteran Howie Morenz in the league scoring race. After leading the Falcons in points again in 1931-32,

Goodfellow saw another team transformation and became a Red Wing. He served the 1934-35 season as team captain, then underwent a huge change himself.

Detroit coach and general manager Jack Adams made an inspired decision. Rich up the middle because of newly acquired centers Marty Barry and Syd Howe, Adams moved Goodfellow back to defense. The results were terrific. In explaining his voting for the 1936 Second All-Star Team, Montreal writer D.A.L. MacDonald of *The Gazette* noted that Goodfellow "is big, rough and a hard hitter, as every defenseman should be."

He quickly settled into his new role, and Detroit won its first Stanley Cup. His versatility drew comparisons years later to a certain ambidextrous winger. "Goodfellow," claimed one observer, "was Gordie Howe before Gordie Howe came along!"

Goodfellow graduated to the First All-Star Team in 1936-37, and the Red Wings successfully defended the Cup.

Named captain again in the autumn of 1938, he had his best personal campaign in 1939-40. His 11 goals and 17 assists, on a weak team that scored only 90 goals, tied him with Boston's Dit Clapper for the most points by a defenseman. Goodfellow was awarded the Hart Trophy and made the First All-Star Team. In the 1941-42 season, he relinquished his captaincy when he moved into a player/coach role, capping his career with Detroit's 1943 Stanley Cup.

EBENEZER "EBBIE" GOODFELLOW
Ottawa, Ontario
April 9, 1907–September 10, 1965
NHL Career: 1929-43
Detroit

	GP	G	A	P	PIM
RS	557	134	190	324	511
PO	45	8	8	16	65

Hart, Stanley Cup (3), A-S Game (2), HOF 1963

JOHNNY GOTTSELIG

LEFT WING

Although Johnny Gottselig was a member of the Regina Pats' 1924-25 Memorial Cup-winning team, he was carried from the championship game with a ruptured appendix. Russian-born but Winnipeg-raised, Gottselig joined the sad-sack Chicago Blackhawks in 1928-29. Rookie Gottselig tallied only 5 goals and 3 assists, but that was good enough for second place in Hawks' scoring.

For the next three seasons, Gottselig was Chicago's top goal scorer, and he blasted home an overtime goal to win game two of the 1931 Stanley Cup finals against the Montreal Canadiens. The Habs prevailed in the close-fought series, but the Blackhawks made it back to the finals in 1934 and won. Gottselig was named team captain for the 1935-36 campaign and led Chicago to a surprising Cup win in 1938. The Blackhawks barely qualified for the playoffs, but Gottselig led all postseason scorers with eight points.

"Gottselig weaved in on the left side by virtue of some of his inimitable stickhandling and picked the far side with a shot that glanced off [Wilf] Cude's glove," reported *The Gazette* in February 1939, in the midst of Gottselig's personal-best campaign. "Black-haired Johnny stepped back to fourth place a week ago after leading the league most of the season and, apparently irked when forced off his pace, scored four points against [the] Canadiens to move right back to the top again." But the Hawks then went 2–11–2 to conclude the season in the league basement, and Gottselig dropped to eighth spot in the NHL scoring race. He still made the Second All-Star Team, though, leading his team in points for the third time with 16 goals and 23 assists.

Early in the 1940-41 season, he retired to become player/coach of Chicago's farm team in Kansas City, but with the Blackhawks' reduced player roster because of the war, Gottselig rejoined the team in 1942-43. He played the full NHL schedule the following season and helped the Hawks back to the Stanley Cup finals. He played one last game in 1944-45 before moving behind the Chicago bench. Gottselig later served the team in a public relations role and was a radio-broadcast analyst.

JOHNNY GOTTSELIG
Odessa, Russia
June 24, 1905–May 15, 1986
NHL Career: 1928-41, 1942-45
Chicago

	GP	G	A	P	PIM
RS	589	176	195	371	203
PO	43	13	13	26	18

Stanley Cup (2), A-S Game (2)

MICHEL GOULET

LEFT WING

In one of the WHA's last underage signings, Michel Goulet became a Birmingham "Baby Bull" in 1978-79. The previous season, he had scored 73 goals and 135 points as a 17-year-old junior with the Quebec Remparts. Goulet returned to Quebec in 1979-80 as the Nordiques' first NHL draft pick. He developed into a strong two-way player, centered primarily by pesky playmaker Dale Hunter, and quickly developed into the top left-wing sniper of the 1980s.

Goulet's 57-goal, 105-point campaign of 1982-83 lifted him to eighth in league scoring and onto the Second All-Star Team. He tallied 56 goals and became a First All-Star Team member in 1983-84. His team-leading career-high 121 points were third highest in the league. He scored 55 goals in 69 games the following season and rejoined the All-Stars in 1985-86 with his last 50-goal campaign. Two more NHL top-10 scoring seasons immediately followed, both honored with All-Star berths.

Traded to Chicago in March 1990, Goulet enjoyed several strong seasons on a line with Jeremy Roenick and Steve Larmer and made a trip to the Stanley Cup finals in 1992, where Pittsburgh prevailed. Goulet's greatest disappointment, however, came on March 16, 1994. "I was skating hard 10 feet from the boards, lost an edge, tripped and went headfirst," said Goulet. His playing days were over, and he spent more than two years in rehabilitation.

His original team, which had become the Colorado Avalanche, celebrated Goulet's full recovery by naming him director of player development for 1996-97. The NHL honored Goulet by inducting him into the Hockey Hall of Fame two years later.

MICHEL GOULET
Péribonka, Quebec
April 21, 1960–
NHL Career: 1979-94
Quebec, Chicago

	GP	G	A	P	PIM
RS	1089	548	604	1152	825
PO	92	39	39	78	110

A-S Game (5), HOF 1998

ADAM GRAVES

 1994

Although he's no choirboy, Adam Graves is admired by friend and foe alike as a dedicated hockey player and a decent man. "Adam was always the type of kid you wanted to make it," said his former coach Colin Campbell. "He is conscientious, nice, hardworking, respectful. And usually, those guys don't make it. Adam is the milk drinker who goes through hell for you." During his years with the New York Rangers, Graves has been the recipient of several awards from his teammates, the fans and the media in recognition of his performance both on and off the ice. The NHL honored Graves with the King Clancy Memorial Trophy in 1994.

He played nine games with Detroit in 1987-88 but didn't latch onto a full-time NHL job until 1989-90. Part of a blockbuster multiplayer deal, Graves went to Edmonton in November and helped the Oilers win the 1990 Stanley Cup. Although he scored five times in the playoffs, he served primarily as an aggressive tough guy. He notched only 7 goals the following season and signed a free-agent contract with the Rangers for 1991-92. Allowed more latitude, Graves promptly doubled his career output with a 26-goal, 33-assist campaign. He still showed evidence of a mean streak, however. His slash to Mario Lemieux's hand in the playoffs warranted a suspension, and Graves watched from the stands as his team went down to defeat.

He tallied 36 goals in 1992-93 and set a franchise record with 52 goals in 1993-94. With 79 points in all, Graves made the Second All-Star Team. He added 10 goals and 17 assists in the playoffs, winning his second Stanley Cup ring. Although frequently playing through back pain, Graves has averaged 30 goals a season since his All-Star campaign.

ADAM GRAVES
Toronto, Ontario
April 12, 1968–
NHL Career: 1987-
Detroit, Edmonton, NY Rangers

	GP	G	A	P	PIM
RS	907	293	248	541	1064
PO	113	35	26	61	113

Clancy, Stanley Cup (2), A-S Game

DEFENSE   ⭐ 1969

Ted Green was involved in one of the ugliest incidents in NHL history, one he'd rather people forgot. "I played 20 years as a pro, and I had a lot of success," said Green. "I've been an All-Star. I was there when there were six teams. And today, years after the injury, people come up to me and say, 'You're Ted Green? How's your head?' That's all they seem to remember of a long career."

A tough, mean and feared defenseman for the Boston Bruins, Green was a ready scrapper, accumulating over 100 penalty minutes in each of his first five NHL seasons. But during the 1967-68 campaign, he adjusted his approach. "I decided I wasn't going to help the team if I was in the penalty box half the time," he told Alan Grayson of the *Christian Science Monitor*. "I used to take runs at players. I'm still ready if the right opportunity arises, but I'm not looking for it the way I used to. I'm enjoying making passes, lugging the puck and manning the point on the power play. I find [this] easier...and I'm going to last a lot longer."

Green had a rewarding 1968-69 season, accumulating a career-high 46 points. He made the Second All-Star Team, and the Bruins were poised for bigger things. In a preseason game in September 1969, however, Green almost died in a vicious stick-swinging fight with Wayne Maki of St. Louis. Three operations on his fractured skull left him with a metal plate in his head and a temporarily partially paralyzed left leg and arm as well as slurred speech. Although Green spent the entire season in rehabilitation, the Boston players voted him a full share of their Stanley Cup winnings that spring.

In a testament to his courage, Green returned to the NHL for the 1970-71 season and had his name inscribed on the Cup in 1972. He then jumped to the Boston-based WHA team, the New England Whalers, and didn't hang up his skates until 1979.

TED GREEN					
Eriksdale, Manitoba					
March 23, 1940–					
NHL Career: 1961-69, 1970-72					
Boston					
	GP	G	A	P	PIM
RS	620	48	206	254	1029
PO	31	4	8	12	54
Stanley Cup, A-S Game (2)					

WAYNE GRETZKY

CENTER 1981, 1982, 1983, 1984, 1985, 1986, 1987, 1991 ⭐2 1980, 1988, 1989, 1990, 1994, 1997, 1998

"The Great One" retired holding or sharing 61 NHL records. Voted an All-Star for 15 of his 20 NHL seasons, Wayne Gretzky won his first awards in his 1979-80 rookie campaign. Disqualified from Calder Trophy voting because he had spent the previous season in the WHA, Gretzky tied Marcel Dionne for the league lead with 137 points. His 51 goals were two fewer than Dionne's, however, which cost him the Art Ross Trophy. Gretzky did win the first of eight consecutive Hart Trophies, as well as his first Lady Byng.

Gretzky won the Ross for the next seven seasons, beginning with a record-breaking 164-point campaign in 1980-81. The following season, he lowered the mark for the fastest 50-goal campaign to 39 games. "I know everything that's been written about you," Flyers captain

Bobby Clarke told him at the time. "I think none of it is adequate." By season's end, Gretzky had 92 tallies and 212 points. Only Gretzky has ever hit 200 points, which he did five times, peaking with 215 in 1985-86.

His assist totals alone would have earned him four of his Art Ross Trophies. In fact, so many setups came from behind the opposition net that the area became known as "Gretzky's office." He captained Edmonton to four Stanley Cups in five seasons and won the Conn Smythe Trophy in 1985 and 1988. Yet the Oilers sold Gretzky to Los Angeles in the summer of 1988. He played the better part of eight seasons with the Kings and deserves much of the credit for hockey's expansion into the southern United States. After a brief sojourn in St. Louis late in the 1995-96 campaign, Gretzky joined the New York

Rangers. He led the league in assists for the next two seasons but decided to retire in the spring of 1999. At his final game, the NHL announced an unprecedented honor: No league player would ever wear Gretzky's number 99 again.

WAYNE GRETZKY
Brantford, Ontario
January 26, 1961–
NHL Career: 1979-99
Edmonton, Los Angeles, St. Louis,
NY Rangers

	GP	G	A	P	PIM
RS	1487	894	1963	2857	577
PO	208	122	260	382	66

Ross (10), Hart (9), Byng (5),
Pearson (5), Smythe (2), Stanley Cup (4),
A-S Game (17), HOF 1999

VIC HADFIELD

LEFT WING 1972

Vic Hadfield saw the New York Rangers develop from a sad-sack club to a Stanley Cup contender. Joining the Rangers in 1961-62, Hadfield

immediately established himself as a tough customer. His 151 penalty minutes in 1963-64 led the league, but he also demonstrated a blistering slap shot. Newcomers Rod Gilbert and Jean Ratelle proved the ideal linemates. "Jean and I knew each other's moves so well, we didn't even have to look," said Gilbert. "We needed someone who could do some of the dirty work in the corners and position himself in front of the net without being pushed around. Vic Hadfield was the perfect complement to us."

Eventually known as the "GAG Line" (for "goal-a-game"), Hadfield, Ratelle and Gilbert helped the Rangers to the playoffs in 1966-67 for the first time in five seasons. Hadfield posted his first of nine straight 20-goals-or-better campaigns the following season. He became team captain in 1971-72 and made the Second All-Star Team. Hadfield scored 50 goals, only the sixth player in NHL history to do so, and finished fourth in league scoring with 106 points, sandwiched between his linemates.

That autumn, Hadfield joined Team Canada for the Summit Series against the Soviet Union. He endured intense criticism for leaving the team before the end of the series, but he had seen only spot duty in two games and knew he wouldn't dress for the remaining matches. He returned to New York and completed two more strong NHL campaigns. Shortly after being injured in the 1974 playoffs, however, Hadfield was traded to Pittsburgh. He scored 31 and 30 goals for the Penguins over the next two seasons but retired only nine games into the 1976-77 campaign.

VIC HADFIELD
Oakville, Ontario
October 4, 1940–
NHL Career: 1961-77
NY Rangers, Pittsburgh

	GP	G	A	P	PIM
RS	1002	323	389	712	1154
PO	73	27	21	48	117

A-S Game (2)

GLENN HALL

Others thought it was nerves, but Glenn Hall believed that being sick to his stomach before every game meant he was ready to compete. There was certainly nothing weak about him. From 1955-56 through part of the 1962-63 season, Hall played 502 consecutive regular-season games, 552 including playoffs. "I was lucky when it came to injuries," he humbly noted, but it was more than good health that led to his iron-man record. The pioneer of the butterfly style of goaltending, Hall was "Mr. Goalie" and an almost perennial All-Star.

Hall broke in with the Detroit Red Wings, first doing spot duty, then usurping the throne of the legendary Terry Sawchuk. He posted a league-high 12 shutouts in 1955-56 and won the Calder Trophy. Although he made the First All-Star Team the following season, his independent spirit during a labor unrest led to his trade in July 1957. "I was sent to Chicago along with Ted Lindsay," said Hall. "Being around him did a lot for my approach to the game. I think I was reasonably talented, but he taught me that if you forced yourself to play harder, you'd get better results."

Hall didn't miss a beat or a game, and he anchored the Hawks to Stanley Cup victory in 1961 and back to the finals in 1962 and 1965. Although he won the Vezina Trophy in 1962-63 and shared it with Denis Dejordy in 1966-67, Chicago left Hall unprotected in the 1967 expansion draft. St. Louis grabbed Hall with its first pick, and he backed the Blues to the Cup finals. Although Montreal, the overwhelming favorite, swept the series, Hall earned the Conn Smythe Trophy. Two games went to overtime, and the other two were 1–0 and 3–2 losses.

In 1968-69, Hall led the league in shutouts for the sixth time and shared the Vezina Trophy with fellow veteran Jacques Plante. He made two more trips to the Cup finals before hanging up his goalie pads. His sweater number 1 was retired by Chicago in 1988.

GLENN HALL
Humboldt, Saskatchewan
October 3, 1931–
NHL Career: 1952-53, 1954-71
Detroit, Chicago, St. Louis

	GP	M	GA	SO	AVE
RS	906	53484	2239	84	2.51
PO	115	6899	321	6	2.79

Calder, Vezina (3), Smythe, Stanley Cup, A-S Game (13), HOF 1975

GLEN HARMON

Glen Harmon participated in the rejuvenation of the NHL's oldest franchise. "I joined the Canadiens in the latter part of 1942-43 after a couple of seasons with the Montreal Royals senior team," he recalled. "We were getting better crowds [at the Forum] than

the Canadiens." That changed when Maurice Richard developed into a star and goalie Bill Durnan arrived the following season. "We knew as long as we got back for the rebound, Bill would stop the first shot," said Harmon. "It was almost guaranteed."

Just over five-foot-eight and 160 pounds, Harmon played a steady defense while contributing 14 points in 27 games. He finished runner-up to Toronto's Gaye Stewart for rookie-of-the-year honors in 1943. Harmon helped lift the Canadiens to first place with a career-high 21 points in 1943-44, and Montreal won the Stanley Cup for the first time in 13 years. The following season, Frank Eddolls became his blue-line partner, and Harmon made the Second All-Star Team. "In practice, [coach] Dick Irvin would send [different line combinations] out against Bill, Frankie and me and bet a dollar they couldn't score twice in five attempts," said Harmon. "He usually won." Harmon and Eddolls went 34 consecutive games without allowing a single goal. Ironically, after Irvin bragged of their streak to the press, his steadiest pair was on the ice for seven goals against in the next game.

The Habs won the Cup again in 1946, and Harmon joined Syl Apps and Sid Abel in forming the first pension plan for NHL players in 1947. Harmon made the Second All-Star Team in 1948-49, finishing just ahead of teammate Ken Reardon in voting. He concluded his NHL career in 1950-51 but played four more seasons for the Montreal Royals before hanging up his skates.

GLEN HARMON
Holland, Manitoba
January 2, 1921–
NHL Career: 1942-51
Montreal

	GP	G	A	P	PIM
RS	452	50	96	146	334
PO	53	5	10	15	37

Stanley Cup (2), A-S Game (2)

DEFENSE

⭐ 1969

Ted Harris spent eight seasons in the minor leagues, more than four of them with the Springfield Indians under Eddie Shore's tutelage. "He taught me how to play the man and the puck," said Harris. "I figure he made me more versatile."

The Montreal Canadiens traded for six-foot-two Harris in June 1963. He played only four NHL games in 1963-64 before joining the Habs full-time the following season. Not coincidentally, Harris won four Stanley Cup rings in five seasons. "He played his position diligently, made the right passes, bodychecked when he had to and never backed down from the toughest opponent," wrote Pat Curran in *The Hockey News*.

Although widely recognized as having his career year in 1968-69, Harris wasn't picked as a starter for the midseason All-Star Game. "I would have been the most surprised guy in hockey if I had made it," he said modestly. The voters didn't forget his strong defensive play at season's end, however, and Harris made the Second All-Star Team.

Little changed in 1969-70, but in an under-the-table deal, Montreal let Minnesota claim Harris in the 1970 intra-league draft. "If Ted Harris can't make a measurable improvement in our defense, I don't know who can," said North Stars general manager Wren Blair. "He's big, tough, durable and smart. At 34, he's got a lot of hockey ahead of him."

Immediately named Minnesota's team captain, Harris didn't disappoint. He even hit a career-high with 7 goals and 23 assists in 1972-73. In November 1973, however, Minnesota swapped him for veteran Red Wing Gary Bergman, and Detroit dealt him to St. Louis in February 1974. Philadelphia bought his services for 1974-75, and Harris retired shortly after hoisting the Cup for the fifth time.

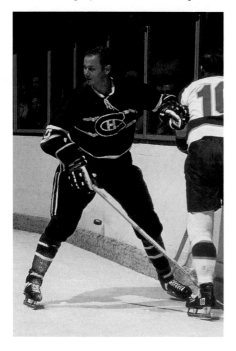

TED HARRIS
Winnipeg, Manitoba
July 18, 1936–
NHL Career: 1963-75
Montreal, Minnesota, Detroit, St. Louis, Philadelphia

	GP	G	A	P	PIM
RS	788	30	168	198	1000
PO	100	1	22	23	230

Stanley Cup (5), A-S Game (5)

DOUG HARVEY

DEFENSE

⭐ 1952, 1953, 1954, 1955, 1956, 1957, 1958, 1960, 1961, 1962 1959

Most people considered Doug Harvey a free spirit, although late in life, he was diagnosed as a manic-depressive. For respite, Harvey developed a dependence on alcohol that ultimately took its toll on both his professional and his personal life. Nonetheless, the man who won the Norris Trophy seven times was described by Toe Blake as "the greatest defenseman who ever played hockey—bar none. Usually, a defenseman specializes in one thing and builds a reputation on that, but Doug could do everything well."

"Harvey was a master at controlling the puck," said Boston's Milt Schmidt. "He'd hang onto it and hang onto it in his own zone until he forced you into a move to check him. Then he'd kill you with his passes."

Harvey had explicit instructions for new members of his team: "If you park yourself near the boards and wait for a pass from me, it won't come. If you want the puck, you'll [only] get it on the fly." He helped Montreal win six Stanley Cups, but management grew tired of his off-ice behavior, and team captain Harvey was traded to the New York Rangers in June 1961.

As player/coach in 1961-62, Harvey lifted the Rangers into the playoffs and won his last Norris Trophy and All-Star berth. "The guys who elected me must have been voting from memory," joked Harvey.

He hated his coaching duties, however, for they separated him from his teammates. "They told him they just wanted him to coach, not play anymore, and that's what ruined him," recalled Gump Worsley

of the Rangers management. "He stayed with us for one more year as a player, but the wheels were coming off." Harvey played in the minors, joined Detroit for a couple of games in 1966-67 and played the 1968-69 season for St. Louis. He died, penniless, in 1989 of cirrhosis of the liver.

DOUG HARVEY
Montreal, Quebec
December 19, 1924–December 26, 1989
NHL Career: 1947-64, 1966-69
Montreal, NY Rangers, Detroit, St. Louis

	GP	G	A	P	PIM
RS	1113	88	452	540	1216
PO	137	8	64	72	152

Norris (7), Stanley Cup (6),
A-S Game (13), HOF 1973

DOMINIK HASEK

GOALTENDER

Drafted by Chicago in 1983, Czechoslovakian star Dominik Hasek didn't join the Blackhawks until 1990-91. Unfortunately, his unorthodox flopping and sprawling style went largely unappreciated. Hasek spent most of two seasons in the IHL, although he did manage to make the 1992 NHL All-Rookie Team with 20 appearances. In August 1992, the Hawks traded him to Buffalo for goalie Stephane Beauregard and a fourth-round draft pick. A year later, the Sabres didn't even protect Hasek in the 1993 expansion draft. But "The Dominator" made the First All-Star Team and won the Vezina Trophy five out of the next six seasons.

Sharing the 1994 William M. Jennings Trophy with Grant Fuhr, Hasek posted the NHL's first sub-2.00 goals-against average in 20 years. His idiosyn-

cratic goaltending methods, including dropping his stick and using his head to block shots, entertained the fans and befuddled the shooters. "It's tough to imagine a game where we earned a win or a tie when Hasek's goaltending was not the dominant factor of our success," said coach John Muckler. Hasek earned the Hart Trophy and the Pearson Award in both 1997 and 1998. His greatest glory, however, came through backstopping the underdog Czech Republic to the 1998 Olympic gold medal. Hundreds of thousands of Hasek's countrymen welcomed him to Prague as a national hero.

Hasek took the Sabres to the Stanley Cup finals in 1999 but, only weeks later, made a shocking announcement: The 1999-2000 campaign would be his last. He would willingly forsake the

final two years and $16.5 million of his contract. After missing half of the season with a groin injury, however, he postponed his retirement plans. His teammates, understandably, were thrilled. Whether he goes out a winner or not, Hasek has proved himself a goaltender for the ages.

DOMINIK HASEK
Pardubice, Czechoslovakia
January 29, 1965–
NHL Career: 1990-
Chicago, Buffalo

	GP	M	GA	SO	AVE
RS	449	25968	977	45	2.26
PO	61	3683	128	5	2.09

Hart (2), Jennings, Vezina (5), Pearson (2), A-S Game (4)

DALE HAWERCHUK

CENTER

Although Dale Hawerchuk had to compete for league honors against Wayne Gretzky and Mario Lemieux, Winnipeg Jets' fans couldn't have been

happier with the timing of his career. "I've been waiting for Dale for two years," said general manager John Ferguson in 1981. Hawerchuk led the Cornwall Royals to consecutive Memorial Cups before the sad-sack Jets drafted him first overall in 1981. Only 18 years old when he entered the NHL, Hawerchuk won the 1982 Calder Trophy with 45 goals and 58 assists. The team improved by 48 points and made the playoffs for the first time.

The following season, Hawerchuk tallied 40 goals. In 1983-84, he set a record with a five-assist period on his way to a second 100-point campaign. At the age of 21, Hawerchuk became team captain for 1984-85. He responded to the added pressure with 53 goals and 77 assists, finishing third in league scoring. Hawerchuk's season ended on an unfortunate note, however, when he was knocked out of the playoffs with broken ribs, but he made the Second All-Star Team and finished runner-up to Gretzky in Hart Trophy voting.

In 1985-86, Hawerchuk tied for ninth

with 105 points, and the following season, he finished seventh with 100 points. He jumped to fourth with a 44-goal, 77-assist campaign in 1987-88 but never cracked the NHL's top-10 again. He agreed to a trade to Buffalo for 1990-91 and led the Sabres in scoring over two seasons. The St. Louis Blues signed him as a free agent for 1995-96 but traded him to Philadelphia in March. Contributing leadership and strong two-way play, Hawerchuk made his only trip to the league finals in 1997. He didn't get a Stanley Cup ring but retired as the tenth-highest scorer in NHL history.

DALE HAWERCHUK
Toronto, Ontario
April 4, 1963–
NHL Career: 1981-97
Winnipeg, Buffalo, St. Louis, Philadelphia

	GP	G	A	P	PIM
RS	1188	518	891	1409	730
PO	97	30	69	99	67

Calder, A-S Game (5)

OTT HELLER

New York Rangers coach and general manager Lester Patrick described Ott Heller as "the perfect hockey player." Heller's flamboyant rushes up the ice and strong defensive play made an immediate impact when he debuted in the NHL midway through the 1931-32 campaign.

That season, the Rangers went to the Stanley Cup finals, and Heller chipped in three playoff goals and an assist. Although still only a second-string defenseman in the 1933 playoffs, Heller notched three more goals, and the Rangers took the Cup from Toronto.

In the 1935-36 season, Heller was paired with rookie Babe Pratt. The Rangers went to the 1937 Cup finals, and Heller hit his offensive high in 1938-39 with 23 assists. He was at his best, however, in 1939-40. Heller scored 5 goals and 14 assists, and he and Pratt were on the ice for only 17 goals against over the entire 48-game season. Their goaltender, Dave Kerr, won the Vezina Trophy, and the Rangers won the 1940 Stanley Cup.

The following spring, Heller received some deserved personal attention when he made the Second All-Star Team. He later captained the Rangers through three last-place seasons, from 1942-43 to 1944-45, but when the team's war veterans returned, Heller was bumped out of the lineup. He played another 10 minor-league seasons of hockey, mixed with some coaching, until finally hanging up his skates for good at the age of 46.

EBERHARDT "OTT" HELLER
Kitchener, Ontario
June 2, 1910–deceased
NHL Career: 1931-46
NY Rangers

	GP	G	A	P	PIM
RS	647	55	176	231	465
PO	61	6	8	14	61

Stanley Cup (2)

CAMILLE HENRY

His slippery moves and slender physique justified Camille Henry's nickname "The Eel." Although his 24 rookie goals earned Henry the 1954 Calder Trophy, his five-foot-nine frame and 140 pounds made the team nervous. "The coaches and trainers would never let the reporters see me on the scales," said Henry, "and they added 20 pounds when they gave the figures out." During the summer of 1954, the Rangers put him through an intensive weight-lifting program, but Henry's new bulk inhibited his natural style. The Rangers sent him to the minors after 21 games, and he didn't return to the NHL until midway through the 1956-57 season.

Henry's feel for the game was fully restored by 1957-58. Possessing the speed to create holes and the savvy to exploit them, he led the Rangers with 32 goals. He made the Second All-Star Team and won the Lady Byng Trophy, having picked up only a single minor penalty all season. Henry averaged 25 goals over the next seven campaigns, peaking in 1962-63 with 37 goals and 60 points.

After Andy Bathgate's trade to Toronto in February 1964, Henry became team captain. A year later, however, the left-winger was on the move himself.

The Rangers dealt him and three teammates to Chicago, where he finally experienced playing for a contender. The Hawks lost the Stanley Cup finals that spring, and Henry spent the 1965-66 season in the minors. He retired for a year but made a comeback with the Rangers in 1967-68. Another trade soon followed, and Henry played just over one season for St. Louis before finishing his hockey career in the Central Hockey League. At the age of 64, he died of complications from epilepsy, alcoholism and diabetes.

CAMILLE HENRY
Quebec City, Quebec
January 31, 1933–September 12, 1997
NHL Career: 1953-55, 1956-65, 1967-70
NY Rangers, Chicago, St. Louis

	GP	G	A	P	PIM
RS	727	279	249	528	88
PO	47	6	12	18	7

Calder, Byng, A-S Game (3)

SUGAR JIM HENRY

GOALTENDER

Known as "Sugar" Jim to many because of his childhood sweet tooth, Jim Henry was simply called "Sam" by his teammates. Henry backed the New York Rangers to first place in the 1941-42 season and led the playoffs with a 2.17 goals-against average. After the Rangers lost the semifinals, Henry enlisted in the Canadian Army and did not return to New York until the autumn of 1945. Manager Lester Patrick alternated him with Chuck Rayner for 20 games, even having his netminders switching every third shift for a time. Henry spent most of two seasons in the AHL before displacing Rayner for the bulk of 1947-48.

After being traded for Emile Francis and Alex Kaleta, Henry spent 1948-49 with the Blackhawks. Frank Brimsek wanted to finish out his career in Chicago, however, and Henry spent two more seasons in the minors before Boston acquired his rights in 1951-52. Herb Ralby of

The Boston Daily Globe gave Henry his vote for the 1952 comeback athlete of the year. "When things were rough around midseason," noted Ralby, "it was Sam's nifty netminding which kept the Bruins from falling out of the league." Henry made the Second All-Star Team, and an observant reporter helped immortalize him after a seventh-game semifinal loss to Montreal. Raccoon-eyed because of a broken nose and bleeding from a cut, Henry was photographed giving a congratulatory handshake to an equally battered Rocket Richard. The image captured for many the brutal but honorable spirit of an era.

Posting seven shutouts for the second consecutive season, Henry backstopped the Bruins to the 1953 Stanley Cup finals. The Canadiens prevailed again, however. Henry tallied a career-best eight shutouts in 1953-54, but the following season, a shot shattered his eye socket, and he never played in the NHL again.

"SUGAR" JIM HENRY
Winnipeg, Manitoba
October 23, 1920–
NHL Career: 1941-42, 1945-49, 1951-55
NY Rangers, Chicago, Boston

	GP	M	GA	SO	AVE
RS	406	24355	1166	27	2.87
PO	29	1741	81	2	2.79

A-S Game

BRYAN HEXTALL SR.

RIGHT WING

Bryan Hextall established a reputation that only grew with time. "He is a very clean-living individual and an excellent ambassador for professional hockey," remarked hockey-promoter Hall of Fame member James Dunn, who had watched Hextall develop his game as an amateur in Manitoba. Hex

tall later helped the Vancouver Lions win the 1934-35 North West Hockey League championship and scored a league-high 27 goals the following season. Although he played only 18 of 48 games, Hextall led the newly formed American Hockey League with 29 goals in 1936-37. The New York Rangers called him up before the season ended.

Hextall had his first 20-goal NHL campaign in 1938-39 and led the league with 24 goals in 1939-40. Named to the First All-Star Team, he capped a glorious season by scoring the overtime Stanley Cup-winning goal against Toronto. Hextall scored a league-high 26 goals in 1940-41 and finished second in points. The following season, he won the scoring crown with 24 goals and 56 points; his linemates Lynn Patrick and Phil Watson finished second and fourth, respectively. Although Hextall hit his career-high in 1942-43 with 27 goals and 59 points, he finished seventh overall, and Toronto's Lorne Carr edged

him onto the Second All-Star Team.

Hextall led the Rangers with 54 points in 1943-44 but spent most of the next two seasons in military service. He scored 20 goals for the seventh and final time in 1946-47, played one more NHL season and one in the AHL and then retired. His sons Bryan Jr. and Dennis both broke into the league with the Rangers in the 1960s and had respectable NHL careers. His grandson, goaltender Ron Hextall, became an All-Star himself in the 1980s.

BRYAN HEXTALL SR.
Grenfell, Saskatchewan
July 31, 1913–July 25, 1984
NHL Career: 1936-44, 1945-48
NY Rangers

	GP	G	A	P	PIM
RS	449	187	175	362	227
PO	37	8	9	17	19

Ross, Stanley Cup, HOF 1969

RON HEXTALL

GOALTENDER

His grandfather, Bryan Hextall Sr., his father, Bryan Jr., and his uncle, Dennis, all had distinguished NHL careers, but Ron Hextall broke new ground for the family by going into goaltending. He had a stunning debut with the Philadelphia Flyers in 1986-87, making the First All-Star Team. Hextall also won the Vezina Trophy and finished second for both the Calder and the William M. Jennings trophies. Although the Flyers lost in the Stanley Cup finals, Hextall pushed Edmonton to a seventh game and received the Conn Smythe Trophy. In his acceptance speech for the Vezina, Hextall boldly announced that he aimed to become the best goalie ever. "I felt sorry for him," said Mark Howe, "because I knew that no goalie could ever have a year like that again."

On December 8, 1987, Hextall became the first goalie in NHL history to fire a puck into the empty opposition net. "I didn't think it was that big a deal," he claimed. "I just fired it up and

over everybody, and it went in." He scored again in the 1989 playoffs, but Hextall became known more for his violent stickwork than for his strong puck-handling and shooting abilities. He tallied a goaltender's record of 113 penalty minutes in 1988-89. Over his career, he sat out three different suspensions, totaling 26 games, for slashing.

Hextall went to Quebec in 1992-93 as part of the package for Eric Lindros. The following season, he joined the New York Islanders but was traded back to Philadelphia for 1994-95. Although Hextall tied for the league lead with a 2.17 goals-against average in 1995-96, he was never again able to translate his sharp competitive edge into memorable play. He retired in 1999, holding the Philadelphia franchise netminding records for appearances and wins for both the regular season and the playoffs.

RON HEXTALL
Brandon, Manitoba
May 3, 1964–
NHL Career: 1986-99
Philadelphia, Quebec, NY Islanders

	GP	M	GA	SO	AVE
RS	608	34750	1723	23	2.97
PO	93	5456	276	2	3.04

Vezina, Smythe, A-S Game

CHARLIE HODGE

GOALTENDER

Although he began his NHL career with 14 games in the 1954-55 season, Charlie Hodge spent the better part of the next decade in the minors. He got his name on the 1958 and 1959 Stanley Cups but filled in only when Montreal's Jacques Plante was injured. Shy, five-foot-six and 150 pounds, Hodge looked every bit the underdog. It was a great surprise, therefore, when the Canadiens traded Plante for Gump

Worsley in the summer of 1963 and Hodge soon emerged as Montreal's starting netminder.

He started the 1963-64 season in the AHL, but when Worsley got hurt, Hodge made the most of his opportunity. "Charlie has been playing some of the best hockey of his career for us this season," said coach Toe Blake that January. "Some of the saves he's made have changed the whole trend of a game and given us just the lift we needed to win."

Hodge finished the campaign with a league-leading eight shutouts. "When Plante was around, I knew I was just filling in whenever I came up," he explained. "This year, I feel more relaxed—more secure—and I guess it's helping me to play a little better." That year, he won the Vezina Trophy and made the Second All-Star Team.

While Worsley returned to the Canadiens late in the 1964-65 season, Hodge

retained his All-Star status. He split the playoffs and a Stanley Cup victory with "The Gumper," and they shared the 1966 Vezina as well. In Montreal's successful 1966 playoff run, though, Worsley got the starting job and Hodge saw no action. Hodge spent one more year with the Habs, then played Oakland's first three seasons. After joining Vancouver for the Canucks' inaugural campaign of 1970-71, he retired.

CHARLIE HODGE
Lachine, Quebec
July 28, 1933–
NHL Career: 1954-55, 1957-61, 1963-71
Montreal, Oakland, Vancouver

	GP	M	GA	SO	AVE
RS	358	20593	927	24	2.70
PO	16	803	32	2	2.39

Vezina (2), Stanley Cup (4), A-S Game (3)

KEN HODGE

RIGHT WING

Ken Hodge was involved in two of the most successful trades in Boston Bruins' franchise history. Unfortunately, as much as he was the bounty in one swap, he was the bait in the other.

Hodge won the 1964-65 Ontario junior scoring championship and moved up to the Chicago Blackhawks. He was still feeling his way when Chicago traded him after the 1966-67 season. Hodge, Phil Esposito and Fred Stanfield became key members of the Boston Bruins in exchange for Gilles Marotte, Pit Martin and Jack Norris. Hodge scored 25 goals in his first season beside Esposito in Boston, but when Wayne Cashman joined them in 1968-69, Hodge jumped to fifth place in league scoring. "Let's face it," said Art Ross Trophy-winner Esposito, "if Kenny wasn't having the season he had, where would I be?" Hodge tallied 45 goals and an equal number of assists.

In 1969-70, Hodge helped Boston win its first Stanley Cup in 29 years and notched 105 points the following sea-

son. Fourth in league scoring, he made the First All-Star Team, but the Bruins were upset in the playoffs. The entire club played the next season with a vengeance. Hodge led the league with 62 penalty minutes in only 15 playoff games. He added 9 goals and 8 assists, and the Bruins reclaimed the Cup.

Hodge scored 50 goals in 1973-74, only the ninth player ever to do so, and made the First All-Star Team again. He matched his career-high with 105 points and added 16 more in the playoffs, but Philadelphia surprised the Bruins in the Cup finals. Hodge's production started to slip, and Boston traded Esposito to the New York Rangers early in the 1975-76 season. In a move designed to reinvigorate both of the veterans' careers, the Rangers acquired Hodge from Boston in May 1976 in exchange for Rick Middleton, who went on to star in the league for many years. New York, however, demoted Hodge to the minors in 1977-78, where he finished out his professional career.

KEN HODGE
Birmingham, England
June 25, 1944–
NHL Career: 1964-78
Chicago, Boston, NY Rangers

	GP	G	A	P	PIM
RS	881	328	472	800	779
PO	97	34	47	81	120

Stanley Cup (2), A-S Game (3)

FLASH HOLLETT

DEFENSE

Bill Hollett was known as "Busher" until he joined the Toronto Maple Leafs in 1933. With Harvey "Busher" Jackson already a Leafs' star, it was time for a new nickname. Some say that Hollett himself suggested "Flash." In any case, the moniker made sense, and it stuck. Hollett finished second to Syl Apps in a 1940s footrace to determine the fastest skater in the NHL.

Hollett was loaned to the Ottawa Senators for the last 30 games of his rookie season. In January 1936, he was sold to Boston. Playing alongside Eddie Shore and, later, Dit Clapper, Hollett developed into a premier rushing defenseman. He helped the Bruins win the

Stanley Cup in 1939 and 1941, scoring in the Cup-clinching game both times.

Hollett tied Harry Cameron's 20-year-old goal-scoring record for blue-liners in 1941-42. Yet it wasn't until the next season, when he again scored 19 times and added a career-best 25 assists, that Hollett made the Second All-Star Team.

Boston traded him to Detroit, however, for the more rugged—and younger—Pat Egan in January 1944. Hollett finally made the First All-Star Team in 1945. His 20-goal season set a new high for defensemen that wasn't surpassed until Bobby Orr scored 21 times in 1968-69.

Hollett was slowed by injuries in 1945-46, and after a contract dispute with Jack Adams, he was out of the league. Adams had reportedly threatened to ensure that he was never inducted into the Hockey Hall of Fame, but Hollett remained unfazed to the end. "If they think I should be in the Hall, I should be, but it doesn't matter to me," he said in his later years. "I know how good I was."

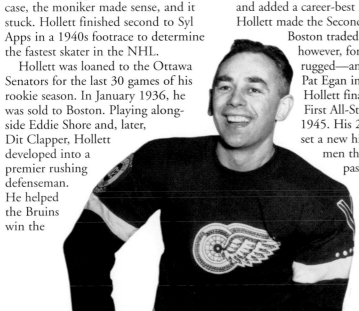

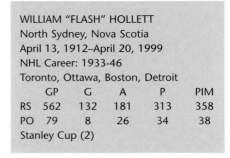

WILLIAM "FLASH" HOLLETT
North Sydney, Nova Scotia
April 13, 1912–April 20, 1999
NHL Career: 1933-46
Toronto, Ottawa, Boston, Detroit

	GP	G	A	P	PIM
RS	562	132	181	313	358
PO	79	8	26	34	38

Stanley Cup (2)

TIM HORTON

⭐ 1964, 1968, 1969 ⭐2 1954, 1963, 1967

Although Tim Horton is remembered more today for the donut chain he founded, he was a dominant defenseman for 22 NHL seasons. His strength allowed him to control the action in front of his own net, and he could rush and shoot the puck with the best of them. Horton made a couple of brief appearances with the Leafs before joining the team full-time in 1952-53. The following season, he made the Second All-Star Team, notching 7 goals and 24 assists as a member of the league's stingiest defense.

Toronto's acquisition of Allan Stanley in 1959 allowed Horton to take his game up another notch. He led his team with 16 points in the 1962 playoffs, winning his first Stanley Cup ring. Horton helped the Leafs successfully defend the Cup the next two seasons and

was runner-up to Pierre Pilote for the 1964 Norris Trophy.

Despite a lineup that featured a host of older veterans, Toronto won the 1967 Stanley Cup, surprising most people, including the favored Montreal Canadiens. But Horton was at the peak of his game, outpointing teenage rookie Bobby Orr in 1967 All-Star voting. "I never knew a player so steady," said teammate Frank Mahovlich. Horton joined Orr on the First All-Star Team defense the following two seasons. He came second on ballots for the 1969 Norris Trophy after notching a career-high 40 points.

It was the end of an era when the Leafs traded Horton to the New York Rangers in March 1970. He played the 1971-72 season for Pittsburgh, and then his old friend Punch Imlach talked him

into playing with the Buffalo Sabres. Horton's life came to a tragic end in February 1974. After earning third-star honors in a game in Toronto, he died when he crashed his sports car early the next morning. The Leafs have honored sweater-number 7 in memory of both Horton and King Clancy, while Buffalo retired Horton's sweater number 2.

MYLES "TIM" HORTON
Cochrane, Ontario
January 12, 1930–February 21, 1974
NHL Career: 1949-50, 1951-74
Toronto, NY Rangers, Pittsburgh, Buffalo

	GP	G	A	P	PIM
RS	1446	115	403	518	1611
PO	126	11	39	50	183

Stanley Cup (4), A-S Game (7), HOF 1977

BRONCO HORVATH

⭐2 1960

His Stetson hat, a nod to the years spent in western Canada, led to Joseph Horvath's nickname "Bronco."

Horvath concluded a long minor-league apprenticeship with the Edmonton Flyers, taking the 1954-55 WHL scoring crown with 50 goals and 110 assists. He tallied a respectable 12 goals and 17 assists for the New York Rangers in 1955-56 but was then sold to the talent-rich Montreal Canadiens. He finished the following season back in the minors.

Boston picked up Horvath in the 1957 intra-league draft, reuniting him with his Edmonton linemates Johnny Bucyk and Vic Stasiuk. The powerful "Uke Line" was born, although Horvath's heritage was Yugoslavian rather than the Ukrainian of his wingers. He scored 30 goals and 36 assists, coming fifth in league scoring. Horvath raced Bobby Hull for the NHL scoring crown throughout most of the 1959-60 campaign. He strung together 22 games in a point-scoring streak from December 27 to February 13 and ended the season tied with Hull for the league lead with 39 goals. Hull, however, had one more assist. "If the Chief [Bucyk] hadn't got injured, I'd have shattered 50 goals or

more," maintained Horvath in later years.

Unfortunately, the "Ukes" were a defensive liability, a factor that put Horvath on the Second All-Star Team that season, although he beat Jean Beliveau in both goals and assists. When Horvath scored only 15 goals in 1960-61, the Bruins left him unprotected, and by January 1963, he had bounced from Chicago to New York to Toronto. He finished the 1962-63 season—and his NHL career, save for a 14-game call-up to the Minnesota North Stars in 1967-68—down in the minors.

JOSEPH "BRONCO" HORVATH
Port Colborne, Ontario
March 12, 1930–
NHL Career: 1955-63, 1967-68
NY Rangers, Montreal, Boston, Chicago, Toronto, Minnesota

	GP	G	A	P	PIM
RS	434	141	185	326	319
PO	36	12	9	21	18

A-S Game (2)

DEFENSE

⭐2 1992

Phil Housley bridged the gap between American high school hockey and the NHL with ease. In 22 games for South St. Paul High in 1981-82, he scored 31 goals and 34 assists. The Buffalo Sabres used their first pick, sixth overall, to select him in the 1982 NHL entry draft, and Housley jumped right onto the Sabres' roster. With 19 goals and 47 assists, he led all first-year blue-liners in points. He made the 1982 All-Rookie Team and finished second in Calder Trophy voting.

In 1983-84, Housley scored a career-best 31 goals. The rearguard posted his highest Buffalo totals in 1989-90 with 60 assists and 81 points. But in a deal that brought Dale Hawerchuk to Buffalo, the swift and smooth-skating Housley was traded to the Winnipeg Jets in June 1990. He made the Second All-Star Team in 1992 with 23 goals and 63 assists. For the first time, he was also a finalist for the Norris Trophy. He followed up with a career-high 79 assists and 97 points in 1992-93, leading all NHL defensemen.

Seen by many as a defensive liability, Housley was traded to St. Louis in 1993-94 and to Calgary the following season. After a brief stint with New Jersey in 1995-96, he joined the Washington Capitals as a free agent. He became the fifth NHL defenseman—and only the second American-born player—to tally 1,000 career points. Picked up on waivers, Housley returned to Calgary in July 1998.

PHIL HOUSLEY
St. Paul, Minnesota
March 9, 1964–
NHL Career: 1982-
Buffalo, Winnipeg, St. Louis, Calgary,
New Jersey, Washington

	GP	G	A	P	PIM
RS	1288	313	817	1130	738
PO	77	13	42	55	32

A-S Game (7)

GORDIE HOWE

RIGHT WING

⭐ 1951, 1952, 1953, 1954, 1957, 1958, 1960, 1963, 1966, 1968, 1969, 1970
⭐2 1949, 1950, 1956, 1959, 1961, 1962, 1964, 1965, 1967

Scoring in his first NHL game, Red Wings rookie Gordie Howe launched a legendary career. On Detroit's "Production Line," with center Sid Abel and left-winger Ted Lindsay, Howe made the 1948-49 Second All-Star Team with 12 goals and 37 points. He never posted a lower point total than this. He came third in league scoring in 1949-50 and did not finish lower than fifth for 20 seasons running.

In 1950-51, Howe won the Art Ross Trophy for the first of four consecutive years with a record-breaking 86 points, and in 1952-53, he set a new high mark with 95 points. He had a strong shot, both right- and left-handed, but he used his stick for more than scoring, and his elbows felled many opponents. "I'm not dirty," Howe maintained. "I'd rather say aggressive." But his kindly manner off the ice was occasionally seen in games.

"I was down, and he had the puck right in front of me," recalled maskless goaltender Gump Worsley. "If he had let it go full force, he would have hit me right in the face. Instead, he just pushed it under me. The whistle went, and he leaned over and said, 'I'll get one later.'"

In addition to scoring, Howe also picked up six Hart Trophies and four Stanley Cup rings on his way to the Hockey Hall of Fame. He tallied a career-high 103 points in 1968-69. "If you can figure out where the puck is going or how a play is going to develop," he told writer Frank Orr, "you can save a lot of energy by skating to where you'll be needed. If I have any secret, that's it." But arthritis in his powerful wrists convinced him to retire in 1971.

In 1973, "Mr. Hockey" took a big risk when the WHA's Houston Aeros offered him a chance to play with his sons Mark and Marty. "If I failed badly," Howe admitted ruefully, "people would remem-ber me more for trying to make a stupid comeback at 45 than for all the other things I did in hockey." But he became a WHA star and added 174 goals and 334 assists to his career totals. When the NHL absorbed the rival league, Howe played all 80 games of the Hartford Whalers' 1979-80 season, scoring 15 goals and 26 assists. He remains the greatest winger the game has ever known.

GORDIE HOWE
Floral, Saskatchewan
March 31, 1928–
NHL Career: 1946-71, 1979-80
Detroit, Hartford

	GP	G	A	P	PIM
RS	1767	801	1049	1850	1685
PO	157	68	92	160	220

Ross (6), Hart (6), Stanley Cup (4),
A-S Game (23), HOF 1972

MARK HOWE

DEFENSE

Mark Howe and his brother Marty turned professional with the WHA's Houston Aeros in 1973-74, joining their father Gordie on a memorable line. Mark won WHA rookie-of-the-year honors and, by the end of the 1978-79 season, had tallied 208 goals and 296 assists. By then, all three Howes were members of the New England Whalers, which would become the NHL's Hartford Whalers in 1979-80. That year, Mark made yet another transition when he switched from forward to defense.

Howe scored 24 goals and 56 assists during his first NHL campaign, finishing third in team scoring. He was lucky, though, that his career didn't end with an injury midseason. Upended at high speed, Howe slid into the sharply pointed center of the net's base. "An inch one way, and it could have gone into my spinal cord," recalled Howe. "An inch the other way, it would have pierced my sphincter muscle, and I would have been walking around with a colostomy bag. When Dad looked at it and almost got sick, I knew it was serious." He missed only a handful of games, however, and developed a reputation as an intelligent and clean-playing blue-liner.

Philadelphia traded for Howe in the summer of 1982. He made the First All-Star Team three out of the next five seasons, finishing runner-up for the Norris Trophy each time. Howe's 58 assists and 82 points in 1985-86 were a career-high, and he led the league with a plus-85. He sandwiched that season with trips to the Stanley Cup finals, but the Flyers fell short to Edmonton each time. Recurrent back problems weren't fully cured by surgery in 1991, yet Howe showed some of his father's longevity. He signed with Detroit in July 1992 and retired, after three seasons, at the age of 40.

MARK HOWE
Detroit, Michigan
May 28, 1955–
NHL Career: 1979-95
Hartford, Philadelphia, Detroit

	GP	G	A	P	PIM
RS	929	197	545	742	455
PO	101	10	51	61	34

A-S Game (4)

SYD HOWE

LEFT WING

Syd Howe, although no relation to Gordie Howe, was himself a great all-round athlete. At one time or another, he played every position but goal. "There's no doubt in my mind that Syd Howe is the most underrated hockey player who ever played in the National Hockey League, past or present," said Bill Cowley in 1975. "If you ask most anybody else who played with or against him, they'd tell you the same thing." This praise is especially noteworthy considering that Howe shattered Cowley's jaw in five places in 1941. Even though the check was clean, Howe regarded the incident as a low point in his career.

After his NHL debut with the Ottawa Senators in 1929-30, Howe went on loan to the Philadelphia Quakers for their sole NHL campaign in 1930-31. He moved to Toronto for the following season, then returned to the Senators. The franchise relocated to St. Louis for 1934-35 and dealt Howe to Detroit on February 11, 1935. He still finished second in league scoring with 22 goals and 25 assists.

Over the next two seasons, Howe helped the Red Wings win the Stanley Cup, but he didn't crack the top-10 scoring list again until 1939-40. He tied for second place the following season. Detroit won the 1943 Stanley Cup, and in 1943-44, Howe hit a personal high with 32 goals, including six in one game, and 60 points. His consistent output allowed him to pass the NHL's all-time scoring leader, Nels Stewart, on March 8, 1945, with 516 career points. At season's end, Howe's tenth-place spot in league scoring lifted him onto the Second All-Star Team. That proved his sole NHL honor, however, and Howe retired the following season.

SYD HOWE
Ottawa, Ontario
September 28, 1911–May 20, 1976
NHL Career: 1929-46
Ottawa, Philadelphia, Toronto, St. Louis, Detroit

	GP	G	A	P	PIM
RS	698	237	291	528	212
PO	70	17	27	44	10

Stanley Cup (3), A-S Game, HOF 1965

DEFENSE 1967

Harry Howell missed only 17 games during his first 16 NHL seasons. In 1955-56, at the age of 22, he became the team captain of the New York Rangers. Although he led the team to the playoffs two seasons in a row, he then gave up the position. Unfortunately, the Rangers never won a playoff round during Howell's lengthy stay in the Big Apple. Yet the defenseman quietly gained respect for his consistent effectiveness.

Howell played a big role on the Rangers' squad, which spent a long stretch of the 1966-67 campaign in first place. Shortly after becoming only the third man to play 1,000 NHL games, he got a big boost in midseason. The team honored him with a "night" in Madison Square Garden, showering him with gifts and accolades. By season's end, he had posted a career-best 12-goal, 28-assist campaign. The Rangers had slipped to fourth place, but Howell was elected to the First All-Star Team and won the Norris Trophy. "I might as well enjoy it now," he noted when he was presented with the trophy, "because I expect it's going to belong to Bobby Orr for the next 10 years."

Although Howell was correct in many ways, there was still a place for a veteran, especially in tutoring a new generation of players that included Brad Park. Howell had to undergo major back surgery in 1969, prompting the Rangers to offer him an off-ice job, but he was far from ready to hang up his skates. He joined the Oakland Seals in 1969-70, which became the California Golden Seals the following season. Sold to Los Angeles in February 1971, Howell concluded his NHL career as a King in 1972-73. Three more campaigns as a WHA player/coach capped the longest professional career of any defenseman.

HARRY HOWELL
Hamilton, Ontario
December 28, 1932–
NHL Career: 1952-73
NY Rangers, Oakland, California,
Los Angeles

	GP	G	A	P	PIM
RS	1411	94	324	418	1298
PO	38	3	3	6	32

Norris, A-S Game (7), HOF 1979

LEFT WING 1960, 1962, 1964, 1965, 1966, 1967, 1968, 1969, 1970, 1972 1963, 1971

A dynamic Adonis with a booming shot and blazing speed, Bobby Hull was dubbed "The Golden Jet" early in his career. He came a close second for 1957-58 rookie of the year, but the decision by Chicago coach Rudy Pilous to switch Hull from center to left wing for 1959-60 was a stroke of genius. Hull won his first scoring championship and earned All-Star status for 11 of the next 12 seasons. He won his Stanley Cup ring in 1961, although he helped the Blackhawks to the league finals three other times.

Hull won his second Art Ross Trophy in 1962, tying Maurice Richard and Bernie Geoffrion for the scoring record with 50 goals. In 1964-65, he won the Hart and Lady Byng trophies. A second

Hart and a third Art Ross came the following season, when he set new highs with 54 goals and 97 points. "Bobby used to go for the far side, your glove hand, 9 times out of 10," recalled goaltender Gump Worsley. "You knew what he was going to do, but he'd still blow it by you." Hull's slap shot was once clocked at 118 miles per hour, and he found the net 58 times in 1968-69.

After completing his fifth 50-goal season in 1971-72, Hull rocked the hockey world by signing the sport's first million-dollar contract with the Winnipeg Jets of the World Hockey Association. He brought the new league immediate respectability and scored 303 goals and 335 assists in the WHA before retiring in 1978. When the WHA was absorbed

in 1979-80, Hull returned to the NHL with Winnipeg. Traded in February 1980 when he had scored only 4 goals and 6 assists in 18 games, he retired for good after a nine-game star turn with Gordie Howe's Hartford Whalers.

BOBBY HULL
Pointe Anne, Ontario
January 3, 1939–
NHL Career: 1957-72, 1979-80
Chicago, Winnipeg, Hartford

	GP	G	A	P	PIM
RS	1063	610	560	1170	640
PO	119	62	67	129	102

Ross (3), Hart (2), Byng, Stanley Cup,
A-S Game (12), HOF 1983

BRETT HULL

RIGHT WING   ★ 1990, 1991, 1992

Son of "The Golden Jet," Brett Hull has surpassed most of his father's scoring feats while forging a career filled with controversy. "All you hear is that Brett is out of shape, that he can't skate, that he can't be coached, that he talks too much," said San Jose winger Tony Granato to *The Dallas Morning News*. Hull had just scored his 600th goal on New Year's Eve 1999. "Brett's answered all of his critics," continued Granato. "He plays hard, and he plays to win. Maybe this will show that he's one of the greatest of all time."

After a couple of brief call-ups to Calgary, Hull played his first full NHL season in 1987-88. He had 26 goals and 24 assists before the Flames traded him to St. Louis in March. He tallied 41 goals for the Blues in 1988-89, then exploded when Adam Oates became his center. For the next three campaigns, "The Golden Brett" made the First All-Star Team and led the NHL in goal scoring. He won the Lady Byng Trophy in 1989-90 with 72 goals, finishing fifth in overall scoring. With 86 goals and 131 points in 1990-91, Hull won both the Hart Trophy and the Pearson Award and finished runner-up for the Byng and Art Ross trophies. In 1991-92, he came fourth overall with 70 goals and 39 assists.

Hull averaged better than 40 goals over each of the next six seasons, but his dream of finishing his career in St. Louis ended when he was unable to secure a no-trade contract for 1998-99. He signed with the Dallas Stars and capped the season by scoring the Stanley Cup-clinching goal. "Somebody asks me every day whether it was a goal," Hull said that summer, referring to his foot being in Dominik Hasek's crease. "I say, 'Wait until I get my ring, and I'll show you.' "

BRETT HULL
Belleville, Ontario
August 9, 1964–
NHL Career: 1985-
Calgary, St. Louis, Dallas

	GP	G	A	P	PIM
RS	940	610	494	1104	371
PO	153	88	71	159	59

Hart, Byng, Pearson, Stanley Cup,
A-S Game (8)

DENNIS HULL

LEFT WING

★ 1973

Dennis Hull's slap shot rivaled that of his superstar brother Bobby. "I scored over 300 goals, but I think if I'd hit the net more, I might have had twice that," he once joked. "But I wasn't as wild as some stories make out." Hull joined the NHL and his brother with the Chicago Blackhawks in 1964-65. He spent much of the following season in the minors but tallied 25 goals for the Hawks in 1966-67.

Hull posted his first 30-goal campaign in 1968-69, his first of eight seasons on a line with center Pit Martin and right-winger Jim Pappin. All three were strong two-way players. "Coach Billy Reay used to tell the press that the only way to stop the Blackhawks was to stop Bobby Hull and Stan Mikita," recalled Hull, "but though we were the third line, we were the highest-scoring line on the team for

those years." Hull notched 40 goals in 1970-71, adding 13 playoff points. The Hawks lost the Stanley Cup finals, but Hull had more success internationally. He contributed 2 goals and 2 assists in four games to help Canada win the 1972 Summit Series, an exciting tune-up for his most productive NHL season. Getting more ice time after his brother Bobby moved to Winnipeg and the WHA, Hull scored 39 goals and 51 assists. He made the Second All-Star Team and led the Blackhawks back to the Cup finals. The unofficial runner-up for the Conn Smythe Trophy, Hull led the play-offs with 15 assists. Unfortunately, Mon-

treal beat the Hawks for the second time in three seasons.

After posting his lowest point totals in a decade, Hull was traded to Detroit in December 1977. He retired after one season with the Red Wings and went on to become a popular speaker on the hockey banquet and charity circuit.

DENNIS HULL
Pointe Anne, Ontario
November 19, 1944–
NHL Career: 1964-78
Chicago, Detroit

	GP	G	A	P	PIM
RS	959	303	351	654	261
PO	104	33	34	67	30
A-S Game (5)					

AL IAFRATE

DEFENSE

★ 1993

Al Iafrate holds the NHL Skills Competition record with a 105.2-mile-per-hour slap shot, which he set at the 1993 All-Star Game. He entered the contest three times during his career and

won it every time. The defenseman possessed more than a powerful shot, though. He showed strong skating and puck-handling skills even as a teenage rookie with the Toronto Maple Leafs. At six-foot-three and 235 pounds, Iafrate could also lay out a devastating hit and clear the front of his net. He tallied two 20-goal seasons for Toronto and, in 1989-90, hit a career-high with 42 assists. That season, Iafrate also started to play a meaner game. After averaging only 0.84 minutes in penalties per game previously, he averaged a hefty 2.25 minutes in each game over the remainder of his career. Leafs management grew tired of Iafrate's idiosyncratic behavior and his biker gear, however, and traded him to Washington in January 1991.

In his second full season with the Capitals, Iafrate made the Second All-Star Team, as much for his strong defensive play as for his 25 goals and 41 assists. The Caps dealt him to Boston for Joe Juneau in March 1994, but after Iafrate played only 12 games for the Bruins, his career

came to a halt. He underwent surgery on his back and both knees and spent two full seasons in recovery. The Bruins criticized his rehabilitation program, but Iafrate made a comeback with the San Jose Sharks in 1996-97. Although he was healthy for seasons of only 38 and 21 games, the Carolina Hurricanes signed Iafrate to an incentive-laden contract in July 1998. Iafrate didn't even make it to training camp, however. He retired in September 1998, generously forsaking his contract by not putting in a token appearance.

AL IAFRATE
Dearborn, Michigan
March 21, 1966–
NHL Career: 1984-94, 1996-98
Toronto, Washington, Boston, San Jose

	GP	G	A	P	PIM
RS	799	152	311	463	1301
PO	71	19	16	35	77
A-S Game (4)					

HARVEY JACKSON

LEFT WING

⭐ 1932, 1934, 1935, 1937   ⭐ 1933

Harvey Jackson brashly refused to help load the team's equipment. "You fresh young busher!" said Toronto Maple Leafs trainer Tim Daley, referring to a character in a Ring Lardner book, a swaggering young baseball player. From then on, the nickname stuck.

Jackson graduated from junior hockey with Charlie Conacher in 1929-30. When Joe Primeau was placed between them at center, the Toronto Maple Leafs' "Kid Line" was born. Jackson won the 1931-32 scoring championship with career-highs of 28 goals and 25 assists. In the opening game of the Stanley Cup finals, he scored a "natural" hat trick—an NHL playoff record—with 3 goals in one period. The Leafs went on to beat the New York Rangers in three straight games.

In 1953, writer Bill Roche remembered a "typical" Jackson goal, with the young left-winger "cutting in behind a defense to take a pass from Joe Primeau …Without seeming to slacken his speed, he nursed the puck from his skate out to his stick, and with a couple of strides, he rode across the goal-mouth on his left skate…Busher jerked his right leg up high to balance himself and ripped a backhand shot just inside the far corner of the goal cage." Jackson was runner-up to Bill Cook in the 1932-33 scoring race and set a record that still survives, with 4 goals in the third period of a 5–2 victory against the St. Louis Eagles on November 20, 1934.

"Busher was hockey's matinee idol," recalled *The Gazette*'s Dink Carroll. "Besides his good looks, he was a neat and careful dresser. He was the one the girls were always asking for autographs." Even when Conacher was injured and Primeau retired in 1936, Jackson continued to produce for Toronto. When he injured his shoulder in the 1938-39 Stanley Cup finals, however, it proved to be his last game as a Maple Leaf. Later that spring, Jackson was part of a package sent to the lowly New York Americans for Sweeney Schriner. After a lengthy hold-out through the fall of 1942, Jackson was sold to the Boston Bruins, where he played on defense for a time. He scored the first overtime shorthanded goal in playoff history to help Boston eliminate Montreal in the 1943 Stanley Cup semifinals. He retired a year later.

HARVEY
"BUSHER" JACKSON
Toronto, Ontario
January 19, 1911–June 25, 1966
NHL Career: 1929-44
Toronto, NY Americans, Boston

	GP	G	A	P	PIM
RS	633	241	234	475	437
PO	71	18	12	30	53

Ross, Stanley Cup, A-S Game (3),
HOF 1971

JAROMIR JAGR

RIGHT WING

⭐ 1995, 1996, 1998, 1999, 2000   ⭐ 1997

Highly touted Czechoslovakian star Jaromir Jagr made the 1991 All-Rookie Team and promptly helped Pittsburgh win two consecutive Stanley Cups. He cracked the top-10 scorers with 99 points in 1993-94. Although his mentor and teammate Mario Lemieux was sidelined the following season, Jagr won the Art Ross Trophy, the first European player to do so. He also made the First All-Star Team and has been an All-Star ever since.

Only Lemieux surpassed him in 1995-96 scoring, when Jagr notched a career-high 62 goals and 87 assists. Jagr tallied 95 points in only 63 games the following season and finished sixth, but when Lemieux retired, he handed Jagr the torch as the league's best player. "He's the key to their team," noted Byron Dafoe. "As Jagr goes, so go the Pittsburgh Penguins." Jagr won the 1998 scoring crown and earned further respect when he then asked for and received the team captaincy. He led the league with 83 assists in 1998-99 and finished 20 points ahead of the pack, collecting the Art Ross and Hart trophies and the Pearson Award.

"When Jaromir came into the league, he was all one-on-one, using his strength and his skills," Paul Kariya told *The Pittsburgh Post-Gazette*. "Now you see him fading, making nice saucer passes through the middle, hitting the late man. And then, when he needs to play one-on-one, he still does it."

Jagr shed his shoulder-length hair for 1999-2000, but little else changed. Despite missing 19 games to injury, he finished first in scoring with 42 goals and 54 assists. "We used to all have our theories about how we're going to work against Gretzky," said Toronto coach Pat Quinn. "Jagr is the same type of player. You stop one thing, and he finds something else to beat you with."

JAROMIR JAGR
Kladno, Czechoslovakia
February 15, 1972–
NHL Career: 1990-
Pittsburgh

	GP	G	A	P	PIM
RS	725	387	571	958	551
PO	124	63	72	135	103

Ross (4), Hart, Pearson (2), Stanley Cup (2),
A-S Game (6)

DEFENSE  ★ 1932, 1933 ★ 1931, 1934

Ivan "Ching" Johnson—also known as "The Chinaman"—made his NHL debut in 1926-27 with an NHL expansion club, the New York Rangers. "I told them I was 28, but I was almost two years older," Johnson later confessed. "I even demanded a three-year contract, because I wasn't sure I could last that long." He'd been a minor-league veteran since 1919, after returning from two years in the trenches during the First World War. The colorful blue-liner was soon a fan favorite, setting career-highs in 1927-28 with 10 goals and 146 penalty minutes. That season, Johnson helped the Rangers to their first Stanley Cup, resting only when he was in the sin bin.

A punishing hitter at five-foot-eleven and 210 pounds, Johnson was paired for years with 240-pound Taffy Abel. "They used to call them the 'Sultan of Suet' and the 'Mountain of Mutton,'" recalled Bun Cook. "They were huge men." Johnson was still at his peak when All-Star voting began in 1931, and he led his team in penalty time for 8 of his 11 seasons as a Blueshirt. But he also had a fun-loving nature. Remembered by George Gamester of *The Toronto Star* as "the balding giant with the pixie grin," Johnson was compared to baseball hero Babe Ruth in his ability "to establish communion with the fans."

Although he tallied no points and only two penalty minutes in his last Rangers campaign in 1936-37, Johnson played one more NHL season for the crosstown Americans before returning to his minor-league roots. He was an AHL All-Star in 1938-39, then changed roles and worked as a linesman. Old habits die hard, though. When a speedy skater crossed the blue line with the puck, Johnson stepped away from the boards and leveled him with a stiff body check. Asked to explain his action, Johnson replied with a shrug, "Instinct, I guess."

IVAN "CHING" JOHNSON
Winnipeg, Manitoba
December 7, 1898–June 17, 1979
NHL Career: 1926-38
NY Rangers, NY Americans

	GP	G	A	P	PIM
RS	436	38	48	86	808
PO	61	5	2	7	161

Stanley Cup (2), A-S Game, HOF 1958

TOM JOHNSON

DEFENSE

Tom Johnson played an inconspicuous but steady game. "It took everyone a long time to know that Johnson was as good as he was," said his coach Toe Blake. "Johnson's trouble," added Emile Francis, "was playing on the most colorful team in hockey history. But he was the real worker on the team." Although

he did occasional spot duty at center, Johnson left most of the offense to his defense partner Doug Harvey and a fleet of high-scoring forwards. Johnson's hard-hitting game contributed to Montreal's incredible success, but he managed to pick up a few enemies along the way.

"Johnson's on my black list," Stan Mikita once said, complaining about Johnson's stickwork. When Johnson entered the Hockey Hall of Fame, Eddie Shore threatened to renounce his membership for the same reason. After a couple of call-ups in previous seasons, Johnson tallied 128 penalty minutes as a rookie in 1950-51. But if he played dirty after that, he was subtle.

He won his first Stanley Cup ring in 1953 and made the 1956 Second All-Star Team as a member of the league's top defense. Johnson played a big part in Montreal's five consecutive Cups between 1956 and 1960, but his 1958-59 campaign was most noteworthy. He made the First All-Star Team, scoring a

personal-best 10 goals and 29 assists, and interrupted Harvey's string of Norris Trophy wins.

Johnson suffered a potentially career-ending eye injury in 1962-63, and the Habs left him unprotected in the intra-league draft. He played the next two seasons for Boston before a terrible gash from a skate resulted in a permanent limp and his retirement. Johnson became a Bruins executive until 1999 and also coached Boston's 1972 Cup-winners.

TOM JOHNSON				
Baldur, Manitoba				
February 18, 1928–				
NHL Career: 1947-48, 1949-65				
Montreal, Boston				
	GP	G	A	P	PIM
RS	978	51	213	264	960
PO	111	8	15	23	109
Norris, Stanley Cup (6), A-S Game (8), HOF 1970				

AURELE JOLIAT

LEFT WING

Sometimes known as hockey's "Little Giant," Aurele Joliat was playing in the Western Canada Hockey League for the Saskatoon Sheiks when the Montreal Canadiens made a daring trade in 1922. Dealing the legendary but aging 35-year-old Newsy Lalonde for the nearly unknown winger paid off in the 1923-24 season. With 4 goals and 4 assists in six playoff games, Joliat was a key contributor as the Canadiens won the Stanley Cup.

Joliat, easily identifiable on the ice because of the black tailor-made cap he always wore, attracted fans wherever he played. Whenever the Canadiens were in New York, Bill Corum of *The Evening Journal* wrote a column titled "Joliatana," full of stories about the easy-

going little winger. "The only way to make Joliat lose his temper," claimed L.S.B. Shapiro of Montreal's *Gazette*, "is to knock his cap off his head."

On the basis of his strong back-checking, combined with a tenth-place finish in the regular-season scoring race, Joliat was named to the inaugural 1931 First All-Star Team. "The 'Mighty Atom' seems to improve every year," noted Shapiro. "He has a genius for making plays, and as a stickhandler, he stands alone in hockey."

"Where does Joliat store all that energy?" asked Howie Morenz admiringly, looking at his linemate stretched out on the rubbing board after the Canadiens had won the 1931 Stanley Cup, their second in a row. According to *The Toronto Star*, "Aurele Joliat played an outstanding game. The 134-pound midget of professional hockey

turned in probably the best performance he has shown this season and made the play for [Johnny] Gagnon's [winning] goal. His stickhandling and trick stops and starts were beautiful to watch."

Joliat's real stature in the game was recognized when he was voted the Hart Trophy for the 1933-34 season. He retired with 270 career goals, matching the all-time record set by Morenz a year earlier.

AURELE JOLIAT				
Ottawa, Ontario				
August 29, 1901–June 2, 1986				
NHL Career: 1922-38				
Montreal				
	GP	G	A	P	PIM
RS	654	270	190	460	757
PO	54	14	19	33	89
Hart, Stanley Cup (3), A-S Game (2), HOF 1947				

MIKE KARAKAS

GOALTENDER

Mike Karakas was Chicago's original "Iron Mike." He won rookie-of-the-year honors in 1935-36, notching nine shutouts, and lost the Vezina Trophy by just two goals. He didn't miss a regular-season game for four consecutive campaigns. The Hawks finished the 1937-38 season with only 37 points, but Karakas demonstrated great agility and a strong glove hand in backstopping his team through two playoff rounds. Unfortunately, he broke his big toe in the last game of the semifinals. Chicago upset the heavily favored Toronto team in the first game of the finals but lost game two 5–1. "Iron Mike" returned to the lineup wearing a custom-made skate with a steel toe guard. After posting a 2–1 victory in game three, his teammates carried him off the ice in triumph. Karakas was just as strong in the fourth game, a 4–1 win, and Chicago took the Stanley Cup three games to one.

The cellar-dwelling Blackhawks demoted Karakas to Providence in December 1939. Although he played five games for Montreal later that season, Karakas didn't return to the NHL full-time until midway through 1943-44. Once again, he backed an underdog Chicago team to the Cup finals, but Montreal swept the series.

The Hawks won only 12 of 50 games in 1944-45, but Karakas led the league with four shutouts and made the Second All-Star Team. The next season, *The Chicago Tribune* quoted coach Johnny Gottselig as saying, "Mike is playing his best hockey and has every player, every manager and most fans singing his praises." Yet when Montreal bombed Chicago 26–7 in a 1946 playoff sweep, Karakas was through in the NHL. He finished out his career in Providence and was an inaugural inductee into the United States Hockey Hall of Fame in 1973.

MIKE KARAKAS
Aurora, Minnesota
December 12, 1911–deceased
NHL Career: 1935-40, 1943-46
Chicago, Montreal

	GP	M	GA	SO	AVE
RS	336	20616	1002	28	2.92
PO	23	1434	72	3	3.01

Calder, Stanley Cup

PAUL KARIYA

LEFT WING

Paul Kariya joined the Anaheim Mighty Ducks in 1994-95 and made the NHL All-Rookie Team. Since then, he's been on the First All-Star Team four out of five seasons. "I don't think there's ever been a more dedicated player in the game than Paul Kariya," wrote rookie *National Post* columnist Wayne Gretzky. "He has such great hockey sense. What sets Paul apart from the rest is that he can do everything at top speed, whereas most players lose half a step when they handle a puck or shoot. He uses his speed to get open, and he gets more good open shots on net than any player I've seen."

In 1995-96, Kariya tallied 50 goals and finished seventh in league scoring with 108 points. He also won the Lady Byng Trophy, as he did the following season, when he came third overall with 44 goals and 55 assists. Unfortunately, Kariya's string of successes nearly came to a permanent end in 1997-98. After sitting out several months because of a contract dispute, he averaged almost a point and a half per game before Chicago's Gary Suter flattened him with a cross-check to the face. Reeling from postconcussion syndrome, Kariya missed a much-anticipated trip to the Nagano Olympics.

Kariya didn't return to action until 1998-99. Although he threatened to defend himself more aggressively with his stick and elbows, he later admitted, "I wouldn't have come back if I felt I had to change my style." With 39 goals and 101 points, he came third in the NHL scoring race that year.

Often criticized in the past for his aloof nature, Kariya believes that he has changed under Teemu Selanne's influence. "He has been great for me," said Kariya, who spends time with linemate Selanne off the ice as well. "Every time I get too serious, he will loosen me up."

In 1999-2000, Kariya's 42 goals and 86 points were good for fourth spot in league scoring. "There is not a guy who works harder on this team than Paul," said Anaheim coach Craig Hartsburg. "There are a lot of good players in this league who, once they get to a certain level, stop doing certain things to improve. Paul's whole day comprises finding ways to get better."

PAUL KARIYA
Vancouver, British Columbia
October 16, 1974–
NHL Career: 1994-
Anaheim

	GP	G	A	P	PIM
RS	376	210	254	464	117
PO	14	8	9	17	4

Byng (2), A-S Game (4)

RED KELLY

In his third NHL season, Red Kelly helped Detroit win the 1949-50 Stanley Cup and made the Second All-Star Team. He graduated to the First Team in 1950-51 when he established a defenseman's record with 54 points and finished ninth in league scoring. That season, he also won the Lady Byng Trophy. Although he was an effective checker and a former welterweight boxing champion, Kelly used speed and savvy more than brawn, taking the Byng again in 1953, 1954 and 1961.

Kelly's play inspired the children of the late James Norris, who had owned the Red Wings, to establish the James Norris Memorial Trophy, to be given annually to the league's best defenseman. Fittingly, Kelly was the inaugural winner in 1954. He played a big part in Cup wins in 1952, 1954 and 1955. Kelly's slip to the Second All-Star Team in 1956 was merely the result of his versatility: He played so many games helping on forward that he received All-Star votes as a center.

In February 1960, Kelly innocently told a reporter that he'd played much of the 1958-59 season with a broken ankle. Detroit manager Jack Adams considered Kelly's admission embarrassing and immediately dealt him to New York. Kelly refused to report, agreeing instead to a trade to Toronto. Playing center full-time for the Maple Leafs, Kelly not only revitalized Frank Mahovlich's career in 1960-61 but notched a career-high 50 assists and 70 points. He successfully ran as a Member of Parliament in 1962 and commuted to Ottawa over four seasons. Meanwhile, Kelly helped the Leafs win four Stanley Cups. Only a handful of Montreal Canadiens has yet matched his total of eight Cup wins.

LEONARD "RED" KELLY
Simcoe, Ontario
July 9, 1927–
NHL Career: 1947-67
Detroit, Toronto

	GP	G	A	P	PIM
RS	1316	281	542	823	327
PO	164	33	59	92	51

Byng (4), Norris, Stanley Cup (8),
A-S Game (13), HOF 1969

TED KENNEDY

All-time scoring-leader Nels Stewart escorted Ted Kennedy to his first meeting with the Toronto Maple Leafs. "The big thing Nels taught me was, if you had that extra bit of a second, take a look before shooting," said Kennedy. "That's something I always remembered."

His coach, "Old Poison" Stewart, had been a plodding centerman, and Kennedy was much the same. "He could do everything but skate," said Howie Meeker. "If he could have skated like I could or like Vic Lynn could, there never would have been a greater center."

Kennedy led the Leafs to the Stanley Cup with a 1945 playoff-leading 7 goals. He was united with Meeker and Lynn in 1946-47, when they formed Toronto's "Second Kid Line." Meeker won the Calder Trophy, and Kennedy finished fifth in league scoring. Kennedy's 4-goal game against Boston in the semifinals was "a belated tribute to the persistence he has shown all season," wrote Jim Coleman of The Globe and Mail. Kennedy later notched the goal that eliminated the Bruins and went on to pot the Cup-clincher against Montreal.

He contributed 8 goals and 6 assists in nine 1948 playoff games, and Toronto retained the Cup. Kennedy was named team captain the following season, and the Leafs won an unprecedented third consecutive title. Although he finished well down in the pack of 1949-50 scorers, Kennedy made the Second All-Star Team. He tied for fourth with 61 points the following campaign and helped the Leafs win the 1951 Stanley Cup. He graciously greeted Princess Elizabeth the next season when she visited the defending champions.

Kennedy made the 1954 Second All-Star Team and won the Hart Trophy the following season—perhaps more an acknowledgment of his career than his seasons. He retired after the 1955 playoffs but returned for a final 30 games when the Leafs faltered in 1956-57.

THEODORE "TEEDER" KENNEDY
Humberstone, Ontario
December 12, 1925–
NHL Career: 1942-55, 1956-57
Toronto

	GP	G	A	P	PIM
RS	696	231	329	560	432
PO	78	29	31	60	32

Hart, Stanley Cup (5), A-S Game (6),
HOF 1966

CENTER

★2 1962, 1971

Initially, the Toronto Maple Leafs worried that five-foot-nine, 165-pound Dave Keon would prove too small for the NHL. But Keon won the 1961 Calder Trophy with 20 goals and 25 assists and quickly developed into a premier checking center. "Trying to move the puck past Keon," said defenseman Bill Gadsby, "was about as easy as shaking your shadow in the sunshine." Although always pressing intensely and an expert at taking his man out of the play, Keon was also an exceptionally clean player. He took an average 6.5 minutes in penalties per NHL season played, won the Lady Byng Trophy in 1962 and 1963 and was runner-up three times.

Keon made the Second All-Star Team in 1962, as much for his defensive skills as for his 61 points. "I could change my style of play and become a scorer," he maintained, "but that is not Toronto's type of game, nor is it mine." Yet Keon was also opportunistic on offense. He led his team in playoff goals when Toronto successfully defended the Stanley Cup in both 1963 and 1964. Whirling about checking, killing penalties and making plays, Keon won the 1967 Conn Smythe Trophy, sparking the Leafs to an upset Cup victory over Montreal.

Named team captain in 1969-70, Keon hit a career-high the following season with 38 goals and 38 assists. Tied for ninth in NHL scoring, he made the Second All-Star Team. In 1972-73, he became the leading scorer in Maple Leaf history. Owner Harold Ballard wouldn't pay Keon his due in 1975, yet when other teams inquired about a trade, the cantankerous Ballard overinflated his value. Keon felt forced to sign with the WHA, where he added 102 goals and 189 assists to his career totals over the next four seasons. He returned to the NHL in 1979-80 with the Hartford Whalers, with whom he concluded a stylish 22-season professional career three seasons later.

DAVE KEON
Noranda, Quebec
March 22, 1940–
NHL Career: 1960-75, 1979-82
Toronto, Hartford

	GP	G	A	P	PIM
RS	1296	396	590	986	117
PO	92	32	36	68	6

Calder, Byng (2), Smythe,
Stanley Cup (4), A-S Game (8), HOF 1986

GOALTENDER

★ 1940 ★2 1938

Dave Kerr was a careful man in a dangerous profession. When there was snow outside or when he was reading, he wore sunglasses to protect the eyesight he regarded as his stock-in-trade. Kerr joined the Montreal Maroons in 1930-31 but was back in the minors when the New York Americans borrowed him for a single game on March 8, 1932. He rejoined the Maroons for 25 games in 1932-33 but was sold to the New York Rangers in December 1934.

"Davey was able to shout at his defensemen," said Ranger teammate Frank Boucher, "giving them guidance without offending them and getting them to do the job he wanted done in front of him, talking continually when the puck was in our end." Defenseman Muzz Patrick had a slightly different recollection.

"Dave was an angle goalie," said Patrick in a 1957 conversation with Kerr and *New York Journal-American* writer Dave Anderson. "Geometrics. He had it all figured out. Remember, Dave, how you'd tell me in practice, 'Just keep your man outside a certain spot. No, not there. Back a couple of feet, Muzz. Now six inches to the left. That's it, keep him outside of there, and if he scores, it's my fault.' " Patrick also noted that Kerr wasn't averse to slashing his own defensemen on the ankle ("some of the worst cracks I ever got in hockey") if they were blocking his view.

Kerr backed the Rangers to within a whisker of beating Detroit for the 1937 Stanley Cup. The following season, he led the NHL with eight shutouts and made the Second All-Star Team. After the Rangers were eliminated from the playoffs, Chicago wanted to use Kerr as a replacement for Mike Karakas, but the Maple Leafs forbade the move. Kerr worked himself back to the 1940 finals.

In 1940, he made the First All-Star Team and took the Vezina Trophy with eight shutouts and a minute 1.54 goals-against average. After he notched three more playoff shutouts, the Rangers took the Stanley Cup. But Kerr soon grew weary of battling Rangers manager Lester Patrick at contract time. He retired after the 1940-41 season and went into the hotel business.

DAVE KERR
Toronto, Ontario
January 11, 1910–May 11, 1978
NHL Career: 1930-41
Montreal Maroons, NY Americans,
NY Rangers

	GP	M	GA	SO	AVE
RS	427	26639	954	51	2.15
PO	40	2616	76	8	1.74

Vezina, Stanley Cup

RIGHT WING

Tim Kerr matched his three-season total of 54 goals and added 39 assists for a team-leading 93 points in 1983-84. "I don't want to have one big year and that's it," said Kerr the following December. "I have to prove that I can keep it going." In 1984-85, he tallied another 54 goals and 98 points.

"Trying to keep him out of the crease," said Rangers defenseman Ron Greschner, "is like trying to tackle a Jaguar—not the animal, the car."

"You try to move him out, and it's like leaning against a tree," agreed Washington assistant coach Terry Murray. "A redwood tree."

Six-foot-three, 230-pound Kerr had more than size, however. "The big thing is that he gets [the puck] away so fast," explained teammate Pelle Lindbergh. "It's a wrist shot, and he takes it so fast, you don't have time to get set. But the really unbelievable thing is that he can get it away with one arm."

Kerr found the net 58 times in 1985-86, finishing third in NHL goal scoring. With another 58 goals in 1986-87, he tied for ninth in league scoring with 95 points and made the Second All-Star Team. But the physical punishment that Kerr absorbed eventually took its toll. He played only eight games the following season. His 48-goal, 40-assist comeback campaign of 1988-89 was rewarded with the Bill Masterton Trophy. A year later, Kerr's wife died shortly after giving birth to their third daughter. On the ice, his output slowed to a trickle. San Jose picked him in the 1991 expansion draft but immediately flipped him to the New York Rangers. Traded to Hartford for 1992-93, Kerr retired after failing to score in 22 games.

TIM KERR
Windsor, Ontario
January 5, 1960–
NHL Career: 1980-93
Philadelphia, NY Rangers, Hartford

	GP	G	A	P	PIM
RS	655	370	304	674	596
PO	81	40	31	71	58

Masterton, A-S Game (3)

OLAF KOLZIG

GOALTENDER

Born in South Africa to German parents, Olaf Kolzig spent most of his youth in Canada. "I'm not a popular choice," he laughed, hearing boos at the Air Canada Centre when he won the 2000 Vezina Trophy over local favorite Curtis Joseph. "[But] I was a big fan of the Leafs and [of] this man right here [Lanny McDonald, who presented the award] when I grew up in Toronto 15 years ago." Kolzig, who competes for Germany in international competition, made

his first two NHL appearances with the Washington Capitals in 1989-90. He got another short call-up in 1992-93 but allowed two goals in one period, maintaining his NHL 6.00 goals-against average.

The following season, Kolzig and his best friend, Byron Dafoe, shared the Harry Holmes Trophy—awarded to the goalies on the AHL team that allows the fewest goals. He gradually saw more game action with Washington but spent time in the minors until the 1996-97 campaign. Kolzig had the Capitals' starting job for 1997-98 and, by season's end, had whittled his NHL career average down to 2.59. He tied the league record with four shutouts in the 1998 playoffs and was the primary reason the Caps got to the Stanley Cup finals. Although Detroit took the Cup in a sweep, Kolzig had a strong .920 save percentage in the four games.

The Capitals failed to make the 1999 playoffs and got off to a poor start the

following autumn. Midseason, however, everything changed. Washington not only qualified for the postseason but won the Southeast Division with a 102-point campaign. "Olie the Goalie," also nicknamed "Godzilla" for his on-ice temperament, made the First All-Star Team. He led all goaltenders with 4,371 minutes played and 1,957 shots faced, won the Vezina and finished fourth in Hart Trophy voting.

OLAF KOLZIG
Johannesburg, South Africa
April 9, 1970–
NHL Career: 1989-90, 1992-
Washington

	GP	M	GA	SO	AVE
RS	272	15374	637	16	2.49
PO	33	2304	72	4	2.14

Vezina, A-S Game (2)

VLADIMIR KONSTANTINOV

DEFENSE

Vladimir Konstantinov spends most of his day in a wheelchair now. His dressing-room stall sits empty. Only six days after winning the 1997 Stanley Cup, Konstantinov was returning home from a Detroit Red Wings' celebration by chauffeured limousine when disaster struck. Unknown to Konstantinov, teammate Slava Fetisov and team masseur Sergei Mnatskanov, their limo driver had a checkered driving history. He crashed the vehicle into a tree. Fetisov sustained minor injuries, Mnatskanov will never walk again, and Konstantinov's massive brain injuries have left him still trying to regain basic speech and memory.

Konstantinov spent seven seasons with the Central Red Army team, joining the club at age 17 and eventually becoming team captain. He helped the Soviet Union win four World Championships, then joined the Red Wings for 1991-92. Known as "Vlad the Impaler" and "The Vladinator," Konstantinov averaged 140 penalty minutes a season over the next

six NHL campaigns. A punishing body checker with a mean edge, he was joined on the Red Wings' blue line by his old friend Fetisov late in the 1994-95 season. Detroit lost the Stanley Cup finals but came back even stronger in 1995-96. Konstantinov tallied a career-high 14 goals, but his main contribution was defensive. Supplying most of the grit to Detroit's dazzling "Russian Five"—a potent lineup that also included Fetisov, Sergei Fedorov, Igor Larionov and Slava Kozlov—Konstantinov made the Second All-Star Team.

He finished runner-up for the 1997 Norris Trophy but somehow failed to become an All-Star. Konstantinov's hard-hitting game played a huge part in Detroit's 1997 Cup win, however, and he also helped motivate the 1997-98 Wings. Moments after accepting the 1998 Cup, Detroit captain Steve Yzerman placed it in Konstantinov's arms. The Wings then steered his wheelchair around the ice in a touching victory lap.

VLADIMIR KONSTANTINOV
Murmansk, U.S.S.R.
March 19, 1967–
NHL Career: 1991-97
Detroit

	GP	G	A	P	PIM
RS	446	47	128	175	838
PO	82	5	14	19	107

Stanley Cup

RIGHT WING

 1985, 1987  1984, 1986, 1989

Jari Kurri arrived in Edmonton in the fall of 1980 as a relatively unknown Finnish player who hardly understood a word of English. By Christmas, the NHL rookie was Wayne Gretzky's right-hand man. They seemed to have a telepathic link. Kurri covered many of Gretzky's defensive responsibilities while becoming an All-Star sniper himself.

After two 32-goal campaigns, he cracked the top-10 scorers in 1982-83 with 45 goals and 59 assists. He also finished runner-up to Bobby Clarke in Frank Selke Trophy voting. "Jari's such a complete hockey player," Gretzky once said. "If we ever told him just to go out and check the other team's top players, he'd put them in his pocket."

With 52 goals and 61 assists in 1983-84, Kurri moved to seventh place in the league. He led the playoffs with 14 goals, and Edmonton won the Stanley Cup for the first of five times in seven seasons. In 1984-85, Kurri jumped to second behind Gretzky in NHL points, with 71 goals and 64 assists. Only six players have ever scored more goals in a season. He also won the Lady Byng Trophy, and his 19 playoff goals that spring remain a league record he shares with Reggie Leach.

Kurri led the NHL with 68 goals in 1985-86, finished second for the Byng and came fourth in total scoring. He finished second the following season with 54 goals and 108 points. Although Gretzky joined Los Angeles in 1988-89, Kurri still managed an eighth-place finish in scoring. He won his fifth Cup ring in 1990. Unable to come to contract terms, Kurri spent the next season playing in Italy before joining Gretzky and the Kings in 1991-92. His scoring tailed off gradually, and by the time he became a New York Ranger in March 1996, his defensive skills were his primary asset. He retired after seasons with Anaheim and Colorado as the ninth-leading goal scorer in NHL history.

JARI KURRI
Helsinki, Finland
May 18, 1960–
NHL Career: 1980-90, 1991-98
Edmonton, Los Angeles, NY Rangers,
Anaheim, Colorado

	GP	G	A	P	PIM
RS	1251	601	797	1398	545
PO	200	106	127	233	123

Byng, Stanley Cup (5), A-S Game (8)

ELMER LACH

 1945, 1948, 1952 ★2 1944, 1946

After breaking his arm in the season opener, Montreal's young "Green Line" center Elmer Lach missed the entire 1941-42 campaign. He was completely recovered for 1942-43, however, notching 40 assists. When coach Dick Irvin gave him wingers Rocket Richard and Toe Blake the following season, the "Punch Line" was born. Lach tallied 24 goals and 48 assists, good for fifth in scoring and a spot on the Second All-Star Team. In the playoffs, his 2 goals and 11 assists helped the Habs end their 13-season Stanley Cup drought—the team's longest ever.

Lach's record-breaking 54 assists were a key to Richard's 50-goal, 50-game 1944-45 campaign. Lach won the scoring title with 80 points, and Richard and Blake were right behind him. The "Punch Line" made the First All-Star Team as well. Although Richard garnered more headlines, Lach was awarded the Hart Trophy as the league's most valuable player. In 1945-46, he tallied a league-high 34 regular-season assists and was named to the Second All-Star Team. He then led all playoff scorers with 17 points to help the Canadiens reclaim the Cup.

Lach's career, threatened when the center suffered a fractured skull and cheekbone that resulted in months of hospital stay in 1946-47, was back on track the following season. He made the First All-Star Team and won his second scoring title, becoming the first player to have his name engraved on the new trophy presented to the NHL by Art Ross earlier that season. Lach passed Bill Cowley and became the all-time NHL points leader in 1951-52, when he fin-

ished third in scoring with 50 assists and 65 points and made the First All-Star Team. He had his final hurrah in 1952-53, when he scored the Cup-clinching overtime goal. "The 35-year-old center raised his stick high in the air," reported

The Gazette's Dink Carroll, "then did something between a cartwheel and a somersault to go rolling and sprawling along the ice." The next season, Richard passed him in points, but Lach retired as the NHL's all-time assists leader.

ELMER LACH
Nokomis, Saskatchewan
January 22, 1918–
NHL Career: 1940-54
Montreal

	GP	G	A	P	PIM
RS	664	215	408	623	478
PO	76	19	45	64	36

Ross (2), Hart, Stanley Cup (3),
A-S Game (3), HOF 1966

GUY LAFLEUR

RIGHT WING

Although he set a modern-era record with three hat tricks during his rookie season, Guy Lafleur struggled under even higher expectations. The heir apparent to Jean Beliveau didn't realize his full potential for three seasons, until he received a public chastising from Beliveau himself. Taking to heart the criticism about his lack of commitment, Lafleur erupted in the 1974-75 season with 53 goals and 66 assists.

"The Flower" won three consecutive Art Ross Trophies, beginning with his 125-point 1975-76 campaign. The following season, he hit his peak with 136 points, and in 1977-78, he tallied 60 goals and 132 points. "We had lots of good players on that team," said Serge Savard, commenting on Montreal's four straight Stanley Cups, "but Lafleur was the most important, because he had the ability to dominate a game." Lafleur led all 1977 playoff scorers, set up Jacques Lemaire for the Cup-winner and earned the Conn Smythe Trophy. He also tallied the overtime marker that eliminated the Boston Bruins in the 1979 semifinals.

Lafleur won the Pearson Award from 1976 to 1978 and the Hart Trophy in 1977 and 1978. He became the first NHL player to score both 50 goals and 100 points in six consecutive seasons while he reigned as the First All-Star Team right-winger. Unfortunately, five years later, he found himself on the bench. Lafleur's disappointment translated into retirement during the 1984-85 season, but it proved temporary. Already a Hall-of-Famer, Lafleur returned to play the 1988-89 campaign for the New York Rangers and tallied a respectable 18 goals and 27 assists. He then played two seasons for the Quebec Nordiques until finally retiring for good.

GUY LAFLEUR				
Thurso, Quebec				
September 20, 1951–				
NHL Career: 1971-85, 1988-91				
Montreal, NY Rangers, Quebec				
	GP	G	A	P	PIM
RS	1126	560	793	1353	399
PO	128	58	76	134	67
Ross (3), Hart (2), Pearson (3), Smythe, Stanley Cup (5), A-S Game (6), HOF 1988				

PAT LaFONTAINE

CENTER

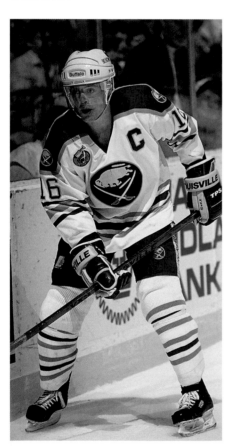

American Pat LaFontaine's 104 goals and 130 assists earned him the Canadian Major Junior Player of the Year award for 1983. Drafted third by the New York Islanders, LaFontaine competed for the United States in the 1984 Olympics before entering the NHL. In 1987-88, with 47 goals and 92 points, he began a four-season streak as the team's leading scorer. He tallied a personal-best 54 goals in 1989-90, finishing eighth in league scoring with 105 points. "When he's really skating, all you can see is the vapor trail," said coach Al Arbour. "Once he gets by you, the only way to get him is with a whaling gun." But the Islanders traded LaFontaine to Buffalo in late October 1991.

LaFontaine led the Sabres that season with 46 goals before posting a career year in 1992-93. Sharing team-captain responsibilities with winger Alexander Mogilny, who notched 76 goals, LaFontaine appeared destined to win the scoring championship. However, Mario Lemieux made a miraculous comeback after undergoing treatment for Hodgkin's disease, and in the end, LaFontaine came second to Lemieux with a 53-goal, 148-point season. He made the Second All-Star Team but sustained knee-ligament damage in the playoffs. The injury cost LaFontaine most of the following two seasons.

Although Mogilny had been traded, LaFontaine nevertheless posted a 40-goal, 51-assist campaign in 1995-96. Awarded the Bill Masterton Trophy, LaFontaine exhibited characteristic determination after suffering from postconcussion syndrome through most of 1996-97. Buffalo doubted his ability to come back for the 1997-98 season, however, and traded LaFontaine to the New York Rangers. He averaged almost a point per game before sustaining another head injury in March that forced his retirement.

PAT LaFONTAINE				
St. Louis, Missouri				
February 22, 1965–				
NHL Career: 1983-98				
NY Islanders, Buffalo, NY Rangers				
	GP	G	A	P	PIM
RS	865	468	545	1013	552
PO	69	26	36	62	36
Masterton, A-S Game (5)				

ROD LANGWAY

DEFENSE

⭐ 1983, 1984 ⭐2 1985

Rod Langway developed his game slowly on a talent-laden Montreal club and won a Stanley Cup ring in his 1978-79 NHL rookie campaign. In 1980-81, he notched a career-best 11 goals and 34 assists. Although Langway tallied 39 points the following season while helping his goaltenders win the Vezina Trophy, playoff failure prompted a roster shake-up.

Langway proved to be the key figure in a September 1982 multiplayer trade with Washington. "The Caps hadn't gotten to the playoffs for so long, but there was a good base of players," said general manager David Poile. "With Rod and the others, we were off to the races." The Capitals named Langway team captain, a position he held until he retired.

The six-foot-three 218-pounder dominated his own end. Washington, which had in fact never made the playoffs before, could not miss with Langway in the lineup. Langway made the First All-Star Team and won the Norris Trophy in both 1983 and 1984. "Nobody wanted to play against him when he was in his prime," said teammate Craig Laughlin.

"The statement that I heard most from opponents was that it was like playing against an octopus. He had the size, the reach and the strength."

Langway finished second in 1984 Hart Trophy voting, a distinction he considered more significant than winning the Norris. He made the Second All-Star Team in 1985 and played consistently solid hockey for the rest of his career. The Capitals officially retired his number-5 sweater in 1997.

ROD LANGWAY
Maag, Formosa
May 3, 1957–
NHL Career: 1978-93
Montreal, Washington

	GP	G	A	P	PIM
RS	994	51	278	329	849
PO	104	5	22	27	97

Norris (2), Stanley Cup, A-S Game (6)

JACQUES LAPERRIERE

DEFENSE

⭐1 1965, 1966 ⭐2 1964, 1970

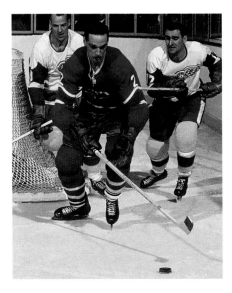

Both as a player and, later, as a coach, Jacques Laperriere helped to make the Montreal Canadiens winners. He first joined the Habs at the tail end of the 1962-63 season. A classic rearguard, Laperriere always preferred to dish the puck rather than shoot it. In 1963-64, his official rookie campaign, he tallied 2 goals and 28 assists. His physically assertive style led to a career-high 102 minutes in penalties, but Laperriere also showed a surprising ability to control the flow of a game. That season, he won the Calder Trophy and a Second All-Star Team berth.

He made the First All-Star Team the following two seasons, helping the Habs win the 1965 Stanley Cup and finishing runner-up to Pierre Pilote in Norris Trophy voting that year. In 1965-66, he beat Pilote for the Norris. Although Laperriere had his name engraved on the Cup that spring, a late-season knee injury had kept him out of the playoffs. His knee caused him intermittent problems thereafter and eventually contributed to an early retirement. He enjoyed Cup victories again in 1968 and 1969, but Montreal missed the 1970 playoffs. Laperriere's efforts hadn't been lacking, however: He tallied a career-high 31 assists and 37 points

and made the Second All-Star Team.

Laperriere enjoyed his most productive playoff in 1971, tallying 13 points in 20 games, and won the Cup again. Two years later, he picked up his sixth ring, but he retired midway through the 1973-74 season. After coaching the Montreal Junior Canadiens, Laperriere returned to the Habs in 1981 as an assistant coach. He moved to Boston in 1997 to assist Pat Burns, one of the six coaches he had served under in Montreal.

JACQUES LAPERRIERE
Rouyn, Quebec
November 22, 1941–
NHL Career: 1962-74
Montreal

	GP	G	A	P	PIM
RS	691	40	242	282	674
PO	88	9	22	31	101

Calder, Norris, Stanley Cup (6),
A-S Game (5), HOF 1987

GUY LAPOINTE

DEFENSE

★ 1973 ★2 1975, 1976, 1977

Guy Lapointe won six Stanley Cup rings with Montreal in the 1970s, but it had taken two auditions before he had latched on with the Canadiens. He appeared in six games over two seasons, becoming a regular in 1970-71. A hefty 205-pound six-footer, Lapointe developed into a smooth-skating two-way defenseman. He notched 44 points in his official rookie campaign, helping the Habs to the 1971 Cup. A 49-point season followed, and he continued to improve in 1972-73, when he scored 19 goals and 35 assists and tallied a career-high 117 penalty minutes. Nominated to the First All-Star Team, he finished runner-up to Bobby Orr in Norris Trophy voting.

Lapointe notched 53 points in 1973-74 and made the Second All-Star Team in the next three seasons. With Larry Robinson and Serge Savard, he became known as one of "The Big Three" on Montreal's blue line. Whether manning the point on the power play or clearing the front of his own net, Lapointe worked with effective precision. The Habs became the NHL's dominant team, winning four straight Cups, beginning with a thrashing of Philadelphia in the 1976 finals. In 1977-78, however, injuries began to take a toll on Lapointe's playing time. Only in 1978-79 did he compete in more than 50 games, and Montreal traded him to St. Louis for a second-round draft pick in March 1982.

Lapointe played for the Blues through the 1982-83 season, then signed with Boston as a free agent for 1983-84. Bruins management contemplated giving Lapointe his familiar number-5 jersey, long retired in Dit Clapper's honor. After a hue and cry from the fans, Lapointe selected number 27 instead. He joined Clapper in the Hall of Fame 10 years later.

GUY LAPOINTE
Montreal, Quebec
March 18, 1948–
NHL Career: 1968-84
Montreal, St. Louis, Boston

	GP	G	A	P	PIM
RS	884	171	451	622	893
PO	123	26	44	70	138

Stanley Cup (6), A-S Game (4), HOF 1993

REGGIE LEACH

RIGHT WING

★2 1976

Reggie Leach was picked third in the 1970 draft by the talent-rich Boston Bruins. Unable to crack the lineup, he was dealt to California in February 1972, where he posted two 20-goal seasons. But Philadelphia captain Bobby Clarke, who had been Leach's junior centerman from Flin Flon, knew the player well and successfully encouraged another trade.

The Flyers had just won the Stanley Cup, and armed with "The Riverton Rifle," they were even stronger in 1974-75. Leach scored 45 goals and 33 assists, adding 8 playoff goals to help defend the Cup. "He gets his shot off so quickly and with so little body movement," said teammate Bernie Parent. "He can change in midshot, aiming for a different area entirely, and still pinpoint it."

Leach modestly commented, "Clarke makes the bombs, and I drop them." He scored 61 goals in 1975-76—only Phil Esposito had ever hit that mark before—and made the Second All-Star Team.

In the 1976 postseason, Leach set new playoff records by scoring in nine consecutive playoff games (breaking Rocket Richard's mark) and tallying 19 goals in all. Although Montreal swept the Flyers in the finals, Leach won the

Conn Smythe Trophy. "It was a great honor," he recalled, "but I didn't really enjoy it at the time because of us getting knocked out in four games."

Leach scored 90 goals over the next three seasons and tallied 50 in 1979-80. "I worked hard on my shot," he said. "Sometimes, I could hit the crossbar 10 times in a row from 30 feet out. Shooting was probably the only thing I worked on, though." Alcoholism ultimately took its toll, and Leach was released in 1982. He played one last season with the Detroit Red Wings before retiring.

REGGIE LEACH
Riverton, Manitoba
April 23, 1950–
NHL Career: 1970-83
Boston, California, Philadelphia, Detroit

	GP	G	A	P	PIM
RS	934	381	285	666	387
PO	94	47	22	69	22

Smythe, Stanley Cup, A-S Game (2)

LEFT WING

★ 1995, 1998 ★2 1996, 1997, 1999

John LeClair developed into a major-leaguer with the Montreal Canadiens, but he became a superstar with Philadelphia. He scored 2 overtime goals for Montreal in the 1993 playoff finals to earn a Stanley Cup ring, but two 19-goal seasons were the best he did as a Hab. The Canadiens traded LeClair to the Flyers in February 1995. Within weeks, the deal looked like a steal for Philadelphia.

"The acquisition of John LeClair saved my career," said Eric Lindros, who soon had the hulking six-foot-three, 225-pound winger on his left side. Right-winger Mikael Renberg completed the original "Legion of Doom" line. LeClair erupted with 25 goals in only 37 games.

"I thought he was a checker. You just get lucky sometimes," admitted Flyers general manager Bob Clarke. LeClair made his first of five consecutive All-Star teams, finishing ninth in scoring with 54 points over the short 48-game schedule.

"The first thing John said [to me] when he came to town was, 'I'll take myself out of the play to allow you to come out in front of the net,'" recalled Lindros. "John will give himself up as a pick to make a play in the offensive zone. And his shot—he has a hammer. I think that's what surprised some of us. He can really bring it."

LeClair notched 51 goals in 1995-96, following up with seasons of 50 and 51. He led the Flyers with 43 goals in 1998-99, while posting the best seasonal plus/minus record for the second time, having done the same in 1996-97. "He has a feel for when to shoot, when to deke, when to pass," observed teammate Ron Hextall. LeClair found the net 40 times in 1999-2000, giving him the most goals over the past five NHL seasons.

JOHN LeCLAIR
St. Albans, Vermont
July 5, 1969–
NHL Career: 1990-
Montreal, Philadelphia

	GP	G	A	P	PIM
RS	665	309	306	615	331
PO	112	37	40	77	72

Stanley Cup, A-S Game (5)

BRIAN LEETCH

DEFENSE

Brian Leetch joined the New York Rangers right after competing in the 1988 Olympics. Officially still a rookie the following season, he set a record for first-year defensemen by notching 23 goals and won the 1989 Calder Trophy.

Leetch cracked his leg in March 1990 but set club rearguard scoring records in 1990-91 with 72 assists and 88 points and made the Second All-Star Team. The following season, he joined the First All-Star Team and was awarded the Norris Trophy. His 80 assists and 102 points led all blue-liners and put him ninth in 1991-92 league scoring.

"He's talented enough to elevate everybody's game, and there is not a part of his game with a hole," said Rangers goalie Mike Richter. "He wants to be great every night. When you have that level of talent and motivation, it's phenomenal." Leetch was an All-Star again in 1994, when he also won the Conn Smythe Trophy. With a playoff-leading 23 assists and 34 points and strong defensive play, he helped the Rangers win the Stanley Cup. Leetch made the Second All-Star Team again in 1996, notching 70 assists and 85 points. "He's a defensive version of [Wayne] Gretzky," said Richter appreciatively, although Leetch's offense has garnered him the most attention. In 1996-97, Leetch led all defensemen in scoring with his fourth 20-goal season and 78 points, made the First All-Star Team and won his second Norris.

He experienced a loss when captain Mark Messier signed with Vancouver for 1997-98. "We were able to read off each other," Leetch explained. "We were the offensive unit for the most part. 'Mess' was able to use his speed and size to create a gap between the other team's defense and forwards, and it was my job to jump into that gap. He looked for me a lot."

Leetch became captain, but both he and the team have struggled. When the Rangers re-signed Messier in July 2000, Leetch immediately returned the captaincy. "I'm glad these three years are over and he's back," he said, smiling.

BRIAN LEETCH
Corpus Christi, Texas
March 3, 1968–
NHL Career: 1987-
NY Rangers

	GP	G	A	P	PIM
RS	857	184	597	781	419
PO	82	28	61	89	30

Calder, Norris (2), Smythe, Stanley Cup, A-S Game (7)

CENTER ★ 1988, 1989, 1993, 1996, 1997 ★2 1986, 1987, 1992

Mario Lemieux rescued the Pittsburgh Penguins for the second time when he took an ownership stake in the team that pulled the franchise out of bankruptcy in 1999. As a player, Lemieux filled a once empty rink as he lifted the perennial also-ran Penguins to the championship. He scored with his first shot in his first game and finished his Calder Trophy-winning 1984-85 rookie campaign with 100 points. In his second season, Lemieux won the Pearson Award and finished just behind Wayne Gretzky in points. "Mario the Magnificent" notched his first 50-goal season in 1986-87 but again finished behind "The Great One" in scoring. When he notched 70 goals and 168 points the following season, he finally surpassed Gretzky, winning his first Hart Trophy the same year. Lemieux won his second Art Ross Trophy in 1988-89

with an 85-goal, 199-point campaign.

The back problems that contributed to Lemieux's early retirement initially flared up in 1989-90. The following season, he missed all but the final 26 games, then returned to the ice fully charged, winning the Conn Smythe Trophy with 16 goals and a playoff-leading 44 points and captaining the Penguins to the 1991 Stanley Cup. Lemieux led the league in both regular-season and playoff scoring in the 1991-92 campaign and picked up his second Cup ring and Smythe Trophy. Yet his 1992-93 heroics are perhaps his greatest accomplishment.

Diagnosed midseason with Hodgkin's disease, Lemieux underwent a month of radiation treatment. After recovering from the setback, he surged into the scoring lead once more, adding the Bill Masterton Trophy to his growing list of awards. Lemieux played only 22 games in 1993-94 and sat out the following

season before making another stirring comeback in 1995-96. With a league-leading 69 goals and 92 assists, Lemieux won the Ross and Hart trophies, the Pearson Award and First All-Star Team honors. He won his last scoring crown the following season, then decided to retire. Only 32 years old, Lemieux immediately entered the Hall of Fame.

MARIO LEMIEUX
Montreal, Quebec
October 5, 1965–
NHL Career: 1984-94, 1995-97
Pittsburgh

	GP	G	A	P	PIM
RS	745	613	881	1494	737
PO	89	70	85	155	83

Calder, Ross (6), Hart (3), Pearson (4), Masterton, Smythe (2), Stanley Cup (2), A-S Game (8), HOF 1997

GOALTENDER ★2 1981

After four seasons as a minor-league pro, Mario Lessard got a shutout in his first NHL start. He blanked the opposition three more times over the Kings' 1978-79 schedule and notched a career-low 3.10 goals-against average.

When Los Angeles faltered in 1979-80, though, management complained that Lessard was overweight. Officially 190 pounds and five-foot-nine (although some pegged him at five-foot-seven), Lessard deemed his heaviness irrelevant. His 1980-81 campaign, played at the same weight, fueled his argument.

Lessard garnered first-star honors in a memorable 3–0 loss in the Montreal Forum. The Kings were outshot 40–14. Lessard led the league with 35 wins at season's end, including a 4–3 victory in March when the Minnesota North Stars fired 69 shots at him, while their goalie faced only 19. "I'm the same as I always was," said Lessard. "I'm just getting more help. When I lose, they say I'm fat. When I win, no one notices my weight." The Kings tallied 99 points, and Lessard made the Second All-Star Team.

Los Angeles slipped well down in the pack with 63 points in 1981-82, while Lessard's average ballooned to 4.36. Although he backed his team to an open-

ing-round playoff victory over Edmonton, the following season was even worse. Averaging only 47 minutes a game, Lessard had but three wins in 19 appearances. Los Angeles sent him to the minors. "I believe I have the talent to play in the National Hockey League," said Lessard, "and I plan on being back there." He played just six more NHL games in 1983-84, however, posting a huge 5.86 average. Demoted once more, Lessard retired after failing to do much better in five AHL contests.

MARIO LESSARD
East Broughton, Quebec
June 25, 1954–
NHL Career: 1978-84
Los Angeles

	GP	M	GA	SO	AVE
RS	240	13529	843	9	3.74
PO	20	1136	83	0	4.38

A-S Game

TONY LESWICK

LEFT WING

Although he was only five-foot-six and 160 pounds, "Mighty Mouse" Tony Leswick quickly proved himself a tough two-way NHL player. He tallied 15 goals in his 1945-46 rookie season with the New York Rangers and led the team with 27 goals and 41 points as a sophomore. Leswick also constantly needled and provoked the best players into taking retaliatory penalties. He hit his career-high with 25 assists and 44 points in 1949-50, making the Second All-Star Team. "Tony Leswick was as busy and effective as a flea in a dog show," reported *The Toronto Daily Star*'s Red Burnett at midseason. "The fiery half-pint spent six minutes in stir, but this did not mar his effectiveness." The Rangers lost the Stanley Cup to Detroit, but the victorious Red Wings were obviously impressed with Leswick's hustle and hitting—in June 1951, they traded Gaye Stewart for him.

Detroit used Leswick primarily as a penalty killer and checker, and he helped the Wings win three Stanley Cups in the next four seasons. In the 1954 finals, he scored a huge goal in double overtime of the seventh game. "Leswick let this high shot go from the blue line," said Butch Bouchard, "only wanting to clear it from his own end to make a change of players." Doug Harvey tried to glove the puck, but it glanced off the tip of his finger into the net. "Even Leswick was surprised," noted Bouchard.

Leswick was traded to Chicago for the 1955-56 campaign, but Detroit bought him back in September 1956. He played in the minors for four seasons, returning to the NHL for only the last quarter of the 1957-58 season, before retiring.

TONY LESWICK
Humboldt, Saskatchewan
March 17, 1923–
NHL Career: 1945-56, 1957-58
NY Rangers, Detroit, Chicago

	GP	G	A	P	PIM
RS	740	165	159	324	900
PO	59	13	10	23	91

Stanley Cup (3), A-S Game (6)

DANNY LEWICKI

LEFT WING

Danny Lewicki made a sparkling debut with the Maple Leafs in 1950-51, scoring 16 goals and 18 assists. "He looks more to me like Aurele Joliat than anybody I've ever seen," said Conn Smythe of his five-foot-eight, 147-pound rookie. Lewicki helped Toronto win the Stanley Cup, but he might not have been physical enough for Smythe's Leafs. He had just 4 goals in 51 games in 1951-52 before being demoted to the AHL's Pittsburgh Hornets. Over the next two seasons, Lewicki made only 11 appearances with the Leafs before Toronto gave up on him entirely.

In July 1954, the Rangers purchased Lewicki's rights. Many scoffed, but not the *Boston Globe*'s Herb Ralby. "Lewicki will be a major-leaguer," he wrote prophetically. "He's contented now, free from pressure. [The] Rangers have picked up an All-Star."

Lewicki led the team with 29 goals and 53 points, finishing tenth in league scoring. "It's all part of the game," he said. "I just never could get on track at Toronto. That's when a change of scenery comes in handy." With only eight penalty minutes, he finished runner-up for the Lady Byng Trophy and made the Second All-Star Team.

Terry Sawchuk maintained that "Dangerous Dan" had one of the hardest shots in the league. "But more than that, few players get it off as quickly as he does—from either side," said Sawchuk, who had just given up a game-tying goal to Lewicki. "That shot wasn't screened. I just didn't move fast enough for it." Lewicki followed up with two 18-goal campaigns but scored only 11 times in 1957-58. Picked up in the intra-league draft, Lewicki played one season with the Chicago Blackhawks before finishing out his pro career tallying 82 goals and 201 points over four American Hockey League campaigns.

DANNY LEWICKI
Fort William, Ontario
March 12, 1931–
NHL Career: 1950-59
Toronto, NY Rangers, Chicago

	GP	G	A	P	PIM
RS	461	105	135	240	177
PO	28	0	4	4	8

Stanley Cup, A-S Game

NICKLAS LIDSTROM

DEFENSE

Through much of the 1998-99 season, Nicklas Lidstrom wrestled with a strong urge to return to Sweden. He wondered whether he should be raising his young children in their native land. Detroit persuaded him to stay, however, and Lidstrom completed another sensational NHL campaign. He had first joined the Red Wings in 1991-92, finishing runner-up for the Calder Trophy with an 11-goal, 49-assist campaign. Partnered with veterans Brad McCrimmon for his first two seasons and Paul Coffey for the next two, Lidstrom continued to improve. He used excellent positioning to defend his net and frequently worked the point on the power play. Detroit made it to the Stanley Cup finals in 1995 for the first time in 29 years, and Lidstrom chipped in 4 goals and made 12 assists in 18 playoff games. "He has great lateral movement, he can skate, and he has really good offensive sense," said coach Scotty Bowman. "He's one of the most underrated defensemen in the league."

Lidstrom tallied 50 assists and 67 points in 1995-96. He helped the Wings win the 1997 Stanley Cup and played an even bigger role in the team's successful title defense. Leading all defensemen in 1997-98 with 59 points, he added 19 playoff points and made the First All-Star Team for the first of three straight seasons, while also finishing runner-up for the Norris Trophy. Lidstrom has finished second for the Norris—to three different opponents— in each of his All-Star campaigns.

He was also runner-up for the 1999 Lady Byng Trophy, the first rearguard nominated for the award since Red Kelly won it in 1954. Lidstrom finished second in Byng voting for the second time with only 18 penalty minutes in 1999-2000, when he led all defensemen in scoring. He posted career-highs with 20 goals, 53 assists and 73 points and looks poised and ready for many future All-Star campaigns.

NICKLAS LIDSTROM
Västerås, Sweden
April 28, 1970–
NHL Career: 1991-
Detroit

	GP	G	A	P	PIM
RS	693	121	375	496	182
PO	123	26	57	83	36

Stanley Cup (2), A-S Game (4)

PELLE LINDBERGH

GOALTENDER ★ 1985

Pelle Lindbergh won Sweden's top goaltending awards several times and backstopped his country to a bronze medal in the 1980 Olympics. "He had great skills, his reflexes were so good, and he was so competitive," said Bobby Clarke. "But he had to learn how to come out and cut down the angles. As great as he was in Sweden, he didn't just step into the NHL. It took him a few years to make it." Tutored by his childhood idol Bernie Parent, Lindbergh spent two award-winning seasons with Philadelphia's AHL farm club.

He played his first eight NHL games in 1981-82, but another opportunity emerged when Philadelphia traded Pete Peeters. Lindbergh made the 1983 NHL All-Rookie Team and, for two seasons, divided the work with Bob Froese. Impressed by Lindbergh's work ethic and his strong start at the 1984-85 training camp, newly hired coach Mike Keenan rewarded him with a league-high 65 starts. Lindbergh responded magnificently, backstopping the Flyers to the Stanley Cup finals. He made the

First All-Star Team and picked up the Vezina Trophy. "The man I really want to thank is the guy standing next to me," said Lindbergh, nodding to the Vezina presenter Parent. "He taught me everything I know about how to play hockey in North America."

Lindbergh got off to another quick start in 1985-86, but tragedy struck on November 10. Driving while intoxicated, Lindbergh lost his life after crashing his Porsche into the wall of an elementary school. Doctors harvested his organs before the respirator was turned off. "It's appropriate," said Keenan. "He died making one more save." NHL fans paid final tribute by nominating Lindbergh posthumously to the February All-Star Game. The Philadelphia players annually award the Pelle Lindbergh Memorial Trophy to the team's most improved player.

PER-ERIK "PELLE" LINDBERGH
Stockholm, Sweden
May 24, 1959–November 10, 1985
NHL Career: 1981-85
Philadelphia

	GP	M	GA	SO	AVE
RS	157	9151	503	7	3.30
PO	23	1214	63	3	3.11

Vezina, A-S Game (2)

ERIC LINDROS

CENTER ★ 1995 ★2 1996

Eric Lindros has been involved in controversy for more than a decade. As "The Next One," Lindros held out for a trade when the Quebec Nordiques selected him in the 1991 NHL draft. On June 30, 1992, the Nordiques traded him to Philadelphia for Peter Forsberg, Steve Duchesne, Kerry Huffman, Mike Ricci, Ron Hextall, Chris Simon, two first-round draft picks and $15 million. Lindros scored 41 goals and 35 assists in 61 games and made the 1993 All-Rookie Team. The following season, he notched 97 points in 67 contests and, only 21 years old, was named team captain.

In 1994-95, Lindros tied for the league lead with 70 points. Although Jaromir Jagr earned the Art Ross Trophy because he had more goals, Lindros made the First All-Star Team and won

both the Hart Trophy and the Pearson Award. He made the Second All-Star Team in 1996, finishing sixth in scoring with a career-high 47 goals, 68 assists and 115 points.

Lindros led the 1997 playoffs with 26 points, but Detroit swept the Flyers in the Stanley Cup finals. When Philadelphia lost the opening round of the 1998 playoffs, general manager Bob Clarke went on record expressing his disappointment in Lindros. After responding with 40 goals and 53 points in 1998-99, however, Lindros suffered a collapsed lung and missed the postseason. Concussions, which ended his younger brother Brett's career in 1996, plagued him in 1999-2000. After playing four games exhibiting symptoms of a severe head injury, Lindros criticized the team medical staff for misdiagnosing

his health. Flyers management reacted angrily, stripping him of his captaincy during his convalescence, yet Lindros did all he could to return to the lineup. Unfortunately, in only his second game back, he sustained another concussion in the Eastern Conference finals. It is uncertain whether Lindros will ever play again.

ERIC LINDROS
London, Ontario
February 28, 1973–
NHL Career: 1992-
Philadelphia

	GP	G	A	P	PIM
RS	486	290	369	659	946
PO	50	24	33	57	118

Hart, Pearson, A-S Game (6)

TED LINDSAY

"Scarface" Lindsay took more than 400 stitches over his career, but it's "Terrible Ted" who is best remembered. He retired as the most penalized player in NHL history. "A little guy has to have plenty of self-confidence, maybe even seem cocky," the five-foot-eight Lindsay told writer Trent Frayne in 1957. "I had the idea that I should beat up every player I tangled with, and I'm still not convinced it wasn't a good idea." He made the First All-Star Team for 8 out of 10 consecutive seasons. In 1949-50, he took the scoring crown with 23 goals and a record-breaking 55 assists, followed by "Production Line" mates Sid Abel and Gordie Howe. Later that spring, he had his name engraved on the Stanley Cup.

Lindsay led all playoff scorers with 5 goals and 2 assists in Detroit's eight-game sweep to the 1951-52 Stanley Cup. He then took formal leadership of the club. "Lindsay is captain because Lindsay is a fighter and a leader," said Red Wings general manager Jack Adams. "He's a player who never quits himself and can stir his team up in the dressing room and on the ice." Lindsay captained the Wings to Stanley Cups in 1954 and 1955. When he secretly organized the first NHL Players' Association in 1957, however, Detroit dealt him to the lowly Chicago Blackhawks.

Lindsay led the NHL in penalty minutes in 1958-59, but he was a disheartened man. Although he helped reinvigorate the franchise, he retired a year before the Blackhawks won the 1961 Stanley Cup, so it came as something of a shock when he announced that he would play the 1964-65 season. "I want to end my career in the Detroit organization," he said. "I want to know that when I hang up [my] skates for keeps, it will be as a Red Wing." Detroit went on to lead the regular season for the first time since 1957 but lost the semifinals.

"Ted Lindsay is an amazing athlete, and those who criticized his comeback, including myself, were wrong," declared NHL president Clarence Campbell. "He's played well and displayed great leadership to the Red Wings." The 39-year-old Lindsay retired at the end of his comeback season and made a quick entrance into the Hockey Hall of Fame.

TED LINDSAY				
Renfrew, Ontario				
July 29, 1925–				
NHL Career: 1944-60, 1964-65				
Detroit, Chicago				
	GP	G	A	P	PIM
RS	1068	379	472	851	1808
PO	133	47	49	96	194
Ross, Stanley Cup (4), A-S Game (11), HOF 1966				

ED LITZENBERGER

The Montreal Canadiens received $15,000 from Chicago for Ed Litzenberger, but the deal was largely altruistic. The Habs were so strong that the Chicago, Boston and New York teams—all controlled by Detroit's Norris family—were starting to complain. Litzenberger had played only five games for Montreal over the 1952-53 and

1953-54 seasons and was still fighting for ice time before his December 1954 trade. After scoring 7 goals and 11 points in 29 games, Litzenberger caught fire with the Blackhawks. He added 16 goals and 24 assists to his official rookie-campaign total and won the Calder Trophy.

In 1955-56, Litzenberger tallied only 10 goals, but he exploded the following season. With 32 goals and an equal number of assists, he came fifth in league scoring and made the Second All-Star Team. He came sixth in 1957-58 scoring with another 32-goal campaign. "He can be as good and as great a player as he wants to be, and of course, he is one of the best in most everyone's book right now," said coach Rudy Pilous in November 1958. "All he has to do to stay at the top is to sell himself on the idea." Litzenberger responded to the vote of confidence with personal bests in 1958-59, finding the net 33 times and finishing fifth in the league with 77 points. Almost perennially in the league basement, the Hawks finally began to become more respectable too.

Litzenberger's production fell over the next two seasons, in part because of injuries. He helped Chicago win the 1961 Stanley Cup, however, before being traded to Detroit. Midway through the 1961-62 season, the Red Wings dealt him to Toronto. Although relegated to spot duty, Litzenberger contributed to three consecutive Toronto Cups before concluding his NHL career in the spring of 1964.

ED LITZENBERGER				
Neudorf, Saskatchewan				
July 15, 1932–				
NHL Career: 1952-64				
Montreal, Chicago, Detroit, Toronto				
	GP	G	A	P	PIM
RS	618	178	238	416	283
PO	40	5	13	18	34
Calder, Stanley Cup (4), A-S Game (6)				

The St. Louis Blues reclaimed Cincinnati Stinger Mike Liut, originally their 1976 draft pick, after the NHL bought out the WHA in 1979. Liut lifted the second-to-last-place Blues into the 1980 playoffs and a brighter future. "There's no doubt in my mind that Mike Liut is the biggest reason for our improvement," team-leading-scorer Bernie Federko told *The St. Louis Post-Dispatch*. "When you have a goalie like him behind you, you can play with so much more confidence."

"He's poised, cool and talented," said coach Red Berenson. "Liut not only looks like [Ken] Dryden, he plays like him too." The Blues tallied a franchise-record 107 points in 1980-81, and Liut made the First All-Star Team.

"Liut has won games for the Blues that they had no business winning," said Los Angeles general manager George Maguire. Liut finished runner-up to Wayne Gretzky for the Hart Trophy, but the NHL players voted him the Pearson Award. He was eager to prove that the players' high regard for him was deserved.

"You want their respect," explained Liut to *The Toronto Star*'s Wayne Parrish at the 1981 Canada Cup in September. "You want them to be impressed by you, to recognize your contribution." Unfortunately, the Soviet Union put eight pucks past Liut to win the championship game 8–1.

Many observers believed Liut's confidence sagged as a result of that loss, to the detriment of his play over the next few seasons. Liut himself disagreed, but he didn't post another superior campaign until 1986-87. The Blues had traded him to Hartford in February 1985, and he made the 1987 Second All-Star Team with a league-leading four shutouts for the Whalers. His average ballooned to 4.25 in 1988-89, however. Although Liut was reportedly earning the league's highest salary, the Whalers benched him for the last month of the schedule and the playoffs. He rebounded the following season and notched the league's lowest average, but Hartford traded him to Washington for journeyman winger Yvon Corriveau in March 1990. Liut retired after spending two seasons as a backup for Don Beaupre.

MIKE LIUT
Weston, Ontario
January 7, 1956–
NHL Career: 1979-92
St. Louis, Hartford, Washington

	GP	M	GA	SO	AVE
RS	663	38155	2219	25	3.49
PO	67	3814	215	2	3.38
Pearson, A-S Game					

HAKAN LOOB

RIGHT WING

The Calgary Flames used a tenth-round pick to select unheralded Swede Hakan Loob in the 1980 NHL draft. By the time he left for Canada two years later, Loob had become a Swedish scoring champion. The five-foot-nine right-winger made an impressive NHL debut with the Flames in 1983-84. Showing speed and grit, Loob scored 30 goals and 25 assists and made the NHL All-Rookie Team. He and fellow Swede Kent Nilsson led Calgary with 37 goals each in 1984-85. The following season, Loob's 31 goals were a team high. Calgary advanced to the Stanley Cup finals but lost to Montreal.

In 1986-87, after Calgary lost the division semifinals, Loob helped Sweden win the 1987 World Championship. He tied for ninth in NHL scoring the following campaign and made the First All-Star Team with a career-best 50 goals and 106 points. Loob tallied 58 assists in 1988-89, tied for second in team scoring with 85 points and added 8 goals and 9 assists in the playoffs, helping the Flames win the Stanley Cup. Sitting on top of the hockey world, he then made a surprising decision.

Loob returned to Sweden, where he won three more scoring titles before breaking the all-time points record in the Swedish Elite League in 1995. He helped Sweden win silver in the 1990 World Championship, gold in 1991 and gold again in the 1994 Olympic Games. "I could've added another four or five years on my NHL career," he told *The Calgary Sun*'s George Johnson in 1998, "but I made a family decision. If I had $3 million to $4 million more in my bank account, would I be any happier? Despite what you might think, the answer is no."

HAKAN LOOB
Karlstad, Sweden
July 3, 1960–
NHL Career: 1983-89
Calgary

	GP	G	A	P	PIM
RS	450	193	236	429	189
PO	73	26	28	54	16

Stanley Cup

HARRY LUMLEY

GOALTENDER

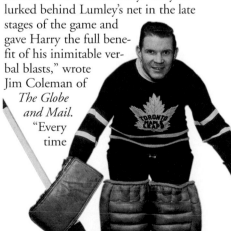

Harry Lumley still holds the record as the youngest NHL goalie. As a 17-year-old, he played two games for Detroit and a single game as a "loaner" with New York in 1943-44. In the sixth game of the 1945 Stanley Cup finals, Toronto owner/manager Conn Smythe thought that he could rattle Lumley. "Smythe lurked behind Lumley's net in the late stages of the game and gave Harry the full benefit of his inimitable verbal blasts," wrote Jim Coleman of *The Globe and Mail*. "Every time Lumley turned aside another Maple Leaf thrust, he would turn and smile sweetly upon Smythe." Lumley posted his second consecutive playoff shutout, but Toronto prevailed 2–1 in game seven.

He backed the Wings to the 1950 Stanley Cup, but rookie Terry Sawchuk then displaced him. Lumley spent two seasons in the league basement with Chicago before the Leafs gave up four good players for him. He posted an NHL-high 10 shutouts for Toronto in 1952-53 and made the First All-Star Team the following season. His 13 shutouts also helped him land the Vezina Trophy. Lumley retained his All-Star status in 1954-55, although he lost the Vezina to Sawchuk by a single goal.

"A big man, Lumley is a harsh competitor—not at all averse to swinging a fist at an opponent or tongue-lashing a careless teammate," wrote *Weekend Magazine*'s Andy O'Brien that season. "The amazing 'Lum' looms as a spectacular and apple-cheeked oddity who, at the age of 28, is in his twelfth NHL season without any signs of nerve wear from vicious rubber. Coach King Clancy bluntly refers to him as 'the key to [the] Leafs' success.'" Yet in May 1956, Lumley was traded back to Chicago. He played most of three seasons in the minors and finished out his NHL career with Boston.

HARRY LUMLEY
Owen Sound, Ontario
November 11, 1926–
NHL Career: 1943-56, 1958-60
Detroit, NY Rangers, Chicago, Toronto, Boston

	GP	M	GA	SO	AVE
RS	804	48104	2210	71	2.76
PO	76	4777	199	7	2.50

Vezina, Stanley Cup, A-S Game (3), HOF 1980

AL MacINNIS

DEFENSE

Al MacInnis won the "Hardest Shot" event in the annual NHL Skills Competition for the sixth time at the 2000 All-Star Game. "[Older players] are taking better care of themselves [now]," he laughed. "After a game, it used to be two dozen chicken wings and some beers." MacInnis broke into the NHL with Calgary, getting brief tryouts over two campaigns before making the team in 1983-84. Increasing his scoring every year, MacInnis led the Flames to the 1986 Stanley Cup finals with a league-high 15 assists. The following season, he notched the first of seven 20-goal campaigns, adding 57 assists and making the Second All-Star Team. An All-Star again in 1989, he led the postseason with 24 assists and 31 points, winning the Conn Smythe Trophy and a Cup ring.

In both of the following two seasons, MacInnis made the First All-Star Team and finished runner-up for the Norris Trophy. His 75-assist, 103-point campaign of 1990-91 placed him ninth in league scoring. MacInnis had 82 points and made the Second All-Star Team in 1993-94. The team, however, hadn't won a playoff round since winning the Cup in 1989. On July 4, 1994, Calgary traded MacInnis and a fourth-round draft pick to St. Louis for Phil Housley and two second-round picks.

En route to leading all defensemen with 62 points in 1998-99, MacInnis broke Red Wing Chris Osgood's hand and Blackhawk Jocelyn Thibault's finger with wicked slap shots. "He was in a class by himself," said coach Joel Quenneville. "He continually got us out of trou-

ble. His puck movement was incredible. His defensive play was terrific. I've seen him play well, but I never saw him play as well for as long as he did this year." MacInnis made the 1999 First All-Star Team and won the Norris Trophy, an award many felt was long overdue.

AL MacINNIS					
Inverness, Nova Scotia					
July 11, 1963–					
NHL Career: 1981-					
Calgary, St. Louis					
	GP	G	A	P	PIM
RS	1203	301	803	1104	1340
PO	149	37	105	142	233
Norris, Smythe, Stanley Cup,					
A-S Game (11)					

FLEMING MACKELL

CENTER

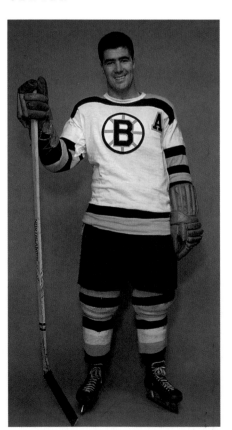

Fleming Mackell weighed 156 pounds and measured five-foot-seven (his father Jack, even smaller than his son, had seen spot duty with the Ottawa Senators in the early 1920s). Over his first three professional seasons, Mackell learned to give as good as he got, bouncing between the Toronto Maple Leafs and their AHL farm team in Pittsburgh. "You could never show that you didn't like the rough stuff, or they would run you out of the league," he said "[but] guys tell me that when I played the game, I was chippy too."

Mackell helped the Leafs win the Stanley Cup in 1949, assisting on two game-winning goals in the finals. He tallied 12 goals and 13 assists in 1950-51, his first full NHL campaign, and Toronto won the Cup again. Possessing great speed and a hard shot, Mackell played well both ways. The Leafs lost patience, however, when he'd scored only two goals halfway through the 1951-52 season, and Mackell was sent to Boston in exchange for defenseman Jim Morrison.

In 1952-53, the Bruins hooked Mackell up with wingers Ed Sandford

and Johnny Peirson, the team's reigning point leader. Mackell made the First All-Star Team after scoring a career-high 27 goals and tying for tenth in the league with 44 points. The following season, he tied Sandford for eighth place in NHL scoring. In 1957-58, he finished seventh overall, tallying a career-high 60 points. In the 1958 playoffs, Mackell scored a record 14 points in one playoff series. The Bruins then lost the finals to Montreal, but Mackell's 19 points were the postseason high. He concluded his NHL career in 1959-60 and spent the next eight seasons in and out of minor-league hockey.

FLEMING MACKELL					
Montreal, Quebec					
April 30, 1929–					
NHL Career: 1947-60					
Toronto, Boston					
	GP	G	A	P	PIM
RS	665	149	220	369	562
PO	80	22	41	63	75
Stanley Cup (2), A-S Game (4)					

LEFT WING 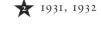 1961, 1963, 1973 — 1962, 1964, 1965, 1966, 1969, 1970

Frank Mahovlich's Hall of Fame career encompassed tremendous peaks and valleys. An imposing figure, with a long, powerful stride, "The Big M" looked lackadaisical when skating alongside a player who did not exhibit his elegance, but his speed, creative stickhandling and heavy shot made Mahovlich a perennial All-Star candidate. He edged out Bobby Hull in 1958 Calder Trophy voting and set a Toronto franchise record with 48 goals in 1960-61, finishing third in league scoring. Mahovlich helped the Leafs win four Stanley Cups in the 1960s and led the team in goals for five straight seasons. Yet his coach and general manager Punch Imlach always expected more, and many fans agreed.

Mahovlich was out of the lineup for a month in 1964-65 recovering from a nervous breakdown, and in 1967-68, he entered hospital again, suffering from depression. In March 1968, he was the key figure in a blockbuster trade with Detroit. Revitalized by the Red Wings, Mahovlich skated on an awesome line with Gordie Howe and Alex Delvecchio. For the first time since 1962-63, he cracked the NHL's top-10 scoring list—twice. Much to his disappointment, however, Detroit dealt him to Montreal midway through the 1970-71 season.

But playing for a strong club proved yet another tonic for Mahovlich. He helped the Habs win the 1971 Stanley Cup with a playoff-record 14 goals and a league-high 27 points. Sixth in 1971-72 scoring, he finished eighth the following season. Back on the First All-Star Team, he also picked up his sixth Cup ring after contributing 23 playoff points toward Montreal's 1973 victory. After one more NHL season, Mahovlich jumped at a lucrative offer from the Toronto Toros in 1974-75 and tallied 89 goals and 143 assists in the WHA before retiring after the 1977-78 season.

FRANK MAHOVLICH
Timmins, Ontario
January 10, 1938–
NHL Career: 1956-74
Toronto, Detroit, Montreal

	GP	G	A	P	PIM
RS	1181	533	570	1103	1056
PO	137	51	67	118	163

Calder, Stanley Cup (6), A-S Game (15), HOF 1981

SYLVIO MANTHA

DEFENSE 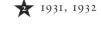 1931, 1932

Although he almost went down in history as the man who literally lost the Stanley Cup, Sylvio Mantha was indeed a winner. He joined the Montreal Canadiens for the 1923-24 season, and that year, the Habs won the Cup. While Mantha was ferrying a group of teammates to a celebration at owner Leo Dandurand's home, his Model T Ford stalled on a hill. Everyone piled out and pushed until the car started again, but they forgot to reload some precious cargo. Not until they arrived at the party did the players realize that the Stanley Cup was missing. Mantha raced back and found the trophy sitting on the curb, right where he had left it.

Mantha had never played defense until partway through his rookie season, but he apprenticed under Sprague Cleghorn and Billy Coutu and soon usurped the two rugged veterans as the team's premier rearguard. Appointed team captain in 1926, Mantha had a career-high 13 goals and 24 points in 1929-30. He led the Canadiens to a Stanley Cup victory that season and in 1930-31 and was a member of the inaugural 1931 Second All-Star Team. That year, as *The Toronto Star* noted, Mantha "is not only effective behind the blue line, but he is one of the shiftiest stickhandlers on the team, and his weaving rushes have saved more than one game."

The Canadiens made him player/coach for the 1935-36 season, but the team finished out of the playoffs for the first time in a decade, and Mantha's days in Montreal were over. He signed a free-agent contract with the Boston Bruins, briefly filling in for holdout Eddie Shore, but retired after playing only four games in 1936-37.

SYLVIO MANTHA
Montreal, Quebec
April 14, 1902–August 7, 1974
NHL Career: 1923-37
Montreal, Boston

	GP	G	A	P	PIM
RS	542	63	72	135	667
PO	46	5	4	9	66

Stanley Cup (3), HOF 1960

LEFT WING

Montreal Junior Canadiens sniper Don Marshall got a one-game tryout with the Habs in 1951-52. Although he failed to score, Marshall finished his junior career that spring with 78 points in 43 games. The following season, he notched 46 goals and 51 assists over the 60-game IHL schedule. In 1953-54, he tallied 94 points in 70 games for the AHL's Buffalo Bisons. Marshall joined the Canadiens early in the 1954-55 campaign, but with left-wingers Bert Olmstead and Dickie Moore already mainstays, the Habs didn't need another scorer.

Although slight at 160 pounds, Marshall had speed, savvy and a habit of staying out of the sin bin. During Montreal's five-season ownership of the Stanley Cup, coach Toe Blake used Marshall as his penalty-killing specialist. "When he'd put me on a steady line, I'd still continue to kill all the penalties too," explained Marshall to The Toronto Star's Jim Proudfoot in 1971. "And in those days, you killed the full two minutes. I'm not the robust type, and when I had

to take a regular turn on top of everything else, I'd just run out of gas. As long as I was a penalty killer, I did my best work in spot assignments."

Marshall joined the New York

Rangers in 1963-64, part of a multi-player trade. He hit career-highs with 26 goals and 54 points in 1965-66. The following season, he made the Second All-Star Team with 24 goals, 22 assists and only two minutes in penalties. "Playing with the Rangers allowed me to play the offensive-minded style of hockey I had wanted to play in Montreal," said Marshall. "I became a pretty good two-way player." The Buffalo Sabres drafted him for their inaugural 1970-71 campaign, and Marshall completed his career in Toronto the following season.

DON MARSHALL
Montreal, Quebec
March 23, 1932–
NHL Career: 1951-52, 1954-72
Montreal, NY Rangers, Buffalo, Toronto

	GP	G	A	P	PIM
RS	1176	265	324	589	127
PO	94	8	15	23	14

Stanley Cup (5), A-S Game (7)

LEFT WING

Gilbert Perreault had been a boarder in Rick Martin's family home before he graduated to the NHL. A year younger than his friend, Martin followed in Perreault's footsteps and joined the Buffalo Sabres in 1971-72. "I was told to go out and score goals and worry about the rest of my game later," said Martin in a 1986 reminiscence with Randy Schultz of The Hockey News. He notched 44 goals, breaking Perreault's record of 38 NHL rookie goals, and finished second to Ken Dryden in Calder Trophy voting.

Martin and Perreault were united with Rene Robert, and the trio became the high-scoring "French Connection" line. Some attributed Martin's success to his linemates, but not Toronto coach Red Kelly. "Martin would succeed with anyone," stated Kelly. "I am intrigued by the way his eyes dart

around and see everything. He is the rare player who anticipates not just one but two or three moves ahead and suddenly is in the right place at the right time." He worked on becoming a two-way player, but Martin scored 52 goals in 1973-74, including a hat trick in the final game. Sixth in league scoring with 86 points, he made his first of four consecutive All-Star Teams.

Martin found the net 52 times again the following season, despite playing only 68 games and having a cast on his thumb from December on. His career-high 95 points earned him a tenth-place spot on the NHL scoring chart. The Sabres lost the 1975 Stanley Cup finals to Philadelphia, the closest Martin came to an NHL championship. He scored 49 goals in 1975-76 and 36 in 1976-77, and he tallied 105 more over the next three seasons.

Unfortunately, he injured his knee badly in November 1980 and never fully recovered. The Sabres traded him to Los Angeles in March 1981. Martin played only one game for the Kings that season and three the next before retiring. Elected to the Buffalo Sabres Hall of Fame in 1989, Martin eventually saw the team retire his number-7 sweater.

RICK MARTIN
Verdun, Quebec
July 26, 1951–
NHL Career: 1971-82
Buffalo, Los Angeles

	GP	G	A	P	PIM
RS	685	384	317	701	477
PO	63	24	29	53	74

A-S Game (7)

BRAD McCRIMMON

DEFENSE 1988

Brad McCrimmon joined the Boston Bruins in 1979-80 and quickly proved himself a tough and dependable NHL rearguard. Although he did score 11 goals in 1980-81, McCrimmon concentrated on defense first. The Bruins didn't fully appreciate his contributions, but Philadelphia coveted him, and McCrimmon was swapped for Flyers goalie Pete Peeters in June 1982. "Brad's a good player, [but] we had a contract disagreement," admitted Boston general manager Harry Sinden. "I'm not sure we did everything right by him."

McCrimmon helped the Flyers to the 1985 Stanley Cup finals. He peaked offensively in 1985-86 with 13 goals and 43 assists, leading the NHL with a plus-83. Despite engaging in a contract squabble with general manager Bob Clarke through the following season, McCrimmon helped lead Philadelphia to the 1987 league finals. Clarke then traded him to Calgary for a couple of draft picks. "Brad has been an integral part of the success of this team," explained

Clarke, "but with the age of our defense, we thought it was in the best interest of our club to work in some youth."

McCrimmon's former teammates weren't happy, however. "You can't replace a guy like him," noted Brian Propp. "He was one of our main team leaders."

In his first season with the Flames, McCrimmon made the Second All-Star Team. In 1989, he finally won a Cup ring. Detroit acquired him in a June 1990 trade, and he patrolled the Red Wings' blue line until 1993. Injuries and age took their toll over the next three seasons with the Hartford Whalers, but McCrimmon's leadership abilities and character enticed an offer from Phoenix in July 1996. The 1996-97 campaign was his last, however, and McCrimmon retired after 18 NHL seasons.

BRAD McCRIMMON
Dodsland, Saskatchewan
March 29, 1959–
NHL Career: 1979-97
Boston, Philadelphia, Calgary, Detroit, Hartford, Phoenix

	GP	G	A	P	PIM
RS	1222	81	322	403	1416
PO	116	11	18	29	176

Stanley Cup, A-S Game

BUCKO McDONALD

DEFENSE 1942

Bucko McDonald was the premier shot-blocking defenseman of his day. Although he didn't skate or play hockey until the professional lacrosse league folded in 1931, McDonald joined the Detroit Red Wings in January 1935. He established a reputation for toughness, which was the source of his nickname "Bucko." In 1935-36, reporter Bill Roche credited him with an unofficial record for "having flattened more opponents in a single game than any player in major pro competition." Yet McDonald also played clean. He never drew a major penalty throughout his career.

According to Andy Lytle of *The Toronto Star*, "it was the shattering body blows handed out by the bold Bucko that cracked the Maroons like Junior putting the screw on a

Brazilian nut" and lifted Detroit into the 1936 Stanley Cup finals against Toronto. McDonald notched a shorthanded goal early in the first game, and the "broad-shouldered idol of the second balconies" scored twice in game two. Detroit won its first Cup and successfully defended it in 1936-37.

McDonald was dealt to Toronto partway through the 1938-39 season. Although he spent some of 1940-41 with the Providence Reds of the AHL, McDonald made the Second All-Star Team a year later. He notched a career-high 19 assists and 21 points, yet his season was somewhat tainted. When the Leafs fell behind Detroit three games to none in the 1942 Cup finals, McDonald was benched during Toronto's miraculous

comeback victory. He was sold to the New York Rangers in November 1943.

McDonald was proud of his final NHL season. Through the 40 games he played in 1944-45, he didn't draw a single penalty. In later years, McDonald coached boys' hockey in Parry Sound, Ontario. There, he moved a young prodigy from forward to defense, and Bobby Orr never forgot his mentor.

WILFRED "BUCKO" McDONALD
Fergus, Ontario
October 31, 1914–July 21, 1991
NHL Career: 1934-45
Detroit, Toronto, NY Rangers

	GP	G	A	P	PIM
RS	446	35	88	123	206
PO	50	6	1	7	24

Stanley Cup (3)

RIGHT WING

 1977, 1983

He retired a grizzled and respected veteran with a bushy mop of a mustache, but a clean-shaven Lanny McDonald had struggled through his first two NHL campaigns. "What Lanny needed was time," said his coach Red Kelly. Everything came together in 1975-76, when Kelly moved McDonald onto a line with Darryl Sittler and Errol Thompson and worked on improving his trademark wrist shot. The trainers sharpened his skates differently, helping him stay on his feet. McDonald scored 37 goals and 56 assists.

In 1976-77, McDonald tallied 46 goals and 44 helpers and made the Second All-Star Team. He cracked the NHL's top-10 scorers that season and the next, becoming a crowd favorite. With his broken wrist heavily taped, McDonald eliminated the New York Islanders from the 1978 playoffs in overtime. He potted 43 more goals in 1978-79, but as a result of a management/player power struggle, Toronto "exiled" him to sad-sack Colorado in December 1979.

McDonald captained the Rockies until early in the 1981-82 campaign, when Calgary traded for him. The following season, he became a co-captain of the Flames, a position he held until his retirement. In 1982-83, McDonald's first full season with Calgary, he notched a career-high 98 points, finished second behind Wayne Gretzky with 66 goals and made the Second All-Star Team.

A leader both on and off the ice, McDonald won the 1983 Bill Masterton Trophy and the 1988 King Clancy Memorial Trophy. Although he gradually moved from first-line sniper to fourth-line specialist, McDonald capped his career in fairy-tale fashion. He finished the 1988-89 season with an even 500 goals. He scored only once in the 1989 playoffs, but that goal was the Cup-clincher. McDonald's number 7 remains the sole sweater retired by Calgary.

LANNY McDONALD
Hanna, Alberta
February 16, 1953–
NHL Career: 1973-89
Toronto, Colorado, Calgary

	GP	G	A	P	PIM
RS	1111	500	506	1006	899
PO	117	44	40	84	120

Masterton, Clancy, Stanley Cup,
A-S Game (4), HOF 1992

RIGHT WING

 1970

John McKenzie bounced around the NHL and the minors for years before he found his niche. In January 1966, Boston sent tough-guy Reggie Fleming to the Rangers in exchange for the equally pugnacious McKenzie. "I've been on a lot of teams," said McKenzie at the time, "and I've never seen one with spirit like this." He had been nicknamed "Pieface" because of the acne he suffered in his younger days, but in Boston, his moniker was more affectionately shortened to "Pie." Only five-foot-nine, McKenzie became hugely popular with Bruins fans. "I just got things going and let the big boys take over," he said, but McKenzie helped define the "Big, Bad Bruins."

His work in the corners and his pesky forechecking were part of his role. "He ignites the rest of us," said Derek Sanderson. "John works so hard, he makes you feel guilty." But McKenzie also emerged as a goal scorer. He played on Boston's second line with Johnny Bucyk and center Fred Stanfield and earned a regular turn on the Bruins' power play as well. McKenzie's 29 goals and 41 assists in 1969-70 moved him into a tie for tenth spot in league scoring and onto the Second All-Star Team. He added 17 points in 14 playoff games as the Bruins took the Stanley Cup.

McKenzie scored a career-high 31 goals and 77 points in 1970-71, eighth in the league. He helped the Bruins reclaim the Stanley Cup in 1971-72 with 69 regular-season and 17 playoff points. But Boston wouldn't match a lucrative WHA offer, and McKenzie never skated in the NHL again. Instead, he played on a handful of different WHA teams, finishing his career with the New England Whalers in 1978-79. McKenzie's enduring popularity was recognized the following season, when the Whalers joined the NHL and officially retired his number-19 sweater.

JOHN McKENZIE
High River, Alberta
December 12, 1937–
NHL Career: 1958-61, 1963-72
Chicago, Detroit, NY Rangers, Boston

	GP	G	A	P	PIM
RS	691	206	268	474	917
PO	69	15	32	47	133

Stanley Cup (2), A-S Game (2)

GOALTENDER 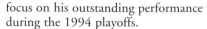 1992

Kirk McLean appeared in six games for New Jersey over two seasons before his trade to Vancouver in September 1987. By 1989-90, he led the league with 63 starts. Although his goals-against average swelled to 3.99 in 1990-91, McLean led the league with a career-high five shutouts the following season. He finished second in 1992 Vezina Trophy voting with a 2.74 average and made the Second All-Star Team. Still, his career-highlight reel will likely focus on his outstanding performance during the 1994 playoffs.

Both McLean and New York Ranger Mike Richter had racked up a playoff-record-tying four shutouts each before meeting in the Stanley Cup finals. "I like facing a lot of shots but, more important, quality shots to keep my focus," McLean once said. The Rangers gave him both. In the opening game, he stopped 52 of 54 shots for a 3–2 victory. New York then took the next three games. Although McLean and the Canucks made a valiant comeback effort, Richter and the Rangers squeaked out a 3–2 victory in the seventh game to win the Cup.

Vancouver foundered over the next few seasons, which prompted the hiring of coach Mike Keenan early in 1997-98. When McLean struggled, Keenan showed little faith in the longest-serving Canuck, and the goaltender was dealt to the Carolina Hurricanes in January 1998 along with Martin Gelinas for Sean Burke, Geoff Sanderson and Enrico Ciccone. McLean didn't display many flashes of his All-Star form until he made 46 saves in a 5–4 overtime victory over Phoenix on March 6, 1998. "Kirk McLean is not a backup goalie," said Carolina coach Paul Maurice. "He's been to a game seven and played tremendous. I'm happy for him." But less than three weeks later, the Hurricanes dealt McLean to Florida for Ray Sheppard, where he played through the 1998-99 season. In an ironic turn, McLean then signed with the New York Rangers as a free agent, backing up his old nemesis Richter.

KIRK McLEAN
Willowdale, Ontario
June 26, 1966–
NHL Career: 1985-
New Jersey, Vancouver, Carolina, Florida, NY Rangers

	GP	M	GA	SO	AVE
RS	589	33869	1833	22	3.25
PO	68	4189	198	6	2.84
A-S Game (2)					

GERRY McNEIL

GOALTENDER

When Bill Durnan suddenly retired in the middle of the 1950 playoffs, Gerry McNeil moved from backup to starter. McNeil backstopped the Habs to the 1951 and 1952 Stanley Cup finals, then made the 1953 Second All-Star Team with a league-leading 10 shutouts and a 2.12 goals-against average. Yet when Chicago took a 3–2 lead in the semifinals, McNeil found his nerves were shot.

Rookie Jacques Plante won the next two games and the Cup opener against Boston. "Gerry is a great goaltender," gloated Plante, "but he's so small that he has to move twice as fast as me to cover the same area."

The Canadiens lost the second game of the finals 4–1, however, and convinced McNeil to return. He shut out the Bruins 3–0. "I was amazed when I found myself running out on the ice to grab Gerry when the game was over," said coach Dick Irvin. "I haven't done that since 1931." After winning game four, McNeil cemented the Cup vic-

tory with a game-five overtime shutout.

He lost his job to Plante again late the following season, but Irvin called on McNeil when the Canadiens faced elimination in game five of the 1954 Cup finals.

McNeil blanked the Wings 1–0 in overtime and won the next game 4–1, and in game seven, regulation time ended with the score tied 1–1. Unfortunately, Doug Harvey inadvertently tipped a harmless shot over McNeil's shoulder. "I've hung up my skates," announced McNeil. "I have a nervous temperament, and I want to do something that involves less worry." He was true to his word for 1954-55, but McNeil played minor-league goal until 1961. He also suited up for Montreal for nine games in 1956-57 and picked up another Cup ring as backup.

GERRY McNEIL
Quebec City, Quebec
April 17, 1926–
NHL Career: 1947-48, 1949-54, 1956-57
Montreal

	GP	M	GA	SO	AVE
RS	276	16535	650	28	2.36
PO	35	2284	72	5	1.89
Stanley Cup (2), A-S Game (3)					

ROLLIE MELANSON

GOALTENDER

Rollie Melanson got his big break when the New York Islanders traded Chico Resch late in the 1980-81 season. Melanson had already made a strong impression during a five-game tryout and when he had started in another six games that season. But he played just 93 minutes of the 1981 playoffs, while First All-Star Team goalie Billy Smith backstopped the team to the second of four straight Stanley Cup victories.

Melanson played 36 games the following campaign but saw only 64 minutes of postseason action. His time with Smith paid dividends, though. "I've learned a lot from Smitty," said Melanson, who also protected his crease aggressively and took a fair share of penalties. "He's helped me

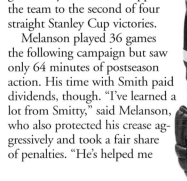

to control my emotions and to get ready for games." Alternating every other game with Smith for the early part of the 1982-83 season, "Rollie the Goalie" began to post numbers equal to those of his veteran partner. "You work yourself up to the playoffs and look forward to them. I'd like to be more a part of it," he admitted to Tim Moriarty of *The Hockey News* in November 1982. "Hopefully, I'll get my chance this season."

The Islander netminders shared the 1983 William M. Jennings Trophy, with Melanson notching a team-low and personal-best 2.66 goals-against average. He made the Second All-Star Team, but Smith won the Conn Smythe Trophy.

The Islanders lost the 1984 finals, and Melanson was traded to Min-

nesota for a first-round draft pick in November 1984. The North Stars dealt him to the New York Rangers in December 1985, who immediately flipped him to Los Angeles. Melanson finished the 1988-89 season in the minors, where he played through 1993-94, except for 20 minutes for New Jersey in 1990-91 and a nine-game 1991-92 stint with Montreal.

ROLAND MELANSON
Moncton, New Brunswick
June 28, 1960–
NHL Career: 1980-89, 1990-92
NY Islanders, Minnesota, Los Angeles, New Jersey, Montreal

	GP	M	GA	SO	AVE
RS	291	16452	995	6	3.63
PO	23	801	59	0	4.42
Jennings, Stanley Cup (3)					

MARK MESSIER

LEFT WING
CENTER

"I may not be able to *carry* a team to a Stanley Cup," said Mark Messier in January 2000, "but I think I can still *lead* a team to a Stanley Cup." While Messier continues to patrol the ice and the dressing room with authority, however, his strength and speed have started to wane. It's been almost two decades since he tallied 50 goals, a career-best, and made the 1982 First All-Star Team on left wing. He retained the honor the following season by finishing seventh in league scoring with 48 goals and 106 points. Messier's 101-point campaign of 1983-84 put him on the Second All-Star Team, and his playoff performance earned him the Conn Smythe Trophy. With 26 points in 19 games and a rugged, aggressive presence that wore down the opposition, he led the Edmonton Oilers to the franchise's first Cup.

Messier had spent some time at center the previous season, but he became a full-time pivot in 1984-85. He helped the Oilers defend the Cup and was a major contributor to Edmonton's titles in 1987 and 1988, finishing tied for third and fifth, respectively, in regular-season scoring. Wayne Gretzky's trade in August 1988 put a tighter spotlight on Messier, and he responded to the pressure. In 1989-90, he finished second in league scoring, making the First All-Star Team and winning both the Hart Trophy and the Pearson Award. He then captained the Oilers to a fifth Cup victory, with a 1990 playoff-leading 22 assists.

The Oilers traded "Moose" to the New York Rangers just before the 1991-92 campaign. He became an All-Star once more and won both the Hart and the Pearson again. His legend grew even greater in 1993-94. Messier almost single-handedly brought the Rangers back from the brink of elimination with a third-period hat trick in a 3–2 game-six win in the semifinals against New Jersey. He then led the Blueshirts to victory over a determined Vancouver squad, the Big Apple's first Cup since 1940. In July 1997, Messier signed with Vancouver, but after failing to make the playoffs three straight times, he returned to Manhattan for 2000-01 as a free agent. He ranks first among active players in points and fourth in NHL history.

MARK MESSIER
Edmonton, Alberta
January 18, 1961–
NHL Career: 1979-
Edmonton, NY Rangers, Vancouver

	GP	G	A	P	PIM
RS	1479	627	1087	1714	1717
PO	236	109	186	295	244

Hart (2), Pearson (2), Smythe,
Stanley Cup (6), A-S Game (14)

RICK MIDDLETON

RIGHT WING

Known variously as "Slick," "Silky" and "Nifty" for his dazzling moves, Rick Middleton developed into a premier two-way player. After a strong junior career and a rookie-of-the-year AHL season with Providence, Middleton made his NHL debut with the New York Rangers in 1974-75. He notched 20 goals before he broke his ankle midseason, losing a shot at the Calder Trophy. He also came under the influence of heavy-drinking playboy Derek Sanderson. "Most of the Rangers still hated Derek from his years with Boston," said Middleton. "I was one of the only guys who would socialize with him."

Although Middleton scored 50 points in 1975-76, his days in New York were numbered. "I was a wild kid with the Rangers," he confessed, "which is part of what led to my trade." The Rangers sent Middleton to Boston for veteran Ken Hodge. That deal ranks among the best Boston ever made. While coach Don

Cherry forced him to polish his defensive game, Middleton consistently increased his scoring totals. Centered at first by Jean Ratelle and later by Barry Pederson, he posted seasons of 42, 60, 86 and 92 points. Leading the Bruins in both goals and assists, Middleton broke into the top-10 scorers in 1980-81 with 103 points.

In 1981-82, his All-Star campaign, Middleton tallied 51 goals and 43 assists. With only 12 penalty minutes, he won the Lady Byng Trophy. The next two seasons, he was Byng runner-up, notching a team-leading 49 and 47 goals, respectively. He set the record of 19 points in a playoff series against Buffalo in 1983 but never won a Cup ring. Middleton co-captained the Bruins with Ray Bourque from 1985-86 until his retirement.

RICK MIDDLETON
Toronto, Ontario
December 4, 1953–
NHL Career: 1974-88
NY Rangers, Boston

	GP	G	A	P	PIM
RS	1005	448	540	988	157
PO	114	45	55	100	19

Byng, A-S Game (3)

STAN MIKITA

CENTER 1962, 1963, 1964, 1966, 1967, 1968 ⭐ 1965, 1970

Stan Mikita spent 22 seasons in a Blackhawks uniform. "You simply don't trade players of his caliber," Chicago general manager Tommy Ivan once said. "If we haven't won in the past, it's because other players have let us down, not Mikita. What more could the man possibly do?" By the time he retired, Mikita owned most of Chicago's scoring and longevity records. His first taste of glory came in the 1961 postseason. His playoff-high 6 goals helped the Hawks win the Stanley Cup. In 1961-62, his first of eight All-Star seasons in nine years, Mikita came fourth in league scoring. His 15 assists and 21 points were both playoff-highs, but Chicago lost the 1962 Cup finals to Toronto.

In 1962-63, Mikita moved up to third place in scoring, and the following season, he won his first Art Ross Trophy. "Mikita can make a defenseman look like a complete fool," said Rangers rearguard Jim Neilson. "You'll hit him, and when he's falling to the ice, he completes a pass to one of his wingers who's moved behind you." Mikita retained the scoring crown in 1964-65 with a record-breaking 59 assists. Yet despite his success, Mikita made a conscious effort to curb the hair-trigger temper that had earned him 154 penalty minutes that season.

"When you're a scorer, you've got to hand it back, or you'll be the target for every elbow, knee and stick in the league," noted Mikita. "I still retaliate, but not right away, when the referees and fans are watching." He reclaimed the Ross Trophy for 1966-67, breaking his own record with 62 assists, won the Hart Trophy and, most surprising, took only 12 minutes in penalties and the Lady Byng Trophy. Mikita swept all three awards again the following season. No other player has ever duplicated the feat once, let alone twice.

STAN MIKITA (NÉ STANISLAV GUOTH)
Sokolce, Czechoslovakia
May 20, 1940–
NHL Career: 1958-80
Chicago

	GP	G	A	P	PIM
RS	1394	541	926	1467	1270
PO	155	59	91	150	169

Ross (4), Hart (2), Byng (2), Stanley Cup, A-S Game (9), HOF 1983

MIKE MODANO

CENTER ⭐ 2000

Mike Modano has developed into a complete hockey player. Drafted first overall by the Minnesota North Stars in 1988, he appeared in two 1989 playoff games before finishing runner-up for the 1990 Calder Trophy with 29 goals and 46 assists. He led the team in scoring for the third straight season when the franchise transferred to Dallas in 1993-94, notching 50 goals.

Modano continued to produce offensively, but in 1996-97, he came fourth in Frank Selke Trophy voting. In 1998-99, he led his team in goals and assists while tying for the top Dallas plus/minus record. He then led the postseason with 18 helpers and happily hoisted the Stanley Cup.

Modano's sole All-Star campaign almost ended in the first game of the 1999-2000 season. Anaheim Mighty Ducks defenseman Ruslan Salei hit Modano from behind and slammed him into the boards. Modano left the ice on a stretcher and was diagnosed in hospital with a broken nose, a concussion and strained neck ligaments. After watching the tape that showed him inches away from being paralyzed, Modano considered retirement: "It's gone through my mind a lot, especially when you know you're a marked man every time you're on the ice." He reacted angrily when the NHL gave Salei only a 10-game suspension, yet the same week, Modano issued a remarkable statement.

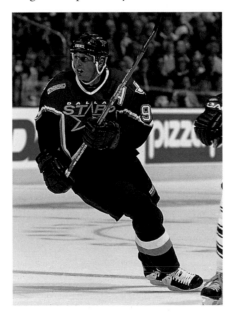

"I am calling on my teammates to set an example for all players," he wrote. "I am looking forward to getting back on the ice and playing as soon as possible but not to getting even. More important, I don't want anyone getting even on my behalf. As professional athletes, we must uphold respect for the game and for each other." Modano recovered and tallied 38 goals and 43 assists, finishing ninth in scoring and making the Second All-Star Team. Although Dallas lost the 2000 Cup finals to New Jersey, Modano came second behind linemate Brett Hull with 23 playoff points.

MIKE MODANO
Livonia, Michigan
June 7, 1970–
NHL Career: 1988-
Minnesota, Dallas

	GP	G	A	P	PIM
RS	787	349	467	816	544
PO	118	42	60	102	86

Stanley Cup, A-S Game (3)

ALEXANDER MOGILNY

RIGHT WING

 1993, 1996

"Hockey is an art," said Alexander Mogilny in 1999. "It's like chess. It's not just going out there and beating the crap out of everybody." But while Mogilny has crafted masterful seasons, he has been inconsistent. In 1986, the 17-year-old joined the Soviet Union's Central Red Army team. He won a gold medal at the 1988 Olympic Games. Mogilny and his linemates Pavel Bure and Sergei Fedorov tallied 38 points in seven games at the 1989 World Junior Championships in Sweden, winning gold. Mogilny's independent nature continually got him into hot water with his coaches and the army, though. He defected as the championship series concluded.

On October 5, 1989, Mogilny scored 20 seconds into his first game for the Buffalo Sabres. He tallied 15 rookie goals and 30 goals as a sophomore. Pat LaFontaine joined the club early in the 1991-92 campaign and helped Mogilny notch 39 goals and 84 points. Mogilny made the Second All-Star Team the following season with a franchise-record 76 goals and tied for seventh in league

scoring with 127 points. "He was great to play with," said LaFontaine. "Those were two years I'll always remember."

Mogilny dropped to 32 goals in 1993-94, then potted only 19 during the short 1994-95 campaign. The

Sabres traded him to Vancouver, where he seemed to rediscover his drive. Mogilny was named to the Second All-Star Team in 1996 with 55 goals and 52 assists, cracking the NHL's top-10 scoring list for the second time. He slumped again, though, scoring 31 goals the following season and 18 in an injury-shortened 1997-98 campaign. The Canucks dealt Mogilny to New Jersey at the 2000 trade deadline. Although he didn't provide the offensive spark the Devils had hoped for, Mogilny did help New Jersey win the Stanley Cup, drawing respect and attention from the opposition as a constant scoring threat.

ALEXANDER MOGILNY
Khabarovsk, U.S.S.R.
February 18, 1969–
NHL Career: 1989-
Buffalo, Vancouver, New Jersey

	GP	G	A	P	PIM
RS	705	353	405	758	351
PO	60	19	27	46	30

Stanley Cup, A-S Game (4)

DICKIE MOORE

LEFT WING

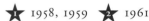 1958, 1959 1961

Hobbled by injuries throughout his NHL career, Dickie Moore relied on his aggressive and rambunctious style for success. He joined the Montreal Canadiens midway through the 1951-52 season and tallied 18 goals and 15 assists in 33 games. Moore missed most of the following season because of injuries but returned in time to help the Habs win the 1953 Stanley Cup. In the opening game of the 1953-54 campaign, he broke his collarbone and didn't play until February. The Habs fell to Detroit in the finals, but Moore led the postseason scoring with 13 points.

He separated his shoulder so many times during his 1954-55 campaign that he had a special protective harness designed. Yet he emerged as an offensive star while helping the Canadiens to

five consecutive Stanley Cup victories. Moore finished eighth in 1956-57 scoring. Despite playing the last three months of the following season with a cast on his broken wrist, Moore won the Art Ross Trophy with 84 points. Named to the First All-Star Team, he was again the league's top left-winger in 1958-59. He broke Gordie Howe's points record, setting personal bests with 41 goals and 55 assists and won his second Ross.

Although he played only 57 games of the 1960-61 season, Moore finished eighth in scoring and made the Second All-Star Team. His fierce loyalty to the Canadiens prompted him to retire in 1963 when he learned that he was being offered in trade discussions. But Toronto's Punch Imlach convinced him to make a one-season comeback with

the Leafs in 1964-65. He lost almost half of the season to injuries, notching only six points. Moore came out of retirement one last time, concluding his NHL career in 1967-68 with the St. Louis Blues and a trip to the Cup finals against Montreal.

RICHARD "DICKIE" MOORE
Montreal, Quebec
January 6, 1931–
NHL Career: 1951-63, 1964-65, 1967-68
Montreal, Toronto, St. Louis

	GP	G	A	P	PIM
RS	719	261	347	608	652
PO	135	46	64	110	122

Ross (2), Stanley Cup (6), A-S Game (6), HOF 1974

CENTER   ★ 1931, 1932 ★ 1933

Howie Morenz, "The Stratford Streak," always played in high gear. "I remember him coming down the ice right at me," recalled King Clancy. "My defense partner and I pulled together and thought we had him stopped. But he never broke stride. He slid the puck between us and leaped about three feet off the ice…picked up the puck and scored."

As a rookie, Morenz helped the Montreal Canadiens win the Stanley Cup in 1923-24, beginning his decade-long string among the top-10 scorers. He led the league in both goals and assists in 1927-28, earning the Hart Trophy. He also helped Montreal win two more Cups, after notching 40 goals in 1929-30 and winning the 1930-31 scoring race.

"He's the hardest player in the league to stop," said Eddie Shore. "Howie comes at you with such speed that it's almost impossible to block him with a body check. When he hits you, he usually comes off a lot better than the defenseman." Morenz made the first two First All-Star Teams while winning the 1931 and 1932 Hart Trophies. He slipped to tenth in 1932-33 scoring and onto the Second Team. After Morenz scored just 8 goals and 13 assists in 1933-34, the Habs shocked the hockey world and dealt him to Chicago.

The Blackhawks traded Morenz to the New York Rangers in January 1936. Montreal bought him back for 1936-37. Unfortunately, a rejuvenated Morenz broke his leg midseason. While he was recovering in hospital, a blood clot

stopped his heart. His body lay in state at center ice in the Montreal Forum while thousands filed past in respect. An inaugural member of the Hockey Hall of Fame, Morenz is officially remembered by the Canadiens through the retirement of his number-7 sweater.

HOWARTH MORENZ
Mitchell, Ontario
September 21, 1902–March 8, 1937
NHL Career: 1923-37
Montreal, Chicago, NY Rangers

	GP	G	A	P	PIM
RS	550	270	197	467	563
PO	47	21	11	32	68

Ross (2), Hart (3), Stanley Cup (3), A-S Game, HOF 1945

GUS MORTSON

DEFENSE   ★ 1950

Gus Mortson tallied the NHL's most penalty minutes in a season four times. He played an aggressive, hard-hitting game; most of his penalty time came from charging, boarding and fighting. The NHL even suspended him twice for deliberate attempts to injure. In 1946-47, the Toronto Maple Leafs paired Mortson with fellow rookie Jimmy Thomson. Known as the "Gold Dust Twins," they anchored the Toronto blue line for six seasons. Mortson quickly showed that he could skate and rush the puck well, but he also led the league with 133 penalty minutes. He picked up 22 more minutes in the playoffs while helping the Leafs win the 1947 Stanley Cup.

Mortson contributed 7 goals in 1947-48, his career-high, but he broke his leg in the first game of the Cup finals. Toronto still triumphed, and Mortson returned in 1948-49 for the Leafs' third of four titles in five seasons. He would later claim that he and Thomson averaged less than one goal against over their years together. Although official statistics weren't kept then, Mortson made the First All-Star Team in 1949-50, while

Thomson made the Second Team the two following seasons.

In September 1952, the Leafs sent Mortson and three teammates to Chicago in exchange for Harry Lumley. Mortson notched a career-high 18 assists and 23 points that season. He led the league with 132 penalty minutes the following campaign and with 147 minutes in 1956-57. He captained the Hawks from 1954-55 to 1956-57, but the team sat solidly in last place. He went to Detroit for future considerations in June 1958, but taken on waivers by the Rangers in January 1959, he finished the season in the minors and never played NHL hockey again.

ANGUS MORTSON
New Liskeard, Ontario
January 24, 1925–
NHL Career: 1946-59
Toronto, Chicago, Detroit

	GP	G	A	P	PIM
RS	797	46	152	198	1380
PO	54	5	8	13	68

Stanley Cup (4), A-S Game (8)

KEN MOSDELL

Che Brooklyn Americans snagged Montreal native Ken Mosdell for the 1941-42 campaign. The Canadiens picked up his rights when the Americans folded after one year, but Mosdell spent two years in the Royal Canadian Air Force. Although he scored 12 goals for Montreal in 1944-45, he spent much of 1945-46 in the minors. He did contribute 4 goals in nine playoff games, however, toward a 1946 Stanley Cup victory.

Lanky, at six-foot-one and 170 pounds, Mosdell played an aggressive checking game that resulted in several injury-plagued seasons. "Milt Schmidt was the hardest player for me to check," recalled Mosdell. "Every time I ran into him, I felt it more than he did. Dick Irvin [told] me not to worry about the puck, just to keep running into Milt, and I'd wind up black-and-blue." Mosdell's ability to play center or wing made his returns to the lineup easier. He helped the Habs win the 1953 Cup before posting his strongest offensive seasons. Centering journeyman Calum MacKay and dependable Floyd Curry in 1953-54, Mosdell notched 22 goals and 24 assists. He tied for tenth in league scoring and made the First All-Star Team. " 'Big Moe' is one of the most valuable hockey machines currently cruising the major ice lanes," wrote *Weekend Magazine*'s Andy O'Brien. "Except in the breakaway department, he is a plodder, seldom flashing—the type who works extra shifts when there's a penalty to kill or a hot scorer on the other team [who] needs cooling. He's the type who gives the pass for the big goal."

In 1954-55, Mosdell tallied a career-high 32 assists and 54 points, finishing in an eighth-place tie in league scoring and making the Second All-Star Team. The Habs won the Cup in 1956, then loaned Mosdell to the fragile Chicago franchise for 1956-57. He returned to the Canadiens for two games in 1957-58 before going to the minors. Substituting for an injured Jean Beliveau, Mosdell played his last three NHL games in the 1959 playoffs and won his fourth Stanley Cup ring.

KEN MOSDELL				
Montreal, Quebec				
July 13, 1922–				
NHL Career: 1941-42, 1944-59				
Brooklyn, Montreal, Chicago				
GP	G	A	P	PIM
RS 693	141	168	309	475
PO 80	16	13	29	48
Stanley Cup (4), A-S Game (5)				

BILL MOSIENKO

RIGHT WING

A few brief seconds of Bill Mosienko's career overshadow all his other accomplishments. On March 23, 1952, Chicago played the New York Rangers in the last game of the regular season. Early in the third period, Mosienko scored 3 goals in only 21 seconds. Although he missed an amazing opportunity to add a fourth goal just moments later, when he got back to the net and hit the post instead, his remarkable flurry remains an NHL record. The Hawks won that game 7–6, but as they did for most of Mosienko's career, they finished the season deep in the NHL basement.

Although Mosienko joined the Blackhawks late in the 1941-42 season, he had only 17 NHL games under his belt before his 1943-44 campaign, the most productive of his career. In it, he tallied 32 goals and 38 assists, eighth best in the league. In 1944-45, he tied for fifth with 54 points in a rare penalty-free season. He was awarded the Lady Byng Trophy and named to the Second All-Star Team.

Joining the Bentley brothers on the "Pony Line" in 1945-46, Mosienko galloped to his second All-Star berth. The quickest of the three, he came ninth in league scoring. The trio was the top-scoring NHL line of 1946-47, but in the 1947-48 preseason, disaster struck.

Mosienko broke his ankle in the All-Star Game, and the Blackhawks panicked. They traded Max Bentley for a handful of Toronto starters, and the "Pony Line" was no more.

Mosienko remained one of the NHL's fastest skaters and won a race against the speediest representatives from the other five teams in 1950. In 1951-52, he cracked the top-10 scorers for the last time. When he retired three seasons later, it was as the top scorer in Chicago Blackhawk history.

BILL MOSIENKO
Winnipeg, Manitoba
November 2, 1921–July 9, 1994
NHL Career: 1941-55
Chicago

	GP	G	A	P	PIM
RS	711	258	282	540	121
PO	22	10	4	14	15

Byng, A-S Game (5), HOF 1965

JOHNNY MOWERS

GOALTENDER

It's an occupational hazard: An NHL goalie's turn in the spotlight can be lamentably short, despite his best efforts. Johnny Mowers had a marvelous rookie season with the Detroit Red Wings in 1940-41. He posted a fine 2.01 goals-against average and lost the Vezina Trophy by only a single percentage point to Toronto's Turk Broda. Mowers was also runner-up to Calder Trophy-winner Johnny Quilty of Montreal. The Wings made it to the Stanley Cup finals that year and again in 1942 but lost both times. The rewards finally came in the 1942-43 season.

After leading the NHL with six shutouts, Mowers made the First All-Star Team. He also earned the Vezina with

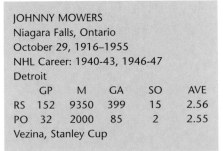

a 2.47 average and the regular-season-champion Wings didn't disappoint their fans in the playoffs. Detroit won the first two games of the Stanley Cup finals against Boston, and Mowers notched a shutout in game three. He was just as brilliantly stingy in the clinching game, blanking the Bruins once more. "One shot he stopped with his head in a tumultuous third period," reported John Walter to *Detroit News* readers. "Blood poured from a gash under his eye. Mowers refused to delay the game to be sewn up. He tended goal the last five minutes with blood streaming down his face." Before the 1943-44 sea-

son began and at his hockey-career peak, Mowers enlisted in the Royal Canadian Air Force. By the time Mowers returned from military service for the 1946-47 NHL campaign, however, Harry Lumley was firmly entrenched in the Detroit net. Mowers didn't count a victory in his seven appearances that season. In a sad conclusion to his brief but respectable NHL career, he let in five goals in two playoff periods before retiring.

JOHNNY MOWERS
Niagara Falls, Ontario
October 29, 1916–1955
NHL Career: 1940-43, 1946-47
Detroit

	GP	M	GA	SO	AVE
RS	152	9350	399	15	2.56
PO	32	2000	85	2	2.55

Vezina, Stanley Cup

JOE MULLEN

Joe Mullen played roller-skate hockey on the streets of New York City's Hell's Kitchen to develop his NHL skills. He suited up for St. Louis once during the 1980 playoffs but didn't become a regular until midway through the 1981-82 campaign. Mullen tied Bernie Federko for the Blues' goal-scoring lead with 41 goals in 1983-84 and led the Blues with 40 the following season. Yet St. Louis traded him to Calgary in February 1986. "I didn't want to leave St. Louis," an upset Mullen told Steve Simmons of *The Hockey News*, "but I have to look at this as another challenge."

Mullen finished the season with 44 goals, then helped the Flames to the Stanley Cup finals. Although Montreal prevailed, Mullen led the playoffs with 12 tallies. He notched 47 goals in 1986-87 and won the Lady Byng Trophy. "It's an award that recognizes ability as well as sportsmanship—the way I think the game should be played," he said. Mullen followed up with a 40-goal 1987-88 campaign, then peaked with a First All-Star Team performance in 1988-89. His strong two-way play earned him the

NHL's plus/minus award. He scored 51 goals and finished seventh in league scoring with 110 points. Awarded his second Byng, Mullen added a playoff-high 16 goals to help Calgary win the Cup.

The Flames traded Mullen to Pittsburgh for 1990-91, and he promptly won two more Cup rings. The first American-born player to hit 1,000 career points, he spent an injury-riddled 1995-96 campaign with Boston before returning to the Penguins. Mullen notched career-goal 500 on March 14, 1997, and retired that spring. He entered the Hockey Hall of Fame in 2000.

JOE MULLEN
New York, New York
February 26, 1957–
NHL Career: 1979-80, 1981-97
St. Louis, Calgary, Pittsburgh, Boston

	GP	G	A	P	PIM
RS	1062	502	561	1063	241
PO	143	60	46	106	42

Byng (2), Stanley Cup (3), A-S Game (3),
HOF 2000

LARRY MURPHY

Larry Murphy trails only Paul Coffey and Ray Bourque in career points by a defenseman. He made an auspicious debut with Los Angeles in 1980-81, when he set rookie-defenseman records (still standing) of 60 assists and 76 points. Since then, however, Murphy hasn't drawn the attention he deserves. "I can't shoot a puck 100 miles per hour, and I'm not going to run the guy through the boards or skate through the whole team," he told Chuck Carlton of *The Hockey News*. But Murphy has been happy with his low-key career.

Traded to Washington early in October 1983, Murphy made the Second All-Star Team in 1987 with a career-high 23 goals and 81 points. Dealt to Minnesota on March 7, 1989, Murphy went to Pittsburgh in December 1990,

where he contributed 23 playoff points toward the Penguins' 1990 Stanley Cup win and notched 16 postseason points in 1991 to aid the team's successful title defense. He joined the Second All-Star Team in 1993 with 63 assists and 85 points, both personal bests. He posted his last All-Star campaign in 1995, picking up 38 points in the lockout-truncated season.

Murphy joined the Toronto Maple Leafs in 1995-96 but, scapegoated for the team's lackluster play, was more or less donated to Detroit at the 1997 trade deadline. "[Coach] Scotty Bowman knew what I could do," he said. "The Red Wings based their assessment of me on what they saw, not what they read." Murphy wasn't on the ice for a single Flyers' goal as Detroit swept

Philadelphia in the 1997 Cup finals. Only his partner Nicklas Lidstrom scored more points among defensemen in the 1998 playoffs, when the Wings repeated as Cup champions. Murphy is now second to Gordie Howe on the NHL's all-time games-played list.

LARRY MURPHY
Scarborough, Ontario
March 8, 1961–
NHL Career: 1980-
Los Angeles, Washington, Minnesota, Pittsburgh, Toronto, Detroit

	GP	G	A	P	PIM
RS	1558	285	910	1195	1072
PO	209	37	114	151	201

Stanley Cup (4), A-S Game (3)

MATS NASLUND

⭐2 1986

In the fall of 1982, Mats Naslund became the first European to join the Montreal Canadiens. Only five-foot seven and 160 pounds, he darted in and out of danger and quickly earned a regular shift and power-play time. "He has proven to everybody that he has heart," said Pierre Mondou. "He reminds me of Yvan Cournoyer at his best."

By season's end, Naslund had broken Guy Lafleur's franchise record for rookies, with 71 points. "The league is not as rough as I thought it might be," said Naslund confidently.

As a sophomore, Naslund tallied 29 goals, then led the Habs in 1984-85 with 42 goals and 79 points. When Mondou retired and Mario Tremblay was injured, Naslund began the following season without his regular linemates. "I took it as a challenge, and so far, it has been working out," he told Glenn Cole of *The Hockey News* in November 1985. "The puck has been going in for me. There is always going to be a tough time of the year when you get cool as a fridge. I just hope I can keep going all year." He did, finishing eighth in league scoring with 43 goals

and 67 assists. Elected to the Second All-Star Team, Naslund also distinguished himself in the playoffs. With 8 goals and 11 assists in 20 games, he helped the Habs to a surprising Stanley Cup victory.

Naslund hit the 80-point mark in each of the next three seasons, leading Montreal scorers twice. He also won the 1988 Lady Byng Trophy, but after notching only 41 points in 1989-90, he returned to Europe. Naslund helped Sweden win the 1991 World Championship and the 1994 Olympic Games. He joined the Boston Bruins in 1994-95 but retired after scoring 22 points in 34 games of the lockout-shortened season.

MATS NASLUND					
Timrå, Sweden					
October 31, 1959–					
NHL Career: 1982-90, 1994-95					
Montreal, Boston					
	GP	G	A	P	PIM
RS	651	251	383	634	111
PO	102	35	57	92	33
Byng, Stanley Cup, A-S Game (3)					

CAM NEELY

 1988, 1990, 1991, 1994

Major injuries punctuated Cam Neely's memorable but too short hockey career. "Power forward" entered hockey's lexicon, and six-foot-one, 218-pound Neely personified the term. Vancouver's 1983 first-round draft pick, Neely posted three mediocre campaigns before the Canucks gave up on him. Boston got a 21-year-old winger in the "Big, Bad Bruins" mold. "The Bruins seemed to be perfect for my style," said Neely. "I was a player who loved to take the body and make a check. I also loved to score."

Neely led the Bruins in goals seven times, beginning with his 36-goal 1986-87 campaign. With 42 goals and 27 assists in 1987-88, he made the Second All-Star Team for the first of four times

in seven seasons. He then helped Boston defeat Montreal in the quarter-finals, the first Boston playoff victory over the Habs since 1943. The Bruins bowed to Edmonton in the Stanley Cup finals, however, as they did in 1990. Neely had scored a career-high 55 goals and 92 points over the 1989-90 season, adding 28 more points in the postseason. He tallied 51 goals and 91 points in 1990-91, but a low hit to the thigh from Pittsburgh's Ulf Samuelsson in the 1991 playoffs almost ended Neely's career.

Over the next two seasons, Neely played only 22 games, but he came back with a vengeance in 1993-94, scoring 50 goals in 44 games. "It made all the rehab and the lonely days worth it," said Neely, who won the Bill Masterton

Trophy. He soon went down with a knee injury, however, and spent more months in recovery. Although Neely led the league with 16 power-play goals in the lockout-shortened 1994-95 season, he retired with a degenerative hip midway through the following campaign.

CAM NEELY					
Comox, British Columbia					
June 6, 1965–					
NHL Career: 1983-96					
Vancouver, Boston					
	GP	G	A	P	PIM
RS	726	395	299	694	1241
PO	93	57	32	89	168
Masterton, A-S Game (5)					

JIM NEILSON

DEFENSE

The son of a Cree woman and a Danish-Canadian man, Jim Neilson grew up in a Saskatchewan orphanage. Although tough and hefty at six-foot-two and 205 pounds, he brought a dignified, respectful presence to the game. "When I came up with the Rangers, there [weren't] one or two things I was weak on," said Neilson. "I would be making six or seven different mistakes a game." Partnered with Doug Harvey for most of his 1962-63 rookie campaign, Neilson exhibited good potential. Dedicated to the defensive side of the game, he played regularly until being benched during the 1967 playoffs. He rebounded strongly the following season, however, finally fulfilling all the promise he had shown.

"Since December 1, Neilson has been the best Blueshirt defenseman, a rusher par excellence and a blocker supreme," reported Norm MacLean in *The Hockey News* in January 1968.

"We now call Neilson 'The Super Chief,'" said coach and general manager Emile Francis. "And you will notice that I am using him as a point man on

the power play." Neilson made the Second All-Star Team that season, finished behind only Bruin defense partners Bobby Orr and Dallas Smith in plus/minus and helped the Rangers to second place in the regular season.

Although Neilson hit personal bests in 1968-69 with 10 goals and 34 assists, he quietly stepped out of the limelight. He was a Stanley Cup finalist in 1972 but became a Golden Seal after being left unprotected during the 1974 intra-

league draft. "Just watching him in different situations was a real education," said California rookie Rick Hampton. "A lot of times, things got a little hairy, and I'd look for Jim. I think a lot of the players did."

Named captain, Neilson was voted the team's most valuable player for 1974-75. "I certainly didn't come prepared to say anything," confessed a surprised Neilson to a packed hall. "In 12 years with the Rangers, it was never necessary." The team transferred to Cleveland in the summer of 1976, and Neilson concluded his pro career with the WHA's Edmonton Oilers in 1978-79.

JIM NEILSON
Big River, Saskatchewan
November 28, 1940–
NHL Career: 1962-78
NY Rangers, California, Cleveland

	GP	G	A	P	PIM
RS	1023	69	299	368	904
PO	65	1	17	18	61
A-S Game (2)					

SCOTT NIEDERMAYER

DEFENSE

Scott Niedermayer became the youngest-ever New Jersey Devil on October 16, 1991, only 46 days after turning 18 years old. He notched an assist, but after three more games, he resumed his stellar junior career with the Kamloops Blazers. Niedermayer was named the 1991 Canadian Major Junior Scholastic Player of the Year. On the ice, he led Kamloops to the 1992 Memorial Cup, tallying 9 goals and 14 assists in 17 playoff games. The following season, Niedermayer joined New Jersey full-time and made the 1993 NHL All-Rookie Team with 11 goals and 29 assists.

The Devils made a coaching change for 1993-94. Under coach Jacques Lemaire's defense-first strategy, Niedermayer's ability to jump up into the play wasn't encouraged, but he still potted

10 goals and 36 assists. In 1994-95, the Devils' system took the team all the way to a Stanley Cup victory. Niedermayer matched his regular-season output with 4 playoff goals, including a solo end-to-end rush that effectively broke the back of the Detroit Red Wings in the finals.

In 1996-97, Niedermayer began to pitch in occasionally at left wing. However, he made his biggest offensive contributions anchoring the New Jersey power play. He led his team in scoring with the man advantage for the second consecutive season in 1997-98, with 29 points. His overall totals of 14 goals, 43 assists and 57 points were all personal bests, and he made the Second All-Star Team. Lemaire resigned, and Niedermayer signed a new contract in the fall of 1998, but the young defenseman's of-

fensive numbers dropped, when the opposite was expected. Still, Niedermayer led the New Jersey blue-line corps for the fifth straight time in 1999-2000 with 38 points. He added another 7 points in the playoffs as the Devils marched confidently all the way to Stanley Cup victory.

SCOTT NIEDERMAYER
Edmonton, Alberta
August 31, 1973–
NHL Career: 1991-
New Jersey

	GP	G	A	P	PIM
RS	597	70	245	315	320
PO	90	14	23	37	58
Stanley Cup (2), A-S Game					

BALDY NORTHCOTT

LEFT WING

He had a full head of thick hair, so it was a tease who first called Lawrence Northcott "Baldy." Writer Marc T. McNeil summarized a March 5, 1932, Maroons 3–1 victory over the Boston Bruins, which offered a preview of the following season. Not even All-Star Hooley Smith, McNeil observed, who normally skated on the Montreal Maroons' famous "S-Line" with Nels Stewart and Babe Siebert, could keep up with wingers Northcott and Jimmy Ward, "who whirled up and down the rink like unlimited expresses." Northcott scored twice and almost pulled off a hat trick. "Baldy came steaming down left wing in the third period, was forced wide at the Boston defense but, keeping possession of the puck, circled to the back of the Bruin net. As he emerged, he slipped the puck around and into the near corner of the goal. It got past [goalie Tiny] Thompson, who was lying flat on his

face, but freak of freaks, it did not cross the goal line."

Stewart and Siebert were sold, and Northcott took a spot on the team's top line for 1932-33. Smith and Ward were coming off their most productive seasons, and with Northcott on left wing, they formed one of the NHL's strongest units. Northcott finished third in league scoring with a career-high 22 goals and 21 assists. Although he made the All-Star Team that season, Northcott achieved his greatest personal glory in the 1934-35 postseason.

In a two-game, total-goals semifinal, the Maroons battled Chicago through two scoreless games, sending the series into sudden-death overtime. "Baldy Northcott...flipped home the winning goal," reported *The Gazette*'s D.A.L. MacDonald in a front-page story, "[and] was carried bodily from the ice by his

cheering teammates, who flung sticks in the air." Northcott scored 3 more goals in the Stanley Cup finals and led all playoff scorers with 5 points as the Maroons swept Toronto in three straight games. The Maroons survived only three more seasons before folding. Northcott played the 1938-39 campaign for Chicago before retiring.

LAWRENCE "BALDY" NORTHCOTT
Calgary, Alberta
September 7, 1908–November 7, 1986
NHL Career: 1928-39
Montreal Maroons, Chicago

	GP	G	A	P	PIM
RS	446	133	112	245	273
PO	31	8	5	13	14

Stanley Cup, A-S Game

ADAM OATES

CENTER

The as-yet-undrafted Adam Oates led Rensselaer Polytechnic Institute, in Troy, New York, to the 1985 NCAA title, igniting a five-team bidding war in the NHL for his services. Oates signed with Detroit. He spent half of the 1985-

86 campaign in the minors but soon developed into a premier NHL playmaker, notching 62 assists and 78 points in 1988-89. In a trade they soon regretted, the Red Wings dealt Oates and Paul MacLean to St. Louis for the Blues' all-time leading scorer Bernie Federko, who retired a year later, and Tony McKegney.

Oates quickly became the perfect setup man for sniper Brett Hull. " 'Hullie' and I were playing together 30 minutes every night," he recalled, "scoring a lot, laughing, going out every night and just having a blast." He tallied 79 assists and 102 points in 1989-90 and tied for tenth in NHL scoring. Although Oates played only 61 games in 1990-91 because of injuries, he jumped to third place in scoring, with 90 helpers and 115 points. He made the Second All-Star Team, but the Blues, unhappy with his salary demands, traded him to Boston in February 1992. Oates finished the 1991-92 campaign with 99 points, tenth in the league, and added 19 points in 15 playoff games.

Although he finished the next two seasons third in league scoring, Oates was shut out of league honors. He set personal-highs with 45 goals, a league-leading 97 assists and 145 points in 1992-93. He also finished runner-up for the Lady Byng Trophy for the first of four consecutive campaigns. Oates tallied 112 points in 1993-94 and tied for tenth in league scoring the following season. Traded to Washington on March 1, 1997, he currently sits in twelfth place among the NHL's all-time assist leaders.

ADAM OATES
Weston, Ontario
August 27, 1962–
NHL Career: 1985-
Detroit, St. Louis, Boston, Washington

	GP	G	A	P	PIM
RS	1049	303	894	1197	335
PO	131	38	103	141	60

A-S Game (5)

BUDDY O'CONNOR

CENTER   ⭐2 1948

A soft-spoken man and just five-foot-eight and 142 pounds, Buddy O'Connor never took more than eight penalty minutes in a season. "I remember the grace and style Buddy possessed," wrote Frank Selke Sr., "the smooth, unhurried way he put his wingers into scoring opportunities, the quiet, almost unobtrusive way he played the game."

Selke witnessed O'Connor's NHL debut with his "Razzle Dazzle" linemates Pete Morin and Gerry Heffernan in 1941-42. O'Connor tallied 25 points in 39 games. He led the Habs with 43 assists in 1942-43 and finished tied for ninth in the league with 58 points. With only two penalty minutes, he came second in Lady Byng Trophy voting.

O'Connor contributed to two Stanley Cup wins before Selke dealt him in August 1947. "Listen, when Buddy was traded to the Rangers, half the kids in Montreal boycotted this place," recalled Montreal reporter Dink Carroll of *The Gazette*. "They'd only come to see the Rangers' games and [to] yell their heads off for O'Connor." The fan favorite finished a single point behind 1947-48 Art Ross Trophy-winner Elmer Lach, with 24 goals and 36 assists. When O'Connor made the Second All-Star Team, he again took a backseat to Lach, but he won both the Hart and the Lady Byng trophies.

Although he missed the first two months of the 1948-49 season because of injuries sustained in a car accident, O'Connor still led his team with 35 points. In 1949-50, at the end of his second last NHL campaign, the Rangers lost to Detroit in double overtime in game seven.

"You do the best you can, and you take the good with the bad," O'Connor later reminisced. "The only difference in the finals of the Stanley Cup is the champagne. The losers don't get it."

HUBERT "BUDDY" O'CONNOR
Montreal, Quebec
June 21, 1916–August 24, 1977
NHL Career: 1941-51
Montreal, NY Rangers

	GP	G	A	P	PIM
RS	509	140	257	397	34
PO	53	15	21	36	6

Hart, Byng, Stanley Cup (2), A-S Game, HOF 1988

JOHN OGRODNICK

LEFT WING   ⭐ 1985

John Ogrodnick broke into the NHL with the Detroit Red Wings halfway through the 1979-80 campaign. He managed to thrive during some of the franchise's lowest periods, scoring 35 goals and 35 assists in 1980-81. In 1982-83, he tallied 41 goals and 44 assists, although the Wings remained in the basement of the Norris Division for the fifth consecutive season. With the addition of veterans Brad Park and Ron Duguay in 1983-84, along with Ogrodnick's rookie centerman Steve Yzerman, Detroit's fortunes began to improve. Although Ogrodnick lost 16 games to injury, he notched 42 goals. "He's playing with drive and determination and making things happen," said coach Nick Polano. "He's taking charge on the ice."

The following season, Ogrodnick broke Mickey Redmond's franchise record with his 54th goal. "It's the best I've felt since being a Red Wing," he said on March 26, 1985. "It sent shivers up my spine." He made the First All-Star Team, finishing the season with 55 tallies and 50 helpers and tying for seventh in league scoring. Although Yzerman and Sergei Fedorov have since scored more goals for Detroit, Ogrodnick still holds the team's record for goals and points in a season by a winger.

He followed up with a 38-goal, 32-assist campaign. Although Ogrodnick was on a point-a-game pace in 1986-87, the Wings traded him to Quebec on January 17. That summer, he threatened to retire if the Nordiques didn't send him elsewhere. He joined the New York Rangers on September 30, 1987. His 43 goals in 1989-90 were the highlight of five seasons in the Big Apple. Ogrodnick returned to Detroit as a free agent for 1992-93 and concluded his NHL career with 6 goals in 19 games.

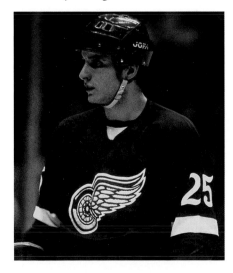

JOHN OGRODNICK
Ottawa, Ontario
June 20, 1959–
NHL Career: 1979-93
Detroit, Quebec, NY Rangers

	GP	G	A	P	PIM
RS	928	402	425	827	260
PO	41	18	8	26	6

A-S Game (5)

BERT OLMSTEAD

LEFT WING

Traded from Chicago, Bert Olmstead quickly passed through Detroit hands and landed with Montreal. There, he got the enviable task of replacing Toe Blake on the famous "Punch Line,"

with Maurice Richard and Elmer Lach. Olmstead tallied 38 points in the last 39 games of the 1950-51 campaign. Known to some as "Dirty Bertie," for his no-holds-barred approach, Olmstead also commanded respect for an unmatched work ethic. "He's the best mucker in the league," said Ken Reardon. With 17 goals and 28 assists, Olmstead finished 1952-53 ninth in NHL scoring. He made the Second All-Star Team, and Montreal won the Cup.

Olmstead moved to fifth place in 1953-54 scoring with 15 goals and 52 points. The following season, he led the league with 48 assists and finished seventh in total scoring. He set an NHL record with 56 helpers in 1955-56 and jumped to fourth spot in league scoring with 70 points. Olmstead earned another Second All-Star Team berth and added 14 playoff points to help the Habs win the Stanley Cup. "Of all the players," Blake once said, "I don't think Olmstead received all the credit he de-

served." After two more Cup wins, the Canadiens left Olmstead unprotected in the 1958 intra-league draft.

Toronto claimed Olmstead and even made him assistant coach for a time. "They're more scared of Bert than they are of me," noted coach Punch Imlach.

When the Leafs won the 1962 Cup, Imlach went over to shake Olmstead's hand but found him too tired to get up. "It's been a long haul, Punch," he said. Left unprotected and chosen by the Rangers that summer, Olmstead retired.

BERT OLMSTEAD
Sceptre, Saskatchewan
September 4, 1926–
NHL Career: 1948-62
Chicago, Montreal, Toronto

	GP	G	A	P	PIM
RS	848	181	421	602	884
PO	115	16	43	59	101

Stanley Cup (5), A-S Game (4), HOF 1985

BOBBY ORR

DEFENSE

Hockey had never seen the likes of Bobby Orr before. "Nobody is a perfect hockey player," said veteran Montreal center Jean Beliveau in 1969. "The important thing is to correct your mistakes. Orr does that. He is always there. He blocks the shots. He can skate. He can shoot. Is there anything more?"

Orr's speed, creativity and passion made him a force to be reckoned with at both ends of the rink. "It's the only way I know how to play," he said. Beginning with his 1966-67 Second All-Star Team rookie-of-the-year campaign, Orr literally revolutionized the role of the rushing defenseman. Although he played only 46 games in 1967-68, he still won the Norris Trophy and graduated to the First All-Star Team. He held his grip on both honors for eight seasons.

Orr earned the Hart Trophy three times and won both the Conn Smythe Trophy and a Stanley Cup ring in 1970

and in 1972. No blue-liner had ever led the league in assists; Orr did so four times. No defenseman had ever scored more than 20 goals; Orr did so in seven consecutive seasons. Most remarkably, Orr remains the only defenseman ever to win the Art Ross Trophy. He won the 1969-70 scoring title with a record 87 assists and 120 points and repeated the feat in 1974-75 with 135 points. He became the first player ever to tally more than 100 assists in a season, with 102 in 1970-71. To date, only centers Wayne Gretzky and Mario Lemieux have bettered that mark.

Orr missed most of the 1975-76 season, and by then, his career was coming to a tragic end. His lawyer, Alan Eagleson, withheld critical information about a lucrative Boston offer and led Orr to sign a free-agent contract with the Chicago Blackhawks in June 1976. That fall, Orr was voted the outstanding player in the Canada Cup tournament, but his knees

lasted only 20 games into the NHL season. He sat out the entire 1977-78 campaign and played only six games in 1978-79. "I worked hard, but I now know for sure that my leg cannot handle playing," he said when he sadly announced his retirement. At the age of 31, Orr entered the Hockey Hall of Fame, the youngest player ever to have done so.

BOBBY ORR
Parry Sound, Ontario
March 20, 1948–
NHL Career: 1966-77, 1978-79
Boston, Chicago

	GP	G	A	P	PIM
RS	657	270	645	915	953
PO	74	26	66	92	107

Calder, Ross (2), Hart (3), Norris (8), Smythe (2), Stanley Cup (2), A-S Game (7), HOF 1979

CHRIS OSGOOD

GOALTENDER

Chris Osgood made a strong NHL debut with the Detroit Red Wings in 1993-94, losing only eight games in 41 appearances. He posted a shutout in his first playoff game. Unfortunately, the San Jose Sharks upset the heavily favored Wings in the opening round. Veteran Mike Vernon was brought in to solidify Detroit's goaltending. During the lockout-shortened 1994-95 season, Osgood played only 19 games and sat on the bench for all but 68 minutes of the 1995 playoffs, as the Red Wings marched to the Stanley Cup finals.

In 1995-96, Osgood got considerably more ice time and led all NHL netminders with 39 victories. On March 6, he scored a goal against the Hartford Whalers, becoming the second goalie ever to fire the puck the length of the ice into a vacant net. The Whalers had pulled their goalie in the last minute, but Osgood salted away a 4–2 victory. He made the 1996 Second All-Star Team with a career-low 2.17 goals-against average. He also finished second in Vezina Trophy voting and shared the William M. Jennings Trophy with Vernon.

Osgood played most of the 1996-97 season, and he and Vernon came second for the Jennings. Although Osgood posted all six of the team's shutouts and a lower average, Vernon got the nod in the playoffs. Initially annoyed, Osgood was a jubilant celebrant when his partner helped the Wings win the Stanley Cup. Vernon was traded over the summer, and Osgood got the starting job for Detroit's title defense. He let in a few questionable long shots along the way but backstopped the Wings to a 1998 Cup victory. "Winning is the thing that gets you a certain respect that other things don't bring you," Osgood proudly told Helene St. James of *The London Free Press*. Although the past two seasons have ended less successfully, he looks ready for a long NHL career.

CHRIS OSGOOD
Peace River, Alberta
November 26, 1972–
NHL Career: 1993-
Detroit

	GP	M	GA	SO	AVE
RS	337	19639	773	29	2.36
PO	62	3624	129	8	2.14

Jennings, Stanley Cup (2), A-S Game (3)

SANDIS OZOLINSH

DEFENSE

In his youth, Sandis Ozolinsh was trained as a figure skater, and it was his speed that led the San Jose Sharks to select him with their third pick in the 1991 NHL draft. Ozolinsh tallied 23 rookie points in 37 games in 1992-93. The following season, he potted 26

goals and notched 64 points. Ozolinsh led all Sharks defensemen in scoring for the third time in 1994-95, prompting his holdout during contract negotiations in the fall of 1995. San Jose signed him. Then, seven games later, he was dealt to the Colorado Avalanche.

Sometimes known as an "offenseman," Ozolinsh led all defensemen with 19 playoff points (10 came with a man advantage). The Avalanche won the 1996 Stanley Cup, and the following season, Ozolinsh led the league with 42 power-play points. He topped all blueliners with 23 goals and finished with 68 points. A Norris Trophy finalist, Ozolinsh made the First All-Star Team.

He scored 51 points in 1997-98 but missed half of the following season because of another contract holdout. Ozolinsh had 52 points in 1999-2000, however. "I don't think there is a word in the dictionary for the kind of game Ozolinsh played tonight," Colorado coach Bob Hartley said after Ozolinsh notched his first career hat trick on December 7, 1999. "He had great puck control, made smart decisions and had a lot of jump." After going almost three months without scoring late in the season, Ozolinsh regained his touch in the playoffs.

"He scored big goals for us, and he played a very solid game," said Patrick Roy after Ozolinsh scored twice in a game against Phoenix. "Not just because he scored points, but the way he played all around. That's what we need from 'Ozo.' " The Avalanche eventually fell to the Dallas Stars in the Western Conference finals. When Ray Bourque agreed to play for Colorado in 2000-01, Ozolinsh became expendable. He was traded to Carolina in June 2000.

SANDIS OZOLINSH
Riga, Latvia
August 3, 1972–
NHL Career: 1992-
San Jose, Colorado, Carolina

	GP	G	A	P	PIM
RS	506	115	254	369	369
PO	107	21	59	80	110

Stanley Cup, A-S Game (4)

GOALTENDER 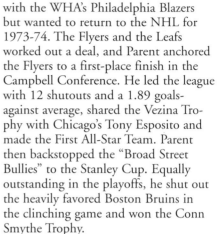 1974, 1975

Bernie Parent played part of two seasons for Boston before Philadelphia claimed him in the 1967 expansion draft. He shared the Flyers' net with Doug Favell for the better part of four seasons before being traded to Toronto in February 1971. Over the next season and a half, Parent's childhood hero Jacques Plante tutored his protégé in the veteran's systematic approach to goaltending. "He didn't really change my style," said Parent. "He just taught me how to use my own system."

Parent spent the 1972-73 campaign with the WHA's Philadelphia Blazers but wanted to return to the NHL for 1973-74. The Flyers and the Leafs worked out a deal, and Parent anchored the Flyers to a first-place finish in the Campbell Conference. He led the league with 12 shutouts and a 1.89 goals-against average, shared the Vezina Trophy with Chicago's Tony Esposito and made the First All-Star Team. Parent then backstopped the "Broad Street Bullies" to the Stanley Cup. Equally outstanding in the playoffs, he shut out the heavily favored Boston Bruins in the clinching game and won the Conn Smythe Trophy.

He repeated his heroics in 1974-75. "What's that they say in Philadelphia— Only God Saves More Than Bernie Parent?" joked Buffalo's Jerry Korab. "Ha! God should have a season so good." The first goalie in 15 years to win back-to-back Vezinas, Parent also won his second All-Star selection. Voted the playoffs' most valuable player again, Parent reluctantly posed with the Smythe Trophy after the Flyers' win. "If you want to take a picture of me with a trophy," he said, "take me with the Stanley Cup. That's what this game is about."

"Bernie always talked about the pressure," said Flyers general manager Keith Allen, "but he seemed immune to it."

Parent lost most of the 1975-76 campaign to injury, and Montreal took ownership of the Cup for the remainder of his playing days. His career ended in February 1979 when an errant stick hit him in the eye. During the following season's home opener, the Flyers retired Parent's number-1 jersey.

BERNIE PARENT
Montreal, Quebec
April 3, 1945–
NHL Career: 1965-72, 1973-79
Boston, Philadelphia, Toronto

	GP	M	GA	SO	AVE
RS	608	35136	1493	54	2.55
PO	71	4302	174	6	2.43

Vezina (2), Smythe (2), Stanley Cup (2),
A-S Game (5), HOF 1984

BRAD PARK

When Brad Park made his debut with the New York Rangers in 1968-69, he drew immediate comparisons to Bobby Orr. His stickhandling and offensive instincts were sharp, he learned to control the pace of the game, and he had good speed. He was as tough a player as any, quick to duke it out with all comers. During his rookie season, Park benefited from the advice of veteran defense partner Harry Howell and honed his defense to a razor-sharp edge. Despite knee problems similar to Orr's, Park picked up seven All-Star selections in his first 10 seasons. Yet in many respects, fate was not kind to him.

Park went to the 1972 Stanley Cup finals with the Rangers, but Orr and the Bruins triumphed. He finished second behind Orr in Norris Trophy voting four times. When he notched a career-high 82 points in 1973-74, cracking the league's top-10 scorers, Orr tallied 122 points. Park proudly became captain of the Rangers for 1974-75 but took a major blow early the next season. In the biggest deal of the decade, Park, Jean Ratelle and Joe Zanussi were sent to archrival Boston for Phil Esposito and Carol Vadnais.

Park played only 10 games with his former nemesis before Orr's years as a Bruin ended. Although Park made the First All-Star Team that season and in 1977-78, he finished second for both the 1976 and 1978 Norris Trophies behind Denis Potvin of the New York Islanders. Park helped the Bruins to the 1977 and 1978 Stanley Cup finals against Montreal, but a Cup ring never materialized. "They had about seven Hall-of-Famers on their club," noted Park (in fact, nine of those Habs made it to the Hall), "so while we lost, there's some consolation in knowing that we were playing an unbelievable opponent."

In 1983-84, Park signed with Detroit as a free agent and tallied 53 assists. He was awarded the Bill Masterton Trophy, an acknowledgment of a dedicated career, and he had a steadying influence as a mentor to young players such as rookie Steve Yzerman. Park retired a year later and briefly coached the last-place Wings in 1985-86. His exceptional playing career was celebrated in 1988, as Park entered the Hockey Hall of Fame.

BRAD PARK
Toronto, Ontario
July 6, 1948–
NHL Career: 1968-85
NY Rangers, Boston, Detroit

	GP	G	A	P	PIM
RS	1113	213	683	896	1429
PO	161	35	90	125	217

Masterton, A-S Game (9), HOF 1988

LEFT WING

Although his pedigree was impeccable, Lynn Patrick did not receive a warm welcome from the New York Rangers' fans. He was the son of Rangers coach and general manager Lester Patrick, so it's not surprising that some doubters called him "Papa's boy." But he was also taunted as "Sonja," after figure skater Sonja Henie. "He was a beautiful skater," recalled Joe Falls of *The Detroit News*, "but he didn't like the corners. The guys in the side balcony of Madison Square Garden used to give it to him pretty good."

His younger brother Muzz, a rugged defenseman, joined the team late in the 1937-38 season. Meanwhile, Patrick's 15 goals and 19 assists during the same campaign offered the first hint that he was capable of being a truly elite scorer. The Rangers won the 1940 Stanley Cup, and Patrick notched his first 20-goal season in 1940-41. He finished second in league scoring with 44 points, tying with four others. The following season, he made the First All-Star Team. With an NHL-high 32 goals, he finished just behind points-leader and linemate Bryan Hextall.

Patrick tallied a career-high 39 assists and 61 points in 1942-43 and made the Second All-Star Team. He spent the next two seasons in the U.S. Army, where he suffered a permanent eye injury while riding a motorcycle through the bush on military maneuvers. Although he returned to the Rangers for the 1945-46 season, Patrick retired after scoring only 8 goals and 6 assists in 38 games. By 1948-49, he was behind the Rangers' bench. In later years, he coached and was general manager of Boston and St. Louis. While watching the Blues play in 1980, Patrick felt ill and left the game early. On his way home, he suffered a fatal heart attack.

LYNN PATRICK
Victoria, British Columbia
February 3, 1912–January 26, 1980
NHL Career: 1934-43, 1945-46
NY Rangers

	GP	G	A	P	PIM
RS	455	145	190	335	240
PO	44	10	6	16	22

Stanley Cup, HOF 1980

PETE PEETERS

GOALTENDER

⭐ 1983

Pete Peeters was a 1978-79 AHL All-Star when he appeared in five NHL games for Philadelphia. He shared Flyers' duties with Phil Myre full-time the following season. Peeters tended goal for 27 of an NHL-team-record 35 consecutive undefeated games. In net for most of the playoffs, he took his club to the 1980 Stanley Cup finals. The next two seasons, the Flyers didn't have as much success, and Philadelphia dealt Peeters to Boston for Brad McCrimmon in June 1982. "You have to remember that the Flyers once traded away Bernie Parent," said Peeters bitterly, "and look what he turned out to be. Sometimes, I think they forgot that I'm 24 years old."

Peeters went on another tear in 1982-83. "He's playing better than anybody I've ever seen over a stretch like this," claimed Brad Park after Peeters had been undefeated in 22 straight games.

"He's probably the best goalie they've had around here since [Frank] Brimsek," said former Bruin Gerry Cheevers modestly, ignoring his own 32-game record. Peeters went 31 games without losing and finished the season with a league-high eight shutouts. He made the First All-Star Team, came runner-up for the Hart Trophy and won the Vezina Trophy with a 2.36 goals-against average.

Over the next two seasons, Peeters' numbers declined. "I'm not making excuses, but we had eight rookies last year," he told *The Hockey News* in October 1985. "Besides [them], we had five new faces." Boston traded Peeters to the Washington Capitals for Pat Riggin several weeks later. Peeters posted an NHL-low 2.78 goals-against average in 1987-88, the highlight of four Washington campaigns. He rejoined the Flyers as a free agent in the summer of 1989 and retired after two more seasons.

PETE PEETERS
Edmonton, Alberta
August 17, 1957–
NHL Career: 1978-91
Philadelphia, Boston, Washington

	GP	M	GA	SO	AVE
RS	489	27699	1424	21	3.08
PO	71	4200	232	2	3.31

Vezina, A-S Game (4)

CENTER

⭐ 1976, 1977

Gilbert Perreault led the Montreal Junior Canadiens to two Memorial Cup championships before becoming the first pick in the 1970 amateur draft.

He was a creative stickhandler, and his bowlegged skating style gave him incredible acceleration, balance and lateral movement. In Buffalo's inaugural 1970-

71 season, he broke a long-standing NHL rookie record with 38 goals to win the Calder Trophy. The following season, he centered Sabres' newcomers Rick Martin and Rene Robert, a line quickly dubbed "The French Connection" after the 1971 movie. Perreault's 48 assists helped Martin to a 44-goal rookie campaign. Robert scored 40 goals in 1972-73, while Perreault notched 60 helpers and 88 points. With only 10 penalty minutes, Perreault won the Lady Byng Trophy.

In 1974-75, the entire "French Connection" made the NHL's top-10 scoring list. Buffalo marched to the Stanley Cup finals to face Philadelphia, the defending champions. "Perreault holds that 'French Connection' together," said Flyers coach Fred Shero. "And Buffalo depends too much on that line. Stop them, and we win." Perreault's shadow Bobby Clarke and goalie Bernie Parent held him a single goal and an assist. The Flyers took the series 4–2 in Perreault's only trip to the Cup finals.

Perreault made the Second All-Star Team the following two seasons. He finished third in 1975-76 scoring, posting career-highs with 44 goals and 69 assists. In 1976-77, his 95 points were good for fifth spot. Perreault finished eighth the following season and fourth in 1979-80. "When he winds up and heads up-ice towards you, beads of sweat build up on your forehead," confessed defenseman Barry Beck, "because you know what he can do." Perreault, team captain from 1981-82 until his retirement, still holds the Buffalo franchise's career records for games, goals, assists and points.

GILBERT PERREAULT
Victoriaville, Quebec
November 13, 1950–
NHL Career: 1970-87
Buffalo

	GP	G	A	P	PIM
RS	1191	512	814	1326	500
PO	90	33	70	103	44

Calder, Byng, A-S Game (5), HOF 1990

PIERRE PILOTE

DEFENSE 1963, 1964, 1965, 1966, 1967 2 1960, 1961, 1962

Pierre Pilote may have been the smallest Chicago defenseman in 1955-56, but he was also the most aggressive. Still honing his skills, Pilote made intimidation an integral part of his game. But he was a canny student, which led to his eight consecutive All-Star seasons. "Sure, I copied [Doug] Harvey," he admitted. "He was the best, so why not? I got to know his techniques so well that I could anticipate most of his moves. I bet I intercepted more of his passes than anyone in the league." By 1960, Pilote was a premier puck rusher and a nasty protector of his own goal. He led the NHL with 165 penalty minutes in 1960-61. In the subsequent playoffs, he tied Gordie Howe for most points and helped the Blackhawks

to their first Stanley Cup win since 1938.

Pilote became team captain in 1961-62, and the Hawks returned to the Cup finals. He graduated to the First All-Star Team in 1963 and won the first of three consecutive Norris Trophies. His 14 goals and 45 assists in 1964-65 broke Babe Pratt's 21-year-old scoring record for defensemen. Yet no one could forget that he was a mean competitor.

"Can't you guys forget about all that fighting stuff?" he complained after leading Chicago to the 1965 Cup finals. "That all took place when I was younger and didn't know any better. I still hit back if someone plays a dirty trick on me. I just don't go looking for trouble anymore." But after breaking his thumb

in a fight, he missed 19 games the following season. Pilote tallied 52 points in 1966-67 but was traded to Toronto for Jim Pappin in May 1968. He played his final season as a Maple Leaf.

PIERRE PILOTE
Kénogami, Quebec
December 11, 1931–
NHL Career: 1955-69
Chicago, Toronto

	GP	G	A	P	PIM
RS	890	80	418	498	1251
PO	86	8	53	61	102

Norris (3), Stanley Cup, A-S Game (8), HOF 1975

GOALTENDER ★ 1956, 1959, 1962 ★ 1957, 1958, 1960, 1971

Known as "Jake the Snake" because of his lightning reflexes, Jacques Plante brought more to the game than physical assets. "So often, your skilled players are not dedicated," said Glenn Hall, "but Plante was."

He was also an innovator. "He is the world's greatest advertisement for wandering goaltenders," wrote the *Boston Globe*'s Harold Kaese during the 1957 Stanley Cup finals. "He plays in front of the net, beside it, behind it. Some night, he'll probably be found on top of it."

When he donned a mask in 1959, Plante faced derision, but his sensational play contradicted the prevalent theory on goalies. "They figured a goalie had to be scared to play well," said Plante. "When shots are coming at you at 100 miles per hour, you're scared whether you have a mask or not." Before long, facial protection became standard goalie equipment.

Plante made his NHL debut in 1952-53 with a Stanley Cup-winning team on the rise, but he earned all his All-Star nominations. For five consecutive years, starting in 1956, Plante also won the Vezina Trophy and a Stanley Cup ring, causing Toe Blake to observe, "For five years, he was the greatest goalie the league has ever seen." Although Plante picked up another Vezina, the Hart Trophy and a First All-Star Team berth in 1962, the Habs eventually grew tired of his idiosyncrasies and experiments and traded him to the lowly New York Rangers in the summer of 1963. After losing too many games and some of his confidence, Plante retired in 1965.

But Plante went on to share his seventh Vezina with fellow veteran Hall when St. Louis drafted the pair in 1968-69. "I don't think I ever played better than I did with St. Louis," claimed Plante, "even in my best years with the Canadiens." Toronto bought Plante's services in the summer of 1970. Although 42 years old, he led the league with a 1.88 goals-against average and made the 1971 Second All-Star Team. Plante was traded to Boston in March 1973, where he finished his NHL career.

JACQUES PLANTE
Mont-Carmel, Quebec
January 17, 1929–February 27, 1986
NHL Career: 1952-65, 1968-73
Montreal, NY Rangers, St. Louis, Toronto, Boston

	GP	M	GA	SO	AVE
RS	837	49533	1965	82	2.38
PO	112	6652	240	14	2.16

Hart, Vezina (7), Stanley Cup (6), A-S Game (8), HOF 1978

BUD POILE

 1948

Hard-shooting Bud Poile scored 16 goals and 19 assists as a 1942-43 Maple Leafs rookie. Early the following season, he entered military service and didn't return to NHL action until late in the 1945-46 campaign. Toronto reunited him with his Fort William hometown friends Gaye Stewart and Gus Bodnar, and they formed "The Flying Forts." Poile notched 19 goals and 36 points in 1946-47, but the Leafs pulled off a stunning trade in November 1947. Poile's entire line, along with Ernie Dickens and Bob Goldham, went to Chicago for Cy Thomas and ace center Max Bentley.

Poile caught fire with the Blackhawks and set career-highs in 1947-48 with 25 goals and 29 assists. He finished the regular season tied with Bentley for fifth place in league scoring. Yet he bounced to Detroit the next season, then split the 1949-50 campaign between the Rangers and the Bruins. "I was sort of always passing through somewhere," he told Dick Beddoes of *The Globe and Mail*. "When the Red Wings sent me

to New York, they were building a new press box in the Detroit Olympia. Jack Adams always said they needed the $35,000 they got for me to pay for it."

Even though Poile tallied 16 goals

and 30 points for Boston in 39 games, the Bruins tried to cut his salary for 1950-51. He refused to sign the contract. "The next day, [Art] Ross sent me as far as he could," said Poile, "which was as playing coach in Tulsa." Although he never made it back to the big league as a player, Poile later served as an NHL coach, general manager and league executive, entering the Hockey Hall of Fame as an NHL builder. His son David, after a long tenure in Washington, became the first general manager of the Nashville Predators.

NORMAN "BUD" POILE
Fort William, Ontario
February 10, 1924–
NHL Career: 1942-44, 1945-50
Toronto, Chicago, Detroit, NY Rangers, Boston

	GP	G	A	P	PIM
RS	311	107	122	229	91
PO	23	4	5	9	8

Stanley Cup, A-S Game (2), HOF 1990

DENIS POTVIN

⭐ 1975, 1976, 1978, 1979, 1981 ⭐ 1977, 1984

Lauded as "the next Bobby Orr," Denis Potvin concluded his five-season junior career under the tutelage of coach Leo Boivin. "Denis will put the hitting back in defense," said Boivin, a premier NHL body checker in the 1950s and 1960s. "I've never seen anybody, I say, anybody, lay them out like Denis does. And they're all good, clean checks." The New York Islanders selected Potvin with the first pick in the 1973 amateur draft, and he didn't disappoint. Potvin accumulated a career-high 175 minutes in penalties as he began to establish his position among the most talented but meanest defensemen in NHL history. Integral to 30 percent of the scoring for the last-place Islanders, he also tallied 54 points and won the 1974 Calder Trophy.

Potvin scored 21 goals and 55 assists

in 1974-75, finished runner-up for the Norris Trophy and made the First All-Star Team. He took the Norris the following season with 31 goals and 98 points. After an 80-point 1976-77 campaign, Potvin won the Norris again. He finished fifth in league scoring in 1977-78 and was awarded his third Norris. He hit career-highs in 1978-79 with 70 assists and 101 points and was seventh in the scoring race. Meanwhile, the Islanders were turning into genuine championship contenders.

In 1979-80, Potvin became team captain, a position he held for eight seasons. He later complained that his coach Al Arbour curbed his offensive freedom, but Potvin's strength lay in his two-way game. He contributed to four straight Stanley Cup wins between 1980 and 1983, averaging 21 points every

playoff. On April 4, 1987, he became the first NHL defenseman to tally 1,000 career points. Feeling that he had little else to prove and unhappy with the Islanders' losing ways, Potvin quit after the 1987-88 season. Not yet 35 years old, he retired holding the rearguard records for goals, assists and points.

DENIS POTVIN
Ottawa, Ontario
October 29, 1953–
NHL Career: 1973-88
NY Islanders

	GP	G	A	P	PIM
RS	1060	310	742	1052	1354
PO	185	56	108	164	253

Calder, Norris (3), Stanley Cup (4), A-S Game (9), HOF 1991

BABE PRATT

★ 1944 ★² 1945

Walter Pratt picked up his nickname "Babe" as a ballplayer, but during the winter, it was the sport of hockey that had his full attention. In one memorable amateur season, Pratt played on five championship teams. In 1935-36, he joined the last-place New York Rangers. The following season, he helped the Rangers to the Stanley Cup finals. Pratt was paired with Ott Heller for most of his years in New York, and their best season together came in 1939-40. They helped lower the team's goals-against average to 1.60, and the Rangers won the Stanley Cup.

Pratt was aggressive as a player and a hellion off the ice. "I was always kind of a bad boy in those days," he laughed in later years. "I did some drinking then—I don't anymore—but the coaches always had to keep an eye on me." Although Pratt notched 24 assists and the Rangers finished first in the 1941-42 regular season, New York traded rapscallion Pratt to Toronto early in 1942-43 for journeymen Hank Goldup and Red Garrett. Pratt notched 25 assists for the Leafs, including a defenseman's record of 6 in one game. In 1943-44, he tallied 40 helpers and 57 points—both rearguard records—and earned the Hart Trophy.

In 1944-45, Pratt scored 18 goals and capped his season with the Stanley Cup-winner late in a 2–1 game-seven victory. But in January 1946, Pratt went from All-Star to outcast when the NHL handed him a lifetime suspension for gambling. After confessing to betting on hockey games, although not against his own team, and vowing never to do so again, Pratt was reinstated. The Leafs dealt him to Boston that summer, and he finished out the 1946-47 season in the minors.

WALTER "BABE" PRATT
Stony Mountain, Manitoba
January 7, 1916–December 16, 1988
NHL Career: 1935-47
NY Rangers, Toronto, Boston

	GP	G	A	P	PIM
RS	517	83	209	292	463
PO	63	12	17	29	90

Hart, Stanley Cup (2), HOF 1966

DEAN PRENTICE

★² 1960

Dean Prentice scored 48 goals and 75 assists for the junior Guelph Biltmores in 1951-52. He jumped straight into the New York Rangers' lineup early the next season and got

off to a tentative start, until his Guelph linemate Andy Bathgate joined him for the 1954-55 season. Prentice led the team with 24 goals in 1955-56 and became a regular contributor thereafter. Although he picked up injuries along the way, *Weekend Magazine* writer Andy O'Brien noted that Prentice "would bust through a brick wall if he thought it would help him score."

Prentice made the Second All-Star Team in 1960. "They once called him punchy and puck-happy," wrote Stan Fischler late that season. "Now they respect him." He finished the campaign with a career-high 32 goals and 66 points, good for tenth in league scoring. Over Prentice's 11 seasons with the Rangers, however, the team never won a playoff round. He notched two more 20-goal seasons before New York swapped him for Don McKenney, Boston's top goal scorer, midway through the 1963-64 campaign. Prentice scored 23 goals in 1964-65, but the Bruins were even more inept than the Rangers. He got his first experience with a contender after his trade to Detroit in February 1966.

Reunited with Bathgate, Prentice scored 5 goals and 5 assists in 12 playoff games. Unfortunately, Montreal defeated the Wings in the 1966 Stanley Cup finals. Prentice averaged more than 20 goals a season for the rest of his career but never got any closer to winning a Cup. Pittsburgh drafted him in 1969 and sold him to the Minnesota North Stars in 1971. When Prentice retired in 1974, only three other players had ever enjoyed longer NHL careers.

DEAN PRENTICE
Schumacher, Ontario
October 5, 1932–
NHL Career: 1952-74
NY Rangers, Boston, Detroit, Pittsburgh, Minnesota

	GP	G	A	P	PIM
RS	1378	391	469	860	484
PO	54	13	17	30	38

A-S Game (4)

JOE PRIMEAU

CENTER

He was "Gentleman Joe" Primeau both on and off the ice. Conn Smythe, just before being fired by New York, offered a contract to Primeau for the Rangers' inaugural 1926-27 season. Out of loyalty, Primeau followed Smythe to Toronto, although his NHL career didn't get into full gear until the 1929-30 season. Smythe put Primeau at center between 18-year-old Charlie Conacher and 20-year-old Harvey "Busher" Jackson, forming one of the league's most famous units. "Joe Primeau was the playmaker on the 'Kid Line,' " recalled coach Dick Irvin. "Charlie and Busher would streak in from the wings, and Joe would set them up."

Precise timing was the key to Primeau's game, and he led the NHL with 32 assists in 1930-31. "All Joe would have to do was to take a short peek, and *zingo*, there was the puck right on the end of your stick," recalled former teammate King Clancy. Primeau tallied a league-leading 37 assists in 1931-32, finishing

runner-up to linemate Jackson in the scoring race. He also won the Lady Byng Trophy for his clean play and finished the season with a playoff-high 6 assists in the Leafs' Stanley Cup triumph.

Always a strong checker and penalty killer as well as a great passer, Primeau could also score. He earned first-star honors for a hat trick against the Montreal Maroons on March 5, 1933. "Primeau climaxed his big night by catching Lionel Conacher napping at the blue line in the final seconds of the third period," reported Bert Perry in *The Globe and Mail*. "He took the puck away from the big defenseman, skimmed around him to get a clear path to the net and stickhandled the rubber into the cage after drawing Dave Kerr out of position." The Leafs went back to the Stanley Cup finals later that spring but lost to the New York Rangers.

Primeau closed out the 1933-34 sea-

son with a career-high 14 goals and a league-high 32 assists, finishing second in scoring to linemate Conacher. He finally made an All-Star Team, but his production started to slip, and he played only two more seasons before turning his attention to a concrete business and coaching. Primeau eventually guided the Leafs to the 1951 Stanley Cup from behind the bench.

JOE PRIMEAU
Lindsay, Ontario
January 29, 1906–May 14, 1989
NHL Career: 1927-36
Toronto

	GP	G	A	P	PIM
RS	310	66	177	243	105
PO	38	5	18	23	12

Byng, Stanley Cup, A-S Game, HOF 1963

CHRIS PRONGER

DEFENSE

The Hartford Whalers selected six-foot-six, 220-pound defenseman Chris Pronger as the second pick in the 1993 entry draft. Although he made the 1994 NHL All-Rookie Team, Pronger's lax work ethic grated on his coaches. The Whalers grew increasingly displeased and, in the summer of 1995, traded him to St. Louis for 50-goal-scorer Brendan Shanahan. Pronger began to hone already strong defensive skills while maturing as a person and as a player. His defense partner Al MacInnis deserves much of the credit for his growth. "I've learned a lot just from the way Al carries himself on and off the ice," said Pronger. "He's a first-class role model and something I'd like to become."

As his intensity increased, so, too, did his penalty minutes, but Pronger's nastiness created space on the ice. He became the youngest captain in St. Louis history

on September 29, 1997, and posted a league-high plus-47 in 1997-98. Pronger made the Second All-Star Team and was a finalist for the Norris Trophy. Although he wasn't an All-Star the following season, he came fourth in Norris voting.

He finished second among NHL rearguards in 1999-2000 scoring, establishing career-highs with 14 goals, 48 assists and 62 points. "He's got such a great stick," Blues assistant coach Mike Kitchen told *The St. Louis Post-Dispatch*. "His hand-eye

coordination is the best I've ever seen." Pronger made the First All-Star Team and won the Norris and Hart trophies. He also led the league with an average of 30.5 minutes of ice time per game. Unfortunately, after coming first in the regular season, the Blues lost the first round of the playoffs to San Jose. "It's nice to win those awards," said team-player Pronger with some disappointment, "but the goal is the Stanley Cup."

CHRIS PRONGER
Dryden, Ontario
October 10, 1974–
NHL Career: 1993-
Hartford, St. Louis

	GP	G	A	P	PIM
RS	508	64	184	248	805
PO	49	7	23	30	124

Hart, Norris, A-S Game (2)

MARCEL PRONOVOST

 1960, 1961  1958, 1959

Marcel Pronovost missed relatively few games, which was more a function of his dedication than anything else. Over his 20-season NHL career, the defenseman suffered a litany of injuries. After sustaining a series of broken noses, Pronovost looked more like a brute than the skillful player he actually was. A smooth skater and strong rusher, he played his first games for the Detroit Red Wings as a teenage replacement. When Gordie Howe was injured in the 1950 Stanley Cup playoffs, Red Kelly moved up to forward, and Pronovost had a chance to pick up his first of four Stanley Cup rings in six consecutive seasons. He received his permanent call-up midway through the following campaign.

He hit his offensive peak in 1954-55, assisting on 25 goals and collecting 34 points. Pronovost's strength, however, was the defensive aspect of the game. He relied more on positional play and stick checking than on hitting, although he lacked nothing in toughness. Pronovost made the Second All-Star Team in both 1958 and 1959. The 1959-60 season proved even more rewarding. The Montreal Canadiens accorded their opponent a rare honor when they sponsored a "night" for Pronovost in the Forum. He received a car from the fans and a diamond ring from his teammates. Kelly's trade in midseason made Pronovost the top Detroit defenseman, and he was named to the First All-Star Team. He held that distinction again in the 1960-61 campaign, when he finished runner-up for the Norris Trophy.

In an eight-player swap, Pronovost was the Toronto Maple Leafs' key acquisition when Andy Bathgate was sent to Detroit in May 1965. The following season, Pronovost became only the seventh player to compete in 1,000 NHL games. He was 36 years old when he helped the Leafs win the 1967 Cup, part of a veteran lineup that upset the Montreal Canadiens. He played his final NHL games for Toronto in 1969-70 but finished his professional career with the Tulsa Oilers in the Central Hockey League the following season.

MARCEL PRONOVOST
Lac la Tortue, Quebec
June 15, 1930–
NHL Career: 1950-70
Detroit, Toronto

	GP	G	A	P	PIM
RS	1206	88	257	345	851
PO	134	8	23	31	104

Stanley Cup (5), A-S Game (11),
HOF 1978

RIGHT WING

⭐ 1965

Content to play most of his career on Montreal's third line, Claude Provost won the inaugural Bill Masterton Trophy in 1968. However, as former Ranger Aldo Guidolin once noted, "Their third line was better than most first lines on other teams." Provost never failed to score at least 10 goals a season throughout his career, but it was his hustle and defensive abilities that kept him in the lineup. He neutralized Bobby Hull in the 1960 semifinals, allowing Montreal to sweep to a fifth consecutive Stanley Cup victory.

In 1961-62, Provost led the Canadiens with 33 goals and finished tenth in the league with 62 points. He credited Gordie Howe with his newfound scoring touch. After he saw Howe cut two inches off the end of his stick at the All-Star Game, Provost decided to follow suit. He topped the Habs again in 1964-65. His 27 goals and 64 points moved him to sixth spot in NHL scoring and onto the First All-Star Team. Provost's offensive

success, however, didn't distract him from his defensive responsibilities.

Provost limited Bobby Hull to a single assist as Montreal won the first two games of the 1965 Cup finals against Chicago. "I know it's tough on him having a guy shadowing him all the time," said Provost, "but that's my job."

Blackhawks coach Billy Reay remained optimistic: "I don't believe there's a player in the league who can stay with Hull game after game after game."

Although Hull did score 2 goals in game four, Montreal won the Cup, and Provost received consideration for the Conn Smythe Trophy. "I've never been checked like that in my life," said Hull wearily. Provost picked up his ninth Cup ring in 1969 and played one more season before retiring.

CLAUDE PROVOST
Montreal, Quebec
September 17, 1933–April 17, 1984
NHL Career: 1955-70
Montreal

	GP	G	A	P	PIM
RS	1005	254	335	589	469
PO	126	25	38	63	86

Masterton, Stanley Cup (9),
A-S Game (11)

GOALTENDER

⭐2 1990

On November 10, 1985, in his first NHL start, Daren Puppa blanked the defending Stanley Cup champion Edmonton Oilers. "Even in your wildest dreams, you don't imagine something like that happening," said Puppa, who made 37 saves. Ten of the shots he faced came from Wayne Gretzky, three of them on breakaways.

Sabres coach Scotty Bowman compared Puppa to his star Tom Barrasso. "They're both tall, both left-handers, and they wear the same style of helmet and face mask," noted Bowman, who also saw similarities to his old netminder with the Canadiens. "Like [Ken] Dryden, Puppa is

a brilliant student, and he's very cool under pressure. He's good with his legs and stands up well."

Despite his exciting debut, Puppa got only six more 1985-86 starts for Buffalo. He played 20 NHL games over the next two seasons while starring for Rochester in the AHL. When Barrasso was traded early in the 1988-89 campaign, Puppa appeared in 37 games for the Sabres. The following season, he played 56 times and recorded 31 wins, tying for the league-high. Puppa finished runner-up in Vezina Trophy voting and made the Second All-Star Team.

In 1990-91, Puppa lost 25 games to injury and struggled to recover his form. Traded to Toronto in February 1993, Puppa was

picked by the Tampa Bay Lightning in the 1993 expansion draft. He played a career-high 63 games in 1993-94 and finished second in 1995-96 with a .918 save percentage in 57 appearances. "It's amazing how having a good goaltender can make you a great coach," said Tampa Bay's Terry Crisp. Sadly, Puppa has suffered from chronic back and groin injuries ever since and has appeared in only 50 games over three seasons.

DAREN PUPPA
Kirkland Lake, Ontario
March 23, 1965–
NHL Career: 1985-
Buffalo, Toronto, Tampa Bay

	GP	M	GA	SO	AVE
RS	429	23816	1204	19	3.03
PO	16	786	51	0	3.89

A-S Game

BILL QUACKENBUSH

★ 1948, 1949, 1951   ★2 1947, 1953

As a fight broke out during a game against the Toronto Maple Leafs in 1946-47, Detroit's gentlemanly Bill Quackenbush paired off with the equally mild-mannered Leaf Harry Watson. "Shall we waltz?" asked Quackenbush with a smile.

"No," laughed Watson. "Let's get in the middle and start shoving a bit. I think they're going to take pictures."

Quackenbush was the first defenseman to be awarded the Lady Byng Trophy. Although he had accumulated only 49 penalty minutes over his first six NHL seasons, it was not until he went penalty-free in 1948-49 that he won the award. Quackenbush established an effective defensive presence without laying on the body or stick. Once he'd broken up the attack, he quickly carried the puck up-ice. Although he scored a career-high 11 goals in 1945-46, Quackenbush was primarily a playmaker.

In 1947-48, he graduated from the Second to the First All-Star Team during his most penalized season, having spent 17 minutes in the sin bin. But he began his streak of clean play that year, sandwiching his Byng-winning campaign in the middle of 137 penalty-free games in total. Quackenbush concluded the streak midway through 1949-50, but by then, he was with the Bruins. His Detroit protégé Red Kelly had come along so well that the Red Wings sent their All-Star rearguard and Pete Horeck to Boston in exchange for four players in August 1949.

Quackenbush was joined on the Bruins' blue line by his younger brother Max in 1950-51. He reclaimed his spot on the First All-Star Team and hit personal-highs with 24 assists and 29 points. Although he helped the Bruins to the 1953 Stanley Cup finals during his last All-Star season, Quackenbush never played for a Cup-winner. He retired after accumulating four penalty minutes and 22 assists over his 70-game 1955-56 campaign. Quackenbush remains the least-penalized defenseman to take a regular shift in any era. Gordie Howe reminisced: "He's one of the best all-around players I've ever played with."

BILL QUACKENBUSH
Toronto, Ontario
March 2, 1922–
NHL Career: 1942-56
Detroit, Boston

	GP	G	A	P	PIM
RS	774	62	222	284	95
PO	80	2	19	21	8

Byng, A-S Game (8), HOF 1976

JEAN RATELLE

★2 1972

Jean Ratelle had a couple of childhood heroes: the elegant Jean Beliveau and the pugnacious Dickie Moore. Beliveau clearly had more influence: With similar size and skills, Ratelle exhibited the same dignified demeanor. He made his first appearances with the New York Rangers in 1960-61, but he didn't complete his first full NHL campaign until 1965-66.

For most of his Ranger seasons, Ratelle centered Rod Gilbert, his childhood friend and a classy playmaker, and Vic Hadfield, a tougher presence. They were eventually tagged the "GAG Line," for "goal-a-game." Ratelle vaulted to fourth in league scoring in 1967-68 with 32 goals and 46 assists. He remained in the top-10 scorers for the next two campaigns and won the 1971 Bill Masterton Trophy for his perseverance.

The "GAG Line" had its greatest success in 1971-72. Unfortunately, Ratelle broke his ankle with 16 games left in the season. He still finished third in league scoring, with Hadfield and Gilbert right behind him. Ratelle's career-high 46 goals and 63 assists earned him both a Second All-Star Team position and the Pearson Award. He was also presented with the Lady Byng Trophy, having taken only four minutes in penalties. Although Ratelle healed in time for the Stanley Cup finals, he reached his career peak with Team Canada's exciting victory that autumn.

Ratelle, Brad Park and Joe Zanussi were traded to Boston early in the 1975-76 season for Phil Esposito and Carol Vadnais. Despite the shock, Ratelle finished the season with 105 points, sixth in the league. He jokingly apologized to his coach Don Cherry for winning his second Byng Trophy. Ratelle became a popular and consistent player in Boston, helping the Bruins to two Cup finals. He retired in 1981 sixth in all-time NHL scoring.

JEAN RATELLE
Lac St. Jean, Quebec
October 3, 1940–
NHL Career: 1960-81
NY Rangers, Boston

	GP	G	A	P	PIM
RS	1281	491	776	1267	276
PO	123	32	66	98	24

Byng (2), Pearson, Masterton, A-S Game (5), HOF 1985

GOALTENDER

Chuck Rayner called Eddie Shore "the greatest goaltending coach I ever had." Under Shore's insistent and innovative tutelage, Rayner developed strong skating and shooting skills. In 1940-41, he broke into the league with the New York Americans, which became the Brooklyn Americans the following season. Rayner then enlisted in the Canadian Navy and missed three NHL seasons. By war's end, the Brooklyn franchise had folded, and the Rangers signed Rayner for 1945-46.

Rayner led the league with five shutouts in 1946-47, and he often brought the crowd to its feet with his unprecedented roaming from the crease. He went behind his net, fielded pucks in the corner and even made rink-long rushes, attempting to become the first NHL netminder to score a goal. "Bonnie Prince Charlie" spent much of the 1947-48 season recovering from a broken cheekbone and was one of the first goalies to use a face mask, although he wore it only in practice.

Rayner made the Second All-Star Team in 1949 for the first of three consecutive seasons. His career year came in 1949-50. "To appreciate the greatness of Rayner," noted Ted Kennedy, "you must remember that he played on some very weak New York teams." Yet Rayner guided the Rangers to the 1950 Stanley Cup finals and was awarded the Hart Trophy. Unfortunately, the circus made its scheduled stop in Madison Square Garden that spring, and the Rangers had to play two "home" games in Toronto. The rest of the series was played in Detroit, and the Red Wings prevailed in the second overtime period of game seven. The Rangers didn't qualify for the playoffs again before Rayner concluded his NHL career in 1952-53.

CLAUDE "CHUCK" RAYNER
Sutherland, Saskatchewan
July 11, 1920–
NHL Career: 1940-42, 1945-53
NY Americans, Brooklyn, NY Rangers

	GP	M	GA	SO	AVE
RS	424	25491	1294	25	3.05
PO	18	1135	46	1	2.43

Hart, A-S Game (3), HOF 1973

KEN REARDON

DEFENSE

 1947, 1950 ⭐ 1946, 1948, 1949

Ken Reardon had a short Hall of Fame career, but as an old-fashioned bruiser, he left vivid memories. "Employing his lumbering 'tiptoe' style of approach, he defends his goal with crashing body checks," wrote Ron McAllister in 1950, "blocking out the enemy with brute strength and, more often than not, ending up in the penalty box." Reardon first laced up with the Montreal Canadiens as a teenager in the autumn of 1940 but joined Canada's war effort after two NHL seasons. He didn't return to the Habs until 1945-46, when he skated with his only Stanley Cup-winning team and was named to the Second All-Star Team.

An All-Star for five consecutive seasons, Reardon was a crowd favorite on home ice but was hated everywhere else.

He once scraped some ice shavings into a ball and fired them into the face of a heckler. In February 1946, he fought a Rangers player and, later, a fan sitting in the front row. "The crowd appeared to think Reardon should have been hung, drawn and quartered," wrote Kerr Petrie in New York's *Herald Tribune*, "but beyond the usual shower of paper and minor refuse, there was no scene worthy of the name." Reardon led his team in 1947-48 with 129 penalty minutes. The following season, an ugly stick-swinging battle with Toronto's Cal Gardner caused Reardon to miss 14 games with a broken shoulder. Both players were fined $250 each, and Reardon swore revenge. NHL president Clarence Campbell made him post a peace bond to ensure that he didn't make good on his threat.

In 1949-50, Reardon scored only one goal but set up 27 others in his best offensive season. Unfortunately, the First All-Star Team blue-liner badly dislocated his shoulder in the second playoff match that spring. Reardon never played another game, but he later worked in Canadiens' management.

KEN REARDON
Winnipeg, Manitoba
April 1, 1921–
NHL Career: 1940-42, 1945-50
Montreal

	GP	G	A	P	PIM
RS	341	26	96	122	604
PO	31	2	5	7	62

Stanley Cup, A-S Game (3), HOF 1966

RIGHT WING

Mark Recchi played 15 games for the Pittsburgh Penguins late in the 1988-89 campaign and scored a goal and an assist. The following season, he finished third in rookie scoring with 30 goals and 67 points. Only five-foot-ten and 185 pounds, Recchi capitalized on his explosive speed and heavy shot. He finished fourth in 1990-91 scoring with 40 goals and 113 points. Adding 10 goals and 34 playoff points, he helped Pittsburgh win the Stanley Cup. It didn't seem necessary to heed coach Scotty Bowman's call for stronger two-way play. Recchi had 70 points by February 1992, but Pittsburgh dealt him to Philadelphia. Shocked about his trade, Recchi nevertheless added 27 points in 22 games for the Flyers and made the Second All-Star Team.

In 1992-93, Recchi hit career-highs with 53 goals, 70 assists and 123 points, finishing tenth in the league. He tied

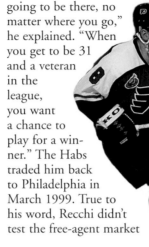

for fifth with 107 points the following season, but in February 1995, the Flyers traded him to Montreal. Although Recchi was the Canadiens' top scorer, the team's futility over several seasons had him thinking about playing elsewhere for 1999-2000. "The money is going to be there, no matter where you go," he explained. "When you get to be 31 and a veteran in the league, you want a chance to play for a winner." The Habs traded him back to Philadelphia in March 1999. True to his word, Recchi didn't test the free-agent market

that summer and, instead, signed a five-year contract with the Flyers.

He led the league with 63 assists in 1999-2000, coming third in total scoring with 91 points. Although right-wingers Jaromir Jagr and Pavel Bure finished ahead of him and denied Recchi All-Star honors, his contributions were noted. " 'Rex' has carried this team," said John LeClair. "You watch his play—it's inspiring."

MARK RECCHI				
Kamloops, British Columbia				
February 1, 1968–				
NHL Career: 1988-				
Pittsburgh, Philadelphia, Montreal				
	GP	G	A	P	PIM
RS	863	361	572	933	619
PO	69	27	50	77	49
Stanley Cup, A-S Game (7)				

RIGHT WING

While he saw only spot duty, Mickey Redmond won two Stanley Cup rings with the Montreal Canadiens. With more ice time—and a blistering slap shot—he tallied 27 goals in 1969-70. In January 1971, the Habs traded Redmond, Guy Charron and Bill Collins to Detroit in exchange for Frank Mahovlich. The Red Wings never qualified for the playoffs during

Redmond's years there, but he blossomed into an elite scorer.

Redmond scored 42 goals and 71 points in 1971-72, then in 1972-73, he became the first Detroit player ever to hit the 50-goal mark. With 52 goals and 93 points, he tied Mahovlich and Johnny Bucyk for seventh in league scoring and also made the First All-Star Team. "I'd say that right now, Mickey has the hardest shot in the league," said Detroit goalie Roy Edwards. "He's also got the second best wrist shot I've ever seen. Gordie Howe had the best."

Wary of losing their star to the WHA, the Red Wings rewarded Redmond with a five-year million-dollar contract in the summer of 1973. "We've long considered Mickey to be the best right-winger in the league," said general manager Ned Harkness. "He just fortified our confidence last season."

Although he lost his centerman Alex Delvecchio to retirement, Redmond made the 1974 Second All-Star Team.

He found the net 51 times, primarily after receiving passes from centers Charron and Bill Hogaboam. "They deserve a lot of the credit," said Redmond. "They were looking for me all the time. When you're getting five, six, seven shots a game, you're going to score." Redmond underwent back surgery in 1974-75. He tried to play the following season, but because of the excruciating leg pain and permanent nerve damage he had suffered, he dressed for his last game on January 18, 1976.

MICKEY REDMOND				
Kirkland Lake, Ontario				
December 27, 1947–				
NHL Career: 1967-76				
Montreal, Detroit				
	GP	G	A	P	PIM
RS	538	233	195	428	219
PO	16	2	3	5	2
Stanley Cup (2), A-S Game				

LEO REISE JR.

Leo Reise Sr. had cracked the NHL's top-10 scoring list with the 1922-23 Hamilton Tigers, but when no NHL club invited Leo Reise Jr. to training camp at the end of his junior career in 1942, he gave up on his dream of following in his father's footsteps to play professional hockey. Instead, Reise enlisted for military service. He became a Navy track-and-field star, then played on the Victoria Navy hockey team with goalie Chuck Rayner in 1943-44. Convinced by Rayner that he had NHL skills, Reise gave hockey his full attention when he resumed civilian life in 1945.

He joined the Chicago Blackhawks organization in 1945-46 and played six NHL games before the season ended. Still a borderline major-leaguer, he was

dealt to Detroit in December 1946. When Reise was paired with veteran Jack Stewart in 1947-48, however, his career took off. He never scored more than 5 goals and 21 points in a season, but he made the Second All-Star Team twice with clean, hard-hitting defense. "A rough, tough customer who packs 211 pounds into a rangy six-foot frame, Reise has forcibly left the stamp of his improvement all around the National Hockey League this season," reported Marshall Dann of *The Hockey News* in January 1950.

"With experience, I've learned to pick my spots for a real hard check and then hand it out," said Reise. "Scoring goals is a thrill, but a defenseman can get a lot of satisfaction out of hitting a player squarely and seeing him rolling on the

ice afterwards. You know that man isn't about to score goals, and after all, that's a defenseman's job—to prevent scoring." Reise helped the Red Wings win the Stanley Cup in 1950 and 1952, then concluded his NHL career playing two seasons with the New York Rangers.

LEO REISE JR.
Stoney Creek, Ontario
June 7, 1922–
NHL Career: 1945-54
Chicago, Detroit, NY Rangers

	GP	G	A	P	PIM
RS	494	28	81	109	399
PO	52	8	5	13	68

Stanley Cup (2), A-S Game (4)

GOALTENDER

⭐ 1976, 1979

His strong resemblance to comedian Freddie Prinze of the mid-1970s TV show *Chico and the Man* led to Glenn Resch's nickname. Resch played two games for the New York Islanders in 1973-74, earning a shot at a starting NHL job the following season. "Resch could be the sleeper at training camp,"

said Islanders general manager Bill Torrey. "I've only seen him play a few games, but in the games I saw, he was the outstanding player." Torrey's hunch proved correct, and Resch began a seven-year partnership with netminder Billy Smith.

Resch played twice as many games as Smith did during the 1975 playoffs, with a goals-against average that was almost half that of Smith. The next season, he notched career-bests with seven shutouts and a 2.07 average, making the Second All-Star Team. A crowd favorite, Resch continually posted better numbers than his cohort and made the 1979 Second All-Star Team as well.

Although Resch split the 1979 postseason almost evenly with Smith, he got only 2 of 21 starts in the Islanders' 1980 successful run to the Stanley Cup. "I was really hot at the end of the season," recalled Resch. "I was sure I was going to start in the playoffs. I actually became a Christian, a committed Christian, through that experience. I learned that my hockey career and my life were not

under my control." Late in the following season, the Islanders decided to trade Resch to the Colorado Rockies.

In the move from a champion team to an inept club, Resch never lost his exuberance. The league rewarded him with the 1982 Bill Masterton Trophy. The Rockies transferred to New Jersey in 1982-83, and in March 1986, Resch was traded to Philadelphia. He concluded his career primarily cheering rookie goalie Ron Hextall, and the Flyers almost won the 1987 Stanley Cup.

GLENN "CHICO" RESCH
Moose Jaw, Saskatchewan
July 10, 1948–
NHL Career: 1973-87
NY Islanders, Colorado, New Jersey, Philadelphia

	GP	M	GA	SO	AVE
RS	571	32279	1761	26	3.27
PO	41	2044	85	2	2.50

Masterton, Stanley Cup, A-S Game (3)

CENTER

⭐ 1958 ⭐ 1959, 1961, 1963

Henri Richard was determined to be a Montreal Canadien like his brother Maurice, 15 years his senior. He was a better skater than "The Rocket" and a stronger two-way player, but at five-foot-seven and 160 pounds, his size was always an issue. "My first coach in junior was Elmer Lach. I don't hold it against him, but he told me I was too small," smiled Richard. "But 20 years in the NHL, that's not too bad."

He brought his nickname, "The Pocket Rocket," from junior hockey to the NHL, where he proved that he belonged. While the younger Richard never displayed his brother's temper, he was aggressive and could not be intimidated. Coach Toe Blake tried him on the right wing—his brother's position—in his rookie season but soon had him at center with new linemates. Centering "The Rocket" and Dickie Moore, Richard and

the Habs embarked on an unprecedented five consecutive Cup-winning seasons.

Richard learned to use his stature to advantage. "One of the things he used to do when he went wide on me was lean into me and actually grab my knee," recalled defenseman Fernie Flaman. "We'd both go down, and I would get the penalty for holding, because it was impossible to see what Henri was doing. It used to drive me crazy." A relentless forechecker, Richard was quick and creative like his sibling but was more of a playmaker than a scorer. He came second in 1957-58 NHL points with 28 goals and a league-high 52 assists and made the First All-Star Team. He made the Second All-Star Team in 1959, 1961 and, again leading the league in assists, 1963.

Richard notched the seventh-game Stanley Cup-winning goal against Detroit in 1966 and against Chicago in 1971. As

team captain, he hoisted his eleventh and last Cup in 1973, an NHL record. His perseverance was acknowledged in 1974 with the Bill Masterton Trophy. "I have been blessed with a lot of great stars over the years," Canadiens general manager Frank Selke Sr. once said, "but game in, game out, Henri Richard may have been the most valuable player I ever had."

HENRI RICHARD
Montreal, Quebec
February 29, 1936–
NHL Career: 1955-75
Montreal

	GP	G	A	P	PIM
RS	1256	358	688	1046	928
PO	180	49	80	129	181

Masterton, Stanley Cup (11), A-S Game (10), HOF 1979

MAURICE RICHARD

RIGHT WING ⭐**1** 1945, 1946, 1947, 1948, 1949, 1950, 1955, 1956 ⭐**2** 1944, 1951, 1952, 1953, 1954, 1957

Most of Quebec's political and cultural elite joined the hockey world at Maurice Richard's state funeral in May 2000. The tributes to one of sport's most charismatic stars and larger-than-life figures flowed for weeks. In 1998-99, the NHL presented, for the first time, the Maurice "Rocket" Richard Trophy, an award that its namesake would have received five times himself as the season's top goal scorer. Although Richard won the Hart Trophy only once, in 1946-47, his value was never in doubt. "As soon as he'd touch the puck, you could feel the electricity in the crowd," said former teammate Bernie Geoffrion. "There's never been another one like him."

Richard broke an ankle in 1940, a wrist in 1941 and an ankle again in his 1942-43 NHL rookie campaign. Montreal considered trading the seemingly brittle young sniper, but the formation of the powerful "Punch Line" early the next season dispelled those thoughts. Coach Dick Irvin moved left-handed shooter Richard to the right side, with Elmer Lach at center and Toe Blake at left wing. Richard became an All-Star for the first of 14 consecutive seasons. In 1944-45, he was the first to score 50 goals in a season. Richard's 6 career playoff overtime goals remain an NHL record. "I've never played well enough to be pleased with myself," Richard admitted to *Maclean's* writer June Callwood in 1959. "If I get three, four goals, I know some of them have been lucky ones."

His passion was sometimes his undoing. Richard responded to a nasty slash late in the 1954-55 season by initiating a wild stick-swinging brawl and punching a linesman. His suspension for the remaining schedule and the ensuing playoffs triggered what became known as "The Richard Riot," a night of destruction that left downtown Montreal a mess.

Richard remained a force right until the end, when he hoisted Montreal's fifth consecutive Stanley Cup—his fourth as team captain—in 1960. "One of the great days in my life," recalled goalie Glenn Hall, "was when I heard Rocket Richard was retiring."

MAURICE "ROCKET" RICHARD
Montreal, Quebec
August 4, 1921–May 27, 2000
NHL Career: 1942-60
Montreal

	GP	G	A	P	PIM
RS	978	544	421	965	1285
PO	133	82	44	126	188

Hart, Stanley Cup (8), A-S Game (13), HOF 1961

PAT RIGGIN

GOALTENDER ⭐**2** 1984

Pat Riggin could claim a genetic predisposition to the netminding profession. His father Dennis enjoyed a lengthy minor pro career and made 18 NHL appearances with Detroit in the early 1960s. "You're born to be a goaltender," noted Riggin. "It comes naturally. You may be able to make a guy a center or a defenseman, but never a goaltender. Goalies are individuals. We have a job to do, and sometimes we just have to be a little different to get it done." After three stellar junior seasons, Riggin became a "Baby Bull" during Birmingham's final 1978-79 campaign in the WHA. The Atlanta Flames claimed him the following season, but it wasn't until the team migrated north to Calgary for 1980-81 that Riggin earned the number-one job.

The Washington Capitals sent the Flames three draft picks and two players for Riggin and winger Ken Houston in June 1982. Riggin shared duties with Al Jensen but had slipped to second string early in the 1983-84 campaign. Riggin was terribly upset when he was demoted to the AHL in Hershey, but he returned to Washington fully renewed after three games. He finished the season with a 2.66 goals-against average, the league's lowest, and made the Second All-Star Team. Riggin and Jensen shared the William M. Jennings Trophy.

By 1985-86, Riggin was struggling again. The Capitals traded him to Boston for Pete Peeters in November 1985. "I get paid to stop pucks, and I wasn't stopping them," admitted Riggin, who spent another stint in the AHL in 1986-87. "But I know I can do the job. I've had these bad stretches before." He never did get fully back on track again, though. Traded to the Pittsburgh Penguins in February 1987, Riggin concluded his NHL career the following season.

PAT RIGGIN
Kincardine, Ontario
May 26, 1959–
NHL Career: 1979-88
Atlanta, Calgary, Washington, Boston, Pittsburgh

	GP	M	GA	SO	AVE
RS	350	19872	1135	11	3.43
PO	25	1336	72	0	3.23

Jennings

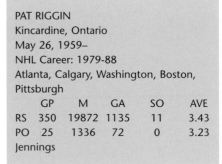

The goaltender of the Toronto St. Patricks was described as "jumpy" —and little wonder. John Ross Roach was only five-foot-five, 130 pounds and 21 years old when he stepped into the Toronto net in 1921-22. But he cleared his crease with authority and soon became known as "Little Napoleon." The rookie netminder led all playoff goalies with a 1.84 goals-against average and helped St. Pats edge the western-champion Vancouver Millionaires 2–1 in the deciding fifth game to win the Stanley Cup.

Although Roach played well, Toronto entered a fallow period. Just prior to the 1926-27 season, Conn Smythe bought the team and changed the club name to the Maple Leafs, but it made little difference. Trying to shake things up in October 1928, Smythe swapped goalies with the New York Rangers. Roach shone on Broadway, backstopping his team to the 1929 Stanley Cup finals.

But even though Roach led all playoff goalies that season, with three shutouts and a minuscule 0.77 goals-against average, it wasn't enough. His Ranger teammates could get only one goal past Boston's Tiny Thompson, and the Bruins won the Cup.

In 1931-32, Roach posted a league-leading nine shutouts and helped the Rangers back to the Cup finals. Unfortunately, the Toronto Maple Leafs put six goals past Roach in each of three straight games to sweep the Cup. Roach was sold to Detroit, and his opening game in Motown on December 13, 1932, marked two milestones: He became the first goalie to record 200 career victories; and the team, formerly the Falcons, played its first game sporting the winged and spoked wheel crest of the newly christened Detroit Red Wings. Roach led all goaltenders that season, with 25 victories and 10 shutouts, earning a spot on the First All-Star Team. The Wings faced Roach's former team in the Stanley Cup semifinals. "Roach has fared well against the Rangers this year," noted *The New York Times*, "having played a prominent role in turning back the New Yorkers four times in six games. Twice, with Roach guarding the cage, the Red Wings blanked the Rangers, and the first of those shutouts shattered an all-time major-league record compiled by the Rangers through 77 straight contests, during which they were not blanked once." New York took the two-game series 6–3, however, and went on to win the Stanley Cup. Roach spent parts of the next two seasons in the minors before retiring in the spring of 1935.

JOHN ROSS ROACH
Port Perry, Ontario
June 23, 1900–July 9, 1973
NHL Career: 1921-35
Toronto, NY Rangers, Detroit

	GP	M	GA	SO	AVE
RS	492	30444	1246	58	2.46
PO	34	2206	69	8	1.88
Stanley Cup					

RENE ROBERT

RIGHT WING

Buffalo fans were quick to embrace Rene Robert as the third member of "The French Connection,"and the Sabres eventually retired his number-14 sweater. Robert had had to pay his dues first, however. He had a five-game tryout with Toronto in 1970-71 and was then selected by Pittsburgh in the intra-league draft. He scored 7 goals in 49 games before being dealt to the Sabres in March 1972. Playing with Gilbert Perreault and Rick Martin, Robert scored 40 goals in 1972-73. "We just happened to click," he later told Randy Schultz of *The Hockey News*. "We fit into each other's patterns and began to know each other's moves. It was something I never experienced before or after I was in Buffalo… a once-in-a-lifetime experience."

Robert tallied another 40 goals in 1974-75, and with 60 assists, he became the first Sabre to notch 100 points. Seventh in league scoring, he made the Second All-Star Team. Robert's memorable overtime goal in the 1975 Stanley Cup

finals—scored while thick fog swirled around the players—proved to be Buffalo's postseason highlight. Robert's scoring slowly began to taper off, however, and in 1978-79, he complained about a

lack of ice time. His subsequent trade to Colorado hurt him deeply. "It was the saddest day of my life," said Robert. "I lost my desire to play the game."

"You're yapping all the time anyway," said Rockies coach Don Cherry. "You might as well wear the 'C' on your sweater." Robert led the team through most of 1979-80 and potted 28 goals, but he relinquished the captaincy to Lanny McDonald before season's end. Robert was traded to Toronto in January 1981, where he finished out his career.

RENE ROBERT					
Trois-Rivières, Quebec					
December 31, 1948–					
NHL Career: 1970-82					
Toronto, Pittsburgh, Buffalo, Colorado					
	GP	G	A	P	PIM
RS	744	284	418	702	597
PO	50	22	19	41	73
A-S Game (2)					

EARL ROBERTSON

GOALTENDER

Earl Robertson had his NHL baptism by fire. After 10 seasons in the minors, he made his major-league debut in the heat of the battle for the 1937 Stanley Cup. When Detroit netminder Normie Smith badly injured his elbow, Robertson had to start game one of the best-of-five final series against the New York Rangers. The teams split the first two games, and the Rangers won the third contest 1–0. Robertson took his sharp play up another notch, shut out the Rangers in game four and blanked them again in the deciding match. "He broke the hearts of the Ranger forwards with his catlike ability," wrote John McManis of *The Detroit News*. "Earl Robertson, the obscure rookie, the man not considered good

enough for major-league hockey, dominated the game."

Despite his heroics, Robertson was quickly traded to the New York Americans for journeyman Red Doran and $7,500 cash. He notched a shutout in his first NHL regular-season game and helped his team get to the 1938 semifinals, posting a league-low 1.52 playoff goals-against average. Unfortunately, the Americans never fared that well again.

"[The] Leafs dominated the second period and should have cashed a goal or two," wrote *The Globe and Mail*'s Bill Roche in March 1939. "But they could not produce any scoring luck in the face of Robertson's fine twine-tending." Two weeks later, Roche reported that the "busiest man at the Gardens last night was Earl Robertson, but the

Amerks' stellar netminder covered himself with glory despite the 7–3 victory [the] Leafs rang up." Although his club missed the 1939 playoffs, Robertson made the Second All-Star Team. He started to get competition from future Hall of Fame goalie Chuck Rayner in 1940-41, however, and lost the number-one job the following season. The then Brooklyn Americans franchise folded, and Robertson retired from the game.

EARL ROBERTSON					
Bengough, Saskatchewan					
November 24, 1910–January 19, 1979					
NHL Career: 1936-42					
Detroit, NY Americans, Brooklyn					
	GP	M	GA	SO	AVE
RS	190	11820	575	16	2.92
PO	15	995	29	2	1.75
Stanley Cup					

LARRY ROBINSON

DEFENSE

Larry Robinson contributed to six Stanley Cup victories and set an NHL record by competing in 20 consecutive playoffs. He joined the Canadiens midseason for their 1972-73 Stanley Cup run, still apprenticing while he built up more strength and toughness. Robinson took a regular shift the following season, and by 1974-75, his offensive skills began to shine as well.

As Montreal launched a four-season string of Cup victories in 1976, Robinson and fellow defensemen Serge Savard and Guy Lapointe became known as "The Big Three." A new tone was set when Robinson thrashed Philadelphia's top enforcer Dave Shultz in the 1976 finals. Robinson rarely had to fight again, for as coach Scotty Bowman noted, "He would just skate into the

middle of any trouble or confusion on the ice, and things would straighten out automatically."

Robinson began a five-season All-Star streak in 1976-77, winning a spot on the First Team. His 19 goals and 66 assists were both career-highs, and he took the Norris Trophy. In 1977-78, he won the Conn Smythe Trophy, matching sharpshooter Guy Lafleur for the playoff scoring lead with 21 points. "Big Bird" Robinson finished runner-up for the Norris in 1978-79 and won it a second time in 1979-80. He returned to the Second All-Star Team in 1986.

Robinson concluded his NHL career with three seasons in Los Angeles, signing a free-agent contract in July 1989. He was an assistant coach for the Stanley Cup-winning New Jersey Devils in 1995,

then became head coach of the Kings for four years. Fired in 1999, Robinson returned to New Jersey as an assistant. With only eight games left in the 1999-2000 season, though, Robinson replaced Robbie Ftorek and steered the Devils to another Cup victory.

LARRY ROBINSON
Winchester, Ontario
June 2, 1951–
NHL Career: 1972-92
Montreal, Los Angeles

	GP	G	A	P	PIM
RS	1384	208	750	958	793
PO	227	28	116	144	211

Norris (2), Smythe, Stanley Cup (6),
A-S Game (10), HOF 1995

LEFT WING   ★ 1988, 1989, 1990, 1991, 1993   ★2 1987, 1992

In Luc Robitaille, most scouts saw only a poor skater. Los Angeles selected him in the ninth round of the 1984 entry draft, pick number 171. But Robitaille scored 340 points in his last two seasons of junior hockey and won the 1986 Canadian Major Junior Player of the Year award. He jumped straight into the NHL and led the Kings and all NHL rookies with a 45-goal, 39-assist campaign. Robitaille won the 1987 Calder Trophy and made the Second All-Star Team, his first of seven consecutive All-Star seasons.

Robitaille's 53 goals and 111 points in 1987-88—good for a fifth-place tie in league scoring—lifted him to the First All-Star Team. He finished tenth in 1988-89 and fifth in 1991-92 before tallying his career-highs. While Wayne Gretzky was recovering from a back injury, Robitaille captained the Kings for the first half of the 1992-93 campaign. After scoring 63 goals and 125 points, "Lucky Luc" then added 22 playoff points as the Kings made their first trip to the Stanley Cup finals.

Although Robitaille notched his eighth straight campaign with at least 44 goals, the Kings missed the 1994 playoffs, and Robitaille was traded to Pittsburgh. He scored 27 goals over the lockout-shortened 1994-95 campaign, but the Penguins then dealt him to the New York Rangers. Robitaille struggled in the Big Apple, notching seasons of 23 and 24 goals, before the Rangers shipped him back to Los Angeles for Kevin Stevens in the summer of 1997. With 39 goals and 74 points in 1998-99, crowd-favorite Robitaille reestablished himself as the Kings' top scorer, a position he shows no signs of relinquishing.

LUC ROBITAILLE
Montreal, Quebec
February 17, 1966–
NHL Career: 1986-
Los Angeles, Pittsburgh, NY Rangers

	GP	G	A	P	PIM
RS	1042	553	597	1150	915
PO	119	49	61	110	154

Calder, A-S Game (7)

RIGHT WING   ⭐ 1966

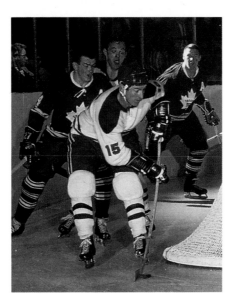

Fleet and possessing a hard, accurate shot, Bobby Rousseau broke in with the Canadiens late in the 1960-61 season, although he didn't see much ice time until the following year. He took a regular shift with center Ralph Backstrom and veteran Don Marshall during his official rookie campaign in 1961-62, tallying 21 goals and 24 assists and winning the Calder Trophy.

Although Rousseau was still developing as a player, the Canadiens trusted him in both power-play and penalty-killing situations. In 1963-64, he finished second on the team with 25 goals, including a 5-goal game against Detroit in February. Rousseau won his first Stanley Cup ring after finishing third in 1965 playoff scoring with 13 points. Playing primarily with Jean Beliveau and John Ferguson in 1965-66, Rousseau led the Habs in both goals and assists. His league-leading 48 helpers and career-high 78 points lifted him into a second-place tie in league scoring with Stan Mikita. He made the Second All-Star Team and helped

Montreal successfully defend the Cup.

Rousseau led the Canadiens with 44 assists and 63 points in 1966-67, despite receiving a two-game suspension for elbowing referee Art Skov. He finished sixth overall, his last top-10 scoring entry, and won two more Cup rings

in the following seasons. Rousseau led Montreal with 46 assists in 1967-68 and notched 30 goals and 70 points the following campaign. In 1970-71, however, Montreal traded him to Minnesota, where he faltered. The North Stars sent him to the New York Rangers the following season, and Rousseau regained his form. After scoring 21 goals and 36 assists, he added 17 playoff points while helping the Rangers to the 1972 Stanley Cup finals. Two less productive campaigns followed, and Rousseau retired after playing only eight games in the 1974-75 season.

BOBBY ROUSSEAU
Montreal, Quebec
July 26, 1940–
NHL Career: 1960-75
Montreal, Minnesota, NY Rangers

	GP	G	A	P	PIM
RS	942	245	458	703	359
PO	128	27	57	84	69

Calder, Stanley Cup (4), A-S Game (3)

GOALTENDER   1989, 1990, 1992   1988, 1991

His idiosyncratic but brilliant netminding technique and his passionate approach have made him a living legend. Patrick Roy played 20 minutes of shutout hockey for the Montreal Canadiens during his last season of junior hockey in 1984-85. He made the NHL All-Rookie Team the following season, then sparked the Canadiens to victory in the 1986 Stanley Cup finals. Roy won the Conn Smythe Trophy with a postseason 1.92 goals-against average. For the next three campaigns, he shared the William M. Jennings Trophy with partner Brian Hayward.

In 1987-88, Roy posted the first of five consecutive All-Star seasons. His first Vezina Trophy came in 1988-89, when he led the league with a 2.47 goals-against average. He went undefeated in the Montreal Forum with a

25–0–4 record, then backstopped the Habs to the Cup finals. Roy picked up the Vezina again in 1990 and 1992. He also won another Jennings single-handedly and finished runner-up for the Hart Trophy in 1992. In 1992-93, the Canadiens finished third in their division, but Roy anchored a record 10 playoff overtime victories en route to winning his second Smythe and another Cup ring. He heroically postponed surgery for appendicitis during the 1994 playoffs, and his position in the Habs net seemed secure. Unfortunately for the Montreal fans, Roy blew up at team president Ronald Corey after taking a nine-goal shellacking in December 1995. Traded to Colorado four days later, Roy led the Avalanche to the 1996 Cup, allowing but four goals during a sweep of the Florida Panthers. "[That performance] puts him

up there with the greatest goalies of all time," said Florida's John Vanbiesbrouck. "I'm not afraid to say that."

Roy's competitive zeal shows no signs of cooling. With a career-low 2.28 goals-against average in 1999-2000, he concluded the season three wins shy of Terry Sawchuk's record of 447 career victories.

PATRICK ROY
Quebec City, Quebec
October 5, 1965–
NHL Career: 1984-
Montreal, Colorado

	GP	M	GA	SO	AVE
RS	841	49100	2155	48	2.63
PO	195	12036	472	15	2.35

Jennings (4), Vezina (3), Smythe (2),
Stanley Cup (3), A-S Game (8)

BORJE SALMING

Not the first Europeans to play in the NHL, Swedes Borje Salming and Inge Hammarstrom were, nevertheless, a novelty. While Hammarstrom enjoyed some success, "B.J." Salming became a star, quickly establishing himself as a tough two-way defenseman, notching 34 assists in his 1973-74 rookie season. Although he was pummeled by Dave "The Hammer" Shultz during his first game in Philadelphia, intimidation never worked with Salming. "You have to admire this guy," former Leafs captain George Armstrong once said. "He can't fight worth beans, but who needs it when you can play hockey like him? Whoever said you can't keep a good man down was right. Salming is that kind of man."

Although he frequently looked as if he were on his last legs as he lugged the puck out of his own end, Salming had surprising speed and good moves. On defense, he was a ready and effective shot-blocker. Taking some of his frustration out during a practice once, he fired his stick into the empty stands. "Who do you think you are?" yelled Jim McKenny jokingly. "King of Sweden?" Salming was frequently called "King" from then on, but the nickname fit his dignified presence on the blue line.

Salming scored 12 goals and 25 assists in 1974-75, making an All-Star Team for the first of six consecutive campaigns, a Toronto record. In 1976-77, he peaked offensively with 78 points, including a career-best 66 assists. Graduating to the First All-Star Team, Salming was also runner-up to Larry Robinson for the Norris Trophy. He finished second behind Robinson in 1980 Norris voting as well.

The Leafs' fortunes sagged in the 1980s, but Salming was a constant bright light. During the 1987-88 season, he became the first European-trained player to play 1,000 NHL games, and his 620 assists with the Leafs remain a franchise record. He completed his NHL career in 1989-90 with the Detroit Red Wings and returned to Sweden. Having resumed play in the Swedish Elite League, he competed for his homeland in the 1991 Canada Cup and in the 1992 Olympics. Salming entered the Hockey Hall of Fame in 1996, but the greatest tribute to him may be in the preponderance of Swedes and Europeans in the NHL today.

BORJE SALMING
Kiruna, Sweden
April 17, 1951–
NHL Career: 1973-90
Toronto, Detroit

	GP	G	A	P	PIM
RS	1148	150	637	787	1344
PO	81	12	37	49	91

A-S Game (3), HOF 1996

ED SANDFORD

Hailed as Milt Schmidt's eventual replacement, Ed Sandford scored modestly for six seasons before exploding with 6 goals against Detroit in the 1953 playoffs. He finished the postseason with a league-high 11 points. "I was the leader," he laughed later, "but not many goals were scored…Guys like Richard and Howe had two men on their backs all the time."

The Bruins switched him from center to left wing for 1953-54. Although the move was made to accommodate Fleming Mackell, Sandford blossomed. "Now I can skate my lane, concentrate on getting into scoring position and think about checking back with my man when

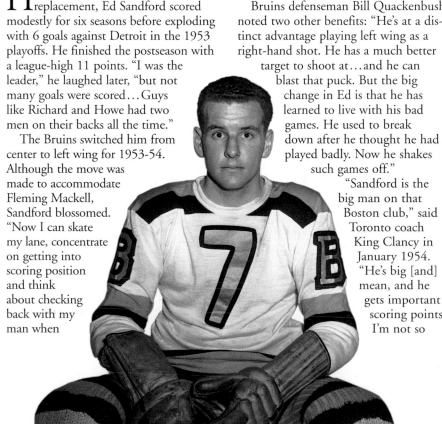

the other team gets the puck," he said.

Bruins defenseman Bill Quackenbush noted two other benefits: "He's at a distinct advantage playing left wing as a right-hand shot. He has a much better target to shoot at…and he can blast that puck. But the big change in Ed is that he has learned to live with his bad games. He used to break down after he thought he had played badly. Now he shakes such games off."

"Sandford is the big man on that Boston club," said Toronto coach King Clancy in January 1954. "He's big [and] mean, and he gets important scoring points. I'm not so sure I'd take [Ted] Lindsay over Sandford at the moment." Sandford made the Second All-Star Team and tied with Mackell for eighth place in league scoring with 47 points. After a more average 1954-55 season, Sandford was included in the Bruins' multiplayer deal with Detroit for Terry Sawchuk that summer. Sandford went to Chicago early in the 1955-56 campaign but retired when the Blackhawks sent him to the minors for the start of the following season.

ED SANDFORD
New Toronto, Ontario
August 20, 1928–
NHL Career: 1947-56
Boston, Detroit, Chicago

	GP	G	A	P	PIM
RS	502	106	145	251	355
PO	42	13	11	24	27

A-S Game (5)

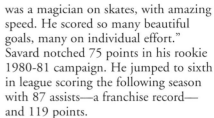
Over three seasons with the Montreal Junior Canadiens, Denis Savard tallied 455 points. Montreal fans could not believe it when their team let him go to Chicago, despite the fact that the Habs had first pick in the 1980 entry draft. "Denis Savard was one of my favorites," said Theoren Fleury, who took inspiration from the five-foot-ten, 175-pound Savard. "He wasn't big, but he was a magician on skates, with amazing speed. He scored so many beautiful goals, many on individual effort." Savard notched 75 points in his rookie 1980-81 campaign. He jumped to sixth in league scoring the following season with 87 assists—a franchise record—and 119 points.

Playing on a line with snipers Steve Larmer and Al Secord, Savard made the Second All-Star Team in 1983. His 86 helpers and 121 points lifted him into third place in overall scoring, and he had three more top-10 finishes in the 1980s. "The thing I live in fear of most in life is making a Denis Savard highlight film," joked Hartford Whalers defenseman Joel Quenneville. "I don't even want to be seen in the background of one of his goals." Savard's 47 goals in 1985-86 were a personal best, and he set another Blackhawk record with 131 points in 1987-88.

Montreal finally acquired Savard in 1990, trading Chris Chelios and a second-round draft pick for him. But Savard's high-scoring days were behind him, and he averaged 60 points a season over three campaigns with the Canadiens. He did earn a Stanley Cup ring in 1993, however, shortly before signing with Tampa Bay as a free agent. Traded back to Chicago in April 1995, Savard retired after picking up only 27 points in 1996-97. The Blackhawks hoisted his jersey number 18 to the rafters the following season. He received another honor two years later. "It's a great day for me and Joey," Savard said after learning that he and Joe Mullen would enter the Hall of Fame in November 2000. "It's something I'll cherish forever."

DENIS SAVARD
Pointe-Gatineau, Quebec
February 4, 1961–
NHL Career: 1980-97
Chicago, Montreal, Tampa Bay

	GP	G	A	P	PIM
RS	1196	473	865	1338	1336
PO	169	66	109	175	256

Stanley Cup, A-S Game (7), HOF 2000

DEFENSE ⭐2 1979

It is surprising that Serge Savard made only one All-Star Team. Consistently dependable and frequently brilliant, he was a key player on seven Stanley Cup-winners. He played his first couple of games for Montreal in 1966-67, then helped the Habs win the Cup the next two seasons. Savard earned the Conn Smythe Trophy for his 1969 playoff performance, a virtuoso effort at both ends of the rink.

He broke his leg midway through the 1970-71 campaign and snapped it again early the following season. There were worries that he was too brittle, but Savard thereafter proved himself a durable competitor. He played for Team Canada in 1972, participating in Canada's four wins and a tie but in none of the team's losses. The following spring, he completed his most productive playoff, scoring 3 goals and 11 points and getting his name on the Cup for the third time.

Savard was the elder statesman of Montreal's "Big Three," a corps of stalwart defensemen that included Guy Lapointe and Larry Robinson. Defense became the backbone of a dynasty in the works, but Savard also showed his playmaking skills. He posted career-highs with 20 goals and 40 assists in 1974-75. While Montreal won the Cup for the next four seasons in a row, Savard tallied 47, 42, 42 and 33 points, respectively. He made the Second All-Star Team for the latter campaign, in 1978-79, and also won the Bill Masterton Trophy.

Savard wore the captain's "C" for two seasons before announcing his retirement at the end of the 1980-81 campaign. But the Winnipeg Jets talked him into joining them instead. Savard helped the Jets make the playoffs for the first time before finishing his playing career in 1982-83.

SERGE SAVARD
Montreal, Quebec
January 22, 1946–
NHL Career: 1966-83
Montreal, Winnipeg

	GP	G	A	P	PIM
RS	1040	106	333	439	592
PO	130	19	49	68	88

Masterton, Smythe, Stanley Cup (7), A-S Game (4), HOF 1986

TERRY SAWCHUK

GOALTENDER   ⭐ 1951, 1952, 1953   ⭐ 1954, 1955, 1959, 1963

Terry Sawchuk's 103 NHL shutouts are an untouchable record, but the goaltender had a tortured and tragic NHL career. Shortly after the 1969-70 season, he sustained injuries when he fell over a barbecue during a fight with teammate Ron Stewart. The 40-year-old Sawchuk subsequently died in hospital of internal bleeding.

While notching a league-leading 11 shutouts in 1950-51, Sawchuk made the First All-Star Team and took the Calder Trophy. The following season, he raised his game still higher. He earned the Vezina Trophy with 12 shutouts and a 1.90 goals-against average. In the play-offs, Sawchuk didn't allow a single goal at home. He lowered his average to 0.63, and Detroit swept to the Stanley Cup in eight straight games. Frank Boucher, then manager of the New York Rangers, agreed in 1952 that people were watching hockey's greatest goalie. "I'm sure that they'll be saying the same thing about Sawchuk years from now." By 1954-55, the goalie had had his name on both the Vezina and the Stanley Cup three times.

Sawchuk made a long-lasting contribution to the game when he pioneered a new goaltending stance. "I found that

I could move more quickly from the crouch position," he explained. "It gave me better balance to go both ways, especially with my legs. Scrambles and shots from the point were becoming the style in hockey when I broke into the NHL. From the crouch, I could keep the puck in my vision much better when it was coming through a maze of players."

Unfortunately, Sawchuk's prowess in the net was the antithesis of his ability to function off the ice. "The first time I met Terry Sawchuk," recalled Joe Falls of *The Detroit Free Press*, "he was raging with anger and shouting obscenities and throwing his skates at a reporter. This was in 1953. In all the years to follow, he never really changed."

In a stunning trade, Sawchuk was sent to Boston for the 1955-56 season. His confidence rattled, he still tallied nine shutouts but suffered a nervous breakdown and temporarily quit the game midway through the following season. The Bruins sent him back to Detroit for 1957-58. Although he recovered most of his form, Sawchuk spent the rest of his career battling a litany of injuries and health problems. "When it came time to waken him," his wife recalled, "I

often had to help him out of bed and, later, into the car for the trip to the rink. Then he'd take a painkiller pill, timing it so he would unstiffen by the time the buzzer sounded to skate out onto the ice."

Nevertheless, Sawchuk made the Second All-Star Team in 1959 and again in 1963. After Toronto picked him up in the 1964 intra-league draft, Sawchuk shared his fourth Vezina with Johnny Bower in 1964-65 and supped from the Stanley Cup in 1967. Playing fewer and fewer games, however, he bounced to Los Angeles, Detroit and New York. Sawchuk's posthumous entry into the Hockey Hall of Fame was in 1971.

TERRY SAWCHUK
Winnipeg, Manitoba
December 28, 1929–May 31, 1970
NHL Career: 1949-70
Detroit, Boston, Toronto, Los Angeles, NY Rangers

	GP	M	GA	SO	AVE
RS	971	57228	2401	103	2.52
PO	106	6290	267	12	2.55

Calder, Vezina (4), Stanley Cup (4), A-S Game (11), HOF 1971

MILT SCHMIDT

Remembered as one of the NHL's best-ever combinations, the "Kraut Line" excelled at tough two-way hockey. Although childhood friends Milt Schmidt, Bobby Bauer and Woody Dumart all played for the Kitchener Greenshirts, which won the 1935 Memorial Cup, they didn't form a line until the autumn of 1936. Their skills and personalities jibed magnificently when coach Aldo Leduc of the AHL's Providence Reds put them on the ice together. Schmidt and Dumart moved up to Boston halfway through the 1936-37 campaign, and Bauer joined them at season's end.

The threesome made an important contribution to Boston's Stanley Cup-winning team of 1939. Schmidt, the youngest and most belligerent of the "Krauts," led the NHL with 30 assists and 52 points the following season. Bauer and Dumart were right behind their First All-Star Team center—

the first time a line finished 1–2–3. The Bruins won the Cup again in 1940-41, but in the early spring of 1942, Schmidt, Bauer and Dumart enlisted in the Royal Canadian Air Force. They served for the last three years of the Second World War, mostly overseas. Not until the 1946-47 season did Schmidt fully recover from his military duty. Finishing fourth in league scoring with a career-high 27 goals and 35 assists, he made the First All-Star Team. With Bauer's retirement at the end of that season, however, the "Kraut Line" dissolved.

Schmidt had another First All-Star Team season in 1950-51, finishing fourth in league scoring and winning the Hart Trophy. Tenth in scoring the following season, Schmidt made the Second All-Star Team. He put in a valiant effort in the 1953 Stanley Cup finals, although Boston lost to Montreal in seven games. "He's surely one of the greatest," wrote Eddie MacCabe in *The Mon-*

treal Star. "He has a heart as big as a pail."

Twenty-three games into the 1954-55 season, Schmidt moved behind the Boston bench. He was the first coach to pull his goalie during a delayed penalty call, a move that quickly became standard practice. Schmidt guided the Bruins to the Stanley Cup finals in 1957 and 1958. As Boston's general manager from 1967 to 1972, he saw his name engraved on the Cup two more times.

MILTON SCHMIDT
Kitchener, Ontario
March 5, 1918–
NHL Career: 1936-42, 1945-55
Boston

	GP	G	A	P	PIM
RS	776	229	346	575	466
PO	86	24	25	49	60

Ross, Hart, Stanley Cup (2),
A-S Game (4), HOF 1961

JIM SCHOENFELD

DEFENSE

He battled injuries throughout his career, but Jim Schoenfeld made an immediate impression as a tower of strength in Buffalo. "They're paying me a lot to hang around and help him, but he's helping me too," said veteran Tim Horton in February 1973. "My old legs don't get me up-ice like they used to, so I let the kid [Schoenfeld] carry the puck. This kid is superstar stuff." Although Schoenfeld was not a great skater, his tough defensive skills made him a 1973 Calder Trophy candidate.

Named team captain during the 1974-75 season, Schoenfeld piled up a career-high 184 penalty minutes and led the Sabres to the 1975 Stanley Cup finals. General manager Punch Imlach deemed him too involved in the NHL Players' Association, however, and stripped him of the captaincy in the summer of 1977. "I was embarrassed by it," admitted Schoenfeld, "but it's hard to hate the old guy when you talk to him face-to-face and he lays out that charm of his."

Schoenfeld hit his offensive peak in 1979-80, notching 9 goals and 27 assists and making the Second All-Star Team. But when the Sabres had a roster shake-up in December 1981, they traded Schoenfeld, Danny Gare and Derek

Smith to the Red Wings. "I like it in Detroit, but all I was hearing was, 'In five years, we'll have a contender,' " said Schoenfeld, explaining his free-agent signing with Boston for 1983-84. "I honestly believe the Bruins can win the Cup this year." Boston bowed out of the playoffs in the semifinals, though, and Schoenfeld began a successful coaching career. Lured back to action by the Sabres in December 1984, when injuries decimated Buffalo's rearguard corps, Schoenfeld went behind the Buffalo bench at season's end.

JIM SCHOENFELD					
Galt, Ontario					
September 4, 1952–					
NHL Career: 1972-85					
Buffalo, Detroit, Boston					
	GP	G	A	P	PIM
RS	719	51	204	255	1132
PO	75	3	13	16	151
A-S Game (2)					

SWEENEY SCHRINER

LEFT WING

Calgary-raised Dave Schriner was so enraptured with his hometown hero, semipro baseball player Bill Sweeney, that he became known as "L'il Sweeney." The "Sweeney" stuck for life. Schriner was foremost a hockey player, however, and he broke into the NHL with the New York Americans in 1934-35. Playing on a line with Art Chapman and Lorne Carr, Schriner tallied 18 goals and 22 assists. Eighth in league scoring, he was named rookie of the year.

The following season, Schriner led the league with 45 points and made the First All-Star Team.

Despite a late-season flourish that left him with 21 goals and 46 points, Schriner was relegated to the Second All-Star Team for 1936-37. "Dave 'Sweeney' Schriner, the poker-

faced Westerner who patrols the left-wing boards for New York's not-so-amazing Amerks," reported Montreal's *Gazette* on March 22, 1937, "broke out in a scoring rush down the stretch in the NHL race. [His] narrow victory made the hard-driving American winger the second man in the league's 20-year history to win the [scoring] championship two years in succession." In 1937-38, Schriner tied for seventh in the league and was runner-up the following season. Shortly thereafter, the Maple Leafs traded five players, including Busher Jackson, for Schriner's services.

Schriner made the First All-Star Team again in 1941 with 24 goals, tenth in league scoring. He led the Leafs with 6 playoff markers in 1942. Toronto rebounded from a 3–0 deficit in games against Detroit

before Schriner potted 2 goals in a 3–1 victory in the deciding game for the Stanley Cup. He missed the 1943-44 season and part of the next because of military service but was back with the Leafs in January 1945. Schriner notched 22 goals in only 26 games, adding 3 playoff goals, and Toronto won the Stanley Cup again. One season later, after scoring a career-low 19 points, Schriner retired.

DAVE "SWEENEY" SCHRINER					
Saratov, Russia					
November 30, 1911–July 4, 1990					
NHL Career: 1934-43, 1944-46					
NY Americans, Toronto					
	GP	G	A	P	PIM
RS	484	201	204	405	148
PO	59	18	11	29	54
Calder, Ross (2), Stanley Cup (2),					
A-S Game, HOF 1962					

DEFENSE ★ 1935, 1942, 1943, 1944 ★ 1936, 1937, 1938, 1939, 1940, 1941

Although he retired in 1946 with more All-Star selections than any player in NHL history before him, Earl Seibert was almost immediately forgotten. With little fanfare, he finally entered the Hockey Hall of Fame in 1963, when he joined his father Oliver, a turn-of-the-century star who'd been posthumously elected two years earlier. "He vanished from the face of the earth when he got out of the game," recalled Art Coulter, reminiscing with *The Toronto Sun*'s Wayne Parrish shortly after Seibert's death in 1990. Coulter had been sent to New York in exchange for Seibert back in January 1936, when the Rangers and the Blackhawks swapped All-Stars.

By 1933, the six-foot-two, 200-pound Seibert was a valuable member of the Rangers' Cup-winning team. He brought his reputation as a hard hitter and an excellent shot-blocker to Chicago and didn't disappoint. In a game against the Montreal Canadiens in 1937, Seibert managed to knock over speedster Howie Morenz. Some claim the hit was a cross-check from behind, but regardless, it was a move that had tragic consequences. With Seibert on top of him as they slid along the ice, Morenz tried to free himself and caught his skate in a rut, badly breaking his leg. The Canadiens' legend died six weeks later when a blood clot that had developed in his leg stopped his heart. For years afterward, the Montreal fans booed the quiet and reserved Seibert. "My father never got over that to the day he died," recalled Seibert's son.

A consistent and feared force on the Chicago blue line for nine years, Seibert helped the Blackhawks to the 1938 Stanley Cup. "He hits just about as hard a body check as any player in hockey but is seldom spilled," boasted the *Chicago Stadium Review* in 1943. "He is cool, steady, fast and a fine stickhandler when carrying the puck." The Red Wings traded defenseman Cully Simon and forwards Don Grosso and Byron McDonald to Chicago for Seibert on January 2, 1945. Seibert finished out his NHL career in Detroit in 1945-46, ending the season in the AHL before briefly turning his attention to coaching.

EARL SEIBERT
Kitchener, Ontario
December 7, 1911–May 12, 1990
NHL Career: 1931-46
NY Rangers, Chicago, Detroit

	GP	G	A	P	PIM
RS	645	89	187	276	746
PO	66	11	8	19	76

Stanley Cup (2), A-S Game, HOF 1963

TEEMU SELANNE

RIGHT WING

Teemu Selanne surprised his NHL opponents in 1992-93 with his speed, desire and creativity. "Most of the season, the guys on the other team didn't know my style," he explained to Mike Brophy of *The Hockey News*. "I was way open all the time. I had at least two breakaways every game." Selanne shattered the rookie scoring records with 76 goals and 132 points, good for a fifth-place tie overall. He made the First All-Star Team and won the Calder Trophy.

"The Finnish Flash" missed almost half of his sophomore season with Winnipeg because of a severed Achilles tendon, then scored 22 goals during the lockout-shortened 1994-95 campaign. Selanne resumed a more productive pace the following season. Anaheim's Paul Kariya

grew even more impressed after spending time with the easygoing right-winger at the 1996 All-Star Game. The Mighty Ducks soon traded for Selanne, putting him on Kariya's line. Anaheim's dynamic duo finished the season tied for seventh in league scoring with 108 points.

Selanne made it back to the First All-Star Team in 1997. His 51 goals and 109 points were each second-best in the NHL. He filled in as team captain for the injured Kariya and led the league in goal scoring with 52 tallies in 1997-98, joining the Second All-Star Team both that season and the next. Selanne also won the inaugural Maurice "Rocket" Richard Trophy for his 47 goals in 1998-99 and was runner-up in total scoring. He finished tied for fifth spot

in 1999-2000, although he counted only 33 goals. "I know when I play well, the numbers will be there," said Selanne, declaring team success more important. "But scoring is magical. It will be a great feeling when the goals come in bunches again. I can't wait."

TEEMU SELANNE
Helsinki, Finland
July 3, 1970–
NHL Career: 1992-
Winnipeg, Anaheim

	GP	G	A	P	PIM
RS	564	346	383	729	197
PO	21	13	7	20	8

Calder, Richard, A-S Game (7)

BRENDAN SHANAHAN

LEFT WING

Big and strong at six-foot-three and 218 pounds, 18-year-old Brendan Shanahan cracked the New Jersey lineup at right wing during the 1987-88 season. The Devils moved him to the left side the following campaign. After four NHL seasons, Shanahan signed a free-agent contract with St. Louis in July 1991. When a dispute over compensation arose, the Blues lost their captain, Scott Stevens, to New Jersey. Shanahan justified the arbitrator's high opinion of him with 33 goals in 1991-92, then erupted for 51 goals and 94 points in 71 games the next season.

Shanahan made the 1994 First All-Star Team with 52 goals and 102 points. Yet Mike Keenan, the new St. Louis coach and general manager for 1994-95, traded him for Hartford's Chris Pronger in July 1995. "I didn't realize the type of player Brendan was in St. Louis," said Pronger, who had a hard time winning over the disgruntled fans. "You knew he scored 50 goals and all those things, but you didn't realize the pillar in the community that he was and [the] things he did off the ice that everybody loved him for."

Captaining the Hartford Whalers for

1995-96, Shanahan led the team with 44 goals. Unhappy with the franchise's precarious state, however, he requested a trade and joined Detroit in October 1996. He has led the Red Wings in goal scoring ever since. Stanley Cup wins in 1997 and 1998 have been highlights, and Shanahan also made the 2000 First All-Star Team with 41 goals and 37 assists. "After the year I had, I wanted to follow it up," he said, upset at reduced ice time in the 2000 playoffs. "I am extremely frustrated. I'm angry, and I'm disappointed that I wasn't given an opportunity to do more for this team." He'll undoubtedly have other chances in the future.

BRENDAN SHANAHAN
Mimico, Ontario
January 23, 1969–
NHL Career: 1987-
New Jersey, St. Louis, Hartford, Detroit

	GP	G	A	P	PIM
RS	947	435	444	879	1854
PO	110	40	46	86	207

Stanley Cup (2), A-S Game (6)

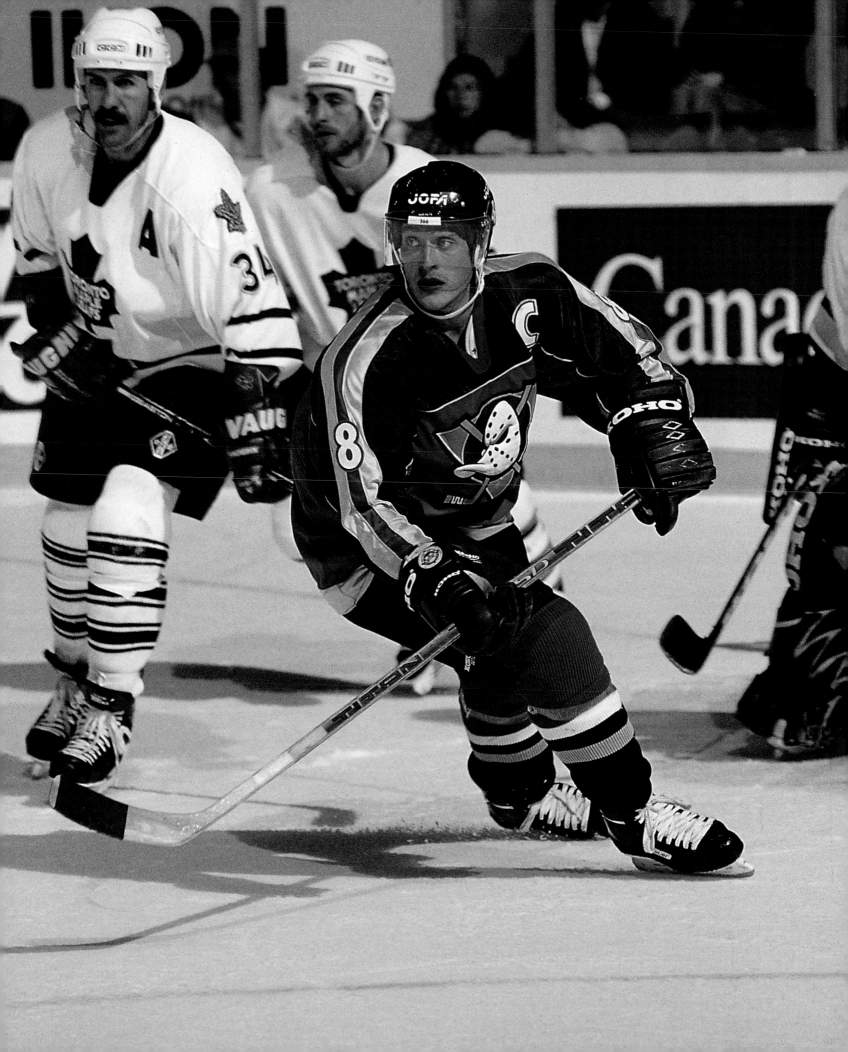

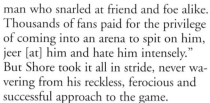 1931, 1932, 1933, 1935, 1936, 1938, 1939 ⭐ 1934

Eddie Shore was an inaugural—and a perennial—All-Star. Only his 16-game suspension in 1933-34 for a hit from behind which had ended the career of Toronto's Ace Bailey explains his demotion to the Second All-Star Team that season. "It is not easy to describe for a younger generation just how mag-

netic a personality he was," wrote Jimmy Powers in a 1962 New York *Daily News* profile. "He seemed to give off sparks in the heat of battle." Yet Shore was likely the most despised man ever to play NHL hockey.

"He was no charmer," recalled Powers. "He was mean and rough, a belligerent

man who snarled at friend and foe alike. Thousands of fans paid for the privilege of coming into an arena to spit on him, jeer [at] him and hate him intensely." But Shore took it all in stride, never wavering from his reckless, ferocious and successful approach to the game.

Because Shore used an unusually long stride to gain tremendous speed to bash and crash his way through and around the opposition, New York Rangers manager Lester Patrick called the four-time Hart Trophy-winner "the human gyroscope." Raymond Schuessler described one of Shore's patented moves in a 1947 issue of *Sportfolio*: "It was a thrill to watch the cyclonic Shore rush down the ice in spectacular solos, bang the puck off the boards while he knocked a defenseman dizzy, retrieve the puck at full speed and pass it back to his roaring forwards who had followed him in."

Shore was also a defensive stalwart who usually played 50 to 55 minutes per game. His NHL career, however, came to an acrimonious end. In 1939, Shore bought the Springfield Indians, a minor pro team. He decided to play for his own team and to join the Bruins when his schedule allowed. Unable to convince or coerce him to do otherwise, Boston sold his contract. Shore played his last 10 NHL games for the New York Americans. As an owner, his notorious penny-pinching, bizarre training techniques and home remedies caused untold grief and eventually sparked revolt among the players. Yet although they were reluctant to admit it, many credited Shore's tutoring as a key to their NHL success.

EDDIE SHORE
Fort Qu'Appelle, Saskatchewan
November 25, 1902–March 17, 1985
NHL Career: 1926-40
Boston, NY Americans

	GP	G	A	P	PIM
RS	550	105	179	284	1047
PO	55	6	13	19	181

Hart (4), Stanley Cup (2), A-S Game (3), HOF 1947

STEVE SHUTT

Rookie Steve Shutt sipped champagne from the Stanley Cup in 1973, but the Montreal Canadiens brought him along slowly. Shutt finished a standout junior career with 133 goals in his last two seasons with the Toronto Marlies. Possessing a hard, accurate shot as well as a knack for getting into shooting position, Shutt made incremental progress in his first two NHL seasons. The 1974-75 campaign marked his evolution into a major contributor. Playing on a line with Guy Lafleur and Pete Mahovlich, who finished fourth and fifth in league scoring, respectively, Shutt scored 30 goals and 35 assists. He tallied 45 goals the following season and added 15 points in 13 playoff games to help the Canadiens win the first of four consecutive Cups.

"During the regular season, the big scorers did a lot of the work," noted Shutt modestly, "but in the playoffs, it was the people I like to call the plumbers—the ones that did all the dirty work—who carried the club. They never get much recognition, but they're the backbone of the team."

Shutt led the NHL with 60 goals in 1976-77, setting a record for left-wingers. His 105 points lifted him into third in NHL scoring and onto the First All-Star Team. When Montreal traded Mahovlich to Pittsburgh, Jacques Lemaire became his regular centerman, and Shutt continued to find the net. He made the Second All-Star Team in 1978 with 49 goals and 37 assists. Two seasons later, when he tallied 47 goals and 42 helpers, he completed his final All-Star campaign.

Not until 1983-84 did Shutt score fewer than 30 goals, but as part of a move toward more defensive hockey, the Habs traded him to Los Angeles the following season. Shutt scored 16 goals and 25 assists for the Kings during the last 59 games of the 1984-85 schedule, then announced that he was quitting.

Although Montreal claimed him in the 1985 waiver draft, Shutt had no desire "to fight for a job with the Canadiens, and I don't want to play in another city." He retired as the twentieth leading goal scorer in NHL history. Shutt has since worked as a Canadiens broadcaster and as an assistant coach.

STEVE SHUTT
Toronto, Ontario
July 1, 1952–
NHL Career: 1972-85
Montreal, Los Angeles

	GP	G	A	P	PIM
RS	930	424	393	817	410
PO	99	50	48	98	65

Stanley Cup (5), A-S Game (3),
HOF 1993

BABE SIEBERT

DEFENSE

Rugged rookie defenseman Babe Siebert was on the Montreal Maroons' 1925-26 championship team, but he made a successful transition to left wing in 1930. "For all his strength, he was a fine skater, a good puck carrier and a really good left-hand shot," noted Frank Selke in his book *Behind the Cheering*. "But…his principal stock-in-trade was an indomitable fighting spirit and the will to win."

As a member of the powerful "S-Line," with Hooley Smith and centerman Nels Stewart, Siebert earned 21 goals and 18 assists, which were good enough to put him in an eighth-place tie in the 1931-32 scoring race.

The New York Rangers opened the checkbook that summer, though, and Siebert moved to the Big Apple. "Lester Patrick is apparently turning Babe Siebert into a defenseman," wrote Marc T. McNeil of *The Gazette* on March 17,

1933. " 'The Flying Dutchman,' of the famous lightning shot, worked beside Ching Johnson." The Rangers won the 1933 Stanley Cup, and the Boston Bruins took note.

When Boston blue-liner Eddie Shore was suspended early in the 1933-34 campaign, the Bruins traded two wingers for Siebert. He filled the hole admirably, and when Shore returned to action, the two formed a fearsome pair. Although they reportedly never exchanged a word together because of a clash they'd had as opponents, Siebert joined Shore on the First All-Star Team of 1936. He was then dealt back to Montreal, this time to play for the Canadiens.

As team captain, Siebert earned the

1937 Hart Trophy and added All-Star honors that season and the next. When he started to slow down, Montreal named him coach for the 1939-40 season. Unfortunately, Siebert drowned while swimming that summer. On October 29, 1939, the Montreal Canadiens played the NHL All-Stars in the "Babe Siebert Memorial Game" as a benefit to raise money for his young family.

ALBERT "BABE" SIEBERT				
Plattsville, Ontario				
January 14, 1904–August 25, 1939				
NHL Career: 1925-39				
Montreal Maroons, NY Rangers, Boston, Montreal				
	GP	G	A	P	PIM
RS	592	140	156	296	982
PO	53	8	7	15	64
Hart, Stanley Cup (2), A-S Game, HOF 1964				

CHARLIE SIMMER

LEFT WING

Charlie Simmer was a rookie with the California Golden Seals in 1974-75 but went up and down between the NHL and the minors until 1978-79. The Seals had moved to Cleveland in August

1976, but Simmer played only 24 games as a Baron. He signed a free-agent contract with Los Angeles in August 1977, and midway through the 1978-79 campaign, he found his niche beside center Marcel Dionne and right-winger Dave Taylor. Simmer tallied 21 goals and 27 assists in 38 games. "We just clicked together right off the bat," recalled Dionne. "Charlie had good range and was the type of guy who goes to the net."

At six-foot-three and 210 pounds, Simmer was the biggest member of the "Triple Crown Line" but was the one most hampered by injuries. He played only 64 games in 1979-80 yet led the league with 56 goals. With 101 points, he came seventh in total scoring and made the First All-Star Team. Simmer took a serious run at one of hockey's enduring markers of greatness the following season and notched his 50th goal in game 51. Unfortunately, he broke his ankle and finished the campaign in seventh place with 56 goals

once again, retaining his All-Star status.

Simmer spent much of 1981-82 healing but rebounded with 80 points the following season and 92 points in 1983-84. A contract dispute led to his trade to Boston in October 1984. Still dogged by injuries, he won the 1986 Bill Masterton Trophy for his perseverance and notched 98 goals over three seasons with the Bruins. Simmer concluded his NHL career by playing the 1987-88 campaign for the Pittsburgh Penguins.

CHARLIE SIMMER				
Terrace Bay, Ontario				
March 20, 1954–				
NHL Career: 1974-88				
California, Cleveland, Los Angeles, Boston, Pittsburgh				
	GP	G	A	P	PIM
RS	712	342	369	711	544
PO	24	9	9	18	32
Masterton, A-S Game (2)				

CENTER 1978

He remains the Maple Leafs' all-time leader in goals and points, but career statistics tell only part of Darryl Sittler's story. "He wasn't the best stick-handler in the world, and he didn't have the greatest shot," said friend and Toronto linemate Lanny McDonald. "He wasn't the toughest guy in the league, either, but probably was in the top three-quarters of every division. You put it all together and add a huge heart, you've got a guy you'd like to go to war with."

Sittler joined the Leafs in 1970-71, and within three seasons, he led the team with 77 points. He made the NHL's top-10 scoring list for the first time in 1974-75 and was named team captain the following season. Although Sittler became the first Toronto player to notch 100 points,

1976 remains significant for other reasons. On February 7, Sittler scored 6 goals and 4 assists against the Boston Bruins, breaking Maurice Richard's record. He reentered "Rocket" territory with a 5-goal game against Philadelphia in the playoffs. In September, Sittler scored the overtime winner against Czechoslovakia that gave his country the Canada Cup.

Sittler tied for eighth in 1976-77 NHL scoring but soared to third the following season. His 45 goals and 72 assists were personal bests, and he made the 1978 Second All-Star Team. A power struggle with management began in 1979-80, however. Although Sittler came ninth in scoring and notched 96 points in 1980-81, general manager Punch Imlach resented his leadership

and independence. Sittler held a "no-trade" contract, but after renouncing his captaincy for a time, he agreed to a move to Philadelphia in January 1982. Sittler tallied 178 points for the Flyers in 2½ seasons and completed his Hall of Fame career in 1984-85 with Detroit.

DARRYL SITTLER
Kitchener, Ontario
September 18, 1950–
NHL Career: 1970-85
Toronto, Philadelphia, Detroit

	GP	G	A	P	PIM
RS	1096	484	637	1121	948
PO	76	29	45	74	137

A-S Game (4), HOF 1989

TOD SLOAN

 1956

Aloysius Sloan was teasingly called Tod as a boy, after the famous 19th-century jockey Tod Sloan, and the nickname stuck. Sloan won the 1945-46 Ontario junior scoring crown with 43 goals and 75 points, then graduated to the AHL. He played one game for Toronto in 1947-48 and dressed for the first 29 NHL matches the following season, earning a Stanley Cup ring. Although slightly built, "Slinker" Sloan played aggressively and had strong offensive skills. Unfortunately, the NHL defensemen could push him around almost at will, and he was sent back to the AHL.

Sloan decided to give up smoking and put on some weight. Five-foot-ten, he eventually weighed in at 175 pounds and earned a full-time spot in the Leafs' lineup for 1950-51. He led the team with 31 regular-season goals, finishing eighth in league scoring with 56 points before helping Toronto win the Stanley Cup. He scored 25 goals and 23 assists in 1951-52, but because of a slew of injuries that he suffered the following season, the Leafs moved him from right wing. "I found I've had to exert myself more since I started playing center, and I don't have as much left to finish off a play," Sloan admitted to Stan Houston of *The Toronto Telegram.* "But, doggone it, I'm not going to be satisfied until I've scored between 15 and 20 goals!"

Sloan led the Leafs in 1953-54 with 32 assists and 43 points, but he didn't hit his goal-scoring target until 1955-56. Erupting with 37 tallies and 29 assists, he made the Second All-Star Team with a fifth-place finish in NHL scoring. "Tod is his own boss," said Conn Smythe. "He does what he likes with the puck. It took us a few years to discover that the best way to handle him is to leave him alone." But two seasons later, Smythe sold Sloan to Chicago because of his involvement with the NHL Players' Association. Sloan helped the Hawks win the 1961 Cup, then retired.

ALOYSIUS "TOD" SLOAN
Vinton, Quebec
November 30, 1927–
NHL Career: 1947-49, 1950-61
Toronto, Chicago

	GP	G	A	P	PIM
RS	745	220	262	482	831
PO	47	9	12	21	47

Stanley Cup (3), A-S Game (2)

BILLY SMITH

1982

Billy Smith played five games for Los Angeles in 1971-72 before the New York Islanders claimed him in the 1972 expansion draft. A fierce protector of his crease, "Battlin' Billy" slashed and fought his way to notoriety while helping the Islanders gradually move from the league basement to being a Stanley Cup contender. "I just try to give myself a little working room," he explained. "But if a guy bothers me, then I retaliate." Smith also routinely refused to shake hands after losing a playoff series, further hardening his image.

On November 28, 1979, the Colorado Rockies pulled their goalie during a delayed penalty call and inadvertently put the puck into their own net. As the last Islander to have touched the puck, Smith became the first NHL net-minder to be credited with scoring a goal. He backstopped his team to the first of four consecutive Stanley Cups later that season. Smith was content to play only half of the regular campaigns and save himself for the playoffs, but he still made the First All-Star Team in 1982. He won 32 of 46 games and earned the Vezina Trophy, voted for by the league's general managers for the first time.

The following season, when the Islanders swept the headline-grabbing Edmonton Oilers in the 1983 Cup finals, Smith shared the William M. Jennings Trophy with Rollie Melanson and won the Conn Smythe Trophy. "There are probably a lot of people in Canada tonight turning over in their beds at the thought of me winning this award," he told a *Hockey Night in Canada* audience, "but a lot of reporters in Canada took cheap shots at us, and that just provoked us. This fourth Cup is so great because we beat Edmonton." Smith retired in 1989, and his sweater number 31 was retired four years later.

BILLY SMITH
Perth, Ontario
December 12, 1950–
NHL Career: 1971-89
Los Angeles, NY Islanders

	GP	M	GA	SO	AVE
RS	680	38431	2031	22	3.17
PO	132	7645	348	5	2.73

Jennings, Vezina, Smythe, Stanley Cup (4), A-S Game, HOF 1993

HOOLEY SMITH

★ 1 1936 ★ 2 1932

He got his nickname from the cartoon character Happy Hooligan, but there was nothing comic about Hooley Smith's skills. He won a gold medal for Canada in the 1924 Winter Olympics, then joined the Ottawa Senators. A strong two-way right-winger, Smith helped the Senators win the 1927 Stanley Cup. An ugly foul against Boston's Harry Oliver in the Cup finals, however, resulted in Smith's month-long suspension the next season. While he sat on the sidelines, Ottawa dealt him to the Montreal Maroons.

Smith found his best linemates when the "S-Line" was formed in 1929-30. He usually played right wing with center Nels Stewart and left-winger Babe Siebert, but he switched position for the 1931-32 season. "The play of the starting lineup, with Hooley Smith at center, was so superb offensively and defensively that it made the Maroons look good as a whole," wrote Marc T. McNeil of *The Gazette* in March 1932. "Hooley was a valuable cog at cen-

ter, with his sweeping hook-check wrecking many a budding Boston attack." Smith edged out Toronto's Joe Primeau for the spot on the Second All-Star Team, but Primeau got postseason satisfaction. In a two-game, total-goals semifinal playoff against the Leafs, Smith scored twice and assisted on his team's other goal. "Hooley Smith played a canny, intelligent and highly effective game," reported McNeil, but the Maroons lost 4–3.

Stewart and Siebert were traded, and Smith centered wingers Jimmy Ward and Baldy Northcott. "Hooley Smith, moving along in the same sensational stride that has characterized his play for a month, was the bright star," reported *The Gazette*'s L.S.B. Shapiro after a late-season 1932-33 game. "The center player was as effective defensively as he was dangerous on the attack." Smith finished tied for fourth in league scoring,

placed eighth in 1933-34 and captained the Maroons to the 1935 Cup. He made the 1936 First All-Star Team with 19 goals and 19 assists, but Smith was sold to Boston for 1936-37 before being dealt to the New York Americans. He played some defense for the Amerks over four seasons and scored his final two NHL goals in 1940-41.

REGINALD "HOOLEY" SMITH				
Toronto, Ontario				
January 7, 1903–August 24, 1963				
NHL Career: 1924-41				
Ottawa, Montreal Maroons, Boston,				
NY Americans				
	GP	G	A	P	PIM
RS	715	200	215	415	1013
PO	54	11	8	19	109
Stanley Cup (2), A-S Game, HOF 1972				

NORMIE SMITH

★ 1937

The "Montreal Marathon" was played on March 24, 1936. The Red Wings squared off against the Montreal Maroons, the team Detroit netminder Normie Smith had played on in 1931-32. "By the end of regulation time, the ice was soft, and it was like skating uphill all the way for both

teams," recalled Smith. "I was afraid that the puck would take a weird bounce and beat me." Both Smith and his Montreal counterpart Lorne Chabot carried shutouts well into the night. "After each period ended, I thought that would be the end of the game—they'd call it off," said Smith. Detroit's rookie Mud Bruneteau finally ended the battle at 16:30 of the sixth overtime period, the longest game in NHL history. Smith made 92 saves for the win.

"Turning in one brilliant performance after another, Normie Smith, Detroit's smiling blond goalkeeper, was the outstanding player in the Red Wings' sweep to the [1936] world championship," wrote Leo Macdonell of the *Detroit Times*. The following season, Smith won the Vezina Trophy and let in only one goal in the first two games of the 1937 playoffs before getting knocked out of action with torn ligaments in his left arm. Detroit lost the

third and fourth games, prompting Smith to dress for the deciding contest. Although barely able to move his arm and in obvious pain, he inspired his team to a 2–1 overtime victory.

Smith was yanked after only one period of the finals, but the Wings still won the Cup. He played all but one game in 1937-38, but Smith had had enough. He retired early in the next season, coming back for only a handful of games during the war years.

NORMAN SMITH				
Toronto, Ontario				
March 18, 1908–February 2, 1988				
NHL Career: 1931-32, 1934-39, 1943-45				
Montreal Maroons, Detroit				
	GP	M	GA	SO	AVE
RS	199	12357	479	17	2.33
PO	12	820	18	3	1.32
Vezina, Stanley Cup (2)				

SID SMITH

LEFT WING

⭐ 1955 ★2 1951, 1952

"Who's Sid Smith?" asked Gordie Howe during the 1949 Stanley Cup finals, honestly puzzled that he didn't know the Toronto sniper. Smith had been a part-time Leaf since 1946-47 and had earned a 1948 Cup ring, but he had played only a single regular-season game in 1948-49. He scored a hat trick in a 3–1 victory in game two of the 1949 finals, though, and helped the Leafs defend the Cup.

The following season, Smith led the Leafs with 45 points, then tallied 30 goals and tied for tenth in 1950-51 scoring with 51 points. He made the Second All-Star Team and helped Toronto reclaim the Cup. Smith moved up to fifth in scoring in 1951-52, tallying 27 goals and a career-best 57 points. Repeating as the Second

All-Star Team left-winger, he also won the Lady Byng Trophy. Smith's 1954-55 campaign would prove to be his best. "He's doing a lot more digging in the corners," noted Ted Kennedy. "He's always been a fine hockey player, but I've never seen him go so well as this year."

Above all, Smith was an opportunist. "Quick reflexes, the ability to change directions in high gear and the alertness to get away a shot without first consulting his road map have been the keys to Smitty's prolific output," wrote Stan Houston in *The Hockey News* in February 1955. Smith's 33 goals and 21 assists gave him another top-10 scoring finish, while he earned his second Byng and was named to the First All-Star Team.

Handed the team captaincy for 1955-

56, Smith struggled until the responsibility was lifted the following season. He recovered his form but retired early in the 1957-58 campaign to become player/coach of the Whitby Dunlops, who won the 1958 World Championship for Canada.

SID SMITH
Toronto, Ontario
July 11, 1925–
NHL Career: 1946-58
Toronto

	GP	G	A	P	PIM
RS	601	186	183	369	94
PO	44	17	10	27	2

Byng (2), Stanley Cup (3), A-S Game (7)

ALLAN STANLEY

DEFENSE

Allan Stanley carried an impossible burden in New York. In December 1948, after acquiring Stanley from the AHL's Providence Reds for three players and a reported $70,000, Rangers coach and general manager Frank Boucher hailed him as the team savior. Although he was runner-up for the Calder Trophy and the Rangers lost the 1950 Stanley Cup finals by only a single goal in the seventh game, Stanley was never able to measure up to the inflated expectations of the Rangers' fans. He became team captain during the 1951-52 season and was a steady defender, yet he faced years of heckling. Stanley suffered a further indignity when he spent most of the 1953-54 season with the Rangers' minor-league affiliate in Vancouver.

Stanley was traded to Chicago in November 1954, but the fan hostility seemed to follow him. He earned an invitation to the 1955 All-Star Game, but it was not until Stanley was sold to

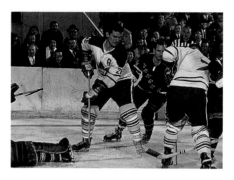

Boston in October 1956 that his plodding but hard-hitting game was fully appreciated. He tallied 6 goals and 25 assists in both 1956-57 and 1957-58, helping the Bruins to the Stanley Cup finals. Yet when Toronto's Punch Imlach picked him up in an October 1958 trade for defenseman Jim Morrison, most observers believed that Stanley was near the end of his career.

Imlach paired "Silent Sam" with Tim Horton, and Stanley blossomed. "Allan

went on to play more than 600 games for Toronto in the next 10 years," noted Imlach, "as honest and dependable a hockey player as a coach could hope for." Stanley made the Second All-Star Team three times as the Leafs developed the league's stingiest defense in preparation for four Stanley Cup wins over the next six seasons. He concluded his 21-season career with the Philadelphia Flyers in 1968-69.

ALLAN STANLEY
Timmins, Ontario
March 1, 1926–
NHL Career: 1948-69
NY Rangers, Chicago, Boston, Toronto, Philadelphia

	GP	G	A	P	PIM
RS	1244	100	333	433	792
PO	109	7	36	43	80

Stanley Cup (4), A-S Game (7), HOF 1981

WALLY STANOWSKI

DEFENSE

As a junior, Wally Stanowski made such a favorable impression on Conn Smythe that the Toronto owner/manager purchased his rights from the New York Americans. Stanowski joined the Maple Leafs for the 1939-40 season but broke his ankle in his first game. On the sidelines until January, he slowly regained his wonderful skating ability. Stanowski made the First All-Star Team in 1941. Known as "The Whirling Dervish" because of his windup for exciting end-to-end rushes, he tallied 7 goals and 14 assists. Stanowski was also strong defensively and an exceptionally hard hitter. "I train on Polish

sausages, the breakfast of champions," he joked.

Although Stanowski missed half of the 1941-42 schedule with injuries, he returned to chip in a couple of goals and 8 assists in 13 playoff games. The Leafs overcame a daunting three-game deficit to Detroit to win the Stanley Cup. Stanowski then enlisted in the Royal Canadian Air Force and didn't return to Toronto until December 1944. He'd been playing hockey with the Winnipeg RCAF team, however, and it didn't take long to adjust to the NHL pace. Stanowski helped the Leafs win the 1945 Cup, although the Red Wings almost got their revenge by pushing the series to seven games after being down 3–0.

A year later, Stanowski was the only experienced defense-

man on the team. His steadying blueline presence contributed to Toronto Cup wins in 1947 and 1948, but the Leafs then traded him to the New York Rangers. Stanowski played the entire 60-game 1948-49 schedule for the Blueshirts, but his "corkscrew" rushes were coming further and further apart. He finished the 1950-51 campaign with the AHL's Cincinnati Mohawks, with whom he played for one more season before retiring from the pro game.

WALLY STANOWSKI
Winnipeg, Manitoba
April 28, 1919–
NHL Career: 1939-42, 1944-51
Toronto, NY Rangers

	GP	G	A	P	PIM
RS	428	23	88	111	160
PO	60	3	14	17	13

Stanley Cup (4), A-S Game

DEFENSE   ★ 1966, 1971, 1972

Nicknamed "Whitey," for his shock of blond hair, Pat Stapleton didn't look like a defenseman at first glance. Although Stapleton was only five-foot-eight, his husky 185-pound build gave him surprising upper-body strength, and he was a quick and nimble skater. He broke into the big leagues with the 1961-62 Boston Bruins. Sent to the minors partway through the following season, he didn't make it back to the NHL until Chicago claimed him in the 1965 intra-league draft.

"One of Stapleton's big strong points is his ability to use his arms and hands to guard the point and keep the puck in offensive position," reported *The Hockey News* in April 1966. "Press-box observers marvel at the way he reaches down with one hand to stop the puck and meanwhile gets his stick in position with the other." Stapleton racked up 4 goals and 30 assists and made the Second All-Star Team. In 1968-69, he set a record for defensemen when he tallied 50 assists. He was voted team captain for the following season but suffered a potentially career-ending knee injury in February 1970, and Hawks management lifted his captaincy.

Bill White aided his partner's recovery. "He took a lot of the load for me at the start, especially in carrying the puck," noted Stapleton, who made the 1971 Second All-Star Team. Although he sustained a horrible 80-stitch gash to his face during the Stanley Cup finals against Montreal, Stapleton didn't miss a single game. Voted an All-Star again in 1972, he had one more trip to the Cup finals in 1973. He then signed a million-dollar contract with the WHA, retiring after the 1977-78 campaign.

PAT "WHITEY" STAPLETON
Sarnia, Ontario
July 4, 1940–
NHL Career: 1961-63, 1965-73
Boston, Chicago

	GP	G	A	P	PIM
RS	635	43	294	337	353
PO	65	10	39	49	38

A-S Game (4)

LEFT WING

 1992 1991, 1993

On January 24, 2000, Kevin Stevens was arrested in the company of a prostitute and charged with possession of crack cocaine. "Anybody who knows Kevin knows he's a quality person," said Mike Richter, typifying the sympathetic reaction expressed around the NHL. "It hits you right in the heart." Most players knew that Stevens had spent time in rehabilitation for substance abuse while with the Los Angeles Kings.

Stevens joined the Pittsburgh Penguins after competing in the 1988 Olympic Games. At six-foot-three and 230 pounds, he had both the archetypal size and the attitude of a power forward. He scored 40 goals and 46 assists in 1990-91 and made the Second All-Star Team. Leading the postseason with 17 goals, Stevens also helped the Penguins win the Stanley Cup. His 54-goal, 123-point, 254-penalty-minute 1991-92 campaign lifted him onto the First All-Star Team and into second place in league scoring. He also finished second with 28 points in playoff scoring, helping Pittsburgh successfully defend the Cup.

He made the Second All-Star Team in 1993 with 55 goals and 56 assists. He was knocked unconscious in the playoffs, however, and suffered a broken nose and sinus bone. Although Stevens tallied 41 goals and 47 assists in 1993-94, many felt that he was never the same player after his injury. The Penguins traded Stevens to Boston in August 1995, but he bounced to Los Angeles in January 1996 and to the Rangers in August 1997. Holding out hope that therapy will resuscitate Stevens' career, the Philadelphia Flyers signed him in July 2000.

KEVIN STEVENS
Brockton, Massachusetts
April 15, 1965–
NHL Career: 1987-
Pittsburgh, Boston, Los Angeles,
NY Rangers

	GP	G	A	P	PIM
RS	787	318	371	689	1372
PO	86	43	57	100	150

Stanley Cup (2), A-S Game (3)

SCOTT STEVENS

DEFENSE

Toronto Maple Leaf Tie Domi praised Scott Stevens during the 2000 playoffs: "That guy can play on my team anytime. He's a warrior." Stevens had taken the same fierce approach when he was a teenager. He joined the 1982-83 All-Rookie Team with 25 points and 195 penalty minutes as a Washington Capital. He hit a career-high with 283 penalty minutes in 1986-87.

"The league was a lot different then," Stevens told Mike Zeisberger of *The Toronto Sun* in the spring of 2000. "You had to prove yourself over and over again, even if it meant fighting. It's not like that anymore." But Stevens brought offense as well as aggression to his game. He had 12 goals and 60 assists in 1987-88, made the First All-Star Team and came runner-up for the Norris Trophy.

Stevens went to St. Louis as a free agent in July 1990 and captained the Blues for 1990-91. When St. Louis similarly signed Brendan Shanahan that summer, New Jersey asked for Stevens as compensation. An arbitrator sided with the Devils, and although Stevens initially refused to report, he made the 1992 Second All-Star Team with New Jersey. He became team captain in 1992-93, a position he still holds. The following season, Stevens made the First All-Star Team with 18 goals and a career-high 78 points. He finished second to Ray Bourque in Norris Trophy voting for the second time. More important, in 1994-95, he led the Devils to Stanley Cup victory.

Stevens became an All-Star for the fourth time in 1997 and shows no signs of slowing down. "He's one of the best pure hitters in the game," said Carolina Hurricanes coach Paul Maurice in 1998.

"He can change the way a game is going with one hit." Stevens proved Maurice's point in the 2000 playoffs, ending Eric Lindros's season with a skull-rattling check in the clinching game of the Eastern Conference finals. He hoisted the Stanley Cup for the second time a couple of weeks later, and his inspired play earned him the Conn Smythe Trophy.

SCOTT STEVENS
Kitchener, Ontario
April 1, 1964–
NHL Career: 1982-
Washington, St. Louis, New Jersey

	GP	G	A	P	PIM
RS	1353	179	649	828	2607
PO	178	22	79	101	347

Smythe, Stanley Cup (2), A-S Game (11)

GAYE STEWART

Gaye Stewart played only game five of the 1942 NHL finals for Toronto, but he earned a Stanley Cup ring. In 1942-43, he won the Calder Trophy with 24 goals and 23 assists. Stewart then enlisted in the Canadian Navy and didn't return to the Leafs until early in the 1945-46 campaign. That spring, he made the First All-Star Team. Setting a franchise record with a league-leading 37 goals, Stewart finished second in NHL scoring with 52 points.

Stewart and his hometown teammates Gus Bodnar and Bud Poile formed "The Flying Forts" line in 1946-47 and helped Toronto win the Cup. Early the following season, however, the Leafs sent the "Forts," Bob Goldham and Ernie Dickens to Chicago for Max Bentley and Cy Thomas. Stewart scored 26 goals and a career-high 29 assists with the Blackhawks, came fourth in league scoring and made the Second All-Star Team.

On July 13, 1950, Stewart went to Detroit in another multiplayer deal, and then the New York Rangers decided to trade Tony Leswick for Stewart's firepower for 1951-52. Stewart started to fizzle the following season, though, and Montreal picked him up on waivers on December 1, 1952. "I'm happy at last," said Stewart. "I think I can help the club, and I'm darn sure I'm not going to admit I'm washed up at 29." He failed to score in five games with the Canadiens, however, and was sent to the minors. Stewart played only three more NHL games, in the 1954 Cup finals. Montreal lost the deciding game on a fluke overtime goal. Perhaps sensing that this was his swan song, Stewart was the only Hab who stuck around to shake hands with the victorious Detroit Red Wings.

GAYE STEWART
Fort William, Ontario
June 28, 1923–
NHL Career: 1941-43, 1945-54
Toronto, Chicago, Detroit, NY Rangers, Montreal

	GP	G	A	P	PIM
RS	502	185	159	344	274
PO	25	2	9	11	16

Calder, Stanley Cup (2), A-S Game (4)

JACK STEWART

Dark-complexioned John Stewart was "Black Jack" to everyone in the NHL, but he insisted that his nickname had another source. "I bodychecked some fellow one night," he told a reporter from the Montreal *Gazette* in 1972, "and when he woke up the next day in the hospital, he asked who'd hit him with a blackjack." True story or not, Stewart was indeed one of the hardest hitters in NHL history.

Although under six feet tall and weighing only 185 pounds, Stewart did much of the Red Wings' heavy work, blocking shots and clearing the slot for 10 years. Stewart made the 1943 First All-Star Team, and with a playoff-high 35 penalty minutes, he then helped the Wings sweep Chicago in the Stanley Cup finals. Stewart spent the next two years in the Royal Canadian Air Force but was an All-Star again in 1946 with an NHL-high 73 minutes in penalties.

Paired with Bill Quackenbush and, later, Red Kelly, Stewart was a capable puck carrier but left most of that to his partner. "Stewart never talks and he never smiles when you're playing against him," Toronto winger Bill Ezinicki told writer Jim Coleman. "He just looks at you coldly through those slits of eyes and then—whammo—he knocks you on your can!"

Coleman recounted a time when Rocket Richard, trying to maneuver around the defense, cut Stewart on the temple with his stick: "Stewart picked up Richard in his mighty arms...lifted 'The Rocket' to shoulder height and ...*threw* him against the boards, six feet away." Stewart got a two-minute penalty for boarding.

He helped Detroit win the Cup again in 1950, but a multiplayer trade with Chicago resulted in Stewart captaining the 1950-51 Blackhawks. He retired the following season after injuring his back and suffering a major concussion.

JOHN "BLACK JACK" STEWART
Pilot Mound, Manitoba
May 6, 1917–May 26, 1983
NHL Career: 1938-43, 1945-52
Detroit, Chicago

	GP	G	A	P	PIM
RS	565	31	84	115	765
PO	80	5	14	19	143

Stanley Cup (2), A-S Game (4), HOF 1964

DEFENSE ⭐2 1988

Gary Suter posted a spectacular NHL debut season with Calgary. "I've seen him make some brilliant plays you just don't expect to see from a rookie defenseman," said teammate Paul Baxter in January 1986.

"He's been unbelievable," agreed goaltender Reggie Lemelin.

Suter received an invitation to the February All-Star Game and, on April 4, 1986, tallied 6 assists, tying the record for defensemen. "Suter's on the

power play, he's killing penalties, he's playing when we're two men short," noted coach Bob Johnson. "He's doing the job." Although Suter had tallied 141 penalty minutes by season's end, he had also notched 18 goals and 50 assists and won the Calder Trophy. Unfortunately, he got hurt in the playoffs, and the Flames lost the Stanley Cup finals.

After a less productive sophomore campaign, Suter had career-highs in 1987-88. His 70 assists and 91 points lifted him onto the Second All-Star Team, and he was a Norris Trophy finalist. He battled injuries the following season but picked up a Cup ring despite playing in only five postseason games. Although the team has never hit such heights again, Suter continued to contribute, scoring 23 goals in 1992-93. In March 1994, he was traded to Chicago via Hartford in two quick multiplayer deals. Suter gained some notoriety with a cross-check to Paul Kariya's face in

January 1998, earning a four-game suspension, but returned to action without tempering his aggressive play.

Suter joined the San Jose Sharks as a free agent in July 1998 but played only one game the following season. He underwent four operations—three on his elbow and one to correct an irregular heartbeat. Suter took a regular turn on the San Jose blue line in 1999-2000, however, earning a nomination for the Bill Masterton Trophy.

GARY SUTER				
Madison, Wisconsin				
June 24, 1964–				
NHL Career: 1985-				
Calgary, Chicago, San Jose				
	GP	G	A	P	PIM
RS	995	187	590	777	1208
PO	95	17	52	69	112
Calder, Stanley Cup, A-S Game (4)				

DEFENSE ⭐ 1962

Jean-Guy Talbot joined the Montreal Canadiens for three games in 1954-55. He became a regular the following season, and the Habs promptly won five consecutive Stanley Cups. Taking inspiration and cues from teammate Doug Harvey, Talbot learned to contribute offensively while patrolling the blue line with vigilance. Although never a strong goal scorer, Talbot had high assist totals for his day. In 1960-61, he tallied 26 helpers and 31 points. He also led the league with 143 penalty minutes. Although some of that time was the result of misconducts, goalie Jacques Plante suggested a way that Talbot could reduce his penalties. By playing slightly farther to the left, Talbot put himself into better position, negating the need to do as much hooking and tripping.

"I'm hoping for my greatest year with the Canadiens," said Talbot in the fall of 1961. "I finished strong last season. I've had a good training camp. And

without Doug Harvey around, I'll probably get a lot more ice. The more you play, the more confidence you get. I've been doing things that I wouldn't try before." That season, he picked up only 90 penalty minutes while notching a career-high 42 assists and 47 points. He joined Harvey, then a New York Ranger, on defense on the 1962 First All-Star Team. By 1964-65, Talbot was the only veteran rearguard left in Montreal, but he solidified the blue-line corps enough that the Habs won the 1965 and 1966 Stanley Cups.

The Minnesota North Stars selected Talbot in the 1967 expansion draft but dealt him to Detroit after only four games. The Red Wings put him on waivers in January 1968, and St. Louis was glad to take Talbot. He helped the Blues to three consecutive Cup finals. Traded again in November 1970, Talbot concluded his career with the Buffalo Sabres during their inaugural season.

JEAN-GUY TALBOT				
Cap-de-la-Madeleine, Quebec				
July 11, 1932–				
NHL Career: 1954-71				
Montreal, Minnesota, Detroit, St. Louis, Buffalo				
	GP	G	A	P	PIM
RS	1056	43	242	285	1006
PO	150	4	26	30	142
Stanley Cup (7), A-S Game (7)				

DAVE TAYLOR

RIGHT WING

⭐ 1981

Although he had made All-American at Clarkson University, Dave Taylor was picked incredibly late in the 1975 NHL amateur draft by the Los Angeles Kings. "I was a little squirt," he explained. "That's why I wasn't selected until the fifteenth round." Over the next two seasons, however, Taylor added three inches and 40 pounds, filling out at a solid six feet and 185 pounds. He won the 1976-77 college scoring championship with 41 goals and a record-tying 108 points in 34 games.

Taylor notched 22 goals in his 1977-78 rookie season, with freewheeling Marcel Dionne as his center, and had even greater success when Charlie Simmer joined them the following season. Taylor always remained the most defensive-minded of what became known as the "Triple Crown Line," yet he still managed to tie for ninth in NHL scoring with 43 goals and 48 assists. His offensive peak came in 1980-81, when

his 47 goals and 65 assists moved him to fifth in the league scoring race and onto the Second All-Star Team. In 1981-82, he made a career-high 67 assists and finished ninth overall.

Taylor's hard-nosed approach to the game earned him even more respect. He captained the Kings from 1985-86

to 1988-89, when he relinquished the position to Wayne Gretzky. The league awarded him both the Bill Masterton and the King Clancy Memorial trophies in 1990-91. Taylor and the Kings made the 1993 Stanley Cup finals, but he retired with the club's longevity record the following season. On April 3, 1995, the team retired his number-18 jersey to the wall of the Great Western Forum. Two years later, Taylor became vice president and general manager of the Kings.

DAVE TAYLOR					
Levack, Ontario					
December 4, 1955–					
NHL Career: 1977-94					
Los Angeles					
	GP	G	A	P	PIM
RS	1111	431	638	1069	1589
PO	92	26	33	59	145
Masterton, Clancy, A-S Game (4)					

PAUL THOMPSON

LEFT WING

⭐ 1938 ⭐ 1936

Paul Thompson looked at rookie Boston goaltender Tiny Thompson, marking the first time that two brothers had faced each other in the Stanley Cup finals. Paul had already been on a Cup-winner the previous year, when his New York Rangers won the 1927-28 championship. But his younger brother stole the show in 1929, holding the Rangers to a single goal in the two-game, total-goals final. Paul's 2 assists were a playoff high, but Boston won the Cup.

Paul Thompson was a strong second-line winger for New York, but more opportunities opened up for him when he was traded. He joined the Chicago Blackhawks for the 1931-32 campaign, beginning eight seasons on the top line with Mush

Marsh and Doc Romnes. Thompson led all Chicago scorers in 1932-33, a feat he repeated five times. He began his five-season streak on the league's top-10 scoring list in 1933-34. During the Blackhawks' successful march to the 1934 Stanley Cup, his 4 goals and 3 assists involved him in more than half of his team's offensive output.

Thompson's 17 goals and 23 assists in 1935-36 tied him with Marty Barry as runner-up to Sweeney Schriner for the scoring title. He made the Second All-Star Team, but 1937-38 proved to be his career year. Thompson's 44 points were good for third place in the league, and he reflected a strong sense of humor when he recalled his most memorable game. "It was in Chicago Stadium [February 3, 1938], the year I had 22 goals," he told the *Calgary Herald*'s Gyle Konotopetz. "This big truck driver was always yelling, 'Take that

bum Thompson off.' Well, I scored four goals that night. After the fourth one, I got a hell of a hand. Then I heard that voice: 'I still think you stink, Thompson!'" The NHL press disagreed, voting him to the First All-Star Team. He capped the year by helping the Blackhawks to the Stanley Cup that spring. Thompson became player/coach in 1938-39 before moving behind the bench, where he steered the Hawks to the 1944 Stanley Cup finals.

PAUL THOMPSON					
Calgary, Alberta					
November 2, 1906–deceased					
NHL Career: 1926-39					
NY Rangers, Chicago					
	GP	G	A	P	PIM
RS	582	153	179	332	336
PO	48	11	11	22	54
Stanley Cup (3)					

TINY THOMPSON

GOALTENDER

 1936, 1938   1931, 1935

Tiny Thompson wasn't really tiny—he'd picked up the nickname as the biggest boy on his midget team. At five-foot-ten, he was actually large for goalies in his day. Thompson joined the Boston Bruins with a splash in 1928-29, notching 12 shutouts in the regular season. He shaved his average down to 0.60 in the playoffs, and Boston won its first Stanley Cup.

Thompson won the Vezina Trophy for the first time in 1930 and made the inaugural Second All-Star Team the following season. But he was far from complacent. Although he missed four games in 1931-32 because of nerves, he grew even more frantic when his replacement played well. "He worries a lot," noted one writer. "Nevertheless, he never has had a nervous breakdown, although he has been jumpy at times." Thompson

regained his composure and won the Vezina Trophy again with a league-high 11 shutouts in 1932-33. He played what he described as his hardest and best game in the ensuing playoffs against Toronto. Thompson blanked the Leafs into a sixth overtime period before losing the epic goaltending battle to Lorne Chabot.

He made the Second All-Star Team again in 1935 and played even better in 1935-36. On January 14, 1936, Thompson became the first goalie to be credited for an assist, and his 10 shutouts and third Vezina Trophy put him on the First All-Star Team. He led the league with six shutouts the following season and captured the top goaltending award again in 1937-38. His days in Boston, however, were numbered.

Citing an eye infection early in the 1938-39 campaign, Thompson rested for

two games, but it was enough to open the door for rookie sensation Frank Brimsek. The Bruins dealt Thompson to Detroit for goalie Normie Smith (who never reported) and $15,000. Thompson finished that season and the next with the Red Wings, then joined his brother Paul in Chicago as a scout.

CECIL "TINY" THOMPSON
Sandon, British Columbia
May 31, 1905–February 11, 1981
NHL Career: 1928-40
Boston, Detroit

	GP	M	GA	SO	AVE
RS	553	34175	1183	81	2.08
PO	44	2972	93	7	1.88

Vezina (4), Stanley Cup, A-S Game, HOF 1959

BILL THOMS

CENTER

Curly-haired Bill Thoms quickly proved himself a capable playmaker with the Toronto Maple Leafs, but he made his biggest mark as a goal scorer. He had two hat tricks in 1935-36, with the second scored in the Montreal Forum on March 12, 1936. "Thoms was the hero of a dazzling assault," reported *The Globe*, "scoring three goals himself and passing to 'Buzz' Boll for a fourth. The center player's sniping made him the first player in the league to score 20 goals this season. It took only a few minutes of the third period for [the] Leafs to draw even on two sparkling goals by Thoms. [He] sagged the corner of the net with a sizzling drive. He scored his second counter soon after the face-off, when he picked up a loose puck [and] cleverly drew [Wilf] Cude out of the nets."

Thoms finished the season tied with teammate Charlie Conacher for most goals, with 23. His 38 points tied for fourth, with Conacher and three others. Voted to the Second All-Star Team, he charged into the playoffs. "Thoms, [the] Leafs' dangerous center player, came through when the going was the toughest, with the most brilliant exhibition of the series," noted *The Gazette* after Toronto won the deciding semifinal game against the New York Americans. "His first goal was a gem, and he made all the play for the second." Thoms led the playoffs with 5 assists, but the Leafs lost the finals to Detroit.

Tallying 38 points once more in 1937-38, Thoms tied for seventh in league scoring. The Leafs lost in the Stanley Cup finals again, but the victorious Chicago Blackhawks obviously liked what they saw of Thoms. Early the next season, Chicago traded 1936 Lady Byng-winner Doc Romnes for Thoms, who led the Blackhawks in scoring with 32 points in 1940-41 and a career-high 45 points in 1941-42, tying for sixth spot in the league. After one more productive season and one mostly lost to injury, Thoms was sold to the Boston Bruins in January 1945, where he concluded his career.

BILL THOMS
Newmarket, Ontario
March 5, 1910–December 26, 1964
NHL Career: 1932-45
Toronto, Chicago, Boston

	GP	G	A	P	PIM
RS	548	135	206	341	154
PO	44	6	10	16	6
A-S Game					

JIMMY THOMSON

DEFENSE

Jimmy Thomson was called up from the Pittsburgh farm team to play five games for the Maple Leafs in 1945-46, then joined Toronto full-time the following season. "We weren't supposed to win anything [in 1946-47]," recalled Thomson. "The defense pairings at the end of the year were Bill Barilko and Garth Boesch, Gus Mortson and myself. Four rookies. As a matter of fact, we got a sound whipping in each series that year. In the semifinals, Detroit beat us in one game 9–1. In the first game of the final, Montreal beat us 6–0, and Bill Durnan was quoted in the papers afterward saying, 'How did these fellows ever get into the playoffs?' " The Leafs rebounded, however, and won the Cup in six games.

Dubbed the "Gold Dust Twins," Thomson and Mortson helped Toronto successfully defend the Cup in both 1948 and 1949. The more defensive-minded of the pair, Thomson played a clean but hard-hitting game and left most of the rushing to Mortson. Thomson fired effective passes, though, and hit his offensive peak in 1950-51, notching 33 assists and 36 points. He made the Second All-Star Team, then led the playoffs with 34 penalty minutes while the Leafs reclaimed the Cup. He failed to score a goal the following season, as he did six times in total throughout his career, but Thomson retained his All-Star status because of his defensive contributions.

He became team captain in 1956-57, although he relinquished the honor for 30 games when Ted Kennedy made a brief comeback. Toronto owner Conn Smythe was furious when Thomson became involved in the formation of the NHL Players' Association, however, and sold his veteran rearguard to Chicago in August 1957. Thomson concluded his NHL career with the Blackhawks the following season, retiring after Toronto bought back his rights in July 1958.

JIMMY THOMSON
Winnipeg, Manitoba
February 23, 1927–deceased
NHL Career: 1945-58
Toronto, Chicago

	GP	G	A	P	PIM
RS	787	19	215	234	920
PO	63	2	13	15	135
Stanley Cup (4), A-S Game (7)					

KEITH TKACHUK

LEFT WING

Like his childhood hero Cam Neely, Keith Tkachuk has an aggressive approach that has been the key to his success. He joined the Winnipeg Jets just after the 1992 Olympic Games and made a strong first impression with his feistiness and deft scoring touch. At six-foot-two and 210 pounds, he hit hard and often. Since entering the NHL, Tkachuk has averaged just under 200 minutes per season in penalties. The Jets named him captain partway through the 1993-94 campaign, and he finished the schedule with 41 goals and 81 points.

Tkachuk made the Second All-Star Team with 51 points in the lockout-shortened 1994-95 season. That summer, he exercised his restricted free agent's rights and agreed to an offer from Chicago. Winnipeg retained Tkachuk by matching the offer, however, then stripped him of the captaincy. Tkachuk nonetheless posted a strong 1995-96 season, scoring 50 goals and 98 points and earning recognition from *The Sporting News* magazine as the league's top left-winger. The team transferred to Phoenix for 1996-97 and restored Tkachuk's captaincy. He responded with a league-leading 52 goals.

He made the 1998 Second All-Star Team with 40 goals and 66 points in 69 games. "I think Keith has finally realized he could score 50 goals a year for the rest of his life," said general manager Bobby Smith in December 1998, "but he was never going to be judged favorably until the franchise started winning something."

Although Tkachuk will earn $8.5 million in 2000-01, the franchise has yet to win a playoff round with him in the lineup. In January 2000, the Carolina Hurricanes leaked a proposed trade. "That's got to be hard on the team and hard on the player," sympathized Jaromir Jagr. Tkachuk tried to shake off the distraction, but his days with the Coyotes may be numbered.

KEITH TKACHUK
Melrose, Massachusetts
March 28, 1972–
NHL Career: 1991-
Winnipeg, Phoenix

	GP	G	A	P	PIM
RS	576	294	258	552	1400
PO	44	19	9	28	100

A-S Game (3)

JOHN TONELLI

LEFT WING

After three WHA seasons, John Tonelli jumped to the New York Islanders for the 1978-79 campaign. On May 24, 1980, he assisted on what is often called the most important goal

in Islander history. "I can still see that puck hitting the back of that net," recalled Tonelli, describing the overtime goal that gave the Islanders their first of four consecutive Stanley Cups. "Bobby Nystrom and I had a two-on-two and crisscrossed at the Philly blue line. That kind of slowed up their defense, and I broke toward the net. I put it on Nystrom's backhand, and he just directed it into the net."

"He is without doubt the hardest worker I have ever seen," said Nystrom, "but some people overlook the fact that he's more than a digger. He's a good stickhandler and playmaker."

Tonelli agreed: "Anybody can go banging into a corner and get the puck, but you have to do something useful after you get it." He made the Second All-Star Team in 1982 with 35 goals and 58 assists. In the playoffs, the Islanders avoided a quarter-final upset by Pittsburgh when Tonelli scored both the tying goal and the overtime winner of the deciding game.

"John has that inner drive to improve," explained Wayne Merrick to Tim Moriarty of *The Hockey News*. "He has all that talent, sure, but [he] works harder and sacrifices more than most guys because he's always striving to get that extra step." Tonelli made the Second All-Star Team again in 1985 with a 42-goal, 100-point campaign that remains a franchise record for left-wingers. Rebuilding, the Islanders traded him to Calgary in March 1986. Tonelli signed with Los Angeles in the summer of 1988 and was twice voted the "most inspirational" King. He split his last NHL season playing for Chicago and the Quebec Nordiques.

JOHN TONELLI
Milton, Ontario
March 23, 1957–
NHL Career: 1978-92
NY Islanders, Calgary, Los Angeles, Chicago, Quebec

	GP	G	A	P	PIM
RS	1028	325	511	836	911
PO	172	40	75	115	200

Stanley Cup (4), A-S Game (2)

DEFENSE

★ 1971 ★₂ 1968

Although capable of brilliance, Jean-Claude Tremblay played a simple game. "If I see a teammate ahead of me in decent scoring position, I'll naturally pass," he said. "Otherwise, I'll shoot as hard as I can from inside the blue line and hope for a goal or a deflection or a goal by one of our guys from the rebound of the shot. Sometimes, I'll move in closer and either pass or shoot it." After two seasons split between the Montreal Canadiens and the minors, Tremblay earned a full-time NHL job in 1961-62.

His strong two-way game and play-off-high 9 assists helped Montreal win the 1965 Stanley Cup. He led the Habs with 11 points as the team successfully defended the Cup the following spring. He couldn't hide his bitterness, though, when Detroit's Roger Crozier was awarded the Conn Smythe Trophy. Tremblay finally got some league recognition when he was named to the 1968 Second All-Star Team.

He picked up more Cup rings in 1968, 1969 and 1971, peaking offensively in 1970-71, when his 11 goals and 52 assists lifted him to the First All-Star Team. After tallying 57 points the following season, he stunned Montreal fans by signing with the WHA's Quebec Nordiques.

"He put Quebec City on the map," said Nordiques' scoring star Marc Tardif.

But the crowd wasn't always kind. "They booed him in Montreal sometimes [too], but it's his style that gets to them," said Toe Blake. "J.C. is very clever with the puck, but he doesn't hit anyone, and that seems to get the fans going." He received many more cheers of appreciation, though. Tremblay was a WHA All-Star three times and led the league twice in assists. He hung up his skates in 1979, having rung up 66 goals and an impressive 358 assists in seven WHA seasons. The Nordiques retired his number-3 sweater.

JEAN-CLAUDE "J.C." TREMBLAY
Bagotville, Quebec
January 22, 1939–deceased
NHL Career: 1959-72
Montreal

	GP	G	A	P	PIM
RS	794	57	306	363	204
PO	108	14	51	65	58

Stanley Cup (5), A-S Game (7)

CENTER

★ 1978, 1979 ★₂ 1982, 1984

Teenager Bryan Trottier won the 1976 Calder Trophy when he set rookie records with 63 assists and 95 points. "It's his poise that really stands out," said teammate Billy Harris. "He's always calm, regardless of the situation. And he's got tremendous hockey sense. He is, if there's such a thing, a natural-born center."

Mike Bossy joined Trottier and Clark Gillies in 1977-78, forming the greatest line in New York Islander history. Trottier leapt up the scoring charts, aided by a record-breaking period against the Rangers, when he notched a hat trick and 3 assists. Second in scoring with 46 goals and a league-leading 77 assists, he made the First All-Star Team both that season and the next. Trottier led the NHL with a career-best 87 assists and 134 points in 1978-79. In addition to

the Art Ross Trophy, he won the Hart Trophy as most valuable player.

The Islanders, meanwhile, had become Stanley Cup contenders. Trottier finished sixth in 1979-80 scoring, then helped the team win its first of four consecutive Cups. He led the 1980 playoffs with 12 goals and 29 points and won the Conn Smythe Trophy. His 18 assists were tops in the 1981 postseason, as were his 23 helpers and 29 points in the 1982 playoffs.

Notching his only 50-goal campaign in 1981-82, Trottier made the Second All-Star Team with a fifth-place finish in league scoring. His final All-Star turn came in 1983-84, when he tallied 40 goals and 111 points. The team lost the 1984 finals to Edmonton and went on a downward slide. Trottier celebrated career-goal 500 on February 13, 1990, but the Islanders bought him out of a

long-term contract that spring. Following a deep depression and bankruptcy, Trottier signed with Pittsburgh as a free agent and quickly won two more Cup rings. After a year spent in the Islanders' sales office, Trottier returned for one final NHL season with the Penguins in 1993-94 before turning to coaching.

BRYAN TROTTIER
Val Marie, Saskatchewan
July 17, 1956–
NHL Career: 1975-92, 1993-94
NY Islanders, Pittsburgh

	GP	G	A	P	PIM
RS	1279	524	901	1425	912
PO	221	71	113	184	277

Calder, Ross, Hart, Clancy, Smythe,
Stanley Cup (6), A-S Game (8), HOF 1997

GOALTENDER

Drafted by the Minnesota North Stars in 1990, Roman Turek was in no hurry to try the NHL. Named the Czech Republic Player of the Year in 1994, he shone at the 1995 World Championship and won a gold medal at the 1996 World Championship. In 1996-97, Turek finally made six NHL appearances with the Stars, who had transferred to Dallas in 1993. The following season, he played in 23 matches. Big, at six-foot-three and 190 pounds, with a right-hand catching glove that can throw off many shooters, Turek was hailed as Dallas's goalie of the future.

He posted great numbers in 1998-99, with a 2.08 average during 16 wins, 3 ties and only 3 losses. Turek shared the William M. Jennings Trophy with Ed Belfour yet saw no playoff action. He earned a Stanley Cup ring but had little opportunity to savor the victory. The Stars couldn't protect both Turek

and Belfour in the expansion draft, so the day after winning the Cup, Dallas traded Turek to the St. Louis Blues.

Turek got the amount of work with St. Louis in 1999-2000 that he'd had in Europe and made the Second All-Star Team. In 67 games, he led the NHL with seven shutouts and won his second Jennings Trophy. Only Philadelphia's Brian Boucher had a lower goals-against average than Turek's 1.95. The Blues

were runaway regular-season leaders, with a franchise-record 114-point campaign. "We were big favorites, and in the middle of the season, when the [St. Louis] Rams won the Super Bowl, people said, 'Now it's your turn,' " said Turek, reflecting on his first NHL playoff experience, an opening-round defeat. "I think some guys probably felt big pressure. But I think everyone learned something. It can't happen again."

ROMAN TUREK
Písek, Czechoslovakia
May 21, 1970–
NHL Career: 1996-
Dallas, St. Louis

	GP	M	GA	SO	AVE
RS	122	6929	235	9	2.08
PO	7	415	19	0	2.75

Jennings (2), Stanley Cup, A-S Game

CENTER

Norm Ullman quietly forged a Hall of Fame career, scoring 20 goals or more in 16 different seasons. Tied for sixth spot in NHL scoring with 28 goals and 42 assists in 1960-61, Ullman finished eighth in the following campaign with 64 points. He led the 1963 play-

offs with 12 assists and 16 points. But he continued to tweak his game plan. "Norm always tried to move past one man too many so he could give the perfect pass," said Gordie Howe. "When he started to shoot, he scored more goals." Ullman raced for the 1964-65 scoring crown, leading with 42 goals and finishing in second spot behind Stan Mikita with 83 points. Ullman, however, got the nod for First All-Star Team honors.

He was declared "the greatest forechecker in hockey" by New York Rangers coach and general manager Emile Francis. "Ullman has perfected the sweep-check and poke-check," added Red Kelly, "and that permits him to avoid being trapped." A tireless skater, Ullman was relentless in pursuit, which led to his playoff record. During the 1965 semifinals, he intercepted a pass and potted his second goal only five seconds after scoring.

Ullman came sixth in 1965-66 scoring and jumped up to third in 1966-67, making the Second All-Star Team. But

late in the following season, shortly after Ullman was elected president of the NHL Players' Association, Detroit traded him to Toronto. He concluded his NHL career with the Maple Leafs, usually centering Ron Ellis and Paul Henderson. He notched a career-high 51 assists and 85 points in 1970-71, finishing sixth in league scoring. After enduring some of the Harold Ballard-inspired organizational rot in Toronto, Ullman played two more seasons in the WHA and tallied 130 points.

NORM ULLMAN
Provost, Alberta
December 26, 1935–
NHL Career: 1955-75
Detroit, Toronto

	GP	G	A	P	PIM
RS	1410	490	739	1229	712
PO	106	30	53	83	67

A-S Game (11), HOF 1982

GOALTENDER   ⭐ 2 1975, 1977

Rookie netminder Rogie Vachon helped Montreal eliminate the New York Rangers to advance to the 1967 Stanley Cup finals. "You can tell that Junior B goaltender he won't be playing against a bunch of peashooters when he plays against the Leafs," sneered Toronto coach and general manager Punch Imlach. "We'll take his head off with our first shot." The Canadiens won the first game 6–2.

"Vachon's got to be the only Junior B goalie in history who has come up and won five straight games in the Stanley Cup playoffs," noted Montreal coach Toe Blake with a smile.

"He's still Junior B," retorted Imlach, "but he's the best damn Junior B in the country." Toronto eventually prevailed, and in 1967-68, Vachon shared the Vezina Trophy with Gump Worsley. He played a backup role during Montreal's 1968 Stanley Cup victory, but the next season, Worsley watched Vachon limit St. Louis to three goals in the Habs' sweep to the Cup.

Vachon played well, but the Canadiens missed the 1970 playoffs. Intending to rest Vachon for the playoffs, Montreal called up an unknown giant late in the 1970-71 campaign. Ken Dryden went on to rock the hockey world and carry the Canadiens to the Cup. Montreal traded Vachon to Los Angeles, a hockey backwater, early the following season. "When you're my size, you've got to be a stand-up kind of person," said five-foot-seven Vachon. "I take my bruises, but I won't back down. Never."

He became immensely popular as he helped lift the Kings from the league basement to a franchise-record 105-point season in 1974-75. With his career-lowest 2.24 goals-against average, Vachon finished runner-up for the Vezina and made the Second All-Star Team. He posted a 1.39 average in the 1976 Canada Cup and became an NHL All-Star again in 1977. Vachon signed a free-agent contract with Detroit in August 1978 and spent his last two seasons in Boston. He returned to Los Angeles in 1984 to become general manager, however, and in 1985, the Kings retired his number 30.

ROGATIEN VACHON
Palmarolle, Quebec
September 8, 1945–
NHL Career: 1966-82
Montreal, Los Angeles, Detroit, Boston

	GP	M	GA	SO	AVE
RS	795	46298	2310	51	2.99
PO	48	2876	133	2	2.77

Vezina, Stanley Cup (3), A-S Game (3)

JOHN VANBIESBROUCK

GOALTENDER ★ 1986 ★ 1994

After playing one game for the New York Rangers in 1981-82, John Vanbiesbrouck did not return to the Big Apple until late in the 1983-84 campaign. Short, at five-foot-eight, but strong positionally with a quick glove hand, he had the starting job by 1985-86. Vanbiesbrouck made the First All-Star Team and won the Vezina Trophy, primarily on the strength of his league-leading 31 victories. The Rangers squeaked into the playoffs with 78 points, but "The Beezer" backstopped them to the Wales Conference finals.

The Rangers didn't fare as well again, but when Mike Richter became Vanbiesbrouck's partner in 1989-90, the Rangers boasted the best goaltending tandem in the game. The NHL expansion for 1993-94 allowed the protection of only one goalie, however. New York traded Vanbiesbrouck, three years older than Richter, to Vancouver four days before the Florida Panthers drafted him. "Respect was uppermost on my mind when I came to Miami," said Vanbiesbrouck. "The new group of us were united in wanting to prove to the rest of the league—and one another—that we could play at a competitive level with the rest, even though we were a new expansion team."

Vanbiesbrouck not only competed but made the Second All-Star Team and was runner-up for the Vezina Trophy during the Panthers' inaugural season. In the 1996 playoffs, he led Florida to the Stanley Cup finals. "I'm exhausted," he said after losing to the Colorado Avalanche. "I'm disappointed, but in the same breath, I'm proud of our accomplishments." In the summer of 1998, Vanbiesbrouck signed with Philadelphia as a free agent. His hot-and-cold play forced the Flyers to go with rookie Brian Boucher in the 2000 playoffs. The Flyers traded Vanbiesbrouck in June 2000 to the New York Islanders, who acquired the veteran so that he could mentor Rick DiPietro, the first 2000 entry draft pick.

JOHN VANBIESBROUCK
Detroit, Michigan
September 4, 1963–
NHL Career: 1981-82, 1983-
NY Rangers, Florida, Philadelphia,
NY Islanders

	GP	M	GA	SO	AVE
RS	829	47549	2367	38	2.99
PO	71	3969	177	5	2.68

Vezina, A-S Game (3)

ELMER VASKO

DEFENSE ★ 1963, 1964

Elmer Vasko felt that it took him three seasons to play NHL hockey with confidence. "A defenseman has to learn to adjust to the pace and to profit by his mistakes. We all make them," admitted Chicago Blackhawk Vasko to Harry Molter of *The Hockey News*. "But you have to mentally shake off worrying about a goal scored against you and concentrate on stopping the next one." Huge in his day, at six-foot-three and 218 pounds, "Moose" Vasko peaked offensively in 1959-60 with 27 assists and 30 points. He also tallied a career-high 110 penalty minutes. The following season, Vasko curbed his aggressiveness and reduced his sentence time to 40 minutes. "I try to hit as many players as I can in our end but pick my spots," he said. "Sometimes, a player tries to get you to check him into the boards to take you out of the play. You have to watch yourself on this."

Increasingly, Vasko left the rushing to his regular partner Pierre Pilote. "I want to play a defensive game," said Vasko. "This is my main job. I still rush with the puck when I get a break, but I always try to guard against being caught up-ice and out of position." He helped Chicago win the 1961 Stanley Cup, then made the Second All-Star Team in 1963 and again the following season.

"[Vasko's] the best defenseman in the National Hockey League this season," said coach Billy Reay in December 1963, although Pilote picked up all the honors at season's end. "You can play anybody with him, and you know you'll be alright."

Vasko retired after the 1965-66 campaign, then returned for Minnesota's first season. He captained the North Stars for 1968-69 but played only three games the following season before concluding his pro career in the minors.

ELMER "MOOSE" VASKO
Duparquet, Quebec
December 11, 1935–
NHL Career: 1956-66, 1967-70
Chicago, Minnesota

	GP	G	A	P	PIM
RS	786	34	166	200	719
PO	78	2	7	9	73

Stanley Cup, A-S Game (4)

Mike Vernon has experienced both the pros and the cons of playing for his hometown teams. He made his first two appearances in the Flames net during his final junior season with the 1982-83 Calgary Wranglers. "There was a lot of pressure playing in Calgary, and at times, it wasn't good for me," he later admitted to broadcaster Dick Irvin. "But it forced me to be a better goaltender. I have no regrets." Vernon came on strong for the Flames late in the 1985-86 campaign and backstopped the team to the Stanley Cup finals. Calgary didn't get out of its own division in the next two playoff years, however, and Vernon picked up an undeserved reputation for being incapable of winning the big game.

He silenced some of the naysayers by leading the Flames to a Stanley Cup victory in 1988-89. Vernon made the Second All-Star Team with a league-high 37 victories and finished runner-up for the Vezina Trophy. Yet he heard the boo-birds frequently in subsequent years. Traded to Detroit in June 1994, Vernon took much of the heat when the Red Wings were swept in the 1995 Cup finals. He shared the 1995-96 William M. Jennings Trophy with young Chris Osgood, posting a career-low 2.26 goals-against average, but he saw action in only 4 of 19 playoff games.

After playing second-string through most of 1996-97, Vernon came through in the postseason and won the Conn Smythe Trophy. "He was unbelievable," said teammate Slava Kozlov. "He was getting stronger and stronger every game...I think he won the Stanley Cup for us." That summer, Detroit traded Vernon to San Jose, and midway through the 1999-2000 season, he joined the Florida Panthers. When Calgary made an unexpected trade for the netminder for 2000-01, however, Vernon's career came full circle: he was back in Cowtown.

MIKE VERNON
Calgary, Alberta
February 24, 1963–
NHL Career: 1982-
Calgary, Detroit, San Jose, Florida

	GP	M	GA	SO	AVE
RS	772	41376	2047	23	2.97
PO	138	8211	367	6	2.68

Jennings, Smythe, Stanley Cup (2), A-S Game (5)

STEVE VICKERS

LEFT WING

Steve Vickers, the New York Rangers' first pick in the 1971 amateur draft, spent a season with the Omaha Knights before graduating to the NHL. Although he lost the rookie scoring race to Philadelphia's Bill Barber, Vickers scored 30 goals in 61 games and won the Calder Trophy. "He doesn't get ruffled, is tough in the corners and is murder in front of the net," noted Toronto goalie Jacques Plante. "He knows how to finish off a play and picks the right spot to convert a pass. I always worry about him, now that I know how good he is."

Vickers notched 34 goals and 24 assists in 1973-74. Brad Park nicknamed him "Pokey," but only because of his off-ice behavior. "He takes everything so easy...doesn't seem to get excited," Park told writer Norm MacLean. "But he's right there coming back to help you out and is always in position for a pass at the line or in front of the net." When the Rangers traded Vic Hadfield to Pittsburgh for 1974-75, Vickers got

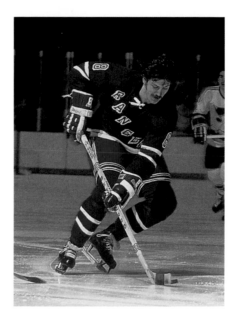

a break. The "GAG II Line" (goal-a-game) formed, with Vickers taking Hadfield's left-wing spot alongside Jean Ratelle and Rod Gilbert. Vickers tallied

a career-high 41 goals and 89 points and made the Second All-Star Team.

Ratelle went to Boston early the next season, and Vickers posted his last 30-goal campaign. He made his only trip to the Stanley Cup finals in 1979 and staked the Rangers to an early lead in their opening-game victory over Montreal. Unfortunately, the Habs swept the remaining games. In the next two seasons, Vickers tallied 62 and 58 points, respectively, but finished the 1981-82 schedule in the minors and retired.

STEVE VICKERS
Toronto, Ontario
April 21, 1951–
NHL Career: 1972-82
NY Rangers

	GP	G	A	P	PIM
RS	698	246	340	586	330
PO	68	24	25	49	58

Calder, A-S Game (2)

PHIL WATSON

CENTER

Phil Watson was dubbed "hockey's most temperamental star" by *The New Yorker* magazine, but his colorful brawling manner, combined with his excellent playmaking ability, brought him success. Watson tied for tenth in NHL scoring in 1938-39 and helped the New York Rangers win the 1940 Stanley Cup. His 1941-42 All-Star campaign was a career-best. Watson led the league with 37 assists and came fourth in league scoring with 52 points. His right-winger Bryan Hextall won the scoring crown, and his left-winger Lynn Patrick came second.

"It doesn't matter where Phil plays," said coach Frank Boucher. "The more I see of him, the more I'm convinced

Phil is one of the greatest team players I've bumped into. I've used him at left wing, at right wing, at center and defense. All he's interested in is being on the ice and in the thick of competition." Unfortunately for New York, Canadian Watson was unable to get a border pass due to wartime travel restrictions. The Rangers loaned him to Montreal for the 1943-44 season in return for four players. Watson anticipated playing only in Montreal and Toronto, but he was later cleared to play the entire schedule. He notched 49 points and helped the Habs win the Stanley Cup before returning to New York.

After the 1947-48 season, Watson moved into coaching, and by 1955-56, he was behind the Rangers' bench. He guided

the team to three consecutive playoff berths, but "Fiery Phil's" volatile nature was his eventual undoing. "If the team was going well," Boucher later recalled, "he'd beam and preen and shout, 'That's my boys.' When we lost, though, he'd grow bitter and shriek at the players, often in front of the writers." With his demoralized team deep in the NHL cellar, Watson was fired during the 1959-60 season.

PHIL WATSON
Montreal, Quebec
April 24, 1914–deceased
NHL Career: 1935-48
NY Rangers, Montreal

	GP	G	A	P	PIM
RS	590	144	265	409	532
PO	45	10	25	35	67

Stanley Cup (2)

COONEY WEILAND

CENTER

★ 1935

Although he was seldom called by his given name Ralph, Cooney Weiland never discovered the origin of his childhood nickname. At only five-foot-seven and 150 pounds, Weiland was a slick stickhandler and hard to knock down. "Besides being an offensive threat," Frank Selke testified while nominating Weiland to the Hockey Hall of Fame, "he was a great exponent of the poke-check, which made him effective defensively, especially killing penalties." But Weiland is best remembered as the sharpshooting center of Boston's "Dynamite Line."

Between wingers Dit Clapper and Dutch Gainor, Weiland helped the Bruins to their first Stanley Cup win in 1929. Forward passing in the offensive zone was allowed for the first time the following season, and the quick-thinking "Dynamite Line" fully exploited the opened-up game. The NHL hurriedly amended the rule midseason and instituted offside,

but the Bruins still finished the regular season with the highest winning percentage of all time, posting a 38–5–1 win-loss-tie record. Weiland simultaneously shattered Howie Morenz's single-season scoring record of 51 points with 43 goals and 30 assists. He led all playoff scorers with 6 goals and 3 assists in five games, but the Montreal Canadiens managed to wrest away the Stanley Cup.

Weiland finished ninth in scoring in 1930-31, with 25 goals and 13 assists, but when his production slipped to 26 points in 1931-32, the Bruins dealt him to the Ottawa Senators. Weiland led his struggling last-place club in scoring, but nine games into the 1933-34 campaign, he was traded to the Detroit Red Wings. The move gave Weiland a new lease on life. Centering fellow playmakers Herbie Lewis

and Larry Aurie, Weiland not only saw playoff action in the spring of 1934 but made the 1935 Second All-Star Team. Traded back to Boston in the summer of 1935, Weiland finished out his NHL career in fine fashion. He captained the Bruins to the 1939 Cup and immediately moved behind the bench to guide the team to the 1941 championship.

RALPH "COONEY" WEILAND
Seaforth, Ontario
November 5, 1904–July 3, 1985
NHL Career: 1928-39
Boston, Ottawa, Detroit

	GP	G	A	P	PIM
RS	509	173	160	333	147
PO	45	12	10	22	12

Ross, Stanley Cup (2), HOF 1971

CY WENTWORTH

DEFENSE

★ 1935

Just prior to the 1932-33 season, the Montreal Maroons bought defenseman Cy Wentworth for $10,000. He immediately had his most productive offensive season, scoring 4 goals and

10 assists, but the 1934-35 campaign was Wentworth's best. He made the Second All-Star Team and enjoyed the ultimate team success.

He starred in the Maroons' first 1935 playoff game, a scoreless tie. "Cy Wentworth, [a] former Hawk who dearly loves to win against Chicago, gave a tremendously fine all-round display," reported *The Gazette*. "Tireless in his rushing and bodychecking, Wentworth was probably the best two-way performer on the ice. He gave just another of those fine displays that have marked his season's work." The Maroons eliminated Chicago two nights later with a 1–0 overtime victory to win the two-game, total-goals series. In the semifinals, Montreal beat the New York Rangers 5–4 in another two-game playoff. Then it was on to Toronto, where they met the powerhouse Leafs in a best-of-five Stanley Cup final.

Wentworth scored one of his rare playoff goals to send the first game into

overtime. "[He] was one of the outstanding stars of the series, culminating a solo rush by making the light flicker for the equalizer," recalled Don Nolan in the 1935-36 *NHL Guide*. Wentworth led all playoff scorers that season, with 3 goals and 5 playoff points, as the Maroons swept the Leafs in three straight games. It was the franchise's final honor. When the Maroons suspended operations prior to the start of the 1938-39 season, Wentworth was sold to the Montreal Canadiens.

MARVIN "CY" WENTWORTH
Grimsby, Ontario
January 24, 1905–deceased
NHL Career: 1927-40
Chicago, Montreal Maroons, Montreal

	GP	G	A	P	PIM
RS	575	39	68	107	355
PO	35	5	6	11	20

Stanley Cup, A-S Game (2)

RIGHT WING

It took Kenny Wharram four tries before he finally latched onto a full-time job with the Chicago Blackhawks in 1958-59. Relatively small at five-foot-nine and 160 pounds, Wharram scored 10 rookie goals. He had more success after getting Stan Mikita, his regular centerman for the next decade, in 1959-60. Ab McDonald replaced veteran Ted Lindsay on their left side in 1960-61, and the swift-skating trio became known as the "Scooter Line." Wharram helped the Hawks win the 1961 Stanley Cup and had his first 20-goal season in 1962-63.

He notched his first hat trick on October 29, 1963. "He's shooting more this season," noted Mikita. "Ken digs into the corners against big [Jean] Beliveau and the others and patrols up and down

that wing all night. He hustles every second on the ice. It's great to see him have [a] big scoring night like this."

Sniper Bobby Hull agreed: "If anyone deserves a night like this, it's this guy for all the work he does up and down the ice." Wharram made the First All-Star Team at season's end with a career-high 39 goals and 71 points, sixth overall in league scoring. He also won the Lady Byng Trophy.

In a 1964-65 exhibition game, Wharram fractured his skull, but he donned a special helmet and quickly returned to the lineup. Although the headgear blocked most of his peripheral vision and Doug Mohns replaced "Scooter" McDonald, Wharram still tallied 24 goals. He returned to the First All-Star Team

in 1967. With 31 goals, he tied Gordie Howe for fourth place in scoring with 65 points. Two seasons of 69 points followed, but Wharram suffered a heart attack during Chicago's 1969-70 training camp and had to retire.

KENNY WHARRAM
North Bay, Ontario
July 2, 1933–
NHL Career: 1951-52, 1953-54,
1955-56, 1958-69
Chicago

	GP	G	A	P	PIM
RS	766	252	281	533	222
PO	80	16	27	43	38

Byng, Stanley Cup, A-S Game (2)

BILL WHITE

DEFENSE

Bill White spent the last five of his seven minor-league apprenticeship seasons playing for the eccentric and notorious Eddie Shore. "That's where I learned to maneuver so well," said the six-foot-two, 195-pound defenseman, grateful for an experience that others found harrowing. "Being a tall and lean person, I looked awkward when I skated, so Shore made me do some very demanding drills. It paid off for me later in my NHL career." The Los Angeles Kings bought Shore's entire Springfield Indians' roster, and White, already 28 years old, made his big-league debut in 1967-68.

He notched a career-high 11 goals as a rookie and always moved the puck well to his forwards, but White's primary contribution was on defense. He went to Chicago on February 20, 1970, in a multiplayer deal. "I've always considered him one of the most underrated defensemen in hockey," Blackhawks coach Billy Reay told Jim Proudfoot of *The Toronto Star* a couple of months later. "He's darn hard to get around because of his height and reach. He is a good, sound player who takes his man to the boards but doesn't get you into trouble with any stupid penalties." Reay paired White with Pat Stapleton, creating a reliable tandem that helped take the Hawks to the Stanley Cup finals in 1971 and 1973.

White made the Second All-Star Team three seasons running, beginning in 1972. He peaked offensively with 38 assists and 47 points in 1972-73, and although Stapleton then jumped to the WHA, White maintained his All-Star status. "It's a shame scoring counts so much in awarding honors to defensemen," said teammate Dick Redmond in 1975. "Playing beside Bill is like going to a school for defensemen." Unfortunately, White suffered nerve damage to his neck and had to retire in 1976.

BILL WHITE
Toronto, Ontario
August 26, 1939–
NHL Career: 1967-76
Los Angeles, Chicago

	GP	G	A	P	PIM
RS	604	50	215	265	495
PO	91	7	32	39	76

A-S Game (6)

DOUG WILSON

DEFENSE

Doug Wilson enjoyed a stellar junior career, and the Ottawa 67s retired his sweater-number 7. He followed his

older brother Murray's footsteps into the NHL and became a Chicago Black-hawk in 1977-78. With a devastating slap shot that eventually made him the all-time leading scorer among Hawk defensemen, Wilson tallied 14 goals and 20 assists as a rookie. Beginning in 1980-81, he led Chicago rearguards in points for 10 consecutive seasons. "I take more pride in playing well in my own end than in the offensive end," explained Wilson. "I feel I'm more than an 'offensive' defenseman."

But it was his 39-goal, 46-assist campaign of 1981-82 that put him onto the First All-Star Team and got him the top defenseman's award. "So many times, the Norris Trophy goes to the guy with the good numbers," he said. "Well, I think the best year I ever had was the year after I won the Norris."

Wilson scored 18 goals and 51 assists in 1982-83 but didn't earn another league honor until 1984-85, when he made the Second All-Star Team with 22 goals and a career-high 54 helpers. His final All-Star campaign came in 1989-90. "He is the Hawks' backbone, the quarterback of the power play, the defensive anchor, the one guy the team could not do without," gushed Tim Sassone of *The Hockey News* in December 1989. Wilson finished the season with 23 goals and 50 assists. The playoffs, however, were an almost complete disappointment.

Although Wilson made his fifth trip to the Campbell Conference finals in 1990, the Hawks never managed to take the next step. He joined San Jose for its inaugural 1991-92 campaign, but back problems restricted his ice time and effectiveness. He captained the Sharks for two seasons before retiring.

DOUG WILSON
Ottawa, Ontario
July 5, 1957–
NHL Career: 1977-93
Chicago, San Jose

	GP	G	A	P	PIM
RS	1024	237	590	827	830
PO	95	19	61	80	88

Norris, A-S Game (7)

GUMP WORSLEY

GOALTENDER

Nicknamed after Andy Gump of the funny papers, Lorne "Gump" Worsley was an unlikely-looking athlete. Yet he didn't conclude his Hall of Fame career until he was 45 years old. When he asked the New York Rangers for a raise after winning the 1953 Calder Trophy, however, Worsley found himself back in the minors for a season. "There's a lot of luck involved in being a goalie," he said, "and sometimes things just go your way. And sometimes you feel like a million bucks starting a game, and you couldn't stop a basketball."

The Rangers traded Worsley to Montreal, but he was injured only eight games into the 1963-64 season. Sent to the minors to recuperate, he didn't get the call to return until a year later. "The Gumper" completed the last quarter of

the 1964-65 campaign sharing duties with Charlie Hodge. Worsley earned his first Stanley Cup ring with a playoff-low 1.68 goals-against average and two shutouts in eight games. Hodge shared the Vezina Trophy with him the following season, when Worsley made the Second All-Star Team and was in the net for every Montreal playoff victory. "Worsley wasn't even tested," griped Detroit's Bill Gadsby as the Canadiens successfully defended the Cup. "His underwear can't even be wet."

Told of the comment, Worsley joked, "What most people don't know is that my underwear is wet before the game even starts."

He shared the Vezina with Rogie Vachon in 1967-68 and was elected to the First All-Star Team. The Habs won

the Cup both that season and the next, but Vachon started getting most of the work. When Montreal tried to demote Worsley to the minors, he refused to report. He eventually agreed to an offer from Minnesota, where he played through the 1973-74 season.

LORNE "GUMP" WORSLEY
Montreal, Quebec
May 14, 1929–
NHL Career: 1952-53, 1954-74
NY Rangers, Montreal, Minnesota

	GP	M	GA	SO	AVE
RS	861	50183	2432	43	2.91
PO	70	4081	192	5	2.82

Calder, Vezina (2), Stanley Cup (4),
A-S Game (4), HOF 1980

Although he stood just five-foot-three, Roy "Shrimp" Worters was larger-than-life. "Roy is probably the most loyal member of any hockey team on skates," wrote former neighbor Gordon Sinclair in 1936. "Only 125 pounds when dressed for the sheet [ice], he's been hurt, cut up and smashed about oftener than any other goaltender in captivity. The gut used to sew him up after gory hockey fracases in his 30 years of netminding would be long enough to string a tennis racquet, but that gut all came from the insides of sheep or whatever they use…Roy still has his full supply."

Worters entered the NHL in 1925-26 with the Pittsburgh Pirates and is credited with being the first goaltender to use his glove as a blocker, steering the puck into the corner instead of trying to catch it. Sold to the New York Americans just before the 1928-29 season, Worters was unhappy with the contract he was offered and refused to report. The league suspended him, but he was reinstated in December. Despite his late start, Worters posted 13 shutouts and became the first goaltender to win the Hart Trophy. He then let in only one goal in a two-game playoff against the Rangers, although his team failed to score even once. It was the last postseason action that Worters and the Amerks would see for seven years.

The basement-dwelling Americans loaned Worters to the league-leading Montreal Canadiens for a single game on February 27, 1930, which might have qualified as a rest. Although the Amerks had the league's eighth-best record in 1930-31, Worters won the Vezina Trophy with a 1.61 goals-against average. When the Americans finally made the playoffs again in 1935-36, Worters posted a shutout in the opener of a two-game, total-goals series to help eliminate Chicago. Toronto, backed by George Hainsworth, proved too strong, but Worters blanked the Leafs once before his team lost the semifinals two games to one. "Worters again played grandly in goal," recounted Andy Lytle of *The Toronto Star* on April 3, 1936. "Hainsworth seemed jumpy, [with] little to do in comparison to Worters. When he and George sat for a picture afterwards, Worters' hand was shaking so he could hardly hold his cigarette."

ROY "SHRIMP" WORTERS
October 19, 1900–November 7, 1957
NHL Career: 1925-37
Pittsburgh, NY Americans, Montreal

	GP	M	GA	SO	AVE
RS	316	19687	664	42	2.02
PO	21	1472	35	5	1.43

Hart, Vezina, HOF 1969

CENTER 1999

In a few short months, Alexei Yashin went from hero to pariah. He made the Second All-Star Team in 1999 with a brilliant 44-goal, 50-assist campaign for the Ottawa Senators. Finishing sixth in league scoring, he was runner-up for the Hart Trophy and was a Pearson Award finalist. He then decided not to honor the final year of his contract, although he would have earned $3.6 million in 1999-2000. Yashin reportedly asked for about $10 million per annum, but the Senators refused to renegotiate his contract or to trade their star to a team that would.

Yashin had used the same ploy successfully with the Senators twice before, but this time, he missed the entire season. Although his teammates fashioned an excellent campaign without him, Ottawa felt Yashin's absence. Off the ice,

his messy, protracted contract negotiations and his withdrawal, in 1998, of most of a much-publicized gift to the National Arts Centre had hurt the club. On the ice, Yashin had always been the best Senator. He tallied 30 goals and 49 assists as a 1993-94 rookie and led the team in scoring every season except for the 1995-96 campaign, when he came second despite having played only 46 games.

"He's our leader on and off the ice," said coach Jacques Martin in 1998. "He is an inspiration to his teammates." Yashin wore the captain's "C" when Randy Cunneyworth missed games in 1997-98 and was officially named captain the following season.

"I think he makes everybody a better player," said linemate Andreas Dackell. "All I have to do is find some open

space, and he'll find me. He has some unbelievable moves." Yashin's next maneuver will be interesting. After spending a year working out with a club team in Switzerland, Yashin successfully argued for permission to compete for Russia in the 2000 World Championship. When he will return to the NHL and where he'll play are still unknown.

ALEXEI YASHIN
Sverdlovsk, U.S.S.R.
November 5, 1973–
NHL Career: 1993-99
Ottawa

	GP	G	A	P	PIM
RS	422	178	225	403	192
PO	22	6	8	14	20
A-S Game (2)					

That it took so long for Steve Yzerman to earn his first All-Star selection speaks volumes about the quality of the competition. Captain of the Detroit Red Wings since 1986-87, he already ranks among the top-10 players of all time in goals, assists and points. "I wouldn't say I'm a classic goal scorer like Mike Bossy or 'The Rocket' [Richard]," said Yzerman, who tallied 39 goals and 87 points as an 18-year-old rookie and had his first 50-goal season in 1987-88. "I came in as a playmaking center, and around my fifth year, they started going in for me." In 1988-89, he came third in scoring and won the Pearson Award after hitting personal-highs with 65 goals, 90 assists and 155 points.

Yzerman came third again the following season, with 62 goals and 65 assists, and stayed in the top-10 scorers through the 1992-93 campaign, when he finished fourth with 58 goals and 79 helpers. "There was definitely an adjustment period when Scotty [Bowman] came in [1993-94]," admitted Yzerman. "I had to adapt my game, but I look back on what is really important, and the only thing that matters is the success we've had in the playoffs. Those are the most enjoyable times, the most fun I've had in the game."

Detroit made the 1995 finals, with Yzerman leading the way with a strong commitment to two-way play. He finally hoisted the Cup in 1997 and 1998, winning the 1998 Conn Smythe Trophy after leading the postseason with 18 assists and 24 points.

"He [has given] this organization a lot of hope and fulfilled it beyond any-body's wildest expectations," said Wings general manager Ken Holland. "The franchise is built around him." Yzerman made the 2000 First All-Star Team, coming tenth in league scoring with 35 goals and 44 assists, while earning the Frank Selke Trophy as the league's best defensive forward.

STEVE YZERMAN
Cranbrook, British Columbia
May 9, 1965–
NHL Career: 1983-
Detroit

	GP	G	A	P	PIM
RS	1256	627	935	1562	816
PO	153	61	91	152	68

Pearson, Selke, Smythe, Stanley Cup (2), A-S Game (9)

CENTER ⭐ 1995

Alexei Zhamnov played four seasons for the Moscow Dynamo, a top Russian club, and won a gold medal for the Unified Team (representing the former U.S.S.R.) at the 1992 Olympic Games. Drafted by the Winnipeg Jets in 1990, Zhamnov scored a career-high 72 points during his inaugural NHL campaign in 1992-93. Unfortunately, fellow rookie and teammate Teemu Selanne's record-shattering 76-goal, 56-assist campaign overshadowed Zhamnov's 25 goals and 47 assists.

After missing 23 games the following season with a bad back, Zhamnov leapt up to third place in league scoring during the 48-game 1994-95 schedule. He made the Second All-Star Team with 65 points, including a career-high 30 goals. With only 20 minutes in penalties, he also became the first Russian player to be nominated for a Lady Byng Trophy. Zhamnov played only 58 games in 1995-96 but tallied 22 goals and 59 points. He qualified for restricted free agency on July 1, 1996, which meant that any team could sign him in return for five first-round draft picks. "You don't let a potential star like Alex go for a draft pick," said general manager John Paddock, assuring other teams that he would invoke his right to match any offers made to his top centerman. But shortly after re-signing with the Jets, who were due to transfer to Phoenix for 1996-97, Zhamnov instead found himself en route to Chicago.

The Blackhawks traded two-time 50-goal-scorer Jeremy Roenick for Zhamnov, junior player Craig Mills and a first-round draft pick. Zhamnov has been a disappointment to the Hawks, although his defensive skills have been welcomed. Over four seasons in Chicago, he has notched 20, 21, 20 and 23 goals, respectively, and is now considered a reliable but unspectacular second-line center. Although his original champion Mike Smith—who was general manager of the Jets back in 1990—took the helm in Chicago for 2000-01, Zhamnov's name frequently crops up in trade rumors.

ALEXEI ZHAMNOV
Moscow, U.S.S.R.
October 1, 1970–
NHL Career: 1992-
Winnipeg, Chicago

	GP	G	A	P	PIM
RS	526	187	312	499	433
PO	12	2	3	5	10

Left Wing Center Right Wing
Defense Defense
Goaltender

LEGEND

ANA: Mighty Ducks of Anaheim	COL: Colorado Avalanche	LA: Los Angeles Kings	NYI: New York Islanders	QUE: Quebec Nordiques
BOS: Boston Bruins	DAL: Dallas Stars	MAR: Montreal Maroons	NYR: New York Rangers	STL: St. Louis Blues
BRO: Brooklyn Americans	DET: Detroit Red Wings	MIN: Minnesota North Stars	OTT: Ottawa Senators	TOR: Toronto Maple Leafs
BUF: Buffalo Sabres	EDM: Edmonton Oilers	MON: Montreal Canadiens	PHI: Philadelphia Flyers	VAN: Vancouver Canucks
CAL: Calgary Flames	FLO: Florida Panthers	NJ: New Jersey Devils	PHO: Phoenix Coyotes	WAS: Washington Capitals
CHI: Chicago Blackhawks	HAR: Hartford Whalers	NYA: New York Americans	PIT: Pittsburgh Penguins	WIN: Winnipeg Jets

First All-Star Team	Season	Second All-Star Team
Aurele Joliat, MON — Howie Morenz, MON — Bill Cook, NYR Eddie Shore, BOS — King Clancy, TOR Chuck Gardiner, CHI	1930-31	Bun Cook, NYR — Frank Boucher, NYR — Dit Clapper, BOS Sylvio Mantha, MON — Ivan Johnson, NYR Tiny Thompson, BOS
Harvey Jackson, TOR — Howie Morenz, MON — Bill Cook, NYR Eddie Shore, BOS — Ivan Johnson, NYR Chuck Gardiner, CHI	1931-32	Aurele Joliat, MON — Hooley Smith, MAR — Charlie Conacher, TOR Sylvio Mantha, MON — King Clancy, TOR Roy Worters, NYA
Baldy Northcott, MAR — Frank Boucher, NYR — Bill Cook, NYR Eddie Shore, BOS — Ivan Johnson, NYR John Ross Roach, DET	1932-33	Harvey Jackson, TOR — Howie Morenz, MON — Charlie Conacher, TOR King Clancy, TOR — Lionel Conacher, MAR Chuck Gardiner, CHI
Harvey Jackson, TOR — Frank Boucher, NYR — Charlie Conacher, TOR King Clancy, TOR — Lionel Conacher, CHI Chuck Gardiner, CHI	1933-34	Aurele Joliat, MON — Joe Primeau, TOR — Bill Cook, NYR Eddie Shore, BOS — Ivan Johnson, NYR Roy Worters, NYA
Harvey Jackson, TOR — Frank Boucher, NYR — Charlie Conacher, TOR Eddie Shore, BOS — Earl Seibert, NYR Lorne Chabot, CHI	1934-35	Aurele Joliat, MON — Cooney Weiland, DET — Dit Clapper, BOS Cy Wentworth, MAR — Art Coulter, CHI Tiny Thompson, BOS
Sweeney Schriner, NYA — Hooley Smith, MAR — Charlie Conacher, TOR Eddie Shore, BOS — Babe Siebert, BOS Tiny Thompson, BOS	1935-36	Paul Thompson, CHI — Bill Thoms, TOR — Cecil Dillon, NYR Earl Seibert, CHI — Ebbie Goodfellow, DET Wilf Cude, MON
Harvey Jackson, TOR — Marty Barry, DET — Larry Aurie, DET Babe Siebert, MON — Ebbie Goodfellow, DET Normie Smith, DET	1936-37	Sweeney Schriner, NYA — Art Chapman, NYA — Cecil Dillon, NYR Earl Seibert, CHI — Lionel Conacher, MAR Wilf Cude, MON
Paul Thompson, CHI — Bill Cowley, BOS — Cecil Dillon, NYR/Gordie Drillon, TOR Eddie Shore, BOS — Babe Siebert, MON Tiny Thompson, BOS	1937-38	Toe Blake, MON — Syl Apps, TOR Art Coulter, NYR — Earl Seibert, CHI Dave Kerr, NYR
Toe Blake, MON — Syl Apps, TOR — Gordie Drillon, TOR Eddie Shore, BOS — Dit Clapper, BOS Frank Brimsek, BOS	1938-39	Johnny Gottselig, CHI — Neil Colville, NYR — Bobby Bauer, BOS Earl Seibert, CHI — Art Coulter, NYR Earl Robertson, NYA
Toe Blake, MON — Milt Schmidt, BOS — Bryan Hextall Sr., NYR Dit Clapper, BOS — Ebbie Goodfellow, DET Dave Kerr, NYR	1939-40	Woody Dumart, BOS — Neil Colville, NYR — Bobby Bauer, BOS Art Coulter, NYR — Earl Seibert, CHI Frank Brimsek, BOS
Sweeney Schriner, TOR — Bill Cowley, BOS — Bryan Hextall Sr., NYR Dit Clapper, BOS — Wally Stanowski, TOR Turk Broda, TOR	1940-41	Woody Dumart, BOS — Syl Apps, TOR — Bobby Bauer, BOS Earl Seibert, CHI — Ott Heller, NYR Frank Brimsek, BOS
Lynn Patrick, NYR — Syl Apps, TOR — Bryan Hextall Sr., NYR Earl Seibert, CHI — Tom Anderson, BRO Frank Brimsek, BOS	1941-42	Sid Abel, DET — Phil Watson, NYR — Gordie Drillon, TOR Pat Egan, BRO — Bucko McDonald, TOR Turk Broda, TOR
Doug Bentley, CHI — Bill Cowley, BOS — Lorne Carr, TOR Earl Seibert, CHI — Jack Stewart, DET Johnny Mowers, DET	1942-43	Lynn Patrick, NYR — Syl Apps, TOR — Bryan Hextall Sr., NYR Jack Crawford, BOS — Flash Hollett, BOS Frank Brimsek, BOS
Doug Bentley, CHI — Bill Cowley, BOS — Lorne Carr, TOR Earl Seibert, CHI — Babe Pratt, TOR Bill Durnan, MON	1943-44	Herb Cain, BOS — Elmer Lach, MON — Maurice Richard, MON Butch Bouchard, MON — Dit Clapper, BOS Paul Bibeault, TOR

First All-Star Team	Season	Second All-Star Team
Toe Blake, MON — Elmer Lach, MON — Maurice Richard, MON; Butch Bouchard, MON — Flash Hollett, BOS; Bill Durnan, MON	1944-45	Syd Howe, DET — Bill Cowley, BOS — Bill Mosienko, CHI; Glen Harmon, MON — Babe Pratt, TOR; Mike Karakas, CHI
Gaye Stewart, TOR — Max Bentley, CHI — Maurice Richard, MON; Jack Crawford, BOS — Butch Bouchard, MON; Bill Durnan, MON	1945-46	Toe Blake, MON — Elmer Lach, MON — Bill Mosienko, CHI; Ken Reardon, MON — Jack Stewart, DET; Frank Brimsek, BOS
Doug Bentley, CHI — Milt Schmidt, BOS — Maurice Richard, MON; Ken Reardon, MON — Butch Bouchard, MON; Bill Durnan, MON	1946-47	Woody Dumart, BOS — Max Bentley, CHI — Bobby Bauer, BOS; Jack Stewart, DET — Bill Quackenbush, DET; Frank Brimsek, BOS
Ted Lindsay, DET — Elmer Lach, MON — Maurice Richard, MON; Bill Quackenbush, DET — Jack Stewart, DET; Turk Broda, TOR	1947-48	Gaye Stewart, CHI — Buddy O'Connor, NYR — Bud Poile, CHI; Ken Reardon, MON — Neil Colville, NYR; Frank Brimsek, BOS
Roy Conacher, CHI — Sid Abel, DET — Maurice Richard, MON; Bill Quackenbush, DET — Jack Stewart, DET; Bill Durnan, MON	1948-49	Ted Lindsay, DET — Doug Bentley, CHI — Gordie Howe, DET; Glen Harmon, MON — Ken Reardon, MON; Chuck Rayner, NYR
Ted Lindsay, DET — Sid Abel, DET — Maurice Richard, MON; Gus Mortson, TOR — Ken Reardon, MON; Bill Durnan, MON	1949-50	Tony Leswick, NYR — Ted Kennedy, TOR — Gordie Howe, DET; Leo Reise Jr., DET — Red Kelly, DET; Chuck Rayner, NYR
Ted Lindsay, DET — Milt Schmidt, BOS — Gordie Howe, DET; Red Kelly, DET — Bill Quackenbush, DET; Terry Sawchuk, DET	1950-51	Sid Smith, TOR — Sid Abel, DET/Ted Kennedy, TOR — Maurice Richard, MON; Jimmy Thomson, TOR — Leo Reise Jr., DET; Chuck Rayner, NYR
Ted Lindsay, DET — Elmer Lach, MON — Gordie Howe, DET; Red Kelly, DET — Doug Harvey, MON; Terry Sawchuk, DET	1951-52	Sid Smith, TOR — Milt Schmidt, BOS — Maurice Richard, MON; Hy Buller, BOS — Jimmy Thomson, TOR; Jim Henry, BOS
Ted Lindsay, DET — Fleming Mackell, BOS — Gordie Howe, DET; Red Kelly, DET — Doug Harvey, MON; Terry Sawchuk, DET	1952-53	Bert Olmstead, MON — Alex Delvecchio, DET — Maurice Richard, MON; Bill Quackenbush, DET — Bill Gadsby, CHI; Gerry McNeil, MON
Ted Lindsay, DET — Ken Mosdell, MON — Gordie Howe, DET; Red Kelly, DET — Doug Harvey, MON; Harry Lumley, TOR	1953-54	Ed Sandford, BOS — Ted Kennedy, TOR — Maurice Richard, MON; Bill Gadsby, CHI — Tim Horton, TOR; Terry Sawchuk, DET
Sid Smith, TOR — Jean Beliveau, MON — Maurice Richard, MON; Doug Harvey, MON — Red Kelly, DET; Harry Lumley, TOR	1954-55	Danny Lewicki, NYR — Ken Mosdell, MON — Bernie Geoffrion, MON; Bob Goldham, DET — Fernie Flaman, BOS; Terry Sawchuk, DET
Ted Lindsay, DET — Jean Beliveau, MON — Maurice Richard, MON; Doug Harvey, MON — Bill Gadsby, NYR; Jacques Plante, MON	1955-56	Bert Olmstead, MON — Tod Sloan, TOR — Gordie Howe, DET; Red Kelly, DET — Tom Johnson, MON; Glenn Hall, DET
Ted Lindsay, DET — Jean Beliveau, MON — Gordie Howe, DET; Doug Harvey, MON — Red Kelly, DET; Glenn Hall, DET	1956-57	Real Chevrefils, BOS — Ed Litzenberger, CHI — Maurice Richard, MON; Fernie Flaman, BOS — Bill Gadsby, NYR; Jacques Plante, MON
Dickie Moore, MON — Henri Richard, MON — Gordie Howe, DET; Doug Harvey, MON — Bill Gadsby, NYR; Glenn Hall, DET	1957-58	Camille Henry, NYR — Jean Beliveau, MON — Andy Bathgate, NYR; Fernie Flaman, BOS — Marcel Pronovost, DET; Jacques Plante, MON
Dickie Moore, MON — Jean Beliveau, MON — Andy Bathgate, NYR; Tom Johnson, MON — Bill Gadsby, NYR; Jacques Plante, MON	1958-59	Alex Delvecchio, DET — Henri Richard, MON — Gordie Howe, DET; Marcel Pronovost, DET — Doug Harvey, MON; Terry Sawchuk, DET
Bobby Hull, CHI — Jean Beliveau, MON — Gordie Howe, DET; Doug Harvey, MON — Marcel Pronovost, DET; Glenn Hall, CHI	1959-60	Dean Prentice, NYR — Bronco Horvath, BOS — Bernie Geoffrion, MON; Allan Stanley, TOR — Pierre Pilote, CHI; Jacques Plante, MON
Frank Mahovlich, TOR — Jean Beliveau, MON — Bernie Geoffrion, MON; Doug Harvey, MON — Marcel Pronovost, DET; Johnny Bower, TOR	1960-61	Dickie Moore, MON — Henri Richard, MON — Gordie Howe, DET; Allan Stanley, TOR — Pierre Pilote, CHI; Glenn Hall, CHI
Bobby Hull, CHI — Stan Mikita, CHI — Andy Bathgate, NYR; Doug Harvey, MON — Jean-Guy Talbot, MON; Jacques Plante, MON	1961-62	Frank Mahovlich, TOR — Dave Keon, TOR — Gordie Howe, DET; Carl Brewer, TOR — Pierre Pilote, CHI; Glenn Hall, CHI
Frank Mahovlich, TOR — Stan Mikita, CHI — Gordie Howe, DET; Pierre Pilote, CHI — Carl Brewer, TOR; Glenn Hall, CHI	1962-63	Bobby Hull, CHI — Henri Richard, MON — Andy Bathgate, NYR; Tim Horton, TOR — Elmer Vasko, CHI; Terry Sawchuk, DET

First All-Star Team	Season	Second All-Star Team
Bobby Hull, CHI — Stan Mikita, CHI — Kenny Wharram, CHI — Pierre Pilote, CHI — Tim Horton, TOR — Glenn Hall, CHI	1963-64	Frank Mahovlich, TOR — Jean Beliveau, MON — Gordie Howe, DET — Elmer Vasko, CHI — Jacques Laperriere, MON — Charlie Hodge, MON
Bobby Hull, CHI — Norm Ullman, DET — Claude Provost, MON — Pierre Pilote, CHI — Jacques Laperriere, MON — Roger Crozier, DET	1964-65	Frank Mahovlich, TOR — Stan Mikita, CHI — Gordie Howe, DET — Bill Gadsby, DET — Carl Brewer, TOR — Charlie Hodge, MON
Bobby Hull, CHI — Stan Mikita, CHI — Gordie Howe, DET — Jacques Laperriere, MON — Pierre Pilote, CHI — Glenn Hall, CHI	1965-66	Frank Mahovlich, TOR — Jean Beliveau, MON — Bobby Rousseau, MON — Allan Stanley, TOR — Pat Stapleton, CHI — Gump Worsley, MON
Bobby Hull, CHI — Stan Mikita, CHI — Kenny Wharram, CHI — Pierre Pilote, CHI — Harry Howell, NYR — Ed Giacomin, NYR	1966-67	Don Marshall, NYR — Norm Ullman, DET — Gordie Howe, DET — Tim Horton, TOR — Bobby Orr, BOS — Glenn Hall, CHI
Bobby Hull, CHI — Stan Mikita, CHI — Gordie Howe, DET — Bobby Orr, BOS — Tim Horton, TOR — Gump Worsley, MON	1967-68	Johnny Bucyk, BOS — Phil Esposito, BOS — Rod Gilbert, NYR — J.C. Tremblay, MON — Jim Neilson, NYR — Ed Giacomin, NYR
Bobby Hull, CHI — Phil Esposito, BOS — Gordie Howe, DET — Bobby Orr, BOS — Tim Horton, TOR — Glenn Hall, STL	1968-69	Frank Mahovlich, DET — Jean Beliveau, MON — Yvan Cournoyer, MON — Ted Green, BOS — Ted Harris, MON — Ed Giacomin, NYR
Bobby Hull, CHI — Phil Esposito, BOS — Gordie Howe, DET — Bobby Orr, BOS — Brad Park, NYR — Tony Esposito, CHI	1969-70	Frank Mahovlich, DET — Stan Mikita, CHI — John McKenzie, BOS — Carl Brewer, DET — Jacques Laperriere, MON — Ed Giacomin, NYR
Johnny Bucyk, BOS — Phil Esposito, BOS — Ken Hodge, BOS — Bobby Orr, BOS — J.C. Tremblay, MON — Ed Giacomin, NYR	1970-71	Bobby Hull, CHI — Dave Keon, TOR — Yvan Cournoyer, MON — Brad Park, NYR — Pat Stapleton, CHI — Jacques Plante, TOR
Bobby Hull, CHI — Phil Esposito, BOS — Rod Gilbert, NYR — Bobby Orr, BOS — Brad Park, NYR — Tony Esposito, CHI	1971-72	Vic Hadfield, NYR — Jean Ratelle, NYR — Yvan Cournoyer, MON — Bill White, CHI — Pat Stapleton, CHI — Ken Dryden, MON
Frank Mahovlich, MON — Phil Esposito, BOS — Mickey Redmond, DET — Bobby Orr, BOS — Guy Lapointe, MON — Ken Dryden, MON	1972-73	Dennis Hull, CHI — Bobby Clarke, PHI — Yvan Cournoyer, MON — Brad Park, NYR — Bill White, CHI — Tony Esposito, CHI
Rick Martin, BUF — Phil Esposito, BOS — Ken Hodge, BOS — Bobby Orr, BOS — Brad Park, NYR — Bernie Parent, PHI	1973-74	Wayne Cashman, BOS — Bobby Clarke, PHI — Mickey Redmond, DET — Bill White, CHI — Barry Ashbee, PHI — Tony Esposito, CHI
Rick Martin, BUF — Bobby Clarke, PHI — Guy Lafleur, MON — Bobby Orr, BOS — Denis Potvin, NYI — Bernie Parent, PHI	1974-75	Steve Vickers, NYR — Phil Esposito, BOS — Rene Robert, BUF — Guy Lapointe, MON — Borje Salming, TOR — Rogie Vachon, LA
Bill Barber, PHI — Bobby Clarke, PHI — Guy Lafleur, MON — Denis Potvin, NYI — Brad Park, BOS — Ken Dryden, MON	1975-76	Rick Martin, BUF — Gilbert Perreault, BUF — Reggie Leach, PHI — Borje Salming, TOR — Guy Lapointe, MON — Chico Resch, NYI
Steve Shutt, MON — Marcel Dionne, LA — Guy Lafleur, MON — Larry Robinson, MON — Borje Salming, TOR — Ken Dryden, MON	1976-77	Rick Martin, BUF — Gilbert Perreault, BUF — Lanny McDonald, TOR — Denis Potvin, NYI — Guy Lapointe, MON — Rogie Vachon, LA
Clark Gillies, NYI — Bryan Trottier, NYI — Guy Lafleur, MON — Denis Potvin, NYI — Brad Park, BOS — Ken Dryden, MON	1977-78	Steve Shutt, MON — Darryl Sittler, TOR — Mike Bossy, NYI — Larry Robinson, MON — Borje Salming, TOR — Don Edwards, BUF
Clark Gillies, NYI — Bryan Trottier, NYI — Guy Lafleur, MON — Denis Potvin, NYI — Larry Robinson, MON — Ken Dryden, MON	1978-79	Bill Barber, PHI — Marcel Dionne, LA — Mike Bossy, NYI — Borje Salming, TOR — Serge Savard, MON — Chico Resch, NYI
Charlie Simmer, LA — Marcel Dionne, LA — Guy Lafleur, MON — Larry Robinson, MON — Ray Bourque, BOS — Tony Esposito, CHI	1979-80	Steve Shutt, MON — Wayne Gretzky, EDM — Danny Gare, BUF — Borje Salming, TOR — Jim Schoenfeld, BUF — Don Edwards, BUF
Charlie Simmer, LA — Wayne Gretzky, EDM — Mike Bossy, NYI — Denis Potvin, NYI — Randy Carlyle, PIT — Mike Liut, STL	1980-81	Bill Barber, PHI — Marcel Dionne, LA — Dave Taylor, LA — Larry Robinson, MON — Ray Bourque, BOS — Mario Lessard, LA
Mark Messier, EDM — Wayne Gretzky, EDM — Mike Bossy, NYI — Doug Wilson, CHI — Ray Bourque, BOS — Billy Smith, NYI	1981-82	John Tonelli, NYI — Bryan Trottier, NYI — Rick Middleton, BOS — Paul Coffey, EDM — Brian Engblom, MON — Grant Fuhr, EDM

First All-Star Team	Season	Second All-Star Team
Mark Messier, EDM — Wayne Gretzky, EDM — Mike Bossy, NYI — Mark Howe, PHI — Rod Langway, WAS — Pete Peeters, BOS	**1982-83**	Michel Goulet, QUE — Denis Savard, CHI — Lanny McDonald, CAL — Ray Bourque, BOS — Paul Coffey, EDM — Rollie Melanson, NYI
Michel Goulet, QUE — Wayne Gretzky, EDM — Mike Bossy, NYI — Rod Langway, WAS — Ray Bourque, BOS — Tom Barrasso, BUF	**1983-84**	Mark Messier, EDM — Bryan Trottier, NYI — Jari Kurri, EDM — Paul Coffey, EDM — Denis Potvin, NYI — Pat Riggin, WAS
John Ogrodnick, DET — Wayne Gretzky, EDM — Jari Kurri, EDM — Paul Coffey, EDM — Ray Bourque, BOS — Pelle Lindbergh, PHI	**1984-85**	John Tonelli, NYI — Dale Hawerchuk, WIN — Mike Bossy, NYI — Rod Langway, WAS — Doug Wilson, CHI — Tom Barrasso, BUF
Michel Goulet, QUE — Wayne Gretzky, EDM — Mike Bossy, NYI — Paul Coffey, EDM — Mark Howe, PHI — John Vanbiesbrouck, NYR	**1985-86**	Mats Naslund, MON — Mario Lemieux, PIT — Jari Kurri, EDM — Larry Robinson, MON — Ray Bourque, BOS — Bob Froese, PHI
Michel Goulet, QUE — Wayne Gretzky, EDM — Jari Kurri, EDM — Ray Bourque, BOS — Mark Howe, PHI — Ron Hextall, PHI	**1986-87**	Luc Robitaille, LA — Mario Lemieux, PIT — Tim Kerr, PHI — Larry Murphy, WAS — Al MacInnis, CAL — Mike Liut, HAR
Luc Robitaille, LA — Mario Lemieux, PIT — Hakan Loob, CAL — Ray Bourque, BOS — Scott Stevens, WAS — Grant Fuhr, EDM	**1987-88**	Michel Goulet, QUE — Wayne Gretzky, EDM — Cam Neely, BOS — Gary Suter, CAL — Brad McCrimmon, CAL — Patrick Roy, MON
Luc Robitaille, LA — Mario Lemieux, PIT — Joe Mullen, CAL — Chris Chelios, MON — Paul Coffey, PIT — Patrick Roy, MON	**1988-89**	Gerard Gallant, DET — Wayne Gretzky, LA — Jari Kurri, EDM — Al MacInnis, CAL — Ray Bourque, BOS — Mike Vernon, CAL
Luc Robitaille, LA — Mark Messier, EDM — Brett Hull, STL — Ray Bourque, BOS — Al MacInnis, CAL — Patrick Roy, MON	**1989-90**	Brian Bellows, MIN — Wayne Gretzky, LA — Cam Neely, BOS — Paul Coffey, PIT — Doug Wilson, CHI — Daren Puppa, BUF
Luc Robitaille, LA — Wayne Gretzky, LA — Brett Hull, STL — Ray Bourque, BOS — Al MacInnis, CAL — Ed Belfour, CHI	**1990-91**	Kevin Stevens, PIT — Adam Oates, STL — Cam Neely, BOS — Chris Chelios, CHI — Brian Leetch, NYR — Patrick Roy, MON
Kevin Stevens, PIT — Mark Messier, NYR — Brett Hull, STL — Brian Leetch, NYR — Ray Bourque, BOS — Patrick Roy, MON	**1991-92**	Luc Robitaille, LA — Mario Lemieux, PIT — Mark Recchi, PIT, PHI — Phil Housley, WIN — Scott Stevens, NJ — Kirk McLean, VAN
Luc Robitaille, LA — Mario Lemieux, PIT — Teemu Selanne, WIN — Chris Chelios, CHI — Ray Bourque, BOS — Ed Belfour, CHI	**1992-93**	Kevin Stevens, PIT — Pat LaFontaine, BUF — Alexander Mogilny, BUF — Larry Murphy, PIT — Al Iafrate, WAS — Tom Barrasso, PIT
Brendan Shanahan, STL — Sergei Fedorov, DET — Pavel Bure, VAN — Ray Bourque, BOS — Scott Stevens, NJ — Dominik Hasek, BUF	**1993-94**	Adam Graves, NYR — Wayne Gretzky, LA — Cam Neely, BOS — Al MacInnis, CAL — Brian Leetch, NYR — John Vanbiesbrouck, FLO
John LeClair, MON, PHI — Eric Lindros, PHI — Jaromir Jagr, PIT — Paul Coffey, DET — Chris Chelios, CHI — Dominik Hasek, BUF	**1994-95**	Keith Tkachuk, WIN — Alexei Zhamnov, WIN — Theoren Fleury, CAL — Ray Bourque, BOS — Larry Murphy, PIT — Ed Belfour, CHI
Paul Kariya, ANA — Mario Lemieux, PIT — Jaromir Jagr, PIT — Chris Chelios, CHI — Ray Bourque, BOS — Jim Carey, WAS	**1995-96**	John LeClair, PHI — Eric Lindros, PHI — Alexander Mogilny, VAN — Vladimir Konstantinov, DET — Brian Leetch, NYR — Chris Osgood, DET
Paul Kariya, ANA — Mario Lemieux, PIT — Teemu Selanne, ANA — Brian Leetch, NYR — Sandis Ozolinsh, COL — Dominik Hasek, BUF	**1996-97**	John LeClair, PHI — Wayne Gretzky, NYR — Jaromir Jagr, PIT — Chris Chelios, CHI — Scott Stevens, NJ — Martin Brodeur, NJ
John LeClair, PHI — Peter Forsberg, COL — Jaromir Jagr, PIT — Nicklas Lidstrom, DET — Rob Blake, LA — Dominik Hasek, BUF	**1997-98**	Keith Tkachuk, PHO — Wayne Gretzky, NYR — Teemu Selanne, ANA — Chris Pronger, STL — Scott Niedermayer, NJ — Martin Brodeur, NJ
Paul Kariya, ANA — Peter Forsberg, COL — Jaromir Jagr, PIT — Al MacInnis, STL — Nicklas Lidstrom, DET — Dominik Hasek, BUF	**1998-99**	John LeClair, PHI — Alexei Yashin, OTT — Teemu Selanne, ANA — Ray Bourque, BOS — Eric Desjardins, PHI — Byron Dafoe, BOS
Brendan Shanahan, DET — Steve Yzerman, DET — Jaromir Jagr, PIT — Chris Pronger, STL — Nicklas Lidstrom, DET — Olaf Kolzig, WAS	**1999-2000**	Paul Kariya, ANA — Mike Modano, DAL — Pavel Bure, FLO — Rob Blake, LA — Eric Desjardins, PHI — Roman Turek, STL

252

WEBSITES

Boston Bruins Legends:
legends.hks.com/

ESPN: espn.go.com/nhl

Hockey Hall of Fame:
www.hhof.com

Hockey Over Time
(Joe Pelletier and Patrick Houda):
www.lcshockey.com/history

National Hockey League:
www.nhl.com

The Sun newspaper chain:
www.canoe.com/Hockey/home.html

BOOKS

Coleman, Charles, *The Trail of the Stanley Cup*, vols. 1-3, National Hockey League, Montreal, 1964, 1969, 1976.

Coleman, Jim, et al., *Legends of Hockey*, Penguin Studio, Toronto, 1996.

Devaney, John, and Burt Goldblatt, *The Stanley Cup: A Complete Pictorial History*, Rand McNally, Chicago, 1975.

Diamond, Dan, ed., *The Official National Hockey League 75th Anniversary Commemorative Book*, McClelland & Stewart, Toronto, 1991.

————, *Total Hockey: The Official Encyclopedia of the National Hockey League*, Andrew McMeel Publishing, Kansas City, 1998.

————, *Years of Glory, 1942-1967: The National Hockey League's Official Book of the Six-Team Era*, McClelland & Stewart, Toronto, 1994.

Dryden, Steve, ed., *The Top 100: NHL Players of All Time*, McClelland & Stewart, Toronto, 1997.

Fischler, Stan, *Bobby Orr and the Big, Bad Bruins*, Dell, New York, 1969.

————, *Golden Ice: The Greatest Teams in Hockey History*, McGraw-Hill Ryerson, Scarborough, 1990.

————, *Hockey Stars Speak*, Warwick Publishing, Toronto, 1996.

———— and Shirley Walton Fischler, *The Hockey Encyclopedia: The Complete Record of Professional Ice Hockey*, Macmillan, New York, 1983.

Greenberg, Jay, *Full Spectrum: The Complete History of the Philadelphia Flyers Hockey Club*, Triumph Books, Chicago, 1996.

Hunt, Jim, *The Men in the Nets*, Ryerson Press, Toronto, 1967.

Hunter, Douglas, *A Breed Apart: An Illustrated History of Goaltending*, Viking, Toronto, 1995.

————, *Champions: The Illustrated History of Hockey's Greatest Dynasties*, Penguin Studio, Toronto, 1997.

Irvin, Dick, *In the Crease: Goaltenders Look at Life in the NHL*, McClelland & Stewart, Toronto, 1995.

Jenish, D'Arcy, *The Stanley Cup: A Hundred Years of Hockey at Its Best*, McClelland & Stewart, Toronto, 1992.

Klein, Jeff Z., and Karl-Eric Reif, *The Coolest Guys on Ice: 32 of Hockey's Greatest Superstars*, Turner Publishing, Atlanta, Georgia, 1996.

Leonetti, Mike, *Hockey's Golden Era: Stars of the Original Six*, Macmillan, Toronto, 1993.

Liebman, Glenn, *Hockey Shorts: 1,001 of the Game's Funniest One-Liners*, Contemporary Books, Chicago, 1996.

McAllister, Ron, *Hockey Stars Today and Yesterday*, McClelland & Stewart, Toronto, 1950.

Obodiac, Stan, ed., *The Leafs: The First Fifty Years*, McClelland & Stewart, Toronto, 1976.

Orr, Frank, *Hockey's Greatest Stars*, Putnam, New York, 1970.

Podnieks, Andrew, *The Red Wings Book: The Most Complete Detroit Red Wings Fact Book Ever Published*, ECW Press, Toronto, 1996.

Roche, Bill, *The Hockey Book*, McClelland & Stewart, Toronto, 1953.

Ross, Sherry, *Hockey Scouting Report: 1998-99*, Greystone Books, Vancouver, 1998.

Taylor, Jim, *Wayne Gretzky: The Authorized Pictorial Biography*, Whitecap Books, Vancouver, 1994.

Ulmer, Michael, *Canadiens Captains: Nine Great Montreal Canadiens*, Macmillan, Toronto, 1996.

————, *Captains*, Macmillan, Toronto, 1995.

Weir, Glenn, Jeff Chapman and Travis Weir, *Ultimate Hockey*, Stoddart, Toronto, 1999.

OTHER REFERENCES

The National Hockey League Official Guide & Record Book, compiled by the NHL Public Relations Department and the NHL clubs' public relations directors.

NHL media guides published by each NHL club.

The Hockey News, a weekly publication during the hockey season, has been of invaluable assistance, particularly issues from 1947 to 1975.

BRIAN BABINEAU
166

STEVE BABINEAU/
HOCKEY HALL OF FAME
18, 25, 32, 96, 107, 122, 124, 141 top,
148, 153, 162, 165, 176 bottom, 194,
214 bottom

PAUL BERESWILL/
HOCKEY HALL OF FAME
90

GRAPHIC ARTISTS/
HOCKEY HALL OF FAME
34 top, 38 top, 58, 82, 83, 89, 92,
100 bottom, 101 top, 103, 104, 120,
129 top, 144, 146, 149 bottom, 167,
178, 184, 201, 232, 234 bottom, 237,
241, 244

HOCKEY HALL OF FAME
15, 17 bottom, 21, 33, 43 top and
bottom, 45 bottom, 46, 47, 52, 53, 55,
61 bottom, 79, 85 bottom, 86, 98 top,
99 bottom, 102, 106, 114, 117, 121,
161 top, 181, 196, 197 bottom, 208,
209, 212, 218 bottom, 227 bottom,
228, 239 bottom, 240 top and bottom

IMPERIAL OIL–TUROFSKY/
HOCKEY HALL OF FAME
14, 16, 22, 24, 26, 27, 28 top, 31, 35,
36, 38 bottom, 40 top, 41 bottom,
45 top, 50, 51 bottom, 56, 57, 60, 63,
65, 66, 67 bottom, 72, 80, 85 top, 93,
95, 98 bottom, 99 top, 101 bottom,
113, 115 top, 118, 119, 125, 134 top,
138, 139, 148, 151 top, 156, 158, 160,
161 bottom, 169 top, 170, 176 top,
179, 182 top and bottom, 183 top,
187, 188, 189, 191, 193, 194, 203,
206, 207, 216, 219, 220, 224, 225,
226 bottom, 229 top and bottom, 245

LONDON LIFE–PORTNOY/
HOCKEY HALL OF FAME
17 top, 19, 42, 47, 54, 62, 64, 67 top,
68, 70, 81, 84, 91, 111 top, 127,
128 top, 129 bottom, 132, 140, 147,
149 top, 154, 171, 174, 175, 177, 180,
186, 190 bottom, 192, 197 top, 198,
202, 205, 208 top, 213, 215, 221, 235,
239 top, 242

DOUG MacLELLAN/
HOCKEY HALL OF FAME
23, 39, 40 bottom, 71, 73, 88, 100 top,
105, 110, 123 bottom, 126, 131, 133,
136, 143, 157, 163, 168 bottom, 172,
173, 185 bottom, 190 top, 199, 200,
210, 222, 223, 236, 248

JAMES McCARTHY/
HOCKEY HALL OF FAME
20

M. NADAL/
HOCKEY HALL OF FAME
29

O-PEE-CHEE/
HOCKEY HALL OF FAME
30, 41 top, 49, 69, 75, 76, 78, 87, 109,
137, 150, 152, 164, 169 bottom, 204,
217, 230, 233, 238, 243

FRANK PRAZAK/
HOCKEY HALL OF FAME
34 bottom, 77, 94, 108, 128 bottom,
134 bottom, 141 bottom, 142, 185 top,
224 top

JAMES RICE/
HOCKEY HALL OF FAME
51 top, 59 top, 115 bottom, 145, 159,
168 top, 214 top, 218 top

DAVE SANDFORD/
HOCKEY HALL OF FAME
28 bottom, 37, 44, 59 bottom, 74, 97,
112, 116, 123 top, 130, 135, 155,
183 bottom, 211, 231, 234, 246, 247